MznLnx

Missing Links Exam Preps

Exam Prep for

Historical Geology

Wicander & Monroe, 4th Edition

The MznLnx Exam Prep is your link from the texbook and lecture to your exams.
The MznLnx Exam Preps are unauthorized and comprehensive reviews of your textbooks.

All material provided by MznLnx and Rico Publications (c) 2010
Textbook publishers and textbook authors do not particpate in or contribute to these reviews.

MznLnx

Rico Publications

Exam Prep for Historical Geology
4th Edition
Wicander & Monroe

Publisher: Raymond Houge
Assistant Editor: Michael Rouger
Text and Cover Designer: Lisa Buckner
Marketing Manager: Sara Swagger
Project Manager, Editorial Production: Jerry Emerson
Art Director: Vernon Lowerui

Product Manager: Dave Mason
Editorial Assitant: Rachel Guzmanji
Pedagogy: Debra Long
Cover Image: Jim Reed/Getty Images
Text and Cover Printer: City Printing, Inc.
Compositor: Media Mix, Inc.

(c) 2010 Rico Publications
ALL RIGHTS RESERVED. No part of this work covered by the copyright may be reproduced or used in any form or by an means--graphic, electronic, or mechanical, including photocopying, recording, taping, Web distribution, information storage, and retrieval systems, or in any other manner--without the written permission of the publisher.

Printed in the United States
ISBN:

For more information about our products, contact us at:
Dave.Mason@RicoPublications.com

For permission to use material from this text or product, submit a request online to:
Dave.Mason@RicoPublications.com

Contents

CHAPTER 1
The Dynamic and Evolving Earth — 1

CHAPTER 2
Earth Materials: Minerals and Rocks — 20

CHAPTER 3
Plate Tectonics: A Unifying Theory — 40

CHAPTER 4
Geologic Time: Concepts and Principles — 64

CHAPTER 5
Rocks, Fossils, and Time-Making Sense of the Geologic Record — 80

CHAPTER 6
Sedimentary Rocks-The Archives of Earth History — 97

CHAPTER 7
Evolution-The Theory and its Supporting Evidence — 113

CHAPTER 8
Precambrian Earth and Life History-The Hadean and Archean — 126

CHAPTER 9
Precambrian Earth and Life History-The Proterozoic Eon — 150

CHAPTER 10
Early Paleozoic Earth History — 175

CHAPTER 11
Late Paleozoic Earth History — 187

CHAPTER 12
Paleozoic Life History: Invertebrates — 198

CHAPTER 13
Paleozoic Lfte History: Vertebrates and Plants — 205

CHAPTER 14
Mesozoic Earth History — 210

CHAPTER 15
Life of the Mesozoic Era — 224

CHAPTER 16
Cenozoic Geologic History: The Tertiary Period — 230

CHAPTER 17
Cenozoic Geologic History: The Quaternary Period — 246

CHAPTER 18
Life of the Cenozoic Era — 261

CHAPTER 19
Primate and Human Evolution — 267

ANSWER KEY — 273

TO THE STUDENT

COMPREHENSIVE

The *MznLnx* Exam Prep series is designed to help you pass your exams. Editors at MznLnx review your textbooks and then prepare these practice exams to help you master the textbook material. Unlike study guides, workbooks, and practice tests provided by the texbook publisher and textbook authors, *MznLnx* gives you **all** of the material in each chapter in exam form, not just samples, so you can be sure to nail your exam.

MECHANICAL

The MznLnx Exam Prep series creates exams that will help you learn the subject matter as well as test you on your understanding. Each question is designed to help you master the concept. Just working through the exams, you gain an understanding of the subject--its a simple mechanical process that produces success.

INTEGRATED STUDY GUIDE AND REVIEW

MznLnx is not just a set of exams designed to test you, its also a comprehensive review of the subject content. Each exam question is also a review of the concept, making sure that you will get the answer correct without having to go to other sources of material. You learn as you go! Its the easiest way to pass an exam.

HUMOR

Studying can be tedious and dry. MznLnx's instructional design includes moderate humor within the exam questions on occassion, to break the tedium and revitalize the brain

Chapter 1. The Dynamic and Evolving Earth

1. _____ is a body of techniques for investigating phenomena and acquiring new knowledge, as well as for correcting and integrating previous knowledge. It is based on gathering observable, empirical and measurable evidence subject to specific principles of reasoning,
   - a. Scientific method0
   - b. Thing
   - c. Undefined
   - d. Undefined

2. The _____ is a cosmological model in which the universe has been expanding for around 13.7 billion years, starting from a tremendously dense and hot state. It is also used in a narrower sense to describe the fundamental 'fireball' that erupted at or close to time t=0 in the history of the universe.
   - a. Event
   - b. Big bang0
   - c. Undefined
   - d. Undefined

3. The _____ consists of the Sun and the other celestial objects gravitationally bound to it: the eight planets, their 165 known moons, three currently identified dwarf planets and their four known moons, and billions of small bodies.
   - a. Thing
   - b. Solar system0
   - c. Undefined
   - d. Undefined

4. A _____, as defined by the International Astronomical Union, is a celestial body orbiting a star or stellar remnant that is massive enough to be rounded by its own gravity, not massive enough to cause thermonuclear fusion in its core, and has cleared its neighboring region of planetesimals.
   - a. Planet0
   - b. Thing
   - c. Undefined
   - d. Undefined

5. The _____ is defined as the summation of all particles and energy that exist and the space-time in which all events occur.
   - a. Place
   - b. Universe0
   - c. Undefined
   - d. Undefined

6. Earth's _____ is a ~2,900 km thick rocky shell comprizing approximately 70% of Earth's volume. It is predominantly solid and overlies the Earth's iron-rich core, which occupies about 30% of Earth's volume. Past episodes of melting and volcanism at the shallower levels of the _____ have produced a very thin crust of crystallized melt products near the surface, upon which we live.
   - a. Mantle0
   - b. Thing
   - c. Undefined
   - d. Undefined

7. In geology, a _____ is the outermost layer of a planet, part of its lithosphere. They are generally composed of a less dense material than its deeper layers.Earths' is composed mainly of basalt and granite. It is cooler and more rigid than the deeper layers of the mantle and core.
   - a. Crust0
   - b. Thing
   - c. Undefined
   - d. Undefined

8. _____ is a field of study within geology concerned generally with the structures within the crust of the Earth, or other planets, and particularly with the forces and movements that have operated in a region to create these structures.
   - a. Thing
   - b. Tectonics0
   - c. Undefined
   - d. Undefined

Chapter 1. The Dynamic and Evolving Earth

9. _____ is a theory of geology that has been developed to explain the observed evidence for large scale motions of the Earth's lithosphere. The theory encompassed and superseded the older theory of continental drift.
   a. Thing
   b. Plate tectonics0
   c. Undefined
   d. Undefined

10. _____ is the science and study of the solid matter that constitute the Earth. Encompassing such things as rocks, soil, and gemstones, _____ studies the composition, structure, physical properties, history, and the processes that shape Earth's components.
    a. Thing
    b. Geology0
    c. Undefined
    d. Undefined

11. _____ refers to the principle that the same processes that shape the universe occurred in the past as they do now, and that the same laws of physics apply in all parts of the knowable universe.
    a. Thing
    b. Uniformitarianism0
    c. Undefined
    d. Undefined

12. The _____ is used by geologists and other scientists to describe the timing and relationships between events that have occurred during the history of Earth.
    a. Thing
    b. Geological time scale0
    c. Undefined
    d. Undefined

13. _____ is the use of the principles of geology to reconstruct and understand the history of the Earth. It focuses on geologic processes that change the Earth's surface and subsurface; and the use of stratigraphy, structural geology and paleontology to tell the sequence of these events. It also focuses on the evolution of plants and animals during different time periods in the geological timescale.
    a. Historical geology0
    b. Thing
    c. Undefined
    d. Undefined

14. A _____ is one of several large landmasses on Earth. They are generally identified by convention rather than any strict criteria, but seven areas are commonly reckoned as continents – they are: Asia, Africa, North America, South America, Antarctica, Europe, and Australia.
    a. Thing
    b. Continent0
    c. Undefined
    d. Undefined

15. _____ is a layer of gases surrounding the planet Earth and retained by the Earth's gravity. This mixture of gases is commonly known as air.
    a. Thing
    b. Earths atmosphere0
    c. Undefined
    d. Undefined

16. An _____ is a mass of glacier ice that covers surrounding terrain and is greater than 19,305 mile². The only current ice sheets are in Antarctica and Greenland. Ice sheets are bigger than ice shelves or glaciers. Masses of ice covering less than 50,000 km² are termed an ice cap. An ice cap will typically feed a series of glaciers around its periphery. Although the surface is cold, the base of an _____ is generally warmer. This process produces fast-flowing channels in the _____.

Chapter 1. The Dynamic and Evolving Earth

a. Ice sheet0
b. Thing
c. Undefined
d. Undefined

17. _____ is the large-scale movement of air, and the means by which heat is distributed on the surface of the Earth. The large-scale structure of the _____ varies from year to year, but the basic structure remains fairly constant.
 a. Thing
 b. Atmospheric circulation0
 c. Undefined
 d. Undefined

18. In geography, a _____ is a landscape form or region that receives very little precipitation. They are defined as areas that receive an average annual precipitation of less than 250 mm. A _____ where vegetation cover is exceedingly sparse correspond to the 'hyperarid' regions of the earth, where rainfall is exceedingly rare and infrequent.
 a. Desert0
 b. Place
 c. Undefined
 d. Undefined

19. A _____ is a wetland that features temporary or permanent inundation of large areas of land by shallow bodies of water, generally with a substantial number of hummocks, or dry-land protrusions, and covered by aquatic vegetation, or vegetation that tolerates periodical inundation.
 a. Swamp0
 b. Thing
 c. Undefined
 d. Undefined

20. _____ are a major group of arthropods and the most diverse group of animals on the Earth, with over a million described species—more than all other animal groups combined. They may be found in nearly all environments on the planet, although only a small number of species occur in the oceans where crustaceans tend to predominate instead.
 a. Thing
 b. Insects0
 c. Undefined
 d. Undefined

21. _____ are tetrapods and amniotes, animals whose embryos are surrounded by an amniotic membrane, and members of the class Sauropsida. They rely on gathering and losing heat from the environment to regulate their internal temperature, e.g, by moving between sun and shade, or by preferential circulation — moving warmed blood into the body core, while pushing cool blood to the periphery.
 a. Reptiles0
 b. Thing
 c. Undefined
 d. Undefined

22. _____ are a taxon of animals that include all living tetrapods or four-legged vertebrates, that do not have amniotic eggs, are ectothermic, term for the animals whose body heat is regulated by the external environment; previously known as cold-blooded, and generally spend part of their time on land.
 a. Thing
 b. Amphibians0
 c. Undefined
 d. Undefined

23. An _____ is a natural unit consisting of all plants, animals and micro organisms in an area functioning together with all the non living physical factors of the environment.
 a. Ecosystem0
 b. Thing
 c. Undefined
 d. Undefined

24. In geography _____ are isolated areas of vegetation in a desert, typically surrounding a spring or similar water source. The location of _____ has been of critical importance for trade and transportation routes in desert areas.

Chapter 1. The Dynamic and Evolving Earth

   a. Oases0
   b. Thing
   c. Undefined
   d. Undefined

25. A _____ is a body of water with a current, confined within a bed and banks. Streams are important as conduits in the water cycle, instruments in aquifer recharge, and corridors for fish and wildlife migration.
   a. Thing
   b. Stream0
   c. Undefined
   d. Undefined

26. A _____ is a naturally occurring substance formed through geological processes that has a characteristic chemical composition, a highly ordered atomic structure and specific physical properties. A rock, by comparison, is an aggregate of minerals and need not have a specific chemical composition. Minerals range in composition from pure elements and simple salts to very complex silicates with thousands of known forms.
   a. Thing
   b. Mineral0
   c. Undefined
   d. Undefined

27. _____ is a general term that includes rocks and materials that are not by definition rocks but are commonly regarded as rocks.
   a. Earth materials0
   b. Thing
   c. Undefined
   d. Undefined

28. An _____ is a layer of gases that may surround a material body of sufficient mass. The gases are attracted by the gravity of the body, and are retained for a longer duration if gravity is high and the _____'s temperature is low. Some planets consist mainly of various gases, and thus have very deep atmospheres.
   a. Atmosphere0
   b. Place
   c. Undefined
   d. Undefined

29. _____ are artificial channels for water. There are two main types of _____: irrigation _____, which are used for the delivery of water, and waterways, which are transportation _____ used for passage of goods and people, often connected to existing lakes, rivers, or oceans.
   a. Canals0
   b. Thing
   c. Undefined
   d. Undefined

30. _____, in everyday life, is most familiar as the agency that endows objects with weight. _____ is responsible for keeping the Earth and the other planets in their orbits around the Sun; for the formation of tides; and for various other phenomena that we observe. _____ is also the reason for the very existence of the Earth, the Sun, and most macroscopic objects in the universe; without it, matter would not have coalesced into these large masses, and life, as we know it, would not exist.
   a. Gravitation0
   b. Thing
   c. Undefined
   d. Undefined

31. A _____ is a landform that extends above the surrounding terrain in a limited area. A _____ is generally steeper than a hill, but there is no universally accepted standard definition for the height of a _____ or a hill although a _____ usually has an identifiable summit.
   a. Mountain0
   b. Place
   c. Undefined
   d. Undefined

Chapter 1. The Dynamic and Evolving Earth

32. _____ is the reprocessing of materials into new products. It prevents useful material resources being wasted, reduces the consumption of raw materials and reduces energy usage, and hence greenhouse gas emissions, compared to virgin production.
   a. Thing
   b. Recycling0
   c. Undefined
   d. Undefined

33. _____ is displacement of solids by the agents of ocean currents, wind, water, or ice by downward or down-slope movement in response to gravity or by living organisms.
   a. Erosion0
   b. Thing
   c. Undefined
   d. Undefined

34. _____ is any product of the condensation of atmospheric water vapor that is deposited on the earth's surface. It occurs when the atmosphere becomes saturated with water vapour and the water condenses and falls out of solution. Air becomes saturated via two processes, cooling and adding moisture.
   a. Precipitation0
   b. Thing
   c. Undefined
   d. Undefined

35. _____ as used in physics, is energy in the form of waves or moving subatomic particles.
   a. Radiation0
   b. Thing
   c. Undefined
   d. Undefined

36. The _____ is the part of the earth, including air, land, surface rocks, and water, within which life occurs, and which biotic processes in turn alter or transform. From the broadest biophysiological point of view, the _____ is the global ecological system integrating all living beings and their relationships, including their interaction with the elements of the lithosphere, hydrosphere, and atmosphere. This _____ is postulated to have evolved, beginning through a process of biogenesis or biopoesis, at least some 3.5 billion years ago.
   a. Thing
   b. Biosphere0
   c. Undefined
   d. Undefined

37. _____ is an all-embracing term for the sciences related to the planet Earth. It is arguably a special case in planetary science, being the only known life-bearing planet. There are both reductionist and holistic approaches to _____. The major historic disciplines use physics, geology, geography, mathematics, chemistry, and biology to build a quantitative understanding of the principal areas or spheres of the Earth system.
   a. Thing
   b. Earth science0
   c. Undefined
   d. Undefined

38. The _____ is Earth's only natural satellite. It makes a complete orbit around the Earth every 27.3 days, and the periodic variations in the geometry of the Earth–_____–Sun system are responsible for the lunar phases that repeat every 29.5 days.
   a. Thing
   b. Moon0
   c. Undefined
   d. Undefined

39. A _____ in physical geography describes the collective mass of water found on, under, and over the surface of a planet.

Chapter 1. The Dynamic and Evolving Earth

a. Hydrosphere0
b. Thing
c. Undefined
d. Undefined

40. A _____ is a massive, gravitationally bound system consisting of stars, an interstellar medium of gas and dust, and dark matter. They typically range from dwarfs with as few as ten million stars up to giants with one trillion stars, all orbiting a common center of mass.
a. Thing
b. Galaxy0
c. Undefined
d. Undefined

41. _____ is the substance of which physical objects are composed. _____ can be solid, liquid, plasma or gas. It constitutes the observable universe.
a. Thing
b. Matter0
c. Undefined
d. Undefined

42. Ocean _____ are any more or less continuous, directed movement of ocean water that flows in one of the Earth's oceans. They are rivers of hot or cold water within the ocean. They are generated from the forces acting upon the water like the earth's rotation, the wind, the temperature and salinity differences and the gravitation of the moon.
a. Currents0
b. Thing
c. Undefined
d. Undefined

43. _____ is a chemical element. An abundant nonmetallic, tetravalent element, _____ has several allotropic forms. This element is the basis of the chemistry of all known life.
a. Thing
b. Carbon0
c. Undefined
d. Undefined

44. The _____ is the biogeochemical cycle by which carbon is exchanged between the biosphere, geosphere, hydrosphere, and atmosphere of the Earth.
a. Carbon cycle0
b. Thing
c. Undefined
d. Undefined

45. A _____ is a rock, sandbar, or other feature lying beneath the surface of the water yet shallow enough to be a hazard to ships. They result from abiotic processes deposition of sand, wave erosion planning down rock outcrops, and other natural processes.
a. Reef0
b. Thing
c. Undefined
d. Undefined

46. _____ is the scientific study of the distribution and abundance of living organisms and how the distribution and abundance are affected by interactions between the organisms and their environment.
a. Ecology0
b. Thing
c. Undefined
d. Undefined

47. Fossils are the mineralized or otherwise preserved remains or traces of animals, plants, and other organisms. The totality of fossils, both discovered and undiscovered, and their placement in fossiliferous rock formations and sedimentary layers is known as the _____ record.

a. Thing
b. Fossil0
c. Undefined
d. Undefined

48. _____ is one of the four fundamental interactions of nature. In the Standard Model of particle physics, it is due to the exchange of the heavy W and Z bosons. Its most familiar effect is beta decay and the associated radioactivity.
   a. Weak nuclear force0
   b. Thing
   c. Undefined
   d. Undefined

49. In physics, the _____ is a subatomic particle with no net electric charge.
   a. Neutron0
   b. Thing
   c. Undefined
   d. Undefined

50. _____ is one of the phenomena by which materials exert attractive or repulsive forces on other materials. Some well known materials that exhibit easily detectable magnetic properties are nickel, iron, some steels, and the mineral magnetite; however, all materials are influenced to greater or lesser degree by the presence of a magnetic field.
   a. Thing
   b. Magnetism0
   c. Undefined
   d. Undefined

51. In physics, the _____ is a subatomic particle with an electric charge of one positive fundamental unit a diameter of about 1.5×10^{-15} m, and a mass of 938.27231(28) MeV/c2 (1.6726×10^{-27} kg), 1.007 276 466 88(13) u or about 1836 times the mass of an electron.
   a. Thing
   b. Proton0
   c. Undefined
   d. Undefined

52. _____ is the process in which an unstable atomic nucleus loses energy by emitting radiation in the form of particles or electromagnetic waves.
   a. Radioactive decay0
   b. Thing
   c. Undefined
   d. Undefined

53. In chemistry, a _____ is defined as a sufficiently stable electrically neutral group of at least two atoms in a definite arrangement held together by strong chemical bonds.
   a. Molecule0
   b. Thing
   c. Undefined
   d. Undefined

54. _____ are the fundamental building blocks of chemistry, and are conserved in chemical reactions.
   a. Thing
   b. Atoms0
   c. Undefined
   d. Undefined

55. _____ is a general term for a variety of phenomena resulting from the presence and flow of charge. This includes many well-known physical phenomena such as lightning, electromagnetic fields and electric currents, and is put to use in industrial applications such as electronics and electric power.
   a. Electricity0
   b. Thing
   c. Undefined
   d. Undefined

56. In physics, the _____ is the force that the field exerts on electrically charged particles. It is this that holds electrons and nuclei together in atoms, and which hold atoms together to make molecules.

Chapter 1. The Dynamic and Evolving Earth

    a. Thing
    b. Electromagnetic force0
    c. Undefined
    d. Undefined

57. _____ is the physics of the electromagnetic field: a field which exerts a force on particles that possess the property of electric charge, and is in turn affected by the presence and motion of those particles. The magnetic field is produced by the motion of electric charges, i.e. electric current.
    a. Electromagnetism0
    b. Thing
    c. Undefined
    d. Undefined

58. _____ is a chemical element represented by the symbol H and an atomic number of 1. At standard temperature and pressure it is a colorless, odorless, nonmetallic, tasteless, highly flammable diatomic gas . With an atomic mass of 1.00794 g/mol, _____ is the lightest element._____ is the most abundant of the chemical elements, constituting roughly 75% of the universe's elemental mass.
    a. Thing
    b. Hydrogen0
    c. Undefined
    d. Undefined

59. A _____ is a massive, luminous ball of plasma. Stars group together to form galaxies, and they dominate the visible universe. The nearest _____ to Earth is the Sun, which is the source of most of the energy on Earth, including daylight. Other stars are visible in the night sky, when they are not outshone by the Sun. A _____ shines because nuclear fusion in its core releases energy which traverses the _____'s interior and then radiates into outer space.
    a. Thing
    b. Star0
    c. Undefined
    d. Undefined

60. An _____ is a type of atom that is defined by its atomic number; that is, by the number of protons in its nucleus.
    a. Element0
    b. Thing
    c. Undefined
    d. Undefined

61. In physics and nuclear chemistry, _____ is the process by which multiple atomic particles join together to form a heavier nucleus. It is accompanied by the release or absorption of energy.
    a. Thing
    b. Nuclear fusion0
    c. Undefined
    d. Undefined

62. A _____ is the process of life. First, an animal or a person is born. Then, they grow, or change. They reproduce themselves, meaning that they give birth to a baby animal/person. Finally, the person/animal dies, and the reproduced baby starts growing. Then the cycle starts again.
    a. Life cycle0
    b. Thing
    c. Undefined
    d. Undefined

63. A _____ is a large, swirling body of water produced by ocean tides.
    a. Thing
    b. Whirlpool0
    c. Undefined
    d. Undefined

64. The _____ is believed to be a gaseous cloud from which Earth's solar system formed. This was first proposed by Emanuel Swedenborg. Immanuel Kant, who was familiar with Swedenborg's work, developed the theory further. He argued that nebulae slowly rotate, gradually collapsing and flattening due to gravity and eventually forming stars and planets.

a. Solar nebula0
b. Thing
c. Undefined
d. Undefined

65. A _____ is an interstellar cloud of dust, hydrogen gas and plasma. It is the first stage of a star's cycle.
    a. Thing
    b. Nebula0
    c. Undefined
    d. Undefined

66. The _____ is a barred spiral galaxy of a Local Group of galaxies within the Virgo Supercluster. The galaxy is estimated to contain 200 billion stars but this number might reach 400 billion if small-mass stars predominate.
    a. Milky Way0
    b. Thing
    c. Undefined
    d. Undefined

67. _____ is the change in matter of a substance to a denser phase, such as a gas to a liquid. _____ commonly occurs when a vapor is cooled to a liquid, but can also occur if a vapor is compressed into a liquid, or undergoes a combination of cooling and compression.
    a. Thing
    b. Condensation0
    c. Undefined
    d. Undefined

68. _____ are solid objects thought to exist in protoplanetary disks and in debris disks. A widely accepted theory of planet formation states that planets form out of dust grains that collide and stick to form larger and larger bodies. When the bodies reach sizes of approximately one kilometer, then they can attract each other directly through their mutual gravity, aiding further growth into moon-sized protoplanets enormously.
    a. Planetesimals0
    b. Thing
    c. Undefined
    d. Undefined

69. _____ refers to things having to do with the land or with the planet Earth.
    a. Thing
    b. Terrestrial0
    c. Undefined
    d. Undefined

70. A _____, telluric planet or rocky planet is a planet that is primarily composed of silicate rocks. Terrestrial planets are substantially different from gas giants, which might not have solid surfaces and are composed mostly of some combination of hydrogen, helium, and water existing in various physical states.
    a. Terrestrial planet0
    b. Thing
    c. Undefined
    d. Undefined

71. _____ is the second-closest planet to the Sun, orbiting it every 224.7 Earth days. It is the brightest natural object in the night sky, except for the Moon, reaching an apparent magnitude of −4.6. Because _____ is an inferior planet, from Earth it never appears to venture far from the Sun: its elongation reaches a maximum of 47.8°.
    a. Thing
    b. Venus0
    c. Undefined
    d. Undefined

72. _____ the fourth planet from the Sun in the Solar System. The planet is named after _____, the Roman god of war. It is also referred to as the "Red Planet" because of its reddish appearance as seen from Earth.
    a. Mars0
    b. Thing
    c. Undefined
    d. Undefined

73. _____ is the eighth and farthest known planet from the Sun in the Solar System. It is the fourth largest planet by diameter, and the third largest by mass.
   a. Neptune0
   b. Place
   c. Undefined
   d. Undefined

74. _____ is the seventh planet from the Sun, and the first discovered in modern times. Although, like the five classical planets, _____ is visible to the naked eye.
   a. Uranus0
   b. Thing
   c. Undefined
   d. Undefined

75. _____ is the sixth planet from the Sun. It is a gas giant and the second largest planet in the Solar System after Jupiter. The planet _____ is primarily composed of hydrogen, with small proportions of helium and trace elements.
   a. Place
   b. Saturn0
   c. Undefined
   d. Undefined

76. In geology the term _____ refers to the system of forces that tend to decrease the volume of or shorten rocks. Compressive strength refers to the maximum compressive stress that can be applied to a material before failure occurs.
   a. Thing
   b. Compression0
   c. Undefined
   d. Undefined

77. A _____ is an approximately circular depression in the surface of a planet, moon or other solid body in the Solar System, formed by the hyper-velocity impact of a smaller body with the surface. Impact craters typically have raised rims, and they range from small, simple, bowl-shaped depressions to large, complex, multi-ringed, impact basins.
   a. Thing
   b. Crater0
   c. Undefined
   d. Undefined

78. _____ is the fifth planet from the Sun and the largest planet within the solar system. It is two and a half times as massive as all of the other planets in our solar system combined. _____, along with Saturn, Uranus and Neptune, is classified as a gas giant.
   a. Jupiter0
   b. Place
   c. Undefined
   d. Undefined

79. _____ are a class of astronomical objects. The term is generally used to indicate a diverse group of small celestial bodies that drift in the solar system in orbit around the Sun.
   a. Asteroids0
   b. Thing
   c. Undefined
   d. Undefined

80. _____ are small bodies in the solar system that orbit the Sun and occasionally exhibit a coma or atmosphere and/or a tail — both primarily from the effects of solar radiation upon its nucleus, which itself is a minor body composed of rock, dust, and ice.
   a. Thing
   b. Comets0
   c. Undefined
   d. Undefined

81. The _____ is the region of the Solar System located roughly between the planets Mars and Jupiter where 98.5% of asteroid orbits can be found. This region is termed the main belt when contrasted with other concentrations of minor planets.

Chapter 1. The Dynamic and Evolving Earth

a. Thing
b. Asteroid belt0
c. Undefined
d. Undefined

82. _____ has the symbol Mg. It is the ninth most abundant element in the universe by mass. It constitutes about 2% of the Earth's crust by mass, and it is the third most abundant element dissolved in seawater. It is essential to all living cells, and is the 11th most abundant element by mass in the human body.
   a. Magnesium0
   b. Thing
   c. Undefined
   d. Undefined

83. An _____ is a chemical compound containing an oxygen atom and other elements. Most of the earth's crust consists of them. They result when elements are oxidized by air.
   a. Oxide0
   b. Thing
   c. Undefined
   d. Undefined

84. _____ is a chemical element metal. It is a lustrous, silvery soft metal. It and nickel are notable for being the final elements produced by stellar nucleosynthesis, and thus are the heaviest elements which do not require a supernova or similarly cataclysmic event for formation.
   a. Thing
   b. Iron0
   c. Undefined
   d. Undefined

85. In geology and astronomy, the term _____ is used to denote types of rock that consist predominantly of _____ minerals. Such rocks include a wide range of igneous, metamorphic and sedimentary types. Most of the Earth's mantle and crust are made up of _____ rocks. The same is true of the Moon and the other rocky planets.
   a. Silicate0
   b. Thing
   c. Undefined
   d. Undefined

86. _____ is a silvery white metal that takes on a high polish. It belongs to the transition metals, and is hard and ductile. It occurs most usually in combination with sulfur and iron in pentlandite, with sulfur in millerite, with arsenic in the mineral niccolite, and with arsenic and sulfur.
   a. Nickel0
   b. Thing
   c. Undefined
   d. Undefined

87. A _____ is a natural object originating in outer space that survives an impact with the Earth's surface without being destroyed. While in space it is called a meteoroid. When it enters the atmosphere, air resistance causes the body to heat up and emit light, thus forming a fireball.
   a. Thing
   b. Meteorite0
   c. Undefined
   d. Undefined

88. A _____ is a chemical substance of two or more different chemically bonded chemical elements, with a fixed ratio determining the composition. The ratio of each element is usually expressed by chemical formula.
   a. Chemical compound0
   b. Thing
   c. Undefined
   d. Undefined

89. _____ is a process by which sediment is added to a tectonic plate. When two tectonic plates collide, one of the plates may slide under the other. This process is called subduction. The plate which is being subducted, is floating on the asthenosphere and is pushed up and against the other plate, which will often be scraped by the subducted plate.

Chapter 1. The Dynamic and Evolving Earth

    a. Accretion0
    b. Thing
    c. Undefined
    d. Undefined

90. _____ is the process of heating a solid substance to a point where it turns into a liquid. An object that has melted is molten.
    a. Thing
    b. Melting0
    c. Undefined
    d. Undefined

91. The _____ of a crystalline solid is the temperature range at which it changes state from solid to liquid. Although the phrase would suggest a specific temperature, most crystalline compounds actually melt over a range of a few degrees or less. At the _____ the solid and liquid phase exist in equilibrium.
    a. Thing
    b. Melting point0
    c. Undefined
    d. Undefined

92. _____ are large geologic basins that are below sea level. Geologically, there are other undersea geomorphological features such as the continental shelves, the deep ocean trenches, and the undersea mountain rangeswhich are not considered to be part of the _____.
    a. Thing
    b. Ocean basins0
    c. Undefined
    d. Undefined

93. _____ is the gas phase component of a another state of matter which does not completely fill its container. It is distinguished from the pure gas phase by the presence of the same substance in another state of matter. Hence when a liquid has completely evaporated, it is said that the system has been completely transformed to the gas phase.
    a. Thing
    b. Vapor0
    c. Undefined
    d. Undefined

94. An _____ is the result from the sudden release of stored energy in the Earth's crust that creates seismic waves. At the Earth's surface, earthquakes may manifest themselves by a shaking or displacement of the ground. An _____ is caused by tectonic plates getting stuck and putting a strain on the ground. The strain becomes so great that rocks give way by breaking and sliding along fault planes.
    a. Thing
    b. Earthquake0
    c. Undefined
    d. Undefined

95. The _____ is a primarily solid sphere about 1220 km in radius situated at Earth's center.The existence of an _____ that is different from the liquid outer core was discovered in 1936 by seismologist Inge Lehman using observations of earthquake-generated seismic waves that partly reflect from its boundary and can be detected by sensitive instruments at Earth's surface called seismographs.
    a. Thing
    b. Inner core0
    c. Undefined
    d. Undefined

96. _____ is a dense, coarse-grained igneous rock, consisting mostly of the minerals olivine and pyroxene. _____ is ultramafic and ultrabasic, as the rock contains less than 45% silica. This type of rock is derived from the Earth's mantle, either as solid blocks and fragments, or as crystals accumulated from magmas that formed in the mantle.
    a. Peridotite0
    b. Thing
    c. Undefined
    d. Undefined

Chapter 1. The Dynamic and Evolving Earth 13

97. _____ rocks form when molten rock, magma, cools and solidifies, with or without crystallization, either below the surface as intrusive, plutonic rocks or on the surface as extrusive, volcanic, rocks.
   a. Thing
   b. Igneous0
   c. Undefined
   d. Undefined

98. _____ forms when rock cools and solidifies either below the surface as intrusive rocks or on the surface as extrusive rocks. This magma can be derived from partial melts of pre-existing rocks in either the Earth's mantle or crust. Typically, the melting is caused by one or more of the following processes -- an increase in temperature, a decrease in pressure, or a change in composition.
   a. Thing
   b. Igneous rock0
   c. Undefined
   d. Undefined

99. _____ is molten rock located beneath the surface of the Earth, and which often collects in a _____ chamber. _____ is a complex high-temperature fluid substance. Most are silicate solutions. It is capable of intrusion into adjacent rocks or of extrusion onto the surface as lava or ejected explosively as tephra to form pyroclastic rock. Environments of _____ formation include subduction zones, continental rift zones, mid-oceanic ridges, and hotspots, some of which are interpreted as mantle plumes.
   a. Thing
   b. Magma0
   c. Undefined
   d. Undefined

100. _____ is a small island located in the middle of San Francisco Bay in California, United States. It served as a lighthouse, then a military fortification, then a military prison followed by a federal prison until 1963, when it became a national recreation area.
   a. Place
   b. Alcatraz Island0
   c. Undefined
   d. Undefined

101. The _____ is the region of the Earth between 100-200 km below the surface that is the weak or "soft" zone in the upper mantle. It lies just below the lithosphere, which is involved in plate movements and isostatic adjustments. In spite of its heat, pressures keep it plastic, and it has a relatively low density. Seismic waves pass relatively slowly through the _____.
   a. Thing
   b. Asthenosphere0
   c. Undefined
   d. Undefined

102. _____ in the most general terms refers to the movement of currents within fluids. _____ is one of the major modes of Heat and mass transfer. In fluids, convective heat and mass transfer take place through both diffusion and by advection, in which matter or heat is transported by the larger-scale motion of currents in the fluid.
   a. Thing
   b. Convection0
   c. Undefined
   d. Undefined

103. A _____ is a phenomenon of fluid dynamics which occurs in situations where there are temperature differences within a body of liquid or gas.
   a. Convection cell0
   b. Thing
   c. Undefined
   d. Undefined

Chapter 1. The Dynamic and Evolving Earth

104. The _____ is the solid outermost shell of a rocky planet. On the Earth, the _____ includes the crust and the uppermost mantle which is joined to the crust across the Mohorovièiæ discontinuity. _____ is underlain by asthenosphere, the weaker, hotter, and deeper part of the upper mantle.
- a. Thing
- b. Lithosphere0
- c. Undefined
- d. Undefined

105. The _____ is the layer of granitic, sedimentary, and metamorphic rocks which form the continents and the areas of shallow seabed close to their shores, known as continental shelves. It is less dense than the material of the Earth's mantle and thus "floats" on top of it. _____ is also less dense than oceanic crust, though it is considerably thicker. About 40% of the Earth's surface is now underlain by _____.
- a. Thing
- b. Continental crust0
- c. Undefined
- d. Undefined

106. _____ is a silvery and ductile member of the poor metal group of chemical elements. It has the symbol Al and atomic number 13.
- a. Aluminum0
- b. Thing
- c. Undefined
- d. Undefined

107. A _____ is an instrument designed for the observation of remote objects. The term usually refers to optical telescopes, but there are telescopes for most of the spectrum of electromagnetic radiation and for other signal types.
- a. Telescope0
- b. Thing
- c. Undefined
- d. Undefined

108. _____ is the part of Earth's lithosphere that surfaces in the ocean basins. _____ is primarily composed of mafic rocks, or sima. It is thinner than continental crust, or sial, generally less than 10 kilometers thick, however it is more dense, having a mean density of about 3.3 grams per cubic centimeter.
- a. Thing
- b. Oceanic crust0
- c. Undefined
- d. Undefined

109. _____ is molten rock expelled by a volcano during an eruption. When first extruded from a volcanic vent, it is a liquid at temperatures from 700 °C to 1,200 °C.
- a. Thing
- b. Lava0
- c. Undefined
- d. Undefined

110. A _____ travels through the Earth, most often as the result of a tectonic earthquake, sometimes from an explosion. They are also continually excited by the pounding of ocean waves and the wind.
- a. Seismic wave0
- b. Thing
- c. Undefined
- d. Undefined

111. A _____ is a disturbance that propagates through space or spacetime, transferring energy and momentum and sometimes angular momentum.
- a. Thing
- b. Wave0
- c. Undefined
- d. Undefined

112. _____ is a common gray to black extrusive volcanic rock. It is usually fine-grained due to rapid cooling of lava on the Earth's surface. It may be porphyritic containing larger crystals in a fine matrix, or vesicular, or frothy scoria.

113. _____ are naturally occurring substances that are considered valuable in their relatively unmodified or natural form. Its value rests in the amount of the material available and the demand for the certain material.
- a. Thing
- b. Natural resources0
- c. Undefined
- d. Undefined

114. In biology and ecology, an _____ is a living complex adaptive system of organs that influence each other in such a way that they function in some way as a stable whole.
- a. Organism0
- b. Thing
- c. Undefined
- d. Undefined

115. _____ can be defined as the solid state recrystallisation of pre-existing rocks due to changes in heat and/or pressure and/or introduction of fluids. There will be mineralogical, chemical and crystallographic changes. _____ produced with increasing pressure and temperature conditions is known as prograde _____. Conversely, decreasing temperatures and pressure characterize retrograde _____.
- a. Thing
- b. Metamorphism0
- c. Undefined
- d. Undefined

116. The _____ is the set of all extant phenomena in a given atmosphere at a given time. The term usually refers to the activity of these phenomena over short periods, as opposed to the term climate, which refers to the average atmospheric conditions over longer periods of time.
- a. Weather0
- b. Thing
- c. Undefined
- d. Undefined

117. A _____ is a section of a river of relatively steep gradient causing an increase in water flow and turbulence. A _____ is a hydrological feature between a run and a cascade. It is characterized by the river becoming shallower and having some rocks exposed above the flow surface.
- a. Rapid0
- b. Thing
- c. Undefined
- d. Undefined

118. _____ is the average and variations of weather over long periods of time. _____ zones can be defined using parameters such as temperature and rainfall.
- a. Climate0
- b. Thing
- c. Undefined
- d. Undefined

119. An _____ is any more or less continuous, directed movement of ocean water that flows in one of the Earth's oceans.Ocean Currents are rivers of hot or cold water within the ocean. The currents are generated from the forces acting upon the water like the earth's rotation, the wind, the temperature and salinity differences and the gravitation of the moon. The depth contours, the shoreline and other currents influence the current's direction and strength.
- a. Thing
- b. Ocean current0
- c. Undefined
- d. Undefined

Chapter 1. The Dynamic and Evolving Earth

120. A _____ is a geological feature that is also known as a Rip in the earth causing magma to flow out and forming an undersea volcano, it also has geological features, a continuous elevational crest for some distance. Ridges are usually termed hills or mountains as well, depending on size.
   a. Thing
   b. Ridge0
   c. Undefined
   d. Undefined

121. Mean _____ is the average height of the sea, with reference to a suitable reference surface.
   a. Thing
   b. Sea level0
   c. Undefined
   d. Undefined

122. An _____ is a period of long-term reduction in the temperature of Earth's climate, resulting in an expansion of the continental ice sheets, polar ice sheets and mountain glaciers .
   a. Thing
   b. Ice Age0
   c. Undefined
   d. Undefined

123. In ecology, a _____ is a term describing the relational position of a species or population in an ecosystem.
   a. Niche0
   b. Thing
   c. Undefined
   d. Undefined

124. _____ is the place where a particular species live and grow. It is essentially the environment—at least the physical environment—that surrounds a species population.
   a. Habitat0
   b. Place
   c. Undefined
   d. Undefined

125. _____ refers to directed, regular, or systematic movement of a group of objects, organisms, or people.
   a. Thing
   b. Migration0
   c. Undefined
   d. Undefined

126. _____ refers to the cyclic rizing and falling of Earth's ocean surface caused by the tidal forces of the Moon and the sun acting on the oceans. They cause changes in the depth of the marine and estuarine water bodies and produce oscillating currents known as tidal streams, making prediction of tides important for coastal navigation.
   a. Thing
   b. Tide0
   c. Undefined
   d. Undefined

127. _____ are the cyclic rizing and falling of Earth's ocean surface caused by the tidal forces of the Moon and the sun acting on the oceans. _____ cause changes in the depth of the marine and estuarine water bodies and produce oscillating currents known as tidal streams, making prediction of _____ important for coastal navigation.
   a. Thing
   b. Tides0
   c. Undefined
   d. Undefined

128. A _____ is a movement of an object in a circular motion. A two-dimensional object rotates around a center of _____. A three-dimensional object rotates around a line called an axis. A circular motion about an external point, e.g. the Earth about the Sun, is called an orbit or more properly an orbital revolution.
   a. Thing
   b. Rotation0
   c. Undefined
   d. Undefined

129. _____ is the process by which favorable traits that are heritable become more common in successive generations of a population of reproducing organisms, and unfavorable traits that are heritable become less common.
   a. Thing
   b. Natural selection0
   c. Undefined
   d. Undefined

130. _____ is the increase in the average temperature of the Earth's near-surface air and oceans in recent decades and its projected continuation. An increase in global temperatures can in turn cause other changes, including sea level rise, and changes in the amount and pattern of precipitation resulting in floods and drought. There may also be changes in the frequency and intensity of extreme weather events.
   a. Global warming0
   b. Thing
   c. Undefined
   d. Undefined

131. _____ is a technique used to date materials based on a knowledge of the decay rates of naturally occurring isotopes, and the current abundances. It is the principal source of information about the age of the Earth and a significant source of information about rates of evolutionary change.
   a. Thing
   b. Radiometric dating0
   c. Undefined
   d. Undefined

132. In optics, _____ is the field that studies the measurement of electromagnetic radiation, including visible light. Note that light is also measured using the techniques of photometry, which deal with brightness as perceived by the human eye, rather than absolute power.
   a. Thing
   b. Radiometry0
   c. Undefined
   d. Undefined

133. In plate tectonics, a _____ is said to occur when tectonic plates slide and grind against each other along a transform fault. The relative motion of such plates is horizontal in either sinistral or dextral direction. Many transform boundaries are locked in tension before suddenly releasing, and causing earthquakes.
   a. Transform boundary0
   b. Thing
   c. Undefined
   d. Undefined

134. A _____ is a type of excavation or depression in the ground. They are generally defined by being deeper than they are wide, and by being narrow compared to their length.
   a. Trench0
   b. Thing
   c. Undefined
   d. Undefined

135. The _____ on the geologic timescale had been intended to cover the world's recent period of repeated glaciations. The _____ follows the Pliocene and is followed by the Holocene. The _____ is the third epoch of the Neogene period or 6th epoch of the Cenozoic era. The end of the _____ corresponds with the end of the Paleolithic age used in archaeology. The _____ is divided into the Early _____, Middle _____ and Late _____, and numerous faunal stages.
   a. Pleistocene0
   b. Thing
   c. Undefined
   d. Undefined

Chapter 1. The Dynamic and Evolving Earth

136. The _____ refers to the sparsity of additional modern mammalian faunas after a burst of evolution during the Eocene. The _____ follows the Eocene epoch and is followed by the Miocene epoch. The _____ is the third and final epoch of the Palaeogene period. The start of the _____ is marked by a major extinction event that may be related to the impact of a large extraterrestrial object in Siberia and/or one near Chesapeake Bay.
- a. Thing
- b. Oligocene0
- c. Undefined
- d. Undefined

137. _____ is a fine-grained sedimentary rock whose original constituents were clays or muds. It is characterized by thin laminae breaking with an irregular curving fracture, often splintery and usually parallel to the often-indistinguishable bedding plane.
- a. Shale0
- b. Thing
- c. Undefined
- d. Undefined

138. _____ was an American paleontologist, evolutionary biologist, and historian of science. He was also one of the most influential and widely-read writers of popular science of his generation, leading many commentators to call him "America's unofficial evolutionist laureate."
- a. Stephen J. Gould0
- b. Person
- c. Undefined
- d. Undefined

139. The _____ is a black shale fossil bed high up in the Canadian Rockies. Fossils were first found in the _____ by Charles Doolittle Walcott, who returned in the following years to collect additional specimens. Walcott recognized the arthropod fossils were new and unique species, but careful reexaminations showed that many in fact constituted entire new phyla of life, and even today some have proven impossible to classify.
- a. Burgess Shale0
- b. Thing
- c. Undefined
- d. Undefined

140. _____ refers to the matter that exists between the stars within a galaxy, the energy, in the form of electromagnetic radiation, that occupies the same volume is called the interstellar radiation field.
- a. Interstellar medium0
- b. Thing
- c. Undefined
- d. Undefined

141. A _____ is a group of mountains bordered by lowlands or separated from other mountain ranges by passes or rivers. Individual mountains within the same _____ do not necessarily have the same geology; they may be a mix of different orogeny, for example volcanoes, uplifted mountains or fold mountains and may, therefore, be of different rock.
- a. Mountain range0
- b. Thing
- c. Undefined
- d. Undefined

142. The _____ is defined as the part of the land adjoining or near the ocean. A coastline is properly a line on a map indicating the disposition of a _____, but the word is often used to refer to the _____ itself. The adjective coastal describes something as being on, near to, or associated with a _____.
- a. Coast0
- b. Place
- c. Undefined
- d. Undefined

143. _____ is a common and widely occurring type of intrusive, felsic, igneous rock. Granites are usually medium to coarsely crystalline, occasionally with some individual crystals larger than the groundmass forming a rock known as porphyry. Granites can be pink to dark gray or even black, depending on their chemistry and mineralogy.

a. Thing
b. Granite0
c. Undefined
d. Undefined

144. The _____ is a mountain range that is almost entirely in the eastern portion of the U.S. state of California. The _____ stretches 400 miles, from Fredonyer Pass in the north to Tehachapi Pass in the south. It is bounded on the west by California's Central Valley, and on the east by the Great Basin.
a. Place
b. Sierra Nevada0
c. Undefined
d. Undefined

Chapter 2. Earth Materials: Minerals and Rocks

1. A _____ is a naturally occurring substance formed through geological processes that has a characteristic chemical composition, a highly ordered atomic structure and specific physical properties. A rock, by comparison, is an aggregate of minerals and need not have a specific chemical composition. Minerals range in composition from pure elements and simple salts to very complex silicates with thousands of known forms.
   - a. Thing
   - b. Mineral0
   - c. Undefined
   - d. Undefined

2. _____ are the fundamental building blocks of chemistry, and are conserved in chemical reactions.
   - a. Atoms0
   - b. Thing
   - c. Undefined
   - d. Undefined

3. An _____ is a type of atom that is defined by its atomic number; that is, by the number of protons in its nucleus.
   - a. Thing
   - b. Element0
   - c. Undefined
   - d. Undefined

4. A _____ is a chemical substance of two or more different chemically bonded chemical elements, with a fixed ratio determining the composition. The ratio of each element is usually expressed by chemical formula.
   - a. Chemical compound0
   - b. Thing
   - c. Undefined
   - d. Undefined

5. The _____ is a fundamental concept in geology that describes the dynamic transitions through geologic time among the three main rock types: sedimentary, metamorphic, and igneous.
   - a. Rock cycle0
   - b. Thing
   - c. Undefined
   - d. Undefined

6. _____ is a small island located in the middle of San Francisco Bay in California, United States. It served as a lighthouse, then a military fortification, then a military prison followed by a federal prison until 1963, when it became a national recreation area.
   - a. Alcatraz Island0
   - b. Place
   - c. Undefined
   - d. Undefined

7. _____ is molten rock located beneath the surface of the Earth, and which often collects in a _____ chamber. _____ is a complex high-temperature fluid substance. Most are silicate solutions. It is capable of intrusion into adjacent rocks or of extrusion onto the surface as lava or ejected explosively as tephra to form pyroclastic rock. Environments of _____ formation include subduction zones, continental rift zones, mid-oceanic ridges, and hotspots, some of which are interpreted as mantle plumes.
   - a. Thing
   - b. Magma0
   - c. Undefined
   - d. Undefined

8. _____ are clastic rocks composed solely or primarily of volcanic materials.
   - a. Pyroclastics0
   - b. Thing
   - c. Undefined
   - d. Undefined

9. _____ rocks form when molten rock, magma, cools and solidifies, with or without crystallization, either below the surface as intrusive, plutonic rocks or on the surface as extrusive, volcanic, rocks.

Chapter 2. Earth Materials: Minerals and Rocks

a. Igneous0
b. Thing
c. Undefined
d. Undefined

10. _____ forms when rock cools and solidifies either below the surface as intrusive rocks or on the surface as extrusive rocks. This magma can be derived from partial melts of pre-existing rocks in either the Earth's mantle or crust. Typically, the melting is caused by one or more of the following processes -- an increase in temperature, a decrease in pressure, or a change in composition.
   a. Igneous rock0
   b. Thing
   c. Undefined
   d. Undefined

11. _____ is an igneous rock of volcanic origin. They often have a vesicular texture, which is the result voids left by volatiles escaping from the molten lava. Pumice is a rock, which is an example of explosive volcanic eruption. It is so vesicular that it floats in water.
   a. Thing
   b. Volcanic rock0
   c. Undefined
   d. Undefined

12. _____ is a geological term used to describe particles of rock derived from pre-existing rock through processes of weathering and erosion.
   a. Thing
   b. Detrital0
   c. Undefined
   d. Undefined

13. _____ is the process of breaking down rocks, soils and their minerals through direct contact with the atmosphere. _____ occurs without movement. Two main classifications of _____ processes exist. Mechanical or physical _____ involves the breakdown of rocks and soils through direct contact with atmospheric conditions. The second classification, chemical _____, involves the direct effect of atmospheric chemicals in the breakdown of rocks, soils and minerals.
   a. Thing
   b. Weathering0
   c. Undefined
   d. Undefined

14. _____ is any particulate matter that can be transported by fluid flow and which eventually is deposited as a layer of solid particles on the bed or bottom of a body of water or other liquid.
   a. Sediment0
   b. Thing
   c. Undefined
   d. Undefined

15. _____ rock is one of the three main rock groups. Rock formed from these covers 75% of the Earth's land area, and includes common types such as chalk, limestone, dolomite, sandstone, and shale.
   a. Thing
   b. Sedimentary0
   c. Undefined
   d. Undefined

16. _____ is one of the three main rock groups. _____ covers 75% of the Earth's land area. Four basic processes are involved in the formation of a clastic _____: weathering caused mainly by friction of waves, transportation where the sediment is carried along by a current, deposition and compaction where the sediment is squashed together to form a rock of this kind.
   a. Thing
   b. Sedimentary rock0
   c. Undefined
   d. Undefined

Chapter 2. Earth Materials: Minerals and Rocks

17. _____ is the result of the transformation of a pre-existing rock type, the protolith, in a process called metamorphism, which means "change in form". The protolith is subjected to heat and extreme pressure causing profound physical and/or chemical change. The protolith may be sedimentary rock, igneous rock or another older rock.
   a. Thing
   b. Metamorphic rock0
   c. Undefined
   d. Undefined

18. Metamorphic rock is the result of the transformation of a pre-existing rock type, the protolith, in a process called metamorphism. The protolith is subjected to heat and extreme pressure causing profound physical and/or chemical change. _____ make up a large part of the Earth's crust. They are formed deep beneath the Earth's surface by great stresses from rocks above and high pressures and temperatures.
   a. Thing
   b. Metamorphic rocks0
   c. Undefined
   d. Undefined

19. _____ can be defined as the solid state recrystallisation of pre-existing rocks due to changes in heat and/or pressure and/or introduction of fluids. There will be mineralogical, chemical and crystallographic changes. _____ produced with increasing pressure and temperature conditions is known as prograde _____. Conversely, decreasing temperatures and pressure characterize retrograde _____.
   a. Thing
   b. Metamorphism0
   c. Undefined
   d. Undefined

20. _____ is the reprocessing of materials into new products. It prevents useful material resources being wasted, reduces the consumption of raw materials and reduces energy usage, and hence greenhouse gas emissions, compared to virgin production.
   a. Recycling0
   b. Thing
   c. Undefined
   d. Undefined

21. _____ is a general term that includes rocks and materials that are not by definition rocks but are commonly regarded as rocks.
   a. Earth materials0
   b. Thing
   c. Undefined
   d. Undefined

22. _____ is a chemical element metal. It is a lustrous, silvery soft metal. It and nickel are notable for being the final elements produced by stellar nucleosynthesis, and thus are the heaviest elements which do not require a supernova or similarly cataclysmic event for formation.
   a. Thing
   b. Iron0
   c. Undefined
   d. Undefined

23. A _____ is any aspect of an object or substance that can be measured or perceived without changing its identity. Physical properties can be intensive or extensive. An intensive property does not depend on the size or amount of matter in the object, while an extensive property does.
   a. Physical property0
   b. Thing
   c. Undefined
   d. Undefined

24. _____ is the characteristic of a solid material expressing its resistance to permanent deformation.

Chapter 2. Earth Materials: Minerals and Rocks

a. Thing
c. Undefined
b. Hardness0
d. Undefined

25. _____ are naturally occurring substances that are considered valuable in their relatively unmodified or natural form. Its value rests in the amount of the material available and the demand for the certain material.
   a. Thing
   b. Natural resources0
   c. Undefined
   d. Undefined

26. _____ is a highly sought-after precious metal which, for many centuries, has been used as money, a store of value and in jewelery. The metal occurs as nuggets or grains in rocks, underground "veins" and in alluvial deposits. It is one of the coinage metals. Itis dense, soft, shiny and the most malleable and ductile of the known metals.
   a. Thing
   b. Gold0
   c. Undefined
   d. Undefined

27. _____ are the hardest natural material known to man and the third-hardest known material. Its hardness and high dispersion of light make it useful for industrial applications and jewelry.
   a. Thing
   b. Diamonds0
   c. Undefined
   d. Undefined

28. A _____ is a highly attractive and valuable piece of mineral, which, when cut and polished, is used in jewelry or other adornments.
   a. Gemstone0
   b. Thing
   c. Undefined
   d. Undefined

29. _____ is a soft white lustrous transition metal, it has the highest electrical and thermal conductivity for a metal.
   a. Silver0
   b. Thing
   c. Undefined
   d. Undefined

30. _____ is a chemical element. A heavy, malleable, ductile, precious, grey-white transition metal, it is resistant to corrosion and occurs in some nickel and copper ores along with some native deposits. It is used in jewelry, laboratory equipment, electrical contacts, dentistry, and automobile emissions control devices.
   a. Thing
   b. Platinum0
   c. Undefined
   d. Undefined

31. _____ is a chemical element. Its ions are variously colored, and are used industrially as pigments and as oxidation chemicals. Its ions function as cofactors for a number of enzymes and the element is thus a required trace mineral for all known living organisms. It is a grey-white metal, resembling iron.
   a. Thing
   b. Manganese0
   c. Undefined
   d. Undefined

32. A _____, in inorganic chemistry, is a salt of phosphoric acid. In organic chemistry it is an ester of phosphoric acid.
   a. Thing
   b. Phosphate0
   c. Undefined
   d. Undefined

Chapter 2. Earth Materials: Minerals and Rocks

33. _____ is the second most common mineral in the Earth's continental crust. It is made up of a lattice of silica tetrahedra. _____ belongs to the rhombohedral crystal system. In nature _____ crystals are often twinned, distorted, or so intergrown with adjacent crystals of _____ or other minerals as to only show part of this shape, or to lack obvious crystal faces altogether and appear massive.
  a. Quartz0
  b. Thing
  c. Undefined
  d. Undefined

34. A _____, is a site for the disposal of waste materials by burial and is the oldest form of waste treatment.
  a. Landfill0
  b. Thing
  c. Undefined
  d. Undefined

35. A _____ is the fringe of land at the edge of a large body of water, such as an ocean, sea, or lake. A strict definition is the strip of land along a water body that is alternately exposed and covered by waves and tides.
  a. Shoreline0
  b. Thing
  c. Undefined
  d. Undefined

36. A _____ is a body of water or other liquid of considerable size contained on a body of land. A vast majority are fresh water, and lie in the Northern Hemisphere at higher latitudes. Most have a natural outflow in the form of a river or stream, but some do not, and lose water solely by evaporation and/or underground seepage.
  a. Thing
  b. Lake0
  c. Undefined
  d. Undefined

37. _____, bounded by Ontario, Canada and Minnesota, USA, to the north and Wisconsin and Michigan, USA, to the south, is the largest of North America's Great Lakes. It is the largest freshwater lake in the world by surface area and is the world's third-largest freshwater lake by volume.
  a. Place
  b. Lake Superior0
  c. Undefined
  d. Undefined

38. _____ in meteorology are large scale patterns in the atmospheric pressure field that are nearly stationary, effectively "blocking" or redirecting migratory cyclones. These _____ can remain in place for several days or even weeks, causing the areas affected by them to have the same kind of weather for an extended period of time.
  a. Thing
  b. Blocks0
  c. Undefined
  d. Undefined

39. _____ is the substance of which physical objects are composed. _____ can be solid, liquid, plasma or gas. It constitutes the observable universe.
  a. Thing
  b. Matter0
  c. Undefined
  d. Undefined

40. In physics, the _____ is a subatomic particle with no net electric charge.
  a. Neutron0
  b. Thing
  c. Undefined
  d. Undefined

41. In physics, the _____ is a subatomic particle with an electric charge of one positive fundamental unit a diameter of about 1.5×10^{-15} m, and a mass of 938.27231(28) MeV/c2 (1.6726×10^{-27} kg), 1.007 276 466 88(13) u or about 1836 times the mass of an electron.

Chapter 2. Earth Materials: Minerals and Rocks

a. Proton0
b. Thing
c. Undefined
d. Undefined

42. The _____ is a fundamental subatomic particle that carries a negative electric charge.
   a. Electron0
   b. Thing
   c. Undefined
   d. Undefined

43. _____ is a chemical element. An abundant nonmetallic, tetravalent element, _____ has several allotropic forms. This element is the basis of the chemistry of all known life.
   a. Carbon0
   b. Thing
   c. Undefined
   d. Undefined

44. _____ are any of the several different forms of an element each having different atomic mass. _____ of an element have nuclei with the same number of protons but different numbers of neutrons.
   a. Isotopes0
   b. Thing
   c. Undefined
   d. Undefined

45. The _____ is the element in group 18 of the periodic table. It is also called helium family or neon family. Chemically, they are very stable due to having the maximum number of valence electrons their outer shell can hold. A thorough explanation requires an understanding of electronic configuration, with references to quantum mechanics.
   a. Thing
   b. Noble gas0
   c. Undefined
   d. Undefined

46. The _____ is the mass of an atom at rest, most often expressed in unified _____ units.[
   a. Atomic mass0
   b. Thing
   c. Undefined
   d. Undefined

47. In chemistry and physics, the _____ is the number of protons found in the nucleus of an atom. It is traditionally represented by the symbol Z.
   a. Atomic number0
   b. Thing
   c. Undefined
   d. Undefined

48. An _____ is an atom or group of atoms which have lost or gained one or more electrons, making them negatively or positively charged.
   a. Thing
   b. Ion0
   c. Undefined
   d. Undefined

49. An _____ is a type of chemical bond based on electrostatic forces between two oppositely-charged ions. In this formation, a metal donates an electron, due to a low electronegativity to form a positive ion or cation.
   a. Thing
   b. Ionic bond0
   c. Undefined
   d. Undefined

50. _____ is the mineral form of sodium chloride. _____ forms isometric crystals. It commonly occurs with other evaporite deposit minerals such as several of the sulfates, halides and borates. _____ occurs in vast lakes of sedimentary evaporite minerals that result from the drying up of enclosed beds, playas, and seas.

Chapter 2. Earth Materials: Minerals and Rocks

  a. Thing
  b. Halite0
  c. Undefined
  d. Undefined

51. In geology and astronomy, the term _____ is used to denote types of rock that consist predominantly of _____ minerals. Such rocks include a wide range of igneous, metamorphic and sedimentary types. Most of the Earth's mantle and crust are made up of _____ rocks. The same is true of the Moon and the other rocky planets.
  a. Silicate0
  b. Thing
  c. Undefined
  d. Undefined

52. A _____ is a concise way of expressing information about the atoms that constitute a particular chemical compound. A _____ is also a short way of showing how a chemical reaction occurs. For molecular compounds, it identifies each constituent element by its chemical symbol and indicates the number of atoms of each element found in each discrete molecule of that compound.
  a. Thing
  b. Chemical formula0
  c. Undefined
  d. Undefined

53. _____ is molten rock expelled by a volcano during an eruption. When first extruded from a volcanic vent, it is a liquid at temperatures from 700 °C to 1,200 °C.
  a. Lava0
  b. Thing
  c. Undefined
  d. Undefined

54. A _____ is a solid in which the constituent atoms, molecules, or ions are packed in a regularly ordered, repeating pattern extending in all three spatial dimensions. Most metals encountered in everyday life are polycrystals. Crystals are often symmetrically intergrown to form _____ twins.
  a. Thing
  b. Crystal0
  c. Undefined
  d. Undefined

55. _____ has the symbol Mg. It is the ninth most abundant element in the universe by mass. It constitutes about 2% of the Earth's crust by mass, and it is the third most abundant element dissolved in seawater. It is essential to all living cells, and is the 11th most abundant element by mass in the human body.
  a. Magnesium0
  b. Thing
  c. Undefined
  d. Undefined

56. The mineral _____ is iron disulfide, FeS2. It has isometric crystals that usually appear as cubes. Its metallic luster and pale-to-normal, brass-yellow hue have earned it a nickname due to many miners mistaking it for the real thing.
  a. Pyrite0
  b. Thing
  c. Undefined
  d. Undefined

57. _____ is the natural mineral form of lead sulfide. It is the most important lead ore mineral. It is one of the most abundant and widely distributed sulfide minerals. It crystallizes in the cubic crystal system often showing octahedral forms. It is often associated with the minerals sphalerite, calcite and fluorite.
  a. Thing
  b. Galena0
  c. Undefined
  d. Undefined

58. A _____ is any polyhedron with twelve faces, but usually a regular one is meant: a Platonic solid composed of twelve regular pentagonal faces, with three meeting at each vertex. It has twenty vertices and thirty edges.

Chapter 2. Earth Materials: Minerals and Rocks

a. Thing
b. Dodecahedron0
c. Undefined
d. Undefined

59. The mineral _____ is a magnesium iron silicate. It is one of the most common minerals on Earth, and has also been identified on the Moon, Mars, and comet Wild 2.
    a. Thing
    b. Olivine0
    c. Undefined
    d. Undefined

60. In organic chemistry, a _____ is a salt of carbonic acid.
    a. Carbonate0
    b. Thing
    c. Undefined
    d. Undefined

61. _____ is the name of a group of rock-forming minerals which make up as much as sixty percent of the Earth's crust. Feldspars crystallize from magma in both intrusive and extrusive rocks, and they can also occur as compact minerals, as veins, and are also present in many types of metamorphic rock.
    a. Thing
    b. Feldspar0
    c. Undefined
    d. Undefined

62. In geology, a _____ is the outermost layer of a planet, part of its lithosphere. They are generally composed of a less dense material than its deeper layers. Earths' is composed mainly of basalt and granite. It is cooler and more rigid than the deeper layers of the mantle and core.
    a. Crust0
    b. Thing
    c. Undefined
    d. Undefined

63. _____ is the oxide of silicon, chemical formula SiO_2, and is known for its hardness as early as the 16th century. It is a principle component in most types of glass and substances such as concrete.
    a. Thing
    b. Silica0
    c. Undefined
    d. Undefined

64. The _____ group of sheet silicate minerals includes several closely related materials having highly perfect basal cleavage. All are monoclinic with a tendency towards pseudo-hexagonal crystals and are similar in chemical composition. The highly perfect cleavage, which is the most prominent characteristic of _____, is explained by the hexagonal sheet-like arrangement of its atoms.
    a. Thing
    b. Mica0
    c. Undefined
    d. Undefined

65. The _____ are a group of important rock-forming silicate minerals found in many igneous and metamorphic rocks. They share a common structure comprised of single chains of silica tetrahedra and they crystalise in the monoclinic and orthorhombic system.
    a. Pyroxenes0
    b. Thing
    c. Undefined
    d. Undefined

66. _____ is a common phyllosilicate mineral within the mica group. Primarily a solid-solution series between the iron-endmember annite, and the magnesium-endmember phlogopite; more aluminous endmembers include siderophyllite.

Chapter 2. Earth Materials: Minerals and Rocks

a. Thing
b. Biotite0
c. Undefined
d. Undefined

67. _____ is a complex inosilicate series of minerals. _____ is not a recognized mineral, in its own right but the name is used as a general or field term, to refer to a dark amphibole. It is an isomorphous mixture of three molecules; a calcium-iron-magnesium silicate, an aluminium-iron-magnesium silicate and an iron-magnesium silicate.
a. Thing
b. Hornblende0
c. Undefined
d. Undefined

68. _____ defines an important group of generally dark-colored rock-forming inosilicate minerals linked at the vertices and generally containing ions of iron and/or magnesium in their structures. Amphiboles crystallize into two crystal systems, monoclinic and orthorhombic.
a. Thing
b. Amphibole0
c. Undefined
d. Undefined

69. _____ is a single chain inosilicate mineral described chemically as $|Ca,Mg,Fe|SiO_3$ or calcium magnesium iron silicate. The crystals are monoclinic and prismatic. _____ has two prominent prismatic cleavages, meeting at angles near 90°.
a. Augite0
b. Thing
c. Undefined
d. Undefined

70. _____ consists of very fine rock and mineral particles less than 2 mm in diameter that are ejected from a volcanic vent. The very fine particles may be carried for many miles, settling out as a dust-like layer across the landscape
a. Ash fall0
b. Thing
c. Undefined
d. Undefined

71. _____ is a phyllosilicate mineral of aluminium and potassium. It has a highly perfect basal cleavage yielding remarkably thin laminae, which are often highly elastic. Sheets of _____ 5 metres by 3 metres have been found in Nellore, India.
a. Thing
b. Muscovite0
c. Undefined
d. Undefined

72. _____ is a very important series of tectosilicate minerals within the feldspar family. Rather than referring to a particular mineral with a specific chemical composition, it is a solid solution series.
a. Thing
b. Plagioclase0
c. Undefined
d. Undefined

73. _____ is a chemical element. It is a soft silvery-white metallic alkali metal that occurs naturally bound to other elements in seawater and many minerals. It oxidizes rapidly in air and is very reactive, especially towards water. In many respects, it and sodium are chemically similar, although organisms in general, and animal cells in particular, treat them very differently.
a. Thing
b. Potassium0
c. Undefined
d. Undefined

Chapter 2. Earth Materials: Minerals and Rocks

74. _____ is an important tectosilicate mineral, which forms igneous rock. _____ is named based on the Greek for "straight fracture," because its two cleavages are at right angles to each other. _____ crystallizes in the monoclinic crystal system. It has a hardness of 6, a specific gravity of 2.56-2.58, and a vitreous to pearly luster. It can be colored white, gray, yellow, pink, or red; rarely green.
   a. Thing
   b. Orthoclase0
   c. Undefined
   d. Undefined

75. _____ refers to the mode of igneous volcanic rock formation in which hot magma from inside the Earth flows out onto the surface as lava or explodes violently into the atmosphere to fall back as pyroclastics or tuff.
   a. Extrusive0
   b. Thing
   c. Undefined
   d. Undefined

76. An _____ is a body of igneous rock that has crystallized from a molten magma below the surface of the Earth.
   a. Intrusion0
   b. Thing
   c. Undefined
   d. Undefined

77. A _____ in geology is an intrusive igneous rock body that crystallized from a magma below the surface of the Earth. Plutons include batholiths, dikes, sills, laccoliths, lopoliths, and other igneous bodies. In practice, "_____" usually refers to a distinctive mass of igneous rock, typically kilometers in dimension, without a tabular shape like those of dikes and sills.
   a. Thing
   b. Pluton0
   c. Undefined
   d. Undefined

78. A _____ is a relatively large and usually conspicuous crystal distinctly larger than the grains of the rock groundmass of a porphyritic igneous rock. They often have euhedral forms either due to early growth within a magma or by post-emplacement recrystallization.
   a. Thing
   b. Phenocryst0
   c. Undefined
   d. Undefined

79. _____ rock is the fine-grained mass of material in which larger grains or crystals are embedded. The _____ of an igneous rock consists of fine-grained, often microscopic, crystals in which larger crystals are embedded. This porphyritic texture is indicative of multi-stage cooling of magma.
   a. Groundmass0
   b. Thing
   c. Undefined
   d. Undefined

80. _____ is a variety of igneous rock consisting of large-grained crystals, such as feldspar or quartz, dispersed in a fine-grained feldspathic matrix or groundmass. The larger crystals are called phenocrysts.
   a. Thing
   b. Porphyry0
   c. Undefined
   d. Undefined

81. In geology, _____ minerals and rocks are silicate minerals, magmas, and volcanic and intrusive igneous rocks that have relatively high concentrations of the heavier elements. The term is a combination of "magnesium" and ferrum.
   a. Thing
   b. Mafic0
   c. Undefined
   d. Undefined

Chapter 2. Earth Materials: Minerals and Rocks

82. _____ is a term used in geology to refer to silicate minerals, magmas, and rocks which are enriched in the lighter elements such as silica, oxygen, aluminium, sodium, and potassium. _____ minerals are usually light in color and have specific gravities less than 3. Common _____ minerals include quartz, muscovite, orthoclase, and the sodium rich plagioclase feldspars.
   a. Felsic0
   b. Thing
   c. Undefined
   d. Undefined

83. _____ is a silvery and ductile member of the poor metal group of chemical elements. It has the symbol Al and atomic number 13.
   a. Thing
   b. Aluminum0
   c. Undefined
   d. Undefined

84. _____ is a dense, coarse-grained igneous rock, consisting mostly of the minerals olivine and pyroxene. _____ is ultramafic and ultrabasic, as the rock contains less than 45% silica. This type of rock is derived from the Earth's mantle, either as solid blocks and fragments, or as crystals accumulated from magmas that formed in the mantle.
   a. Peridotite0
   b. Thing
   c. Undefined
   d. Undefined

85. _____ are pyroclastic rocks formed by explosive eruption of lava and any rocks which are entrained within the eruptive column. This may include rocks plucked off the wall of the magma conduit, or physically picked up by the ensuing pyroclastic surge.
   a. Thing
   b. Volcanic breccia0
   c. Undefined
   d. Undefined

86. _____ refers to a size classification term for tephra, which is material that falls out of the air during a volcanic eruption. They are in some senses similar to ooids or pisoids in calcareous sediments.
   a. Lapillus0
   b. Thing
   c. Undefined
   d. Undefined

87. _____ is a rock composed of angular fragments of rocks or minerals in a matrix, that is a cementing material, that may be similar or different in composition to the fragments.
   a. Thing
   b. Breccia0
   c. Undefined
   d. Undefined

88. _____ is a type of naturally-occurring glass formed as an extrusive igneous rock. It is produced when felsic lava erupted from a volcano cools rapidly through the glass transition temperature and freezes without sufficient time for crystal growth. _____ is commonly found within the margins of rhyolitic lava flows known as _____ flows, where cooling of the lava is rapid.
   a. Thing
   b. Obsidian0
   c. Undefined
   d. Undefined

89. _____ is a highly vesicular pyroclastic extrusive igneous rock of intermediate to siliceous magmas including rhyolite, trachyte and phonolite. _____ is usually light in color ranging from white, yellowish, gray, gray brown, and a dull red. Most of the time, it is white. As an extrusive rock it was made from a volcanic eruption.

Chapter 2. Earth Materials: Minerals and Rocks

a. Pumice0
b. Thing
c. Undefined
d. Undefined

90. In cell biology, a _____ is a relatively small and enclosed compartment, separated from the cytosol by at least one lipid bilayer.
   a. Vesicle0
   b. Thing
   c. Undefined
   d. Undefined

91. A _____, is a tall, conical volcano composed of many layers of hardened lava, tephra, and volcanic ash. These volcanoes are characterized by a steep profile and periodic, explosive eruptions. The lava that flows from them is viscous, and cools and hardens before spreading very far.
   a. Stratovolcano0
   b. Thing
   c. Undefined
   d. Undefined

92. A _____ is an opening, or rupture, in the Earth's surface or crust, which allows hot, molten rock, ash and gases to escape from deep below the surface.
   a. Thing
   b. Volcano0
   c. Undefined
   d. Undefined

93. A _____ coastline occurs where bands of differing rock type run perpendicular to the coast.
   a. Thing
   b. Discordant0
   c. Undefined
   d. Undefined

94. A _____ coastline occurs where the bands of differing rock types run parallel to the coast. The outer hard rock provides a protective barrier to erosion of the softer rocks further inland.
   a. Concordant0
   b. Thing
   c. Undefined
   d. Undefined

95. _____ is the geological process whereby material is added to a landform. This is the process by which wind and water create a sediment deposit, through the laying down of granular material that has been eroded and transported from another geographical location.
   a. Thing
   b. Deposition0
   c. Undefined
   d. Undefined

96. _____ is the process in which sediments compact under pressure, expel connate fluids, and gradually become solid rock.
   a. Thing
   b. Lithification0
   c. Undefined
   d. Undefined

97. A _____ is a disturbance that propagates through space or spacetime, transferring energy and momentum and sometimes angular momentum.
   a. Wave0
   b. Thing
   c. Undefined
   d. Undefined

Chapter 2. Earth Materials: Minerals and Rocks

98. A _____ is a large, slow moving river of ice, formed from compacted layers of snow, that slowly deforms and flows in response to gravity. _____ ice is the largest reservoir of fresh water on Earth, and second only to oceans as the largest reservoir of total water. Glaciers cover vast areas of polar regions but are restricted to the highest mountains in the tropics.
 a. Thing
 b. Glacier0
 c. Undefined
 d. Undefined

99. A _____ is a body of water with a current, confined within a bed and banks. Streams are important as conduits in the water cycle, instruments in aquifer recharge, and corridors for fish and wildlife migration.
 a. Thing
 b. Stream0
 c. Undefined
 d. Undefined

100. The _____ the bottom of the ocean. At the bottom of the continental slope is the continental rise, which is caused by sediment cascading down the continental slope.
 a. Seafloor0
 b. Thing
 c. Undefined
 d. Undefined

101. _____ is the process of a material being more closely packed together.
 a. Thing
 b. Compaction0
 c. Undefined
 d. Undefined

102. _____ is rock that is of a certain particle size range. In geology, _____ is any loose rock that is at least two millimeters in its largest dimension and no more than 75 millimeters.
 a. Gravel0
 b. Thing
 c. Undefined
 d. Undefined

103. _____ is any product of the condensation of atmospheric water vapor that is deposited on the earth's surface. It occurs when the atmosphere becomes saturated with water vapour and the water condenses and falls out of solution. Air becomes saturated via two processes, cooling and adding moisture.
 a. Thing
 b. Precipitation0
 c. Undefined
 d. Undefined

104. _____ is the process of deposition of dissolved mineral components in the interstices of sediments. It is an important factor in the consolidation of coarse-grained clastic sedimentary rocks such as sandstones, conglomerates, or breccias during diagenesis or lithification. Cementing materials may include silica, carbonates, iron oxides, or clay minerals.
 a. Cementation0
 b. Thing
 c. Undefined
 d. Undefined

105. An _____ is a chemical compound containing an oxygen atom and other elements. Most of the earth's crust consists of them. They result when elements are oxidized by air.
 a. Thing
 b. Oxide0
 c. Undefined
 d. Undefined

106. _____ is a very common mineral, colored black to steel or silver-gray, brown to reddish brown, or red. It is mined as the main ore of iron. Varieties include kidney ore, martite iron rose and specularite. While the forms of it vary, they all have a rust-red streak. it is harder than pure iron, but much more brittle.

Chapter 2. Earth Materials: Minerals and Rocks 33

a. Hematite0
b. Thing
c. Undefined
d. Undefined

107. _____ is an ore consisting in a mixture of hydrated iron oxide-hydroxide of varying composition. It often contains a varying amount of oxide compared to hydroxide.
- a. Limonite0
- b. Thing
- c. Undefined
- d. Undefined

108. In biology, _____ is non-living particulate organic material. It typically includes the bodies of dead organisms or fragments of organisms or faecal material. _____ is normally colonised by communities of microorganisms which act to decompose the material.
- a. Thing
- b. Detritus0
- c. Undefined
- d. Undefined

109. A _____ is a section of a river of relatively steep gradient causing an increase in water flow and turbulence. A _____ is a hydrological feature between a run and a cascade. It is characterized by the river becoming shallower and having some rocks exposed above the flow surface.
- a. Thing
- b. Rapid0
- c. Undefined
- d. Undefined

110. _____ is a common and widely occurring type of intrusive, felsic, igneous rock. Granites are usually medium to coarsely crystalline, occasionally with some individual crystals larger than the groundmass forming a rock known as porphyry. Granites can be pink to dark gray or even black, depending on their chemistry and mineralogy.
- a. Granite0
- b. Thing
- c. Undefined
- d. Undefined

111. _____ is an igneous, volcanic rock, of felsic composition. It may have any texture from aphanitic to porphyritic. The mineral assemblage is usually quartz, alkali feldspar and plagioclase. Biotite and pyroxene are common accessory minerals.
- a. Thing
- b. Rhyolite0
- c. Undefined
- d. Undefined

112. In materials science, _____ is the distribution of crystallographic orientations of a sample.
- a. Thing
- b. Crystalline texture0
- c. Undefined
- d. Undefined

113. _____ are a class of sedimentary rocks composed primarily of carbonate minerals. The two major types are limestone and dolomite, composed of calcite and the mineral dolomite respectively. Chalk and tufa are also minor sedimentary carbonates.
- a. Thing
- b. Carbonate rocks0
- c. Undefined
- d. Undefined

114. _____ is a sedimentary carbonate rock that contains a high percentage of the mineral dolomite. It is usually referred to as dolomite rock. In old U.S.G.S. publications it was referred to as magnesian limestone.

Chapter 2. Earth Materials: Minerals and Rocks

a. Dolostone0
b. Thing
c. Undefined
d. Undefined

115. _____, in everyday life, is most familiar as the agency that endows objects with weight. _____ is responsible for keeping the Earth and the other planets in their orbits around the Sun; for the formation of tides; and for various other phenomena that we observe. _____ is also the reason for the very existence of the Earth, the Sun, and most macroscopic objects in the universe; without it, matter would not have coalesced into these large masses, and life, as we know it, would not exist.

a. Gravitation0
b. Thing
c. Undefined
d. Undefined

116. _____ is a grey to dark grey intermediate intrusive igneous rock composed principally of plagioclase feldspar, biotite, hornblende, and/or pyroxene. It may contain small amounts of quartz, microcline and olivine.

a. Diorite0
b. Thing
c. Undefined
d. Undefined

117. _____ is a dark, coarse-grained, intrusive igneous rock chemically equivalent to basalt. It is a plutonic rock, formed when molten magma is trapped beneath the Earth's surface and cools into a crystalline mass.

a. Thing
b. Gabbro0
c. Undefined
d. Undefined

118. _____ is an igneous, volcanic rock, of intermediate composition, with aphanitic to porphyritic texture.

a. Andesite0
b. Thing
c. Undefined
d. Undefined

119. _____ is a common gray to black extrusive volcanic rock. It is usually fine-grained due to rapid cooling of lava on the Earth's surface. It may be porphyritic containing larger crystals in a fine matrix, or vesicular, or frothy scoria.

a. Thing
b. Basalt0
c. Undefined
d. Undefined

120. _____ is a type of rock consisting of consolidated volcanic ash ejected from vents during a volcanic eruption.

a. Thing
b. Tuff0
c. Undefined
d. Undefined

121. _____ is a sedimentary rock composed mainly of sand-size mineral or rock grains. Most _____ is composed of quartz and/or feldspar because these are the most common minerals in the Earth's crust. Like sand, _____ may be any color, but the most common colors are tan, brown, yellow, red, gray and white.

a. Sandstone0
b. Thing
c. Undefined
d. Undefined

122. A _____ is a rock consisting of individual stones that have become cemented together. Conglomerates are sedimentary rocks consisting of rounded fragements and are thus differentiated from breccias, which consist of angular clasts. Both conglomerates and breccias are characterized by clasts larger than sand.

a. Thing
b. Conglomerate0
c. Undefined
d. Undefined

Chapter 2. Earth Materials: Minerals and Rocks

123. _____ refers to water-soluble, mineral sediments that result from the evaporation of bodies of surficial water.
a. Evaporite0
b. Thing
c. Undefined
d. Undefined

124. _____ is a sedimentary rock composed largely of the mineral calcite. _____ often contains variable amounts of silica in the form of chert or flint, as well as varying amounts of clay, silt and sand as disseminations, nodules, or layers within the rock. The primary source of the calcite in _____ is most commonly marine organisms. These organisms secrete shells that settle out of the water column and are deposited on ocean floors as pelagic ooze or alternatively is conglomerated in a coral reef.
a. Thing
b. Limestone0
c. Undefined
d. Undefined

125. _____ is a fine-grained silica-rich cryptocrystalline sedimentary rock that may contain small fossils. It varies greatly in color from white to black, but most often manifests as gray, brown, grayish brown and light green to rusty red; its color is an expression of trace elements present in the rock, and both red and green are most often related to traces of iron.
a. Thing
b. Chert0
c. Undefined
d. Undefined

126. _____ is a very soft mineral composed of calcium sulfate dihydrate, with the chemical formula $CaSO_4 \cdot 2H_2O$. _____ occurs in nature as flattened and often twinned crystals and transparent cleavable masses. It may also occur silky and fibrous. Finally it may also be granular or quite compact.
a. Gypsum0
b. Thing
c. Undefined
d. Undefined

127. _____ is a fossil fuel formed in swamp ecosystems where plant remains were saved by water and mud from oxidization and biodegradation. It is a sedimentary rock, but the harder forms, such as anthracite _____, can be regarded as metamorphic rocks because of later exposure to elevated temperature and pressure. It is composed primarily of carbon along with assorted other elements, including sulfur.
a. Thing
b. Coal0
c. Undefined
d. Undefined

128. Fossils are the mineralized or otherwise preserved remains or traces of animals, plants, and other organisms. The totality of fossils, both discovered and undiscovered, and their placement in fossiliferous rock formations and sedimentary layers is known as the _____ record.
a. Thing
b. Fossil0
c. Undefined
d. Undefined

129. _____ has penetrative planar fabric present within it. It is common to rocks affected by regional metamorphic compression typical of orogenic belts.
a. Thing
b. Foliated metamorphic rock0
c. Undefined
d. Undefined

130. A _____ is a process that results in the interconversion of chemical substances. The substance or substances initially involved in a _____ are called reactants. Chemical reactions are characterized by a chemical change, and they yield one or more products which are, in general, different from the reactants.

Chapter 2. Earth Materials: Minerals and Rocks

a. Thing
c. Undefined
b. Chemical reaction0
d. Undefined

131. _____ are large emplacements of igneous intrusive rock that forms from cooled magma deep in the Earth's crust. They are almost always made mostly of felsic or intermediate rock-types, such as granite, quartz monzonite, or diorite.
a. Thing
c. Undefined
b. Batholiths0
d. Undefined

132. Overburden, or _____ pressure, is a term used in geology to denote the pressure imposed on a stratigraphic layer by the weight of overlying layers of material.
a. Lithostatic0
c. Undefined
b. Thing
d. Undefined

133. _____ is a term used in geology to denote the pressure imposed on a stratigraphic layer by the weight of overlying layers of material.
a. Event
c. Undefined
b. Lithostatic pressure0
d. Undefined

134. A _____ is a large emplacement of igneous intrusive rock that forms from cooled magma deep in the Earth's crust. They are almost always made mostly of felsic or intermediate rock-types, such as granite, quartz monzonite, or diorite.
a. Batholith0
c. Undefined
b. Thing
d. Undefined

135. In plate tectonics, a _____ a linear feature that exists between two tectonic plates that are moving away from each other. These areas can form in the middle of continents but eventually form ocean basins.
a. Thing
c. Undefined
b. Divergent plate boundary0
d. Undefined

136. _____ is a common and widely distributed type of rock formed by high-grade regional metamorphic processes from preexisting formations that were originally either igneous or sedimentary rocks. Gneissic rocks are usually medium to coarse foliated and largely recrystallized but do not carry large quantities of micas, chlorite or other platy minerals.
a. Gneiss0
c. Undetined
b. Thing
d. Undetined

137. _____ is a term used to describe a group of hydrous aluminium phyllosilicate minerals, that are typically less than 2 micrometres in diameter. _____ consists of a variety of phyllosilicate minerals rich in silicon and aluminium oxides and hydroxides which include variable amounts of structural water. Clays are generally formed by the chemical weathering of silicate-bearing rocks by carbonic acid but some are formed by hydrothermal activity.
a. Thing
c. Undefined
b. Clay0
d. Undefined

138. _____ is a calcium aluminium iron sorosilicate mineral, crystallizing in the monoclinic system. It occurs in crystalline limestones and schistose rocks of metamorphic origin. It is also a product of hydrothermal alteration of various minerals composing igneous rocks.

a. Thing
b. Epidote0
c. Undefined
d. Undefined

139. A _____ is a compound that contains this group, with chlorine in oxidation state +3. They are also known as salts of chlorous acid.
a. Chlorite0
b. Thing
c. Undefined
d. Undefined

140. _____ is the group designation for a series of contact metamorphic rocks that have been baked and indurated by the heat of intrusive igneous masses and have been rendered massive, hard, splintery, and in some cases exceedingly tough and durable. Most _____ are fine-grained.
a. Hornfels0
b. Thing
c. Undefined
d. Undefined

141. _____ is a hard, compact variety of mineral coal that has a high luster. It has the highest carbon count and contains the fewest impurities of all coals, despite its lower calorific content.
a. Anthracite0
b. Thing
c. Undefined
d. Undefined

142. _____ is a field of study within geology concerned generally with the structures within the crust of the Earth, or other planets, and particularly with the forces and movements that have operated in a region to create these structures.
a. Tectonics0
b. Thing
c. Undefined
d. Undefined

143. _____ is a theory of geology that has been developed to explain the observed evidence for large scale motions of the Earth's lithosphere. The theory encompassed and superseded the older theory of continental drift.
a. Plate tectonics0
b. Thing
c. Undefined
d. Undefined

144. _____ is a fine-grained, homogeneous, metamorphic rock derived from an original shale-type sedimentary rock composed of clay or volcanic ash through low grade regional metamorphism. The result is a foliated rock in which the foliation may not correspond to the original sedimentary layering.
a. Slate0
b. Thing
c. Undefined
d. Undefined

145. The _____ refers to a group of medium-grade metamorphic rocks, chiefly notable for the preponderance of lamellar minerals such as micas, chlorite, talc, hornblende, graphite, and others. Quartz often occurs in drawn-out grains to such an extent that a particular form called quartz _____ is produced.
a. Thing
b. Schist0
c. Undefined
d. Undefined

146. _____ is a rock at the frontier between igneous and metamorphic rocks. They can also be known as diatexite.
a. Migmatite0
b. Thing
c. Undefined
d. Undefined

Chapter 2. Earth Materials: Minerals and Rocks

147. _____ is the part of Earth's lithosphere that surfaces in the ocean basins. _____ is primarily composed of mafic rocks, or sima. It is thinner than continental crust, or sial, generally less than 10 kilometers thick, however it is more dense, having a mean density of about 3.3 grams per cubic centimeter.
- a. Thing
- b. Oceanic crust0
- c. Undefined
- d. Undefined

148. A _____ is a landform that extends above the surrounding terrain in a limited area. A _____ is generally steeper than a hill, but there is no universally accepted standard definition for the height of a _____ or a hill although a _____ usually has an identifiable summit.
- a. Place
- b. Mountain0
- c. Undefined
- d. Undefined

149. _____ is displacement of solids by the agents of ocean currents, wind, water, or ice by downward or down-slope movement in response to gravity or by living organisms.
- a. Thing
- b. Erosion0
- c. Undefined
- d. Undefined

150. _____ is the use of the principles of geology to reconstruct and understand the history of the Earth. It focuses on geologic processes that change the Earth's surface and subsurface; and the use of stratigraphy, structural geology and paleontology to tell the sequence of these events. It also focuses on the evolution of plants and animals during different time periods in the geological timescale.
- a. Historical geology0
- b. Thing
- c. Undefined
- d. Undefined

151. The _____ is used by geologists and other scientists to describe the timing and relationships between events that have occurred during the history of Earth.
- a. Thing
- b. Geological time scale0
- c. Undefined
- d. Undefined

152. _____ is the science and study of the solid matter that constitute the Earth. Encompassing such things as rocks, soil, and gemstones, _____ studies the composition, structure, physical properties, history, and the processes that shape Earth's components.
- a. Geology0
- b. Thing
- c. Undefined
- d. Undefined

153. The _____ A, also called atomic _____ or nucleon number, is the number of nucleons in an atomic nucleus. The _____ is unique for each isotope of an element and is written either after the element name or as a superscript to the left of an element's symbol. For example, carbon-12 has 6 protons and 6 neutrons.
- a. Mass number0
- b. Thing
- c. Undefined
- d. Undefined

154. _____ are those minerals containing the carbonate ion: CO_3^{2-}.
- a. Carbonate minerals0
- b. Thing
- c. Undefined
- d. Undefined

155. _____ rocks are rocks formed from fragments of pre-existing rock.

Chapter 2. Earth Materials: Minerals and Rocks

a. Clastic0
b. Thing
c. Undefined
d. Undefined

156. _____ is a measure of the void spaces in a material, and is measured as a fraction, between 0–1, or as a percentage between 0–100%.
a. Thing
b. Porosity0
c. Undefined
d. Undefined

157. The carbonate mineral _____ is a chemical or biochemical calcium carbonate and is one of the most widely distributed minerals on the Earth's surface. It is a common constituent of sedimentary rocks, limestone in particular. It is also the primary mineral in metamorphic marble
a. Calcite0
b. Thing
c. Undefined
d. Undefined

158. _____ is water from a sea or ocean. On average, _____ in the world's oceans has a salinity of ~3.5%, or 35 parts per thousand. This means that every 1 kg of _____ has approximately 35 grams of dissolved salts.
a. Seawater0
b. Thing
c. Undefined
d. Undefined

Chapter 3. Plate Tectonics: A Unifying Theory

1. _____ refers to the movement of the Earth's continents relative to each other. _____ is a concept that said the shapes of continents on either side of the Atlantic Ocean seem to fit together and the similarity of southern continent fossil faunae could mean that all the continents had once been joined into a supercontinent. It was suggested that the continents had been pulled apart by the centrifugal pseudoforce of the Earth's rotation.
   - a. Thing
   - b. Continental drift0
   - c. Undefined
   - d. Undefined

2. A _____ column is a column of rizing air in the lower altitudes of the Earth's atmosphere. Thermals are created by the uneven heating of the Earth's surface from solar radiation, and are an example of convection. The Sun warms the ground, which in turn warms the air directly above it.
   - a. Thing
   - b. Thermal0
   - c. Undefined
   - d. Undefined

3. The _____ the bottom of the ocean. At the bottom of the continental slope is the continental rise, which is caused by sediment cascading down the continental slope.
   - a. Thing
   - b. Seafloor0
   - c. Undefined
   - d. Undefined

4. _____ occurs at mid-ocean ridges, where new oceanic crust is formed through volcanic activity and then gradually moves away from the ridge. _____ helps explain continental drift in the theory of plate tectonics.
   - a. Thing
   - b. Seafloor spreading0
   - c. Undefined
   - d. Undefined

5. _____ in the most general terms refers to the movement of currents within fluids. _____ is one of the major modes of Heat and mass transfer. In fluids, convective heat and mass transfer take place through both diffusion and by advection, in which matter or heat is transported by the larger-scale motion of currents in the fluid.
   - a. Thing
   - b. Convection0
   - c. Undefined
   - d. Undefined

6. A _____ is a phenomenon of fluid dynamics which occurs in situations where there are temperature differences within a body of liquid or gas.
   - a. Convection cell0
   - b. Thing
   - c. Undefined
   - d. Undefined

7. An _____ is the result from the sudden release of stored energy in the Earth's crust that creates seismic waves. At the Earth's surface, earthquakes may manifest themselves by a shaking or displacement of the ground. An _____ is caused by tectonic plates getting stuck and putting a strain on the ground. The strain becomes so great that rocks give way by breaking and sliding along fault planes.
   - a. Earthquake0
   - b. Thing
   - c. Undefined
   - d. Undefined

8. _____ are naturally occurring substances that are considered valuable in their relatively unmodified or natural form. Its value rests in the amount of the material available and the demand for the certain material.
   - a. Thing
   - b. Natural resources0
   - c. Undefined
   - d. Undefined

Chapter 3. Plate Tectonics: A Unifying Theory

9. _____ is an active stratovolcano located on the island of Luzon in the Philippines, at the intersection of the borders of the provinces of Zambales, Tarlac, and Pampanga.
   a. Thing
   b. Mount Pinatubo0
   c. Undefined
   d. Undefined

10. An _____ is a layer of gases that may surround a material body of sufficient mass. The gases are attracted by the gravity of the body, and are retained for a longer duration if gravity is high and the _____'s temperature is low. Some planets consist mainly of various gases, and thus have very deep atmospheres.
    a. Atmosphere0
    b. Place
    c. Undefined
    d. Undefined

11. A _____ is an opening, or rupture, in the Earth's surface or crust, which allows hot, molten rock, ash and gases to escape from deep below the surface.
    a. Thing
    b. Volcano0
    c. Undefined
    d. Undefined

12. _____ is molten rock located beneath the surface of the Earth, and which often collects in a _____ chamber. _____ is a complex high-temperature fluid substance. Most are silicate solutions. It is capable of intrusion into adjacent rocks or of extrusion onto the surface as lava or ejected explosively as tephra to form pyroclastic rock. Environments of _____ formation include subduction zones, continental rift zones, mid-oceanic ridges, and hotspots, some of which are interpreted as mantle plumes.
    a. Magma0
    b. Thing
    c. Undefined
    d. Undefined

13. A _____ is a landform that extends above the surrounding terrain in a limited area. A _____ is generally steeper than a hill, but there is no universally accepted standard definition for the height of a _____ or a hill although a _____ usually has an identifiable summit.
    a. Place
    b. Mountain0
    c. Undefined
    d. Undefined

14. _____ are large geologic basins that are below sea level. Geologically, there are other undersea geomorphological features such as the continental shelves, the deep ocean trenches, and the undersea mountain rangeswhich are not considered to be part of the _____.
    a. Ocean basins0
    b. Thing
    c. Undefined
    d. Undefined

15. A _____ is one of several large landmasses on Earth. They are generally identified by convention rather than any strict criteria, but seven areas are commonly reckoned as continents – they are: Asia, Africa, North America, South America, Antarctica, Europe, and Australia.
    a. Thing
    b. Continent0
    c. Undefined
    d. Undefined

16. _____ is a layer of gases surrounding the planet Earth and retained by the Earth's gravity. This mixture of gases is commonly known as air.

a. Earths atmosphere0
b. Thing
c. Undefined
d. Undefined

17. _____ is the average and variations of weather over long periods of time. _____ zones can be defined using parameters such as temperature and rainfall.
   a. Climate0
   b. Thing
   c. Undefined
   d. Undefined

18. In biology and ecology, _____ is the cessation of existence of a species or group of taxa, reducing biodiversity. The moment of _____ is generally considered to be the death of the last individual of that species.
   a. Thing
   b. Extinction0
   c. Undefined
   d. Undefined

19. _____ is a field of study within geology concerned generally with the structures within the crust of the Earth, or other planets, and particularly with the forces and movements that have operated in a region to create these structures.
   a. Thing
   b. Tectonics0
   c. Undefined
   d. Undefined

20. The southern supercontinent _____ included most of the landmasses in today's southern hemisphere, including Antarctica, South America, Africa, Madagascar, Australia-New Guinea, and New Zealand, as well as Arabia and the Indian subcontinent, which are in the Northern Hemisphere.
   a. Thing
   b. Gondwana0
   c. Undefined
   d. Undefined

21. Fossils are the mineralized or otherwise preserved remains or traces of animals, plants, and other organisms. The totality of fossils, both discovered and undiscovered, and their placement in fossiliferous rock formations and sedimentary layers is known as the _____ record.
   a. Thing
   b. Fossil0
   c. Undefined
   d. Undefined

22. _____, both meaning "Earth", and graphein meaning "to describe" or "to write"or "to map", is the study of the earth and its features, inhabitants, and phenomena. A literal translation would be "to describe the Earth". The first person to use the word "_____" was Eratosthenes. Four historical traditions in geographical research are the spatial analysis of natural and human phenomena, area studies, study of man-land relationship, and research in earth sciences.
   a. Thing
   b. Geography0
   c. Undefined
   d. Undefined

23. The _____ is defined as the part of the land adjoining or near the ocean. A coastline is properly a line on a map indicating the disposition of a _____, but the word is often used to refer to the _____ itself. The adjective coastal describes something as being on, near to, or associated with a _____.
   a. Coast0
   b. Place
   c. Undefined
   d. Undefined

24. The _____ is the earliest of three geologic eras of the Phanerozoic eon. The _____ is subdivided into six geologic periods; from oldest to youngest they are: the Cambrian, Ordovician, Silurian, Devonian, Carboniferous, and Permian.

Chapter 3. Plate Tectonics: A Unifying Theory

a. Thing
c. Undefined
b. Paleozoic0
d. Undefined

25. _____ was a geologist who was an expert on the geography of the Alps. He is responsible for discovering two of the Earth's major now-lost geographical features, the supercontinent Gondwana and the Tethys Ocean.
   a. Person
   c. Undefined
   b. Edward Suess0
   d. Undefined

26. _____ is a small island located in the middle of San Francisco Bay in California, United States. It served as a lighthouse, then a military fortification, then a military prison followed by a federal prison until 1963, when it became a national recreation area.
   a. Place
   c. Undefined
   b. Alcatraz Island0
   d. Undefined

27. A _____ is a large, slow moving river of ice, formed from compacted layers of snow, that slowly deforms and flows in response to gravity. _____ ice is the largest reservoir of fresh water on Earth, and second only to oceans as the largest reservoir of total water. Glaciers cover vast areas of polar regions but are restricted to the highest mountains in the tropics.
   a. Thing
   c. Undefined
   b. Glacier0
   d. Undefined

28. _____ is a fossil fuel formed in swamp ecosystems where plant remains were saved by water and mud from oxidization and biodegradation. It is a sedimentary rock, but the harder forms, such as anthracite _____, can be regarded as metamorphic rocks because of later exposure to elevated temperature and pressure. It is composed primarily of carbon along with assorted other elements, including sulfur.
   a. Thing
   c. Undefined
   b. Coal0
   d. Undefined

29. The _____ is a secondary effect of the force of gravity and is responsible for the tides. It arises because the gravitational field is not constant across a body's diameter.
   a. Tidal force0
   c. Undefined
   b. Thing
   d. Undefined

30. The _____ is Earth's only natural satellite. It makes a complete orbit around the Earth every 27.3 days, and the periodic variations in the geometry of the Earth–_____–Sun system are responsible for the lunar phases that repeat every 29.5 days.
   a. Thing
   c. Undefined
   b. Moon0
   d. Undefined

31. _____ is a naturally occurring liquid found in formations in the Earth consisting of a complex mixture of hydrocarbons of various lengths.
   a. Thing
   c. Undefined
   b. Petroleum0
   d. Undefined

32. The _____ in the Southwest Asian region, is an extension of the Gulf of Oman located between Iran and the Arabian Peninsula. The _____ was the focus of the Iraq-Iran War that lasted from 1980 to 1988, with each side attacking the other's oil tankers.
   a. Place
   b. Persian Gulf0
   c. Undefined
   d. Undefined

33. _____ is the study of the ancient geologic environments of the Earth's surface as preserved in the stratigraphic record.
   a. Thing
   b. Palaeogeography0
   c. Undefined
   d. Undefined

34. An _____ is a long period of time with different technical and colloquial meanings, and usages in language. It begins with some beginning event known as an epoch, epochal date, epochal event or epochal moment.
   a. Thing
   b. Era0
   c. Undefined
   d. Undefined

35. The _____ is one of three geologic eras of the Phanerozoic eon. The _____ was a time of tectonic, climatic and evolutionary activity, shifting from a state of connectedness into their present configuration. The climate was exceptionally warm throughout the period, also playing an important role in the evolution and diversification of new animal species. By the end of the era, the basis of modern life was in place.
   a. Thing
   b. Mesozoic0
   c. Undefined
   d. Undefined

36. The _____ Era meaning "new life", is the most recent of the three classic geological eras. It covers the 65.5 million years since the Cretaceous-Tertiary extinction event at the end of the Cretaceous that marked the demise of the last non-avian dinosaurs and the end of the Mesozoic Era. The _____ era is ongoing.
   a. Thing
   b. Cenozoic0
   c. Undefined
   d. Undefined

37. The _____ is the most recent of the three classic geological eras. It covers the 65.5 million years since the Cretaceous-Tertiary extinction event at the end of the Cretaceous that marked the demise of the last non-avian dinosaurs and the end of the Mesozoic Era.
   a. Thing
   b. Cenozoic era0
   c. Undefined
   d. Undefined

38. The _____ is the longest geological period and constitutes nearly half of the Mesozoic. The end of the Cretaceous defines the boundary between the Mesozoic and Cenozoic eras. The Cretaceous as a separate period was first defined using strata in the Paris Basin and named for the extensive beds of chalk.
   a. Thing
   b. Cretaceous Period0
   c. Undefined
   d. Undefined

39. _____ is any particulate matter that can be transported by fluid flow and which eventually is deposited as a layer of solid particles on the bed or bottom of a body of water or other liquid.
   a. Sediment0
   b. Thing
   c. Undefined
   d. Undefined

Chapter 3. Plate Tectonics: A Unifying Theory

40. The _____ is the extended perimeter of each continent and associated coastal plain, which is covered during interglacial periods such as the current epoch by relatively shallow seas and gulfs. The shelf usually ends at a point of increasing slope.
    a. Thing
    b. Continental shelf0
    c. Undefined
    d. Undefined

41. In biology and ecology, an _____ is a living complex adaptive system of organs that influence each other in such a way that they function in some way as a stable whole.
    a. Organism0
    b. Thing
    c. Undefined
    d. Undefined

42. In chemistry, a _____ is defined as a sufficiently stable electrically neutral group of at least two atoms in a definite arrangement held together by strong chemical bonds.
    a. Thing
    b. Molecule0
    c. Undefined
    d. Undefined

43. The _____ is a largely continental tectonic plate covering the Arabian peninsula and extending northward to Turkey.
    a. Arabian plate0
    b. Thing
    c. Undefined
    d. Undefined

44. _____ in meteorology are large scale patterns in the atmospheric pressure field that are nearly stationary, effectively "blocking" or redirecting migratory cyclones. These _____ can remain in place for several days or even weeks, causing the areas affected by them to have the same kind of weather for an extended period of time.
    a. Thing
    b. Blocks0
    c. Undefined
    d. Undefined

45. In geology, a _____ zone is an area on Earth where two tectonic plates meet and move towards one another, with one sliding underneath the other and moving down into the mantle, at rates typically measured in centimeters per year. An oceanic plate ordinarily slides underneath a continental plate; this often creates an orogenic zone with many volcanoes and earthquakes.
    a. Thing
    b. Subduction0
    c. Undefined
    d. Undefined

46. The _____ is an inlet of the Indian Ocean between Africa and Asia. The connection to the ocean is in the south through the Bab el Mandeb sound and the Gulf of Aden. In the north are the Sinai Peninsula, the Gulf of Aqaba and the Gulf of Suez. The _____ is a Global 200 ecoregion.
    a. Red Sea0
    b. Place
    c. Undefined
    d. Undefined

47. The _____ is located in the Indian Ocean between Yemen on the south coast of the Arabian Peninsula and Somalia in Africa. In the northwest it connects with the Red Sea through the Bab el Mandeb sound.
    a. Gulf of Aden0
    b. Place
    c. Undefined
    d. Undefined

Chapter 3. Plate Tectonics: A Unifying Theory

48. An _____ is a term for any perforation through the Earth's surface designed to find and release both petroleum oil and gas hydrocarbons.
   a. Oil well0
   b. Thing
   c. Undefined
   d. Undefined

49. A _____ is a geological feature that is also known as a Rip in the earth causing magma to flow out and forming an undersea volcano, it also has geological features, a continuous elevational crest for some distance. Ridges are usually termed hills or mountains as well, depending on size.
   a. Ridge0
   b. Thing
   c. Undefined
   d. Undefined

50. The _____ is the second-largest of the world's oceanic divisions; with a total area of about 106.4 million square kilometres, it covers approximately one-fifth of the Earth's surface. The _____ occupies an elongated, S-shaped basin extending longitudinally between the Americas to the west, and Eurasia and Africa to the east.
   a. Atlantic Ocean0
   b. Place
   c. Undefined
   d. Undefined

51. _____ was a German interdisciplinary scientist and meteorologist, who became famous for his theory of continental drift.
   a. Thing
   b. Alfred Wegener0
   c. Undefined
   d. Undefined

52. _____ is the supercontinent that existed during the Paleozoic and Mesozoic eras before each of the component continents were separated into their current configuration.
   a. Pangaea0
   b. Event
   c. Undefined
   d. Undefined

53. In geology, a _____ is a land mass comprizing more than one continental core, or craton.
   a. Thing
   b. Supercontinent0
   c. Undefined
   d. Undefined

54. The _____ is the southernmost point on the surface of the Earth, on the opposite side of the Earth from the North Pole. It is the site of the US Amundsen-Scott _____ Station, which was established in 1956 and has been permanently staffed since that date
   a. South Pole0
   b. Place
   c. Undefined
   d. Undefined

55. In geology, glacial _____ are grooves or lines inscribed on the surface of a rock, produced by a geological process such as glacial flow.
   a. Thing
   b. Striations0
   c. Undefined
   d. Undefined

56. _____ was a genus of Early Triassic Period therapsids, which lived approximately 250 million years ago in what is now Antarctica, India and South Africa. Specifically it was a dicynodont, which means "having two dog-teeth", they were heavily-built barrel-chested medium-sized about 3 feet long herbivorous animals, approximately the size of a pig, with very stout limbs.

Chapter 3. Plate Tectonics: A Unifying Theory

a. Thing
c. Undefined
b. Lystrosaurus0
d. Undefined

57. The _____ is the last period of the Palaeozoic Era. As the _____ opened, the Earth was still in the grip of an ice age, so the polar regions were covered with deep layers of ice. During the _____, all the Earth's major land masses except portions of East Asia were collected into a single supercontinent known as Pangaea. The _____ ended with the most extensive extinction event recorded in paleontology: the _____-Triassic extinction event.
a. Permian0
c. Undefined
b. Thing
d. Undefined

58. _____ is an extinct genus of anapsid reptile from the Permian period. It was about 1 m long.
a. Thing
c. Undefined
b. Mesosaurus0
d. Undefined

59. _____ contains low concentrations of dissolved salts and other total dissolved solids. It is an important renewable resource, necessary for the survival of most terrestrial organisms, and required by humans for drinking and agriculture, among many other uses.
a. Fresh water0
c. Undefined
b. Thing
d. Undefined

60. _____ are tetrapods and amniotes, animals whose embryos are surrounded by an amniotic membrane, and members of the class Sauropsida.They rely on gathering and losing heat from the environment to regulate their internal temperature, e.g. by moving between sun and shade, or by preferential circulation — moving warmed blood into the body core, while pushing cool blood to the periphery.
a. Reptiles0
c. Undefined
b. Thing
d. Undefined

61. _____ is the first period of the Mesozoic Era. Both the start and end of the _____ are marked by major extinction events. During the _____, both marine and continental life show an adaptive radiation beginning from the starkly impoverished biosphere that followed the Permian-_____ extinction. Corals of the hexacorallia group made their first appearance. The first flowering plants may have evolved during the _____, as did the first flying vertebrates, the pterosaurs.
a. Triassic0
c. Undefined
b. Event
d. Undefined

62. _____ was a metre-long predator of the Lower Triassic. It was one of the more mammal-like of the "mammal-like reptiles", a member of a grouping called Eucynodontia. The genus _____ had a more-or-less worldwide distribution. Fossils have so far been recovered from South Africa, South America, China and Antarctica.
a. Thing
c. Undefined
b. Cynognathus0
d. Undefined

63. _____ a South African geologist. From 1903 to 1920 he worked for the Geological Commission of the Cape of Good Hope mapping the local geology.
a. Alexander Du Toit0
c. Undefined
b. Person
d. Undefined

Chapter 3. Plate Tectonics: A Unifying Theory

64. The _____ is an imaginary line on the Earth's surface equidistant from the North Pole and South Pole. It thus divides the Earth into a Northern Hemisphere and a Southern Hemisphere.
   a. Equator0
   b. Thing
   c. Undefined
   d. Undefined

65. _____ is the place where a particular species live and grow. It is essentially the environment—at least the physical environment—that surrounds a species population.
   a. Habitat0
   b. Place
   c. Undefined
   d. Undefined

66. In physics, a _____ is a solenoidal vector field in the space surrounding moving electric charges and magnetic dipoles, such as those in electric currents and magnets.
   a. Magnetic field0
   b. Thing
   c. Undefined
   d. Undefined

67. _____ is one of the phenomena by which materials exert attractive or repulsive forces on other materials. Some well known materials that exhibit easily detectable magnetic properties are nickel, iron, some steels, and the mineral magnetite; however, all materials are influenced to greater or lesser degree by the presence of a magnetic field.
   a. Thing
   b. Magnetism0
   c. Undefined
   d. Undefined

68. _____ refers to the study of the record of the Earth's magnetic field preserved in various magnetic minerals through time. The study of _____ has demonstrated that the Earth's magnetic field varies substantially in both orientation and intensity through time.
   a. Paleomagnetism0
   b. Thing
   c. Undefined
   d. Undefined

69. _____ is the magnetic north pole is constantly shifting relative to the axis of rotation. This is responsible for the shifting magnetic declination required for compass work and orienteering.
   a. Polar wandering0
   b. Thing
   c. Undefined
   d. Undefined

70. In physics, there are two kinds of dipoles . An electric _____ is a separation of positive and negative charge. The simplest example of this is a pair of electric charges of equal magnitude but opposite sign, separated by some, usually small, distance. By contrast, a magnetic _____ is a closed circulation of electric current. A simple example of this is a single loop of wire with some constant current flowing through it.
   a. Dipole0
   b. Thing
   c. Undefined
   d. Undefined

71. _____, are either of two fixed points on the surface of a spinning body or planet, at 90 degrees from the equator, based on the axis around which a body spins. For the purposes of cartography, it provides an agreed upon absolute point of measurement. These should not be confused with magnetic poles, which can also exist on a planet.
   a. Thing
   b. Geographic poles0
   c. Undefined
   d. Undefined

Chapter 3. Plate Tectonics: A Unifying Theory

72. A _____ is a movement of an object in a circular motion. A two-dimensional object rotates around a center of _____. A three-dimensional object rotates around a line called an axis. A circular motion about an external point, e.g. the Earth about the Sun, is called an orbit or more properly an orbital revolution.
   a. Thing
   b. Rotation0
   c. Undefined
   d. Undefined

73. Earth's _____ is a ~2,900 km thick rocky shell comprizing approximately 70% of Earth's volume. It is predominantly solid and overlies the Earth's iron-rich core, which occupies about 30% of Earth's volume. Past episodes of melting and volcanism at the shallower levels of the _____ have produced a very thin crust of crystallized melt products near the surface, upon which we live.
   a. Thing
   b. Mantle0
   c. Undefined
   d. Undefined

74. _____ is a chemical element metal. It is a lustrous, silvery soft metal. It and nickel are notable for being the final elements produced by stellar nucleosynthesis, and thus are the heaviest elements which do not require a supernova or similarly cataclysmic event for formation.
   a. Thing
   b. Iron0
   c. Undefined
   d. Undefined

75. A _____ is a naturally occurring substance formed through geological processes that has a characteristic chemical composition, a highly ordered atomic structure and specific physical properties. A rock, by comparison, is an aggregate of minerals and need not have a specific chemical composition. Minerals range in composition from pure elements and simple salts to very complex silicates with thousands of known forms.
   a. Mineral0
   b. Thing
   c. Undefined
   d. Undefined

76. The _____ is a term in physics and materials science and refers to a characteristic property of a ferromagnetic or piezoelectric material.
   a. Thing
   b. Curie point0
   c. Undefined
   d. Undefined

77. The Earth's _____ is the wandering point on the Earth's surface at which the Earth's magnetic field points vertically downwards i.e. the "dip" is 90°. It should not be confused with the lesser known North Geomagnetic Pole.
   a. Magnetic north0
   b. Thing
   c. Undefined
   d. Undefined

78. The _____ is a major division of the geologic timescale that extends from the end of the Ordovician period to the beginning of the Devonian period. The base of the _____ is set at a major extinction event when 60% of marine species were wiped out.
   a. Silurian0
   b. Thing
   c. Undefined
   d. Undefined

79. _____ is molten rock expelled by a volcano during an eruption. When first extruded from a volcanic vent, it is a liquid at temperatures from 700 °C to 1,200 °C.

a. Thing
b. Lava0
c. Undefined
d. Undefined

80. The Earth's _____ is the wandering point on the Earth's surface where the geomagnetic field lines are directed vertically upwards. The _____ is constantly shifting due to changes in the Earth's magnetic field. It is moving north west by about 10 to 15 kilometers per year.
   a. South magnetic pole0
   b. Thing
   c. Undefined
   d. Undefined

81. _____ is the extraction of valuable minerals or other geological materials from the earth, usually from an ore body, vein, or seam. Any material that cannot be grown from agricultural processes, or created artificially in a laboratory or factory, is usually extracted from the earth by this method.
   a. Mining0
   b. Thing
   c. Undefined
   d. Undefined

82. _____ is the part of Earth's lithosphere that surfaces in the ocean basins. _____ is primarily composed of mafic rocks, or sima. It is thinner than continental crust, or sial, generally less than 10 kilometers thick, however it is more dense, having a mean density of about 3.3 grams per cubic centimeter.
   a. Thing
   b. Oceanic crust0
   c. Undefined
   d. Undefined

83. _____ rocks form when molten rock, magma, cools and solidifies, with or without crystallization, either below the surface as intrusive, plutonic rocks or on the surface as extrusive, volcanic, rocks.
   a. Igneous0
   b. Thing
   c. Undefined
   d. Undefined

84. _____ forms when rock cools and solidifies either below the surface as intrusive rocks or on the surface as extrusive rocks. This magma can be derived from partial melts of pre-existing rocks in either the Earth's mantle or crust. Typically, the melting is caused by one or more of the following processes – an increase in temperature, a decrease in pressure, or a change in composition.
   a. Igneous rock0
   b. Thing
   c. Undefined
   d. Undefined

85. In geology, a _____ is the outermost layer of a planet, part of its lithosphere. They are generally composed of a less dense material than its deeper layers. Earths' is composed mainly of basalt and granite. It is cooler and more rigid than the deeper layers of the mantle and core.
   a. Crust0
   b. Thing
   c. Undefined
   d. Undefined

86. A _____ is a group of mountains bordered by lowlands or separated from other mountain ranges by passes or rivers. Individual mountains within the same _____ do not necessarily have the same geology; they may be a mix of different orogeny, for example volcanoes, uplifted mountains or fold mountains and may, therefore, be of different rock.
   a. Mountain range0
   b. Thing
   c. Undefined
   d. Undefined

Chapter 3. Plate Tectonics: A Unifying Theory

87. _____ was an American geologist. He was considered one of the "founding fathers" of the unifying theory of plate tectonics. He is best known for his theories on sea floor spreading, specifically work on relationships between island arcs, seafloor gravity anomalies, and serpentinized peridotite, suggesting that the convection of the Earth's mantle was the driving force behind this process. This work provided a conceptual base for the development of the theory of plate tectonics.
   a. Person
   b. Harry Hess0
   c. Undefined
   d. Undefined

88. A _____ is an underwater mountain range, formed by plate tectonics. This uplifting of the ocean floor occurs when convection currents rise in the mantle beneath the oceanic crust and create magma where two tectonic plates meet at a divergent boundary.
   a. Oceanic ridge0
   b. Thing
   c. Undefined
   d. Undefined

89. _____ are minute disruptions in the earths magnetic field due to either a greater or lesser difference in surrounding constant normal values.
   a. Magnetic Anomalies0
   b. Thing
   c. Undefined
   d. Undefined

90. An _____ phenomenon is an observed event which deviates from what is expected according to existing rules or scientific theory.
   a. Anomalous0
   b. Thing
   c. Undefined
   d. Undefined

91. _____ is a technique used to date materials based on a knowledge of the decay rates of naturally occurring isotopes, and the current abundances. It is the principal source of information about the age of the Earth and a significant source of information about rates of evolutionary change.
   a. Thing
   b. Radiometric dating0
   c. Undefined
   d. Undefined

92. In optics, _____ is the field that studies the measurement of electromagnetic radiation, including visible light. Note that light is also measured using the techniques of photometry, which deal with brightness as perceived by the human eye, rather than absolute power.
   a. Thing
   b. Radiometry0
   c. Undefined
   d. Undefined

93. The _____ is the layer of granitic, sedimentary, and metamorphic rocks which form the continents and the areas of shallow seabed close to their shores, known as continental shelves. It is less dense than the material of the Earth's mantle and thus "floats" on top of it. _____ is also less dense than oceanic crust, though it is considerably thicker. About 40% of the Earth's surface is now underlain by _____.
   a. Thing
   b. Continental crust0
   c. Undefined
   d. Undefined

94. A _____ is a type of excavation or depression in the ground. They are generally defined by being deeper than they are wide, and by being narrow compared to their length.

a. Thing
b. Trench0
c. Undefined
d. Undefined

95. The _____ is the solid outermost shell of a rocky planet. On the Earth, the _____ includes the crust and the uppermost mantle which is joined to the crust across the Mohorovièiæ discontinuity. _____ is underlain by asthenosphere, the weaker, hotter, and deeper part of the upper mantle.
a. Lithosphere0
b. Thing
c. Undefined
d. Undefined

96. The _____ is the region of the Earth between 100-200 km below the surface that is the weak or "soft" zone in the upper mantle. It lies just below the lithosphere, which is involved in plate movements and isostatic adjustments. In spite of its heat, pressures keep it plastic, and it has a relatively low density. Seismic waves pass relatively slowly through the _____.
a. Asthenosphere0
b. Thing
c. Undefined
d. Undefined

97. The _____ are hemispheric-scale long but narrow topographic depressions of the sea floor. They are also the deepest parts of the ocean floor. Trenches define one of the most important natural boundaries on the Earth's solid surface, that between two lithospheric plates. There are three types of lithospheric plate boundaries: divergent, convergent, and transform. Trenches are the spectacular and distinctive morphological features of convergent plate boundaries.
a. Thing
b. Oceanic trenches0
c. Undefined
d. Undefined

98. Ocean _____ are any more or less continuous, directed movement of ocean water that flows in one of the Earth's oceans. They are rivers of hot or cold water within the ocean. They are generated from the forces acting upon the water like the earth's rotation, the wind, the temperature and salinity differences and the gravitation of the moon.
a. Currents0
b. Thing
c. Undefined
d. Undefined

99. _____ is a theory of geology that has been developed to explain the observed evidence for large scale motions of the Earth's lithosphere. The theory encompassed and superseded the older theory of continental drift.
a. Thing
b. Plate tectonics0
c. Undefined
d. Undefined

100. A _____ is a scientific instrument used to measure the strength and/or direction of the magnetic field in the vicinity of the instrument.
a. Thing
b. Magnetometer0
c. Undefined
d. Undefined

101. An _____ is a body of igneous rock that has crystallized from a molten magma below the surface of the Earth.
a. Intrusion0
b. Thing
c. Undefined
d. Undefined

Chapter 3. Plate Tectonics: A Unifying Theory

102. The _____ is the first epoch of the Palaeogene Period in the modern Cenozoic era. The _____ immediately followed the mass extinction event at the end of the Cretaceous, which marks the demise of the dinosaurs. The die-off of the dinosaurs left unfilled ecological niches worldwide, and the name _____ refers to the older, new fauna that arose during the epoch, prior to the emergence of modern mammalian orders in the Eocene.
 a. Paleocene0
 b. Thing
 c. Undefined
 d. Undefined

103. The _____ on the geologic timescale had been intended to cover the world's recent period of repeated glaciations. The _____ follows the Pliocene and is followed by the Holocene. The _____ is the third epoch of the Neogene period or 6th epoch of the Cenozoic era. The end of the _____ corresponds with the end of the Paleolithic age used in archaeology. The _____ is divided into the Early _____, Middle _____ and Late _____, and numerous faunal stages.
 a. Pleistocene0
 b. Thing
 c. Undefined
 d. Undefined

104. The _____ epoch is the period in the geologic timescale that extends from 5.332 million to 1.806 million years before present.
 a. Thing
 b. Pliocene0
 c. Undefined
 d. Undefined

105. The _____ Epoch is a period of time that extends from about 23.03 to 5.332 million years before the present. As with other older geologic periods, the rock beds that define the start and end are well identified but the exact dates of the start and end of the period are uncertain.
 a. Miocene0
 b. Thing
 c. Undefined
 d. Undefined

106. The _____ refers to the sparsity of additional modern mammalian faunas after a burst of evolution during the Eocene. The _____ follows the Eocene epoch and is followed by the Miocene epoch. The _____ is the third and final epoch of the Palaeogene period. The start of the _____ is marked by a major extinction event that may be related to the impact of a large extraterrestrial object in Siberia and/or one near Chesapeake Bay.
 a. Oligocene0
 b. Thing
 c. Undefined
 d. Undefined

107. The _____ is a geological eon representing a period before the first abundant complex life on Earth. The _____ Eon extended from 2500 million years ago to 542.0 ± 1.0 million years ago. The _____ is the most recent part of the old informal Precambrian time.
 a. Thing
 b. Proterozoic0
 c. Undefined
 d. Undefined

108. A _____, as defined by the International Astronomical Union, is a celestial body orbiting a star or stellar remnant that is massive enough to be rounded by its own gravity, not massive enough to cause thermonuclear fusion in its core, and has cleared its neighboring region of planetesimals.
 a. Planet0
 b. Thing
 c. Undefined
 d. Undefined

Chapter 3. Plate Tectonics: A Unifying Theory

109. In plate tectonics, a _____ a linear feature that exists between two tectonic plates that are moving away from each other. These areas can form in the middle of continents but eventually form ocean basins.
   a. Divergent plate boundary0
   b. Thing
   c. Undefined
   d. Undefined

110. _____ the fourth planet from the Sun in the Solar System. The planet is named after _____, the Roman god of war. It is also referred to as the "Red Planet" because of its reddish appearance as seen from Earth.
   a. Thing
   b. Mars0
   c. Undefined
   d. Undefined

111. _____ is the science and study of the solid matter that constitute the Earth. Encompassing such things as rocks, soil, and gemstones, _____ studies the composition, structure, physical properties, history, and the processes that shape Earth's components.
   a. Geology0
   b. Thing
   c. Undefined
   d. Undefined

112. _____ is the process of heating a solid substance to a point where it turns into a liquid. An object that has melted is molten.
   a. Melting0
   b. Thing
   c. Undefined
   d. Undefined

113. A _____ is an intrusion into a cross-cutting fissure, meaning a _____ cuts across other pre-existing layers or bodies of rock, this means that a _____ is always younger than the rocks that contain it. The thickness is usually much smaller than the other two dimensions. Thickness can vary from sub-centimeter scale to many meters in thickness and the lateral dimensions can extend over many kilometers.
   a. Dike0
   b. Thing
   c. Undefined
   d. Undefined

114. The _____ is a tectonic plate covering the continent of Africa and extending westward to the Mid-Atlantic Ridge.
   a. Thing
   b. African plate0
   c. Undefined
   d. Undefined

115. In geology, a _____ is a tabular pluton that has intruded between older layers of sedimentary rock, beds of volcanic lava or tuff, or even along the direction of foliation in metamorphic rock. The term _____ is synonymous with concordant intrusive sheet. This means that the _____ does not cut across preexisting rocks. Contrast this with dikes.
   a. Thing
   b. Sill0
   c. Undefined
   d. Undefined

116. In geology, a _____ is a place where the Earth's crust and lithosphere are being pulled apart.
   a. Rift0
   b. Thing
   c. Undefined
   d. Undefined

117. _____ rock is one of the three main rock groups. Rock formed from these covers 75% of the Earth's land area, and includes common types such as chalk, limestone, dolomite, sandstone, and shale.

Chapter 3. Plate Tectonics: A Unifying Theory 55

a. Sedimentary0
b. Thing
c. Undefined
d. Undefined

118. Faults are planar rock fractures, which show evidence of relative movement. Large faults within the Earth's crust are the result of shear motion and active _____ zones are the causal locations of most earthquakes. Earthquakes are caused by energy release during rapid slippage along faults. The largest examples are at tectonic plate boundaries but many faults occur far from active plate boundaries. Since faults do not usually consist of a single, clean fracture, the term _____ zone is used when referring to the zone of complex deformation that is associated with the _____ plane.

a. Fault0
b. Thing
c. Undefined
d. Undefined

119. _____ can be defined as the solid state recrystallisation of pre-existing rocks due to changes in heat and/or pressure and/or introduction of fluids. There will be mineralogical, chemical and crystallographic changes. _____ produced with increasing pressure and temperature conditions is known as prograde _____. Conversely, decreasing temperatures and pressure characterize retrograde _____.

a. Thing
b. Metamorphism0
c. Undefined
d. Undefined

120. _____ is the process of building mountains, and may be studied as a tectonic structural event, as a geographical event and a chronological event, in that orogenic events cause distinctive structural phenomena and related tectonic activity, affect certain regions of rocks and crust and happen within a time frame.

a. Orogeny0
b. Thing
c. Undefined
d. Undefined

121. In plate tectonics, a _____ is an actively deforming region where two tectonic plates or fragments of lithosphere move towards one another. When two plates move toward one another, they form either a subduction zone or a continental collision.

a. Thing
b. Convergent boundary0
c. Undefined
d. Undefined

122. Mean _____ is the average height of the sea, with reference to a suitable reference surface.

a. Thing
b. Sea level0
c. Undefined
d. Undefined

123. In geology, a _____ is a depression with predominant extent in one direction. The terms U-shaped and V-shaped are descriptive terms of geography to characterize the form of valleys. Most valleys belong to one of these two main types or a mixture of them, at least with respect of the cross section of the slopes or hillsides.

a. Thing
b. Valley0
c. Undefined
d. Undefined

124. _____ is an accumulate in the abyssal plain of the deep ocean, far away from terrestrial sources that provide terrigenous sediments; the latter are primarily limited to the continental shelf, and deposited by rivers.

a. Thing
b. Pelagic sediment0
c. Undefined
d. Undefined

125. _____ is an igneous, volcanic rock, of intermediate composition, with aphanitic to porphyritic texture.

Chapter 3. Plate Tectonics: A Unifying Theory

a. Andesite0
b. Thing
c. Undefined
d. Undefined

126. The _____ is the largest of the Earth's oceanic divisions. It extends from the Arctic in the north to the Antarctic in the south, bounded by Asia and Australia on the west and the Americas on the east. At 169.2 million square kilometres in area, this largest division of the World Ocean – and, in turn, the hydrosphere – covers about 46% of the Earth's water surface and about 32% of its total surface area, making it larger than all of the Earth's land area combined.
a. Pacific Ocean0
b. Place
c. Undefined
d. Undefined

127. The _____ is an island nation located in Southeast Asia, with Manila as its capital city. The Philippine Archipelago comprises 7,107 islands in the western Pacific Ocean. The country reflects diverse indigenous Austronesian cultures from its many islands, as well as European and American influence from Spain, Latin America and the United States.
a. Philippine Islands0
b. Place
c. Undefined
d. Undefined

128. An _____ is any piece of land that is completely surrounded by water, above high tide. There are two main types of islands: continental islands and oceanic islands. There are also artificial islands. A grouping of geographically and/or geologically related islands is called an archipelago.
a. Thing
b. Island0
c. Undefined
d. Undefined

129. The _____ are a chain of more than 300 small volcanic islands forming an island arc in the Northern Pacific Ocean, occupying an area of 6,821 sq mi westward from the Alaska Peninsula toward the Kamchatka Peninsula.
a. Place
b. Aleutian Islands0
c. Undefined
d. Undefined

130. A _____ in geology is a valley created by the formation of a rift.
a. Rift valley0
b. Thing
c. Undefined
d. Undefined

131. The _____ is a vast geographical and geological feature, approximately 6,000 kilometres in length, which runs from northern Syria in Southwest Asia to central Mozambique in East Africa. Caused by the geological process of rifting, it is a complex feature where several plates of the earth's crust join.
a. East African Rift0
b. Place
c. Undefined
d. Undefined

132. A _____ is a body of water or other liquid of considerable size contained on a body of land. A vast majority are fresh water, and lie in the Northern Hemisphere at higher latitudes. Most have a natural outflow in the form of a river or stream, but some do not, and lose water solely by evaporation and/or underground seepage.
a. Lake0
b. Thing
c. Undefined
d. Undefined

133. _____ is the process by which molecules in a liquid state become a gas.

Chapter 3. Plate Tectonics: A Unifying Theory

a. Thing
c. Undefined
b. Evaporation0
d. Undefined

134. _____ is the natural or artificial removal of surface and sub-surface water from a given area. Many agricultural soils need _____ to improve production or to manage water supplies.
a. Thing
c. Undefined
b. Drainage0
d. Undefined

135. The _____, named after the Nazca region of southern Peru, is an oceanic tectonic plate in the eastern Pacific Ocean basin off the west coast of South America.
a. Thing
c. Undefined
b. Nazca plate0
d. Undefined

136. A _____ is a chain of volcanic islands or mountains formed by plate tectonics as an oceanic tectonic plate subducts under another tectonic plate and produces magma.
a. Thing
c. Undefined
b. Volcanic arc0
d. Undefined

137. The _____ are South America's longest mountain range, forming a continuous chain of highland along the western coast of South America.
a. Andes Mountains0
c. Undefined
b. Place
d. Undefined

138. A _____ is a natural depression or hole in the surface topography caused by the removal of soil or bedrock, often both, by water. They may vary in size from less than a meter to several hundred meters both in diameter and depth, and vary in form from soil-lined bowls to bedrock-edged chasms.
a. Thing
c. Undefined
b. Sinkhole0
d. Undefined

139. A _____ is an area on Earth where two tectonic plates meet and move towards one another, with one sliding underneath the other and moving down into the mantle, at rates typically measured in centimeters per year. In a sense, subduction zones are the opposite of divergent boundaries, areas where material rises up from the mantle and plates are moving apart.
a. Thing
c. Undefined
b. Subduction zone0
d. Undefined

140. _____ is the result of the transformation of a pre-existing rock type, the protolith, in a process called metamorphism, which means "change in form". The protolith is subjected to heat and extreme pressure causing profound physical and/or chemical change. The protolith may be sedimentary rock, igneous rock or another older rock.
a. Metamorphic rock0
c. Undefined
b. Thing
d. Undefined

141. Metamorphic rock is the result of the transformation of a pre-existing rock type, the protolith, in a process called metamorphism. The protolith is subjected to heat and extreme pressure causing profound physical and/or chemical change. _____ make up a large part of the Earth's crust. They are formed deep beneath the Earth's surface by great stresses from rocks above and high pressures and temperatures.

Chapter 3. Plate Tectonics: A Unifying Theory

| a. Thing | b. Metamorphic rocks0 |
| c. Undefined | d. Undefined |

142. _____ is one of the three main rock groups. _____ covers 75% of the Earth's land area. Four basic processes are involved in the formation of a clastic _____: weathering caused mainly by friction of waves, transportation where the sediment is carried along by a current, deposition and compaction where the sediment is squashed together to form a rock of this kind.

| a. Thing | b. Sedimentary rock0 |
| c. Undefined | d. Undefined |

143. _____ is a 16-ton, manned deep-ocean research submersible owned by the United States Navy and operated by the Woods Hole Oceanographic Institution in Woods Hole, Massachusetts. The three-person vessel allows for two scientists and one pilot to dive for up to nine hours at 4500 metersor 15,000 feet.

| a. Alvin0 | b. Thing |
| c. Undefined | d. Undefined |

144. _____ is a dense, coarse-grained igneous rock, consisting mostly of the minerals olivine and pyroxene. _____ is ultramafic and ultrabasic, as the rock contains less than 45% silica. This type of rock is derived from the Earth's mantle, either as solid blocks and fragments, or as crystals accumulated from magmas that formed in the mantle.

| a. Thing | b. Peridotite0 |
| c. Undefined | d. Undefined |

145. _____ is a dark, coarse-grained, intrusive igneous rock chemically equivalent to basalt. It is a plutonic rock, formed when molten magma is trapped beneath the Earth's surface and cools into a crystalline mass.

| a. Thing | b. Gabbro0 |
| c. Undefined | d. Undefined |

146. _____ refers to sections of the oceanic crust and the subjacent upper mantle that have been uplifted or emplaced to be exposed within continental crustal rocks.

| a. Thing | b. Ophiolite0 |
| c. Undefined | d. Undefined |

147. The _____ are a mountain range in Asia, separating the Indian subcontinent from the Tibetan Plateau. By extension, it is also the name of the massive mountain system which includes the Himalaya proper, the Karakoram, the Hindu Kush, and a host of minor ranges extending from the Pamir Knot.

| a. Himalayas0 | b. Place |
| c. Undefined | d. Undefined |

148. The _____ is the name for one of the great mountain range systems of Europe, stretching from Austria and Slovenia in the east, through Italy, Switzerland, Liechtenstein and Germany to France in the west.

| a. Place | b. Alps0 |
| c. Undefined | d. Undefined |

149. In plate tectonics, a _____ is said to occur when tectonic plates slide and grind against each other along a transform fault. The relative motion of such plates is horizontal in either sinistral or dextral direction. Many transform boundaries are locked in tension before suddenly releasing, and causing earthquakes.

Chapter 3. Plate Tectonics: A Unifying Theory

a. Thing
c. Undefined
b. Transform boundary0
d. Undefined

150. A _____ is a geological fault that is a special case of strike-slip faulting which terminates abruptly, at both ends, at a major transverse geological feature. Also known as a conservative plate boundary.
a. Transform fault0
c. Undefined
b. Thing
d. Undefined

151. The _____ which forms the country of Japan extends from north to south along the eastern coast of the Eurasian Continent, the western shore of the Pacific Ocean.
a. Japanese Islands0
c. Undefined
b. Place
d. Undefined

152. A _____ linear oceanic feature--often hundreds, even thousands of kilometers long--resulting from the action of offset mid-ocean ridge axis segments; they are a consequence of plate tectonics.
a. Thing
c. Undefined
b. Fracture zone0
d. Undefined

153. The _____ is a geological fault that runs a length of roughly 800 miles through western and southern California in the United States. The fault, a right-lateral strike-slip fault, marks a transform boundary between the Pacific Plate and the North American Plate.
a. San Andreas fault0
c. Undefined
b. Thing
d. Undefined

154. The _____ is an oceanic tectonic plate beneath the Pacific Ocean.
a. Pacific plate0
c. Undefined
b. Thing
d. Undefined

155. The _____ is a tectonic plate covering most of North America, extending eastward to the Mid-Atlantic Ridge and westward to the Cherskiy Range in East Siberia.
a. North American Plate0
c. Undefined
b. Thing
d. Undefined

156. _____ was a Greek captain employed by Spain to sail northward from Mexico and look for a northern passage from the Pacific Ocean to the Atlantic Ocean. In 1592, his exploration took him into the body of water, the Strait of _____.
a. Person
c. Undefined
b. Juan de Fuca0
d. Undefined

157. The _____ is a body of water that separates the Baja California Peninsula from the Mexican mainland. It is bordered by the states of Baja California, Baja California Sur, Sonora, and Sinaloa.
a. Thing
c. Undefined
b. Sea of Cortez0
d. Undefined

158. _____ is a location on the Earth's surface that has experienced active volcanism for a long period of time. J. Tuzo Wilson came up with the idea in 1963 that volcanic chains like the Hawaiian Islands result from the slow movement of a tectonic plate across a "fixed" hot spot deep beneath the surface of the planet.

Chapter 3. Plate Tectonics: A Unifying Theory

a. Thing
b. Hot spots0
c. Undefined
d. Undefined

159. A _____ is an upwelling of abnormally hot rock within the Earth's mantle. As the heads of mantle plumes can partly melt when they reach shallow depths, they are thought to be the cause of volcanic centers known as hotspots and probably also to have caused flood basalts.
a. Mantle plume0
b. Event
c. Undefined
d. Undefined

160. The _____ is a large enclosed plain, approximately 50 miles long and up to 15 miles across, in eastern San Luis Obispo County, California. It contains the 180,000 acre _____ National Monument, and it is the largest single native grassland remaining in California.
a. Carrizo Plain0
b. Place
c. Undefined
d. Undefined

161. _____, in everyday life, is most familiar as the agency that endows objects with weight. _____ is responsible for keeping the Earth and the other planets in their orbits around the Sun; for the formation of tides; and for various other phenomena that we observe. _____ is also the reason for the very existence of the Earth, the Sun, and most macroscopic objects in the universe; without it, matter would not have coalesced into these large masses, and life, as we know it, would not exist.
a. Gravitation0
b. Thing
c. Undefined
d. Undefined

162. _____ is an igneous rock of volcanic origin. They often have a vesicular texture, which is the result voids left by volatiles escaping from the molten lava. Pumice is a rock, which is an example of explosive volcanic eruption. It is so vesicular that it floats in water.
a. Volcanic rock0
b. Thing
c. Undefined
d. Undefined

163. The _____ are a mountain range that runs roughly north and south through western Russia. They are sometimes considered as the natural boundary between Europe and Asia. It extends 2,500 km from the Kazakh steppes along the northern border of Kazakhstan to the coast of the Arctic ocean.
a. Place
b. Ural Mountains0
c. Undefined
d. Undefined

164. The _____ describes the periodic opening and closing of ocean basins.
a. Wilson cycle0
b. Thing
c. Undefined
d. Undefined

165. The _____ are a vast system of mountains in eastern North America.
a. Appalachian Mountains0
b. Place
c. Undefined
d. Undefined

166. A _____ in paleogeography is an accretion that has collided with a continental nucleus, or "craton" but can be recognized by the foreign origin of its rock strata. The boundaries of a _____ are usually represented by crustal faults. In the lithospheric scheme of plate tectonics, a _____ is not a microplate, but a piece of crust "riding" atop another plate.

a. Thing
b. Terrane0
c. Undefined
d. Undefined

167. An _____ is any more or less continuous, directed movement of ocean water that flows in one of the Earth's oceans. Ocean Currents are rivers of hot or cold water within the ocean. The currents are generated from the forces acting upon the water like the earth's rotation, the wind, the temperature and salinity differences and the gravitation of the moon. The depth contours, the shoreline and other currents influence the current's direction and strength.
a. Ocean current0
b. Thing
c. Undefined
d. Undefined

168. _____ refers to directed, regular, or systematic movement of a group of objects, organisms, or people.
a. Migration0
b. Thing
c. Undefined
d. Undefined

169. _____ is a collective term for animal life of any particular region or time. Paleontologists usually use _____ to refer to a typical collection of animals found in a specific time or place. Paleontologists sometimes refer to a sequence of 80 or so faunal stages, which are a series of rocks all containing similar fossils.
a. Fauna0
b. Thing
c. Undefined
d. Undefined

170. _____ in biology is an anatomical structure, physiological process or behavioral trait of an organism that has evolved over a short or long period of time by the process of natural selection such that it increases the expected long-term reproductive success of the organism. The term _____ is also sometimes used as a synonym for natural selection, but most biologists discourage this usage. Organisms that are adapted to their environment are able to: obtain air, water, food and nutrients, cope with physical conditions such as temperature, light and heat, defend themselves from their natural enemies, reproduce, and respond to changes around them
a. Adaptation0
b. Thing
c. Undefined
d. Undefined

171. _____ is an English word that describes any animal without a spinal column.
a. Invertebrate0
b. Thing
c. Undefined
d. Undefined

172. The _____ is a tropical sea in the Western Hemisphere, part of the Atlantic Ocean, southeast of the Gulf of Mexico.
a. Caribbean Sea0
b. Place
c. Undefined
d. Undefined

173. An _____ is a volume of rock containing components or minerals in a mode of occurrence that renders it valuable for mining.
a. Ore0
b. Thing
c. Undefined
d. Undefined

174. _____ is a variety of igneous rock consisting of large-grained crystals, such as feldspar or quartz, dispersed in a fine-grained feldspathic matrix or groundmass. The larger crystals are called phenocrysts.

a. Thing
b. Porphyry0
c. Undefined
d. Undefined

175. _____ is a ductile metal with excellent electrical conductivity, and finds extensive use as an electrical conductor, heat conductor, as a building material, and as a component of various alloys.
a. Copper0
b. Thing
c. Undefined
d. Undefined

176. _____ is any product of the condensation of atmospheric water vapor that is deposited on the earth's surface. It occurs when the atmosphere becomes saturated with water vapour and the water condenses and falls out of solution. Air becomes saturated via two processes, cooling and adding moisture.
a. Thing
b. Precipitation0
c. Undefined
d. Undefined

177. A _____, is a fissure in a planet's surface from which geothermally heated water issues. Hydrothermal vents are commonly found near volcanically active places, tectonic plates that are moving apart, ocean basins, and hotspots.
a. Hydrothermal vent0
b. Thing
c. Undefined
d. Undefined

178. _____ is a highly sought-after precious metal which, for many centuries, has been used as money, a store of value and in jewelery. The metal occurs as nuggets or grains in rocks, underground "veins" and in alluvial deposits. It is one of the coinage metals. Itis dense, soft, shiny and the most malleable and ductile of the known metals.
a. Thing
b. Gold0
c. Undefined
d. Undefined

179. _____ is a soft white lustrous transition metal, it has the highest electrical and thermal conductivity for a metal.
a. Silver0
b. Thing
c. Undefined
d. Undefined

180. _____ is a chemical element in the periodic table that has the symbol Zn and atomic number 30. In some historical and sculptural contexts, it is known as spelter.
a. Thing
b. Zinc0
c. Undefined
d. Undefined

181. The term _____ refers to several types of chemical compounds containing sulfur in its lowest oxidation number of −2.
a. Thing
b. Sulfide0
c. Undefined
d. Undefined

182. The _____ is an open-pit mine extracting a large porphyry copper deposit southwest of Salt Lake City, Utah, USA, in the Oquirrh Mountains. It is owned by Rio Tinto plc through Kennecott Utah Copper Corporation which operates the mine, a concentrator and a smelter. The mine has been in production since 1906, and has resulted in the creation of a pit over 0.75 miles wide, and covering 1,900 acres.
a. Place
b. Bingham Mine0
c. Undefined
d. Undefined

Chapter 3. Plate Tectonics: A Unifying Theory

183. In physics, _____ is defined as the rate of change of displacement or the rate of displacement. Simply put, it is distance per units of time.
    a. Thing
    b. Velocity0
    c. Undefined
    d. Undefined

184. _____ was a supercontinent that most recently existed as a part of the split of the Pangaean supercontinent in the late Mesozoic era. It included most of the landmasses which make up today's continents of the northern hemisphere, chiefly Laurentia, Baltica, Siberia, Kazakhstania, and the North China and East China Cratons.
    a. Thing
    b. Laurasia0
    c. Undefined
    d. Undefined

185. The _____ form an archipelago of nineteen islands and atolls, numerous smaller islets, and undersea seamounts trending northwest by southeast in the North Pacific Ocean between latitudes 19° N and 29° N. The archipelago takes its name from the largest island in the group and extends some 1500 miles from the Island of Hawai'i in the south to northernmost Kure Atoll.
    a. Hawaiian Islands0
    b. Place
    c. Undefined
    d. Undefined

186. A _____ is a deep valley between cliffs often carved from the landscape by a river. Most were formed by a process of long-time erosion from a plateau level. The cliffs form because harder rock strata that are resistant to erosion and weathering remain exposed on the valley walls.
    a. Canyon0
    b. Thing
    c. Undefined
    d. Undefined

187. The _____ is a very colorful, steep-sided gorge, carved by the Colorado River in the U.S. state of Arizona. It is one of the first national parks in the United States.
    a. Grand Canyon0
    b. Place
    c. Undefined
    d. Undefined

Chapter 4. Geologic Time: Concepts and Principles

1. Before the advent of absolute dating in the 20th century, archaeologists and geologists were largely limited to the use of _____ techniques. Estimates of the order of prehistoric and geological events were determined by using basic stratigraphic rules, and by observing where fossil organisms lay in the geological record, stratified bands of rocks present throughout the world.
   a. Relative dating0
   b. Thing
   c. Undefined
   d. Undefined

2. _____ is a discredited and obsolete scientific theory of geology proposed by Abraham Werner in the late 18th century that proposed rocks formed from the crystallisation of minerals in the early Earth's oceans.
   a. Neptunism0
   b. Thing
   c. Undefined
   d. Undefined

3. _____ refers to the principle that the same processes that shape the universe occurred in the past as they do now, and that the same laws of physics apply in all parts of the knowable universe.
   a. Uniformitarianism0
   b. Thing
   c. Undefined
   d. Undefined

4. _____ is the theory that Earth has been affected by sudden, short-lived, violent events that were sometimes worldwide in scope. The dominant paradigm of geology has been uniformitarianism, but recently a more inclusive and integrated view of geologic events has developed resulting in a gradual change in the scientific consensus, reflecting acceptance of some catastrophic events.
   a. Catastrophism0
   b. Thing
   c. Undefined
   d. Undefined

5. _____ is the science and study of the solid matter that constitute the Earth. Encompassing such things as rocks, soil, and gemstones, _____ studies the composition, structure, physical properties, history, and the processes that shape Earth's components.
   a. Geology0
   b. Thing
   c. Undefined
   d. Undefined

6. _____ is the process in which an unstable atomic nucleus loses energy by emitting radiation in the form of particles or electromagnetic waves.
   a. Radioactive decay0
   b. Thing
   c. Undefined
   d. Undefined

7. _____ is the process of determining a specific date for an archaeological site or artifact. _____ is usually based on the physical or chemical properties of the materials of artifacts, buildings, or other items that have been modified by humans.
   a. Thing
   b. Absolute dating0
   c. Undefined
   d. Undefined

8. In optics, _____ is the field that studies the measurement of electromagnetic radiation, including visible light. Note that light is also measured using the techniques of photometry, which deal with brightness as perceived by the human eye, rather than absolute power.
   a. Radiometry0
   b. Thing
   c. Undefined
   d. Undefined

Chapter 4. Geologic Time: Concepts and Principles 65

9. _____ rocks form when molten rock, magma, cools and solidifies, with or without crystallization, either below the surface as intrusive, plutonic rocks or on the surface as extrusive, volcanic, rocks.
   a. Igneous0
   b. Thing
   c. Undefined
   d. Undefined

10. _____ forms when rock cools and solidifies either below the surface as intrusive rocks or on the surface as extrusive rocks. This magma can be derived from partial melts of pre-existing rocks in either the Earth's mantle or crust. Typically, the melting is caused by one or more of the following processes -- an increase in temperature, a decrease in pressure, or a change in composition.
    a. Igneous rock0
    b. Thing
    c. Undefined
    d. Undefined

11. A _____ is a deep valley between cliffs often carved from the landscape by a river. Most were formed by a process of long-time erosion from a plateau level. The cliffs form because harder rock strata that are resistant to erosion and weathering remain exposed on the valley walls.
    a. Canyon0
    b. Thing
    c. Undefined
    d. Undefined

12. The _____ is a river in the southwestern United States and northwestern Mexico, approximately 1,450 mi long, draining a part of the arid regions on the western slope of the Rocky Mountains. The natural course of the river flows into the Gulf of California, but the heavy use of the river as an irrigation source for the Imperial Valley has desiccated the lower course of the river in Mexico such that it no longer consistently reaches the sea.
    a. Colorado River0
    b. Place
    c. Undefined
    d. Undefined

13. The _____ is a very colorful, steep-sided gorge, carved by the Colorado River in the U.S. state of Arizona. It is one of the first national parks in the United States.
    a. Grand Canyon0
    b. Place
    c. Undefined
    d. Undefined

14. _____ was a U.S. soldier, geologist, and explorer of the American West. He is famous for the 1869 Powell Geographic Expedition, a three-month river trip down the Green and Colorado rivers that included the first passage through the Grand Canyon.
    a. Person
    b. John Wesley Powell0
    c. Undefined
    d. Undefined

15. A _____ is a section of a river of relatively steep gradient causing an increase in water flow and turbulence. A _____ is a hydrological feature between a run and a cascade. It is characterized by the river becoming shallower and having some rocks exposed above the flow surface.
    a. Rapid0
    b. Thing
    c. Undefined
    d. Undefined

16. A _____ is a body of water with a current, confined within a bed and banks. Streams are important as conduits in the water cycle, instruments in aquifer recharge, and corridors for fish and wildlife migration.

a. Stream0
b. Thing
c. Undefined
d. Undefined

17. A _____, as defined by the International Astronomical Union, is a celestial body orbiting a star or stellar remnant that is massive enough to be rounded by its own gravity, not massive enough to cause thermonuclear fusion in its core, and has cleared its neighboring region of planetesimals.
   a. Thing
   b. Planet0
   c. Undefined
   d. Undefined

18. A _____ is a landform that extends above the surrounding terrain in a limited area. A _____ is generally steeper than a hill, but there is no universally accepted standard definition for the height of a _____ or a hill although a _____ usually has an identifiable summit.
   a. Mountain0
   b. Place
   c. Undefined
   d. Undefined

19. _____ is the process of building mountains, and may be studied as a tectonic structural event, as a geographical event and a chronological event, in that orogenic events cause distinctive structural phenomena and related tectonic activity, affect certain regions of rocks and crust and happen within a time frame.
   a. Thing
   b. Orogeny0
   c. Undefined
   d. Undefined

20. _____ is a small island located in the middle of San Francisco Bay in California, United States. It served as a lighthouse, then a military fortification, then a military prison followed by a federal prison until 1963, when it became a national recreation area.
   a. Alcatraz Island0
   b. Place
   c. Undefined
   d. Undefined

21. The _____ is used by geologists and other scientists to describe the timing and relationships between events that have occurred during the history of Earth.
   a. Thing
   b. Geological time scale0
   c. Undefined
   d. Undefined

22. _____ is a technique used to date materials based on a knowledge of the decay rates of naturally occurring isotopes, and the current abundances. It is the principal source of information about the age of the Earth and a significant source of information about rates of evolutionary change.
   a. Thing
   b. Radiometric dating0
   c. Undefined
   d. Undefined

23. _____ is a chemical element metal. It is a lustrous, silvery soft metal. It and nickel are notable for being the final elements produced by stellar nucleosynthesis, and thus are the heaviest elements which do not require a supernova or similarly cataclysmic event for formation.
   a. Thing
   b. Iron0
   c. Undefined
   d. Undefined

Chapter 4. Geologic Time: Concepts and Principles

24. _____ is the geological process whereby material is added to a landform. This is the process by which wind and water create a sediment deposit, through the laying down of granular material that has been eroded and transported from another geographical location.
    a. Thing
    b. Deposition0
    c. Undefined
    d. Undefined

25. _____ is the average and variations of weather over long periods of time. _____ zones can be defined using parameters such as temperature and rainfall.
    a. Thing
    b. Climate0
    c. Undefined
    d. Undefined

26. _____ is the substance of which physical objects are composed. _____ can be solid, liquid, plasma or gas. It constitutes the observable universe.
    a. Thing
    b. Matter0
    c. Undefined
    d. Undefined

27. _____ is any particulate matter that can be transported by fluid flow and which eventually is deposited as a layer of solid particles on the bed or bottom of a body of water or other liquid.
    a. Sediment0
    b. Thing
    c. Undefined
    d. Undefined

28. A _____ is a body of water or other liquid of considerable size contained on a body of land. A vast majority are fresh water, and lie in the Northern Hemisphere at higher latitudes. Most have a natural outflow in the form of a river or stream, but some do not, and lose water solely by evaporation and/or underground seepage.
    a. Thing
    b. Lake0
    c. Undefined
    d. Undefined

29. _____ is matter that has come from a recently living organism; is capable of decay, or the product of decay; or is composed of organic compounds. The definition of _____ varies upon the subject it is being used for.
    a. Organic matter0
    b. Thing
    c. Undefined
    d. Undefined

30. In biology and ecology, an _____ is a living complex adaptive system of organs that influence each other in such a way that they function in some way as a stable whole.
    a. Organism0
    b. Thing
    c. Undefined
    d. Undefined

31. An _____ is a core sample from the accumulation of snow and ice over many years that have recrystallized and have trapped air bubbles from previous time periods. The composition of these ice cores, especially the presence of hydrogen and oxygen isotopes, provides a picture of the climate at the time.
    a. Ice core0
    b. Thing
    c. Undefined
    d. Undefined

32. _____ is a chemical element. An abundant nonmetallic, tetravalent element, _____ has several allotropic forms. This element is the basis of the chemistry of all known life.

a. Carbon0
b. Thing
c. Undefined
d. Undefined

33. _____ is an English word that describes any animal without a spinal column.
   a. Invertebrate0
   b. Thing
   c. Undefined
   d. Undefined

34. Fossils are the mineralized or otherwise preserved remains or traces of animals, plants, and other organisms. The totality of fossils, both discovered and undiscovered, and their placement in fossiliferous rock formations and sedimentary layers is known as the _____ record.
   a. Fossil0
   b. Thing
   c. Undefined
   d. Undefined

35. _____ refers to the variation in the Earth's global climate or in regional climates over time. It describes changes in the variability or average state of the atmosphere over time scales ranging from decades to millions of years. These changes can be caused by processes internal to the Earth, external forces or, more recently, human activities.
   a. Thing
   b. Climate change0
   c. Undefined
   d. Undefined

36. A _____ is a type of speleothem that rises from the floor of a limestone cave due to the dripping of mineralized solutions and the deposition of calcium carbonate. The corresponding formation on the ceiling of a cave is known as a stalactite. If these formations grow together, meeting in the middle, the result is known as a column.
   a. Thing
   b. Stalagmite0
   c. Undefined
   d. Undefined

37. A _____ is a natural underground void large enough for a human to enter. Some people suggest that the term '_____' should only apply to cavities that have some part which does not receive daylight; however, in popular usage, the term includes smaller spaces like a sea _____, rock shelters, and grottos.
   a. Place
   b. Cave0
   c. Undefined
   d. Undefined

38. In organic chemistry, a _____ is a salt of carbonic acid.
   a. Thing
   b. Carbonate0
   c. Undefined
   d. Undefined

39. _____ is approximately 70% more dense than lead and is weakly radioactive. It occurs naturally in low concentrations in soil, rock and water.
   a. Thing
   b. Uranium0
   c. Undefined
   d. Undefined

40. _____ is a general term for the plant life of a region; it refers to the ground cover provided by plants, and is, by far, the most abundant biotic element of the biosphere. Primeval redwood forests, coastal mangrove stands, sphagnum bogs, desert soil crusts, roadside weed patches, wheat fields, cultivated gardens and lawns; are all encompassed by the term _____.

a. Place
b. Vegetation0
c. Undefined
d. Undefined

41. A _____ is a tropical or subtropical woodland ecosystem. They are characterized by the trees being sufficiently small or widely spaced so that the canopy does not close. It is often believed that they are characterized by widely spaced, scattered trees, however in many _____ communities tree densities are higher and trees are more regularly spaced than in forest communities.
   a. Place
   b. Savanna0
   c. Undefined
   d. Undefined

42. _____ refers to an area of land of low topographic relief that historically supported grasses and herbs, with few trees, and having generally a mesic climate.
   a. Prairie0
   b. Place
   c. Undefined
   d. Undefined

43. A _____ is an area with a high density of trees, historically, a wooded area set aside for hunting. These plant communities cover large areas of the globe and function as animal habitats, hydrologic flow modulators, and soil conservers, constituting one of the most important aspects of the Earth's biosphere.
   a. Thing
   b. Forest0
   c. Undefined
   d. Undefined

44. _____ is the term given to land colonised or sown with plant communities dominated by grasses and herbaceous plants. They are very varied; they can be found in most terrestrial climates.
   a. Place
   b. Grassland0
   c. Undefined
   d. Undefined

45. _____ refers to the interaction between electrons in a quantum system whose electronic structure is being considered.
   a. Electron correlation0
   b. Thing
   c. Undefined
   d. Undefined

46. _____ is the saltiness or dissolved salt content of a body of water. In oceanography, it has been traditional to express halinity not as percent, but as parts per thousand, which is approximately grams of salt per liter of solution.
   a. Salinity0
   b. Thing
   c. Undefined
   d. Undefined

47. _____ was an Irish scientist, possibly most famous for his development of radiotherapy in the treatment of cancer. He is also known for developing techniques to accurately estimate the age of a geological period, based on radioactive elements present in minerals.
   a. John Joly0
   b. Person
   c. Undefined
   d. Undefined

48. _____ are large geologic basins that are below sea level. Geologically, there are other undersea geomorphological features such as the continental shelves, the deep ocean trenches, and the undersea mountain rangeswhich are not considered to be part of the _____.

a. Thing
b. Ocean basins0
c. Undefined
d. Undefined

49. _____ rock is one of the three main rock groups. Rock formed from these covers 75% of the Earth's land area, and includes common types such as chalk, limestone, dolomite, sandstone, and shale.
a. Thing
b. Sedimentary0
c. Undefined
d. Undefined

50. _____ is one of the three main rock groups. _____ covers 75% of the Earth's land area. Four basic processes are involved in the formation of a clastic _____: weathering caused mainly by friction of waves, transportation where the sediment is carried along by a current, deposition and compaction where the sediment is squashed together to form a rock of this kind.
a. Thing
b. Sedimentary rock0
c. Undefined
d. Undefined

51. The _____ states that layers of sediment initially extend laterally in all directions; in other words, they are laterally continuous. As a result, rocks that are otherwise similar, but are now separated by a valley or other erosional feature, can be assumed to be originally continuous.
a. Principle of lateral continuity0
b. Thing
c. Undefined
d. Undefined

52. _____ was a Scottish geologist, noted for formulating uniformitarianism and the Plutonist School of thought. He is considered by many to be the father of modern geology.
a. James Hutton0
b. Person
c. Undefined
d. Undefined

53. _____ is the use of the principles of geology to reconstruct and understand the history of the Earth. It focuses on geologic processes that change the Earth's surface and subsurface; and the use of stratigraphy, structural geology and paleontology to tell the sequence of these events. It also focuses on the evolution of plants and animals during different time periods in the geological timescale.
a. Thing
b. Historical geology0
c. Undefined
d. Undefined

54. An _____ is a body of igneous rock that has crystallized from a molten magma below the surface of the Earth.
a. Thing
b. Intrusion0
c. Undefined
d. Undefined

55. Faults are planar rock fractures, which show evidence of relative movement. Large faults within the Earth's crust are the result of shear motion and active _____ zones are the causal locations of most earthquakes. Earthquakes are caused by energy release during rapid slippage along faults. The largest examples are at tectonic plate boundaries but many faults occur far from active plate boundaries. Since faults do not usually consist of a single, clean fracture, the term _____ zone is used when referring to the zone of complex deformation that is associated with the _____ plane.
a. Fault0
b. Thing
c. Undefined
d. Undefined

Chapter 4. Geologic Time: Concepts and Principles

56. _____ is the discipline concerned with the questions of how one should live ; what sorts of things exist and what are their essential natures ; what counts as genuine knowledge; and what are the correct principles of reasoning.
   a. Thing
   b. Philosophy0
   c. Undefined
   d. Undefined

57. _____ is an Earth Science focused around the chemistry, crystal structure, and physical properties of minerals. Specific studies within _____ include the processes of mineral origin and formation, classification of minerals, their geographical distribution, as well as their utilization.
   a. Thing
   b. Mineralogy0
   c. Undefined
   d. Undefined

58. _____ was a German geologist who set out a controversial theory about the stratification of the Earth's crust and coined the now obsolete word Neptunism. The basic concept of Wernerian geology was the belief in an all encompassing ocean that gradually receded to its present location while precipitating or depositing virtually all the rocks and minerals in the Earth's crust.
   a. Abraham Gottlob Werner0
   b. Thing
   c. Undefined
   d. Undefined

59. _____ is a common and widely occurring type of intrusive, felsic, igneous rock. Granites are usually medium to coarsely crystalline, occasionally with some individual crystals larger than the groundmass forming a rock known as porphyry. Granites can be pink to dark gray or even black, depending on their chemistry and mineralogy.
   a. Thing
   b. Granite0
   c. Undefined
   d. Undefined

60. A _____ is the fringe of land at the edge of a large body of water, such as an ocean, sea, or lake. A strict definition is the strip of land along a water body that is alternately exposed and covered by waves and tides.
   a. Shoreline0
   b. Thing
   c. Undefined
   d. Undefined

61. A _____ is an intrusion into a cross-cutting fissure, meaning a _____ cuts across other pre-existing layers or bodies of rock, this means that a _____ is always younger than the rocks that contain it. The thickness is usually much smaller than the other two dimensions. Thickness can vary from sub-centimeter scale to many meters in thickness and the lateral dimensions can extend over many kilometers.
   a. Dike0
   b. Thing
   c. Undefined
   d. Undefined

62. _____, bounded by Ontario, Canada and Minnesota, USA, to the north and Wisconsin and Michigan, USA, to the south, is the largest of North America's Great Lakes. It is the largest freshwater lake in the world by surface area and is the world's third-largest freshwater lake by volume.
   a. Place
   b. Lake Superior0
   c. Undefined
   d. Undefined

63. _____ is water from a sea or ocean. On average, _____ in the world's oceans has a salinity of ~3.5%, or 35 parts per thousand. This means that every 1 kg of _____ has approximately 35 grams of dissolved salts.

Chapter 4. Geologic Time: Concepts and Principles

a. Thing
b. Seawater0
c. Undefined
d. Undefined

64. _____ is a common gray to black extrusive volcanic rock. It is usually fine-grained due to rapid cooling of lava on the Earth's surface. It may be porphyritic containing larger crystals in a fine matrix, or vesicular, or frothy scoria.
a. Thing
b. Basalt0
c. Undefined
d. Undefined

65. _____ was a Scottish lawyer, geologist, and populariser of uniformitarianism. Principles of Geology, his first book, was also his most famous, most influential, and most important. First published in three volumes in 1830-33, it established his credentials as an important geological theorist and introduced the doctrine of uniformitarianism.
a. Person
b. Charles Lyell0
c. Undefined
d. Undefined

66. _____ is displacement of solids by the agents of ocean currents, wind, water, or ice by downward or down-slope movement in response to gravity or by living organisms.
a. Erosion0
b. Thing
c. Undefined
d. Undefined

67. The _____ the bottom of the ocean. At the bottom of the continental slope is the continental rise, which is caused by sediment cascading down the continental slope.
a. Seafloor0
b. Thing
c. Undefined
d. Undefined

68. A _____ is one of several large landmasses on Earth. They are generally identified by convention rather than any strict criteria, but seven areas are commonly reckoned as continents – they are: Asia, Africa, North America, South America, Antarctica, Europe, and Australia.
a. Continent0
b. Thing
c. Undefined
d. Undefined

69. _____ is molten rock located beneath the surface of the Earth, and which often collects in a _____ chamber. _____ is a complex high-temperature fluid substance. Most are silicate solutions. It is capable of intrusion into adjacent rocks or of extrusion onto the surface as lava or ejected explosively as tephra to form pyroclastic rock. Environments of _____ formation include subduction zones, continental rift zones, mid-oceanic ridges, and hotspots, some of which are interpreted as mantle plumes.
a. Thing
b. Magma0
c. Undefined
d. Undefined

70. _____ is the process of heating a solid substance to a point where it turns into a liquid. An object that has melted is molten.
a. Melting0
b. Thing
c. Undefined
d. Undefined

71. An _____ is a buried erosion surface separating two rock masses or strata of different ages, indicating that sediment deposition was not continuous. In general, the older layer was exposed to erosion for an interval of time before deposition of the younger, but the term is used to describe any break in the sedimentary geologic record.

Chapter 4. Geologic Time: Concepts and Principles

    a. Thing
    b. Unconformity0
    c. Undefined
    d. Undefined

72. _____ is a rocky promontory in the county of Berwickshire on the east coast of Scotland. It is famous in the history of geology as a result of a boat trip in 1788 in which James Hutton, with James Hall and John Playfair, observed the angular unconformity which Hutton regarded as conclusive proof of the theory of geological evolution.
    a. Place
    b. Siccar Point0
    c. Undefined
    d. Undefined

73. _____ is the result of the transformation of a pre-existing rock type, the protolith, in a process called metamorphism, which means "change in form". The protolith is subjected to heat and extreme pressure causing profound physical and/or chemical change. The protolith may be sedimentary rock, igneous rock or another older rock.
    a. Metamorphic rock0
    b. Thing
    c. Undefined
    d. Undefined

74. Metamorphic rock is the result of the transformation of a pre-existing rock type, the protolith, in a process called metamorphism. The protolith is subjected to heat and extreme pressure causing profound physical and/or chemical change. _____ make up a large part of the Earth's crust. They are formed deep beneath the Earth's surface by great stresses from rocks above and high pressures and temperatures.
    a. Metamorphic rocks0
    b. Thing
    c. Undefined
    d. Undefined

75. _____ can be defined as the solid state recrystallisation of pre-existing rocks due to changes in heat and/or pressure and/or introduction of fluids. There will be mineralogical, chemical and crystallographic changes. _____ produced with increasing pressure and temperature conditions is known as prograde _____. Conversely, decreasing temperatures and pressure characterize retrograde _____.
    a. Thing
    b. Metamorphism0
    c. Undefined
    d. Undefined

76. _____ is an unconformity where horizontally parallel strata of sedimentary rock are deposited on tilted and eroded layers that may be either vertical or at an angle to the overlying horizontal layers
    a. Angular unconformity0
    b. Thing
    c. Undefined
    d. Undefined

77. _____ was a mathematical physicist, engineer, and outstanding leader in the physical sciences of the 19th century. He did important work in the mathematical analysis of electricity and thermodynamics, and did much to unify the emerging discipline of physics in its modern form. He is widely known for developing the Kelvin scale of absolute temperature measurement.
    a. Lord Kelvin0
    b. Person
    c. Undefined
    d. Undefined

78. A _____ is a process that results in the interconversion of chemical substances. The substance or substances initially involved in a _____ are called reactants. Chemical reactions are characterized by a chemical change, and they yield one or more products which are, in general, different from the reactants.

Chapter 4. Geologic Time: Concepts and Principles

    a. Thing
    c. Undefined
    b. Chemical reaction0
    d. Undefined

79. The term _____, taken literally, refers to movement that goes on forever. This is possible in the current theoretical understanding of physics as in Newton's First Law of Motion. However, _____ usually refers to a device or system that stores and/or outputs more energy than is put into it.
    a. Thing
    c. Undefined
    b. Perpetual motion0
    d. Undefined

80. _____ was already eminent as an English naturalist when he proposed and provided evidence for the theory that all species have evolved over time from one or a few common ancestors through the process of natural selection. The fact that evolution occurs became accepted by the scientific community and the general public in his lifetime, while his theory of natural selection came to be widely seen as the primary explanation of the process of evolution in the 1930s, and now forms the basis of modern evolutionary theory. In modified form, Darwin's theory remains a cornerstone of biology, as it provides a unifying explanation for the diversity of life.
    a. Charles Darwin0
    c. Undefined
    b. Person
    d. Undefined

81. A _____ is a barrier across flowing water that obstructs, directs or slows down the flow, often creating a reservoir, lake or impoundment.
    a. Dam0
    c. Undefined
    b. Thing
    d. Undefined

82. _____ are any of the several different forms of an element each having different atomic mass. _____ of an element have nuclei with the same number of protons but different numbers of neutrons.
    a. Isotopes0
    c. Undefined
    b. Thing
    d. Undefined

83. An _____ is a type of atom that is defined by its atomic number; that is, by the number of protons in its nucleus.
    a. Thing
    c. Undefined
    b. Element0
    d. Undefined

84. _____ was a Polish-French physicist and chemist. She was a pioneer in the field of radioactivity, the first twice-honored Nobel laureate and the first female professor at the Sorbonne.
    a. Marie Curie0
    c. Undefined
    b. Thing
    d. Undefined

85. _____ are the fundamental building blocks of chemistry, and are conserved in chemical reactions.
    a. Thing
    c. Undefined
    b. Atoms0
    d. Undefined

86. In physics, the _____ is a subatomic particle with no net electric charge.
    a. Thing
    c. Undefined
    b. Neutron0
    d. Undefined

Chapter 4. Geologic Time: Concepts and Principles 75

87. In physics, the _____ is a subatomic particle with an electric charge of one positive fundamental unit a diameter of about 1.5×10^{-15} m, and a mass of 938.27231(28) MeV/c2 (1.6726×10^{-27} kg), 1.007 276 466 88(13) u or about 1836 times the mass of an electron.
   a. Thing
   b. Proton0
   c. Undefined
   d. Undefined

88. In chemistry and physics, the _____ is the number of protons found in the nucleus of an atom. It is traditionally represented by the symbol Z.
   a. Thing
   b. Atomic number0
   c. Undefined
   d. Undefined

89. The _____ is a fundamental subatomic particle that carries a negative electric charge.
   a. Thing
   b. Electron0
   c. Undefined
   d. Undefined

90. In nuclear physics, _____ is a type of radioactive decay in which a beta particle, an electron or a positron, is emitted.
   a. Thing
   b. Beta decay0
   c. Undefined
   d. Undefined

91. The _____ A, also called atomic _____ or nucleon number, is the number of nucleons in an atomic nucleus. The _____ is unique for each isotope of an element and is written either after the element name or as a superscript to the left of an element's symbol. For example, carbon-12 has 6 protons and 6 neutrons.
   a. Mass number0
   b. Thing
   c. Undefined
   d. Undefined

92. The _____ is the mass of an atom at rest, most often expressed in unified _____ units.[
   a. Atomic mass0
   b. Thing
   c. Undefined
   d. Undefined

93. The _____ of an atom is the very small dense region, of positive charge, in its centre consisting of nucleons. The size of the nucleus is in the range of 1.6 fm to about 15 fm. These dimensions are much smaller than the size of the atom itself by a factor of about 23,000 to about 145,000.
   a. Atomic nucleus0
   b. Thing
   c. Undefined
   d. Undefined

94. _____ is a type of radioactive decay in which an atomic nucleus emits an alpha particle and transforms into an atom with a mass number 4 less and atomic number 2 less.
   a. Alpha decay0
   b. Thing
   c. Undefined
   d. Undefined

95. A _____ is an optical instrument used to measure properties of light over a specific portion of the electromagnetic spectrum. The variable measured is most often the light's intensity but could also, for instance, be the polarization state.
   a. Thing
   b. Spectrometer0
   c. Undefined
   d. Undefined

Chapter 4. Geologic Time: Concepts and Principles

96. Mass spectrometry or informally is an analytical technique used to measure the mass-to-charge ratio of ions. It is most generally used to find the composition of a physical sample by generating a mass spectrum representing the masses of sample components. The mass spectrum is measured by a _____.
   a. Thing
   b. Mass spectrometer0
   c. Undefined
   d. Undefined

97. A _____ is a naturally occurring substance formed through geological processes that has a characteristic chemical composition, a highly ordered atomic structure and specific physical properties. A rock, by comparison, is an aggregate of minerals and need not have a specific chemical composition. Minerals range in composition from pure elements and simple salts to very complex silicates with thousands of known forms.
   a. Thing
   b. Mineral0
   c. Undefined
   d. Undefined

98. A _____ is a solid in which the constituent atoms, molecules, or ions are packed in a regularly ordered, repeating pattern extending in all three spatial dimensions. Most metals encountered in everyday life are polycrystals. Crystals are often symmetrically intergrown to form _____ twins.
   a. Crystal0
   b. Thing
   c. Undefined
   d. Undefined

99. A _____ is a unique arrangement of atoms in a crystal. It is composed of a unit cell, a set of atoms arranged in a particular way, which is periodically repeated in three dimensions on a lattice. The spacing between unit cells in various directions is called its lattice parameters. The symmetry properties of the crystal are embodied in its space group.
   a. Thing
   b. Crystal structure0
   c. Undefined
   d. Undefined

100. _____ is a phyllosilicate mineral. It crystallizes with monoclinic geometry. The name is derived from the Greek glaucos meaning 'gleaming' or 'silvery', to describe the appearance of the blue-green color, presumably relating to the sheen and blue-green color of the sea's surface. Its color ranges from olive green, black green to bluish green. It is probably the result of the iron content of the mineral.
   a. Thing
   b. Glauconite0
   c. Undefined
   d. Undefined

101. In nuclear physics, a decay product, also known as a _____, daughter isotope or daughter nuclide, is a nuclide resulting from the radioactive decay of a parent isotope or precursor nuclide. The _____ may be stable or it may decay to form a _____ of its own. The daughter of a _____ is sometimes called a granddaughter product.
   a. Thing
   b. Daughter product0
   c. Undefined
   d. Undefined

102. _____ is a chemical element. It is a soft silvery-white metallic alkali metal that occurs naturally bound to other elements in seawater and many minerals. It oxidizes rapidly in air and is very reactive, especially towards water. In many respects, it and sodium are chemically similar, although organisms in general, and animal cells in particular, treat them very differently.
   a. Potassium0
   b. Thing
   c. Undefined
   d. Undefined

Chapter 4. Geologic Time: Concepts and Principles

103. _____ is the process of formation of solid crystals from a uniform solution. It is also a chemical solid-liquid separation technique, in which mass transfer of a solute from the liquid solution to a pure solid crystalline phase occurs.
   a. Thing
   b. Crystallization0
   c. Undefined
   d. Undefined

104. In thermodynamics, a _____ can exchange heat and work, but not matter, with its surroundings.
   a. Thing
   b. Closed system0
   c. Undefined
   d. Undefined

105. A _____ coastline occurs where the bands of differing rock types run parallel to the coast. The outer hard rock provides a protective barrier to erosion of the softer rocks further inland.
   a. Concordant0
   b. Thing
   c. Undefined
   d. Undefined

106. A _____ coastline occurs where bands of differing rock type run perpendicular to the coast.
   a. Thing
   b. Discordant0
   c. Undefined
   d. Undefined

107. The _____ is a major division of the geologic timescale. The _____ is the earliest period in whose rocks are found numerous large, distinctly fossilizable multicellular organisms that are more complex than sponges or medusoids. During this time, roughly fifty separate major groups of organisms or "phyla" emerged suddenly, in most cases without evident precursors. This radiation of animal phyla is referred to as the _____ explosion.
   a. Cambrian0
   b. Event
   c. Undefined
   d. Undefined

108. A _____ is a natural object originating in outer space that survives an impact with the Earth's surface without being destroyed. While in space it is called a meteoroid. When it enters the atmosphere, air resistance causes the body to heat up and emit light, thus forming a fireball.
   a. Meteorite0
   b. Thing
   c. Undefined
   d. Undefined

109. _____ is an igneous rock of volcanic origin. They often have a vesicular texture, which is the result voids left by volatiles escaping from the molten lava. Pumice is a rock, which is an example of explosive volcanic eruption. It is so vesicular that it floats in water.
   a. Thing
   b. Volcanic rock0
   c. Undefined
   d. Undefined

110. _____ dating is a radiometric dating technique based on analyses of the damage trails left by fission fragments in certain uranium bearing minerals and glasses. The fragments emitted by this fission process leave trails of damage in the crystal structure of the minerals enclosing the uranium. Etching of polished surfaces of these minerals reveals the spontaneous fission tracks for counting by optical microscopic means. The number of tracks correlates directly with the age of the sample and the uranium content.
   a. Fission track0
   b. Thing
   c. Undefined
   d. Undefined

Chapter 4. Geologic Time: Concepts and Principles

111. _____, is a radioactive isotope of carbon discovered on February 27, 1940, by Martin Kamen and Sam Ruben. Its nucleus contains 6 protons and 8 neutrons. Its presence in organic materials is used extensively as basis of the _____ dating method to date archaeological, geological, and hydrogeological samples.
   a. Thing
   b. Radiocarbon0
   c. Undefined
   d. Undefined

112. _____ is a group of phosphate minerals, usually referring to hydroxylapatite, fluorapatite, and chlorapatite, named for high concentrations of OH-, F-, or Cl- ions, respectively, in the crystal.
   a. Thing
   b. Apatite0
   c. Undefined
   d. Undefined

113. _____ is a rock formation rizing nearly 1,800 feet above the high-desert plain on the Navajo reservation, about 20 kilometers southwest of the northern New Mexico town of _____, which is named for the peak.
   a. Place
   b. Shiprock0
   c. Undefined
   d. Undefined

114. An _____ is a layer of gases that may surround a material body of sufficient mass. The gases are attracted by the gravity of the body, and are retained for a longer duration if gravity is high and the _____'s temperature is low. Some planets consist mainly of various gases, and thus have very deep atmospheres.
   a. Place
   b. Atmosphere0
   c. Undefined
   d. Undefined

115. _____ is a chemical element which has the symbol N and atomic number 7. Elemental _____ is a colorless, odourless, tasteless and mostly inert diatomic gas at standard conditions, constituting 78.1% by volume of Earth's atmosphere.
   a. Thing
   b. Nitrogen0
   c. Undefined
   d. Undefined

116. The _____ is the biogeochemical cycle by which carbon is exchanged between the biosphere, geosphere, hydrosphere, and atmosphere of the Earth.
   a. Carbon cycle0
   b. Thing
   c. Undefined
   d. Undefined

117. _____ as used in physics, is energy in the form of waves or moving subatomic particles.
   a. Thing
   b. Radiation0
   c. Undefined
   d. Undefined

118. Biological _____ refers to those processes by which a species maintains or expands the distribution of a population. _____ implies movement—movement away from an existing population or away from the parent organisms.
   a. Dispersal0
   b. Thing
   c. Undefined
   d. Undefined

119. A _____ is one of two main structural axes of a vascular plant. It is normally divided into nodes and internodes, the nodes hold buds which grow into one or more leaves, inflorescence, cones etc.

Chapter 4. Geologic Time: Concepts and Principles

a. Stem0
b. Thing
c. Undefined
d. Undefined

120. A _____, is a tall, conical volcano composed of many layers of hardened lava, tephra, and volcanic ash. These volcanoes are characterized by a steep profile and periodic, explosive eruptions. The lava that flows from them is viscous, and cools and hardens before spreading very far.
   a. Thing
   b. Stratovolcano0
   c. Undefined
   d. Undefined

121. _____ have an extremely low yearly precipitation, receiving much less rain or snowfall annually than would satisfy the climatological demand for evaporation and transpiration.
   a. Thing
   b. Arid lands0
   c. Undefined
   d. Undefined

122. The basic idea of this is that an object, event or entity can be spanned across multiple realities or universes. When combined, these multiple, unique, pan-dimensional segments of the object, consciousness or event, make up parts or constituents of its _____.
   a. Superposition0
   b. Thing
   c. Undefined
   d. Undefined

123. The principle or _____ states that sediments are deposited under the influence of gravity as nearly horizontal beds. Observations in a wide variety of sedimentary environments support this principle. If we find folded or faulted strata, we know that the layers were deformed by tectonic forces after the sediments were deposited. This principle can be combined with the principle of superposition.
   a. Original horizontality0
   b. Thing
   c. Undefined
   d. Undefined

124. _____ is a sedimentary rock composed mainly of sand-size mineral or rock grains. Most _____ is composed of quartz and/or feldspar because these are the most common minerals in the Earth's crust. Like sand, _____ may be any color, but the most common colors are tan, brown, yellow, red, gray and white.
   a. Sandstone0
   b. Thing
   c. Undefined
   d. Undefined

125. _____ is the name of a group of rock-forming minerals which make up as much as sixty percent of the Earth's crust. Feldspars crystallize from magma in both intrusive and extrusive rocks, and they can also occur as compact minerals, as veins, and are also present in many types of metamorphic rock.
   a. Thing
   b. Feldspar0
   c. Undefined
   d. Undefined

126. _____ is a 14,000 acre park near Kimberly, Oregon. Located within the John Day River Basin, this U.S. National Monument is world-renowned for its well-preserved, remarkably complete record of fossil plants and animals, a record that spans more than 40 of the 65 million years of the Cenozoic Era.
   a. Place
   b. John Day Fossil Beds National Monument0
   c. Undefined
   d. Undefined

Chapter 5. Rocks, Fossils, and Time-Making Sense of the Geologic Record

1. A _____ is a geologic event during which sea level rises relative to the land and the shoreline moves toward higher ground, resulting in flooding. Transgressions can be caused either by the land sinking or the ocean basins filling with water.
   a. Transgression0
   b. Thing
   c. Undefined
   d. Undefined

2. Mean _____ is the average height of the sea, with reference to a suitable reference surface.
   a. Thing
   b. Sea level0
   c. Undefined
   d. Undefined

3. A _____ is one of several large landmasses on Earth. They are generally identified by convention rather than any strict criteria, but seven areas are commonly reckoned as continents – they are: Asia, Africa, North America, South America, Antarctica, Europe, and Australia.
   a. Continent0
   b. Thing
   c. Undefined
   d. Undefined

4. _____ rock is one of the three main rock groups. Rock formed from these covers 75% of the Earth's land area, and includes common types such as chalk, limestone, dolomite, sandstone, and shale.
   a. Sedimentary0
   b. Thing
   c. Undefined
   d. Undefined

5. _____ is one of the three main rock groups. _____ covers 75% of the Earth's land area. Four basic processes are involved in the formation of a clastic _____: weathering caused mainly by friction of waves, transportation where the sediment is carried along by a current, deposition and compaction where the sediment is squashed together to form a rock of this kind.
   a. Thing
   b. Sedimentary rock0
   c. Undefined
   d. Undefined

6. Fossils are the mineralized or otherwise preserved remains or traces of animals, plants, and other organisms. The totality of fossils, both discovered and undiscovered, and their placement in fossiliferous rock formations and sedimentary layers is known as the _____ record.
   a. Thing
   b. Fossil0
   c. Undefined
   d. Undefined

7. The basic idea of this is that an object, event or entity can be spanned across multiple realities or universes. When combined, these multiple, unique, pan-dimensional segments of the object, consciousness or event, make up parts or constituents of its _____.
   a. Thing
   b. Superposition0
   c. Undefined
   d. Undefined

8. A _____, is a tall, conical volcano composed of many layers of hardened lava, tephra, and volcanic ash. These volcanoes are characterized by a steep profile and periodic, explosive eruptions. The lava that flows from them is viscous, and cools and hardens before spreading very far.
   a. Stratovolcano0
   b. Thing
   c. Undefined
   d. Undefined

9. The _____ is used by geologists and other scientists to describe the timing and relationships between events that have occurred during the history of Earth.

Chapter 5. Rocks, Fossils, and Time-Making Sense of the Geologic Record 81

a. Geological time scale0
b. Thing
c. Undefined
d. Undefined

10. _____ is a technique used to date materials based on a knowledge of the decay rates of naturally occurring isotopes, and the current abundances. It is the principal source of information about the age of the Earth and a significant source of information about rates of evolutionary change.
   a. Radiometric dating0
   b. Thing
   c. Undefined
   d. Undefined

11. In optics, _____ is the field that studies the measurement of electromagnetic radiation, including visible light. Note that light is also measured using the techniques of photometry, which deal with brightness as perceived by the human eye, rather than absolute power.
   a. Radiometry0
   b. Thing
   c. Undefined
   d. Undefined

12. _____ is the result of the transformation of a pre-existing rock type, the protolith, in a process called metamorphism, which means "change in form". The protolith is subjected to heat and extreme pressure causing profound physical and/or chemical change. The protolith may be sedimentary rock, igneous rock or another older rock.
   a. Metamorphic rock0
   b. Thing
   c. Undefined
   d. Undefined

13. Metamorphic rock is the result of the transformation of a pre-existing rock type, the protolith, in a process called metamorphism. The protolith is subjected to heat and extreme pressure causing profound physical and/or chemical change. _____ make up a large part of the Earth's crust. They are formed deep beneath the Earth's surface by great stresses from rocks above and high pressures and temperatures.
   a. Thing
   b. Metamorphic rocks0
   c. Undefined
   d. Undefined

14. _____ can be defined as the solid state recrystallisation of pre-existing rocks due to changes in heat and/or pressure and/or introduction of fluids. There will be mineralogical, chemical and crystallographic changes. _____ produced with increasing pressure and temperature conditions is known as prograde _____. Conversely, decreasing temperatures and pressure characterize retrograde _____.
   a. Metamorphism0
   b. Thing
   c. Undefined
   d. Undefined

15. _____ rocks form when molten rock, magma, cools and solidifies, with or without crystallization, either below the surface as intrusive, plutonic rocks or on the surface as extrusive, volcanic, rocks.
   a. Thing
   b. Igneous0
   c. Undefined
   d. Undefined

16. _____ the fourth planet from the Sun in the Solar System. The planet is named after _____, the Roman god of war. It is also referred to as the "Red Planet" because of its reddish appearance as seen from Earth.
   a. Thing
   b. Mars0
   c. Undefined
   d. Undefined

Chapter 5. Rocks, Fossils, and Time-Making Sense of the Geologic Record

17. A _____ is an opening, or rupture, in the Earth's surface or crust, which allows hot, molten rock, ash and gases to escape from deep below the surface.
  a. Volcano0
  b. Thing
  c. Undefined
  d. Undefined

18. _____ is a chemical element in the periodic table that has the symbol Hg and atomic number 80. A heavy, silvery transition metal, _____ is one of five elements that are liquid at or near room temperature and pressure.
  a. Mercury0
  b. Thing
  c. Undefined
  d. Undefined

19. The _____ is Earth's only natural satellite. It makes a complete orbit around the Earth every 27.3 days, and the periodic variations in the geometry of the Earth–_____–Sun system are responsible for the lunar phases that repeat every 29.5 days.
  a. Moon0
  b. Thing
  c. Undefined
  d. Undefined

20. A _____, as defined by the International Astronomical Union, is a celestial body orbiting a star or stellar remnant that is massive enough to be rounded by its own gravity, not massive enough to cause thermonuclear fusion in its core, and has cleared its neighboring region of planetesimals.
  a. Thing
  b. Planet0
  c. Undefined
  d. Undefined

21. The _____ is the part of the earth, including air, land, surface rocks, and water, within which life occurs, and which biotic processes in turn alter or transform. From the broadest biophysiological point of view, the _____ is the global ecological system integrating all living beings and their relationships, including their interaction with the elements of the lithosphere, hydrosphere, and atmosphere. This _____ is postulated to have evolved, beginning through a process of biogenesis or biopoesis, at least some 3.5 billion years ago.
  a. Biosphere0
  b. Thing
  c. Undefined
  d. Undefined

22. A _____ in physical geography describes the collective mass of water found on, under, and over the surface of a planet.
  a. Hydrosphere0
  b. Thing
  c. Undefined
  d. Undefined

23. An _____ is a layer of gases that may surround a material body of sufficient mass. The gases are attracted by the gravity of the body, and are retained for a longer duration if gravity is high and the _____'s temperature is low. Some planets consist mainly of various gases, and thus have very deep atmospheres.
  a. Atmosphere0
  b. Place
  c. Undefined
  d. Undefined

24. _____ is an atmospheric discharge of electricity, which usually, but not always, occurs during rain storms, and frequently during volcanic eruptions or dust storms.
  a. Thing
  b. Lightning0
  c. Undefined
  d. Undefined

Chapter 5. Rocks, Fossils, and Time-Making Sense of the Geologic Record   83

25. _____, a branch of geology, studies rock layers and layering. It is primarily used in the study of sedimentary and layered volcanic rocks. _____ includes two related subfields: lithologic or lithostratigraphy and biologic _____ or biostratigraphy.
   a. Thing
   b. Stratigraphy0
   c. Undefined
   d. Undefined

26. _____ are where one sedimetary deposit ends and another one begins. The rock is prone to breakage at these points because of the weakness between the layers.
   a. Bedding planes0
   b. Thing
   c. Undefined
   d. Undefined

27. _____ is any particulate matter that can be transported by fluid flow and which eventually is deposited as a layer of solid particles on the bed or bottom of a body of water or other liquid.
   a. Thing
   b. Sediment0
   c. Undefined
   d. Undefined

28. _____ is a common and widely occurring type of intrusive, felsic, igneous rock. Granites are usually medium to coarsely crystalline, occasionally with some individual crystals larger than the groundmass forming a rock known as porphyry. Granites can be pink to dark gray or even black, depending on their chemistry and mineralogy.
   a. Granite0
   b. Thing
   c. Undefined
   d. Undefined

29. _____ is a common gray to black extrusive volcanic rock. It is usually fine-grained due to rapid cooling of lava on the Earth's surface. It may be porphyritic containing larger crystals in a fine matrix, or vesicular, or frothy scoria.
   a. Basalt0
   b. Thing
   c. Undefined
   d. Undefined

30. _____ is molten rock expelled by a volcano during an eruption. When first extruded from a volcanic vent, it is a liquid at temperatures from 700 °C to 1,200 °C.
   a. Thing
   b. Lava0
   c. Undefined
   d. Undefined

31. In geology, a _____ is a tabular pluton that has intruded between older layers of sedimentary rock, beds of volcanic lava or tuff, or even along the direction of foliation in metamorphic rock. The term _____ is synonymous with concordant intrusive sheet. This means that the _____ does not cut across preexisting rocks. Contrast this with dikes.
   a. Thing
   b. Sill0
   c. Undefined
   d. Undefined

32. _____ is the geological process whereby material is added to a landform. This is the process by which wind and water create a sediment deposit, through the laying down of granular material that has been eroded and transported from another geographical location.
   a. Deposition0
   b. Thing
   c. Undefined
   d. Undefined

Chapter 5. Rocks, Fossils, and Time-Making Sense of the Geologic Record

33. An _____ is a buried erosion surface separating two rock masses or strata of different ages, indicating that sediment deposition was not continuous. In general, the older layer was exposed to erosion for an interval of time before deposition of the younger, but the term is used to describe any break in the sedimentary geologic record.
    a. Unconformity0
    b. Thing
    c. Undefined
    d. Undefined

34. _____ is displacement of solids by the agents of ocean currents, wind, water, or ice by downward or down-slope movement in response to gravity or by living organisms.
    a. Erosion0
    b. Thing
    c. Undefined
    d. Undefined

35. _____ is the process in which sediments compact under pressure, expel connate fluids, and gradually become solid rock.
    a. Lithification0
    b. Thing
    c. Undefined
    d. Undefined

36. _____: a _____ is an ion with a positive charge. It is the inverse anion.
    a. Thing
    b. Cation0
    c. Undefined
    d. Undefined

37. _____ was a pioneer in both anatomy and geology. He first studied anatomy, beginning with a focus on the muscular system and the nature of muscle contraction. He used geometry to show that a contracting muscle changes its shape but not its volume.
    a. Nicolas Steno0
    b. Person
    c. Undefined
    d. Undefined

38. The _____ states that layers of sediment initially extend laterally in all directions; in other words, they are laterally continuous. As a result, rocks that are otherwise similar, but are now separated by a valley or other erosional feature, can be assumed to be originally continuous.
    a. Thing
    b. Principle of lateral continuity0
    c. Undefined
    d. Undefined

39. Faults are planar rock fractures, which show evidence of relative movement. Large faults within the Earth's crust are the result of shear motion and active _____ zones are the causal locations of most earthquakes. Earthquakes are caused by energy release during rapid slippage along faults. The largest examples are at tectonic plate boundaries but many faults occur far from active plate boundaries. Since faults do not usually consist of a single, clean fracture, the term _____ zone is used when referring to the zone of complex deformation that is associated with the _____ plane.
    a. Fault0
    b. Thing
    c. Undefined
    d. Undefined

40. A _____ is an unconformity between parallel layers of sedimentary rocks which represents a period of erosion or non-deposition.
    a. Thing
    b. Disconformity0
    c. Undefined
    d. Undefined

Chapter 5. Rocks, Fossils, and Time-Making Sense of the Geologic Record 85

41. A _____ is a rock consisting of individual stones that have become cemented together. Conglomerates are sedimentary rocks consisting of rounded fragements and are thus differentiated from breccias, which consist of angular clasts. Both conglomerates and breccias are characterized by clasts larger than sand.
- a. Thing
- b. Conglomerate0
- c. Undefined
- d. Undefined

42. The _____ is an epoch of the Carboniferous period lasting from roughly 325 Ma to 299 Ma. As with most other geologic periods, the rock beds that define the period are well identified, but the exact date of the start and end are uncertain by a few million years.
- a. Thing
- b. Pennsylvanian0
- c. Undefined
- d. Undefined

43. The _____ Era meaning "new life", is the most recent of the three classic geological eras. It covers the 65.5 million years since the Cretaceous-Tertiary extinction event at the end of the Cretaceous that marked the demise of the last non-avian dinosaurs and the end of the Mesozoic Era. The _____ era is ongoing.
- a. Cenozoic0
- b. Thing
- c. Undefined
- d. Undefined

44. _____ is an unconformity where horizontally parallel strata of sedimentary rock are deposited on tilted and eroded layers that may be either vertical or at an angle to the overlying horizontal layers
- a. Angular unconformity0
- b. Thing
- c. Undefined
- d. Undefined

45. The _____ is a major division of the geologic timescale. The _____ is the earliest period in whose rocks are found numerous large, distinctly fossilizable multicellular organisms that are more complex than sponges or medusoids. During this time, roughly fifty separate major groups of organisms or "phyla" emerged suddenly, in most cases without evident precursors. This radiation of animal phyla is referred to as the _____ explosion.
- a. Event
- b. Cambrian0
- c. Undefined
- d. Undefined

46. In horticulture, _____ is the process of pretreating seeds to simulate natural conditions that a seed must endure before germination.
- a. Stratification0
- b. Thing
- c. Undefined
- d. Undefined

47. The _____ is an informal name for the eons of the geologic timescale that came before the current Phanerozoic eon. It spans from the formation of Earth around 4500 Ma to the evolution of abundant macroscopic hard-shelled animals, which marked the beginning of the Cambrian, the first period of the first era of the Phanerozoic eon, some 542 Ma.
- a. Thing
- b. Precambrian0
- c. Undefined
- d. Undefined

48. A _____ is a landform that extends above the surrounding terrain in a limited area. A _____ is generally steeper than a hill, but there is no universally accepted standard definition for the height of a _____ or a hill although a _____ usually has an identifiable summit.

a. Mountain0	b. Place
c. Undefined	d. Undefined

49. A _____ should ideally be a distinctive rock that forms under certain conditions of sedimentation, reflecting a particular process or environment.

a. Thing	b. Facies0
c. Undefined	d. Undefined

50. _____ are usually further subdivided, for example, you might refer to a "tan, cross-bedded oolitic limestone facies" or a "shale facies". The characteristics of the rock unit come from the depositional environment and original composition. _____ reflect depositional environment, each facies being a distinct kind of sediment for that area or environment.

a. Sedimentary facies0	b. Thing
c. Undefined	d. Undefined

51. _____ is a fine-grained sedimentary rock whose original constituents were clays or muds. It is characterized by thin laminae breaking with an irregular curving fracture, often splintery and usually parallel to the often-indistinguishable bedding plane.

a. Thing	b. Shale0
c. Undefined	d. Undefined

52. _____ is a sedimentary rock composed mainly of sand-size mineral or rock grains. Most _____ is composed of quartz and/or feldspar because these are the most common minerals in the Earth's crust. Like sand, _____ may be any color, but the most common colors are tan, brown, yellow, red, gray and white.

a. Thing	b. Sandstone0
c. Undefined	d. Undefined

53. _____ is a sedimentary rock composed largely of the mineral calcite. _____ often contains variable amounts of silica in the form of chert or flint, as well as varying amounts of clay, silt and sand as disseminations, nodules, or layers within the rock. The primary source of the calcite in _____ is most commonly marine organisms. These organisms secrete shells that settle out of the water column and are deposited on ocean floors as pelagic ooze or alternatively is conglomerated in a coral reef.

a. Limestone0	b. Thing
c. Undefined	d. Undefined

54. A _____ is a deep valley between cliffs often carved from the landscape by a river. Most were formed by a process of long-time erosion from a plateau level. The cliffs form because harder rock strata that are resistant to erosion and weathering remain exposed on the valley walls.

a. Thing	b. Canyon0
c. Undefined	d. Undefined

55. The _____ is a very colorful, steep-sided gorge, carved by the Colorado River in the U.S. state of Arizona. It is one of the first national parks in the United States.

a. Place	b. Grand Canyon0
c. Undefined	d. Undefined

Chapter 5. Rocks, Fossils, and Time-Making Sense of the Geologic Record 87

56. A _____ is the fringe of land at the edge of a large body of water, such as an ocean, sea, or lake. A strict definition is the strip of land along a water body that is alternately exposed and covered by waves and tides.
   a. Shoreline0
   b. Thing
   c. Undefined
   d. Undefined

57. In geology, engineering, and surveying, _____ is the motion of a surface as it shifts downward relative to a datum such as sea-level. The opposite of _____ is uplift, which results in an increase in elevation. In meteorology, _____ refers to the downward movement of air.
   a. Subsidence0
   b. Thing
   c. Undefined
   d. Undefined

58. A _____ is a large, slow moving river of ice, formed from compacted layers of snow, that slowly deforms and flows in response to gravity. _____ ice is the largest reservoir of fresh water on Earth, and second only to oceans as the largest reservoir of total water. Glaciers cover vast areas of polar regions but are restricted to the highest mountains in the tropics.
   a. Thing
   b. Glacier0
   c. Undefined
   d. Undefined

59. A _____ is a section of a river of relatively steep gradient causing an increase in water flow and turbulence. A _____ is a hydrological feature between a run and a cascade. It is characterized by the river becoming shallower and having some rocks exposed above the flow surface.
   a. Thing
   b. Rapid0
   c. Undefined
   d. Undefined

60. A _____ is a geological feature that is also known as a Rip in the earth causing magma to flow out and forming an undersea volcano, it also has geological features, a continuous elevational crest for some distance. Ridges are usually termed hills or mountains as well, depending on size.
   a. Ridge0
   b. Thing
   c. Undefined
   d. Undefined

61. The _____ the bottom of the ocean. At the bottom of the continental slope is the continental rise, which is caused by sediment cascading down the continental slope.
   a. Seafloor0
   b. Thing
   c. Undefined
   d. Undefined

62. _____ occurs at mid-ocean ridges, where new oceanic crust is formed through volcanic activity and then gradually moves away from the ridge. _____ helps explain continental drift in the theory of plate tectonics.
   a. Seafloor spreading0
   b. Thing
   c. Undefined
   d. Undefined

63. _____ is water from a sea or ocean. On average, _____ in the world's oceans has a salinity of ~3.5%, or 35 parts per thousand. This means that every 1 kg of _____ has approximately 35 grams of dissolved salts.
   a. Thing
   b. Seawater0
   c. Undefined
   d. Undefined

Chapter 5. Rocks, Fossils, and Time-Making Sense of the Geologic Record

64. _____ are large geologic basins that are below sea level. Geologically, there are other undersea geomorphological features such as the continental shelves, the deep ocean trenches, and the undersea mountain ranges which are not considered to be part of the _____.
   a. Ocean basins0
   b. Thing
   c. Undefined
   d. Undefined

65. _____ are clastic rocks composed solely or primarily of volcanic materials.
   a. Thing
   b. Pyroclastics0
   c. Undefined
   d. Undefined

66. An _____ is a type of atom that is defined by its atomic number; that is, by the number of protons in its nucleus.
   a. Thing
   b. Element0
   c. Undefined
   d. Undefined

67. A _____ is a structure preserved in sedimentary rocks that record biological activity. While we are most familiar with relatively spectacular, fossilized hard-part remains such as shells and bones, a _____ is often less dramatic, but nonetheless very important.
   a. Trace fossil0
   b. Thing
   c. Undefined
   d. Undefined

68. In biology and ecology, an _____ is a living complex adaptive system of organs that influence each other in such a way that they function in some way as a stable whole.
   a. Organism0
   b. Thing
   c. Undefined
   d. Undefined

69. _____ is the name given to the mineral that results when human or animal dung is fossilized. _____ may range in size from the size of a BB all the way up to that of a large appliance.
   a. Coprolite0
   b. Thing
   c. Undefined
   d. Undefined

70. _____ is an English word that describes any animal without a spinal column.
   a. Thing
   b. Invertebrate0
   c. Undefined
   d. Undefined

71. The _____ is one of three geologic eras of the Phanerozoic eon. The _____ was a time of tectonic, climatic and evolutionary activity, shifting from a state of connectedness into their present configuration. The climate was exceptionally warm throughout the period, also playing an important role in the evolution and diversification of new animal species. By the end of the era, the basis of modern life was in place.
   a. Thing
   b. Mesozoic0
   c. Undefined
   d. Undefined

72. _____ is a perennial flowering plant cultivated as an important forage crop. _____ is one of the most important legumes used in agriculture.
   a. Thing
   b. Alfalfa0
   c. Undefined
   d. Undefined

Chapter 5. Rocks, Fossils, and Time-Making Sense of the Geologic Record

73. _____ are people who study prehistoric life forms on Earth through the examination of plant and animal fossils. This includes the study of body fossils, tracks, burrows, cast-off parts, fossilised faeces, palynomorphs and chemical residues.
   a. Person
   b. Paleontologists0
   c. Undefined
   d. Undefined

74. A _____ is any of a number of an extinct genus of proboscidean, often with long curved tusks and, in northern species, a covering of long hair. They lived from the Pliocene epoch from to around 4,000 years ago.
   a. Mammoth0
   b. Thing
   c. Undefined
   d. Undefined

75. _____ refers to all species of microscopic fungi that grow in the form of multicellular filaments, called hyphae.
   a. Thing
   b. Mold0
   c. Undefined
   d. Undefined

76. A _____ is a naturally occurring substance formed through geological processes that has a characteristic chemical composition, a highly ordered atomic structure and specific physical properties. A rock, by comparison, is an aggregate of minerals and need not have a specific chemical composition. Minerals range in composition from pure elements and simple salts to very complex silicates with thousands of known forms.
   a. Mineral0
   b. Thing
   c. Undefined
   d. Undefined

77. _____ are extinct arthropods. They appeared in the second Epoch of the Cambrian period and flourished throughout the lower Paleozoic era before beginning a drawn-out decline to extinction when all _____, with the sole exception of Proetida, died out. The last of the _____ disappeared in the mass extinction at the end of the Permian.
   a. Trilobites0
   b. Thing
   c. Undefined
   d. Undefined

78. _____ were vertebrate animals that dominated terrestrial ecosystems for over 160 million years, first appearing approximately 230 million years ago. At the end of the Cretaceous Period, approximately 65 million years ago, a catastrophic extinction event ended _____' dominance on land.
   a. Dinosaurs0
   b. Thing
   c. Undefined
   d. Undefined

79. Before the advent of absolute dating in the 20th century, archaeologists and geologists were largely limited to the use of _____ techniques. Estimates of the order of prehistoric and geological events were determined by using basic stratigraphic rules, and by observing where fossil organisms lay in the geological record, stratified bands of rocks present throughout the world.
   a. Thing
   b. Relative dating0
   c. Undefined
   d. Undefined

80. A _____ is a special-purpose map made to show geological features. The stratigraphic contour lines are drawn on the surface of a selected deep stratum, so that they can show the topographic trends of the strata under the ground. It is not always possible to properly show this when the strata are extremely fractured, mixed, in some discontinuities, or where they are otherwise disturbed.

Chapter 5. Rocks, Fossils, and Time-Making Sense of the Geologic Record

a. Thing
b. Geologic map0
c. Undefined
d. Undefined

81. _____ are artificial channels for water. There are two main types of _____: irrigation _____, which are used for the delivery of water, and waterways, which are transportation _____ used for passage of goods and people, often connected to existing lakes, rivers, or oceans.

a. Canals0
b. Thing
c. Undefined
d. Undefined

82. _____ was an English geologist, credited with creating the first nationwide geologic map. He is known as the "Father of English Geology", however recognition was slow in coming. His work was plagiarised, he was financially ruined, and he spent time in debtors' prison. It was only much later in his life that Smith received recognition for his accomplishments.

a. William Smith0
b. Person
c. Undefined
d. Undefined

83. The _____ is an axiom that forms one of the bases of the sciences of geology, archaeology, and other fields dealing with stratigraphy. In its plainest form, that is: layers are arranged in a time sequence, with the oldest on the bottom and the youngest on the top, unless later processes disturb this arrangement.

a. Law of Superposition0
b. Thing
c. Undefined
d. Undefined

84. _____ refers to the reduction of the body of a formerly living organism into simpler forms of matter.

a. Thing
b. Decomposition0
c. Undefined
d. Undefined

85. _____ refer to marine animals from the class Anthozoa and exist as small sea anemone-like polyps, typically in colonies of many identical individuals. The group includes the important reef builders that are found in tropical oceans, which secrete calcium carbonate to form a hard skeleton.

a Thing
b. Coral0
c. Undefined
d. Undefined

86. A _____ is a ruminant mammal belonging to the family Cervidae. A number of broadly similar animals from related families within the order Artiodactyla are often also called this.

a. Thing
b. Deer0
c. Undefined
d. Undefined

87. The _____ Epoch is a period of time that extends from about 23.03 to 5.332 million years before the present. As with other older geologic periods, the rock beds that define the start and end are well identified but the exact dates of the start and end of the period are uncertain.

a. Miocene0
b. Thing
c. Undefined
d. Undefined

88. A _____ is an extended period of months or years when a region notes a deficiency in its water supply. Generally, this occurs when a region receives consistently below average precipitation.

Chapter 5. Rocks, Fossils, and Time-Making Sense of the Geologic Record

a. Thing
b. Drought0
c. Undefined
d. Undefined

89. _____ are the two species of elephants in the genus Loxodonta, one of the two existing genera in Elephantidae.
a. African elephants0
b. Thing
c. Undefined
d. Undefined

90. The term _____ is ambiguous: it can refer to all cetaceans, to just the larger ones, or only to members of particular families within the order Cetacea.
a. Thing
b. Whales0
c. Undefined
d. Undefined

91. A _____ is a type of underwater vessel with limited mobility which is typically transported to its area of operation by a surface vessel or large submarine
a. Thing
b. Submersible0
c. Undefined
d. Undefined

92. The _____ is the ninth largest body of water in the world. It is an ocean basin largely surrounded by the North American continent and the island of Cuba. It is bounded on the northeast, north and northwest by the Gulf Coast of the United States, on the southwest and south by Mexico, and on the southeast by Cuba.
a. Gulf of Mexico0
b. Place
c. Undefined
d. Undefined

93. A _____ is the most rapid up to 80 km/h and fluid type of downhill mass wasting.
a. Thing
b. Mudflow0
c. Undefined
d. Undefined

94. The _____ is a tributary of the Colorado River, 730 mi long, in the western United States. The _____ Basin covers parts of Wyoming, Utah, and Colorado. The river begins in the Wind River Mountains of Wyoming, and flows through Utah for much of its course, draining the northeastern portion of the state while looping for 40 mi into western Colorado.
a. Place
b. Green River0
c. Undefined
d. Undefined

95. The _____ is an Eocene geologic formation that records the sedimentation in a series of intermontane lakes. The sedimentary layers were formed in a large area of interconnecting lakes.
a. Place
b. Green River Formation0
c. Undefined
d. Undefined

96. _____ consists of very fine rock and mineral particles less than 2 mm in diameter that are ejected from a volcanic vent. The very fine particles may be carried for many miles, settling out as a dust-like layer across the landscape
a. Ash fall0
b. Thing
c. Undefined
d. Undefined

97. The _____ is the centerpiece of the Greater Yellowstone Ecosystem, the largest intact ecosystem in the Earth's northern temperate zone. Located mostly in the U.S. state of Wyoming, the park extends into Montana and Idaho. The park is known for its wildlife and geothermal features; Old Faithful Geyser is one of the most popular features in the park.

Chapter 5. Rocks, Fossils, and Time-Making Sense of the Geologic Record

a. Place
b. Yellowstone National Park0
c. Undefined
d. Undefined

98. A _____ is a body of water with a current, confined within a bed and banks. Streams are important as conduits in the water cycle, instruments in aquifer recharge, and corridors for fish and wildlife migration.
a. Stream0
b. Thing
c. Undefined
d. Undefined

99. A _____ is an area with a high density of trees, historically, a wooded area set aside for hunting. These plant communities cover large areas of the globe and function as animal habitats, hydrologic flow modulators, and soil conservers, constituting one of the most important aspects of the Earth's biosphere.
a. Forest0
b. Thing
c. Undefined
d. Undefined

100. The _____ are a famous cluster of tar pits located in Hancock Park in the urban heart of Los Angeles, California, USA. Asphalt has seeped up from the ground in this area for tens of thousands of years, forming hundreds of sticky pools that trapped animals and plants which happened to enter.
a. La Brea tar pits0
b. Thing
c. Undefined
d. Undefined

101. The _____ is a body of water that separates the Baja California Peninsula from the Mexican mainland. It is bordered by the states of Baja California, Baja California Sur, Sonora, and Sinaloa.
a. Thing
b. Sea of Cortez0
c. Undefined
d. Undefined

102. A _____ is a type of open-pit mine from which rock or minerals are extracted. They are generally used for extracting building materials, such as dimension stone. They are usually shallower than other types of open-pit mines.
a. Thing
b. Quarry0
c. Undefined
d. Undefined

103. _____ is a chemical element. An abundant nonmetallic, tetravalent element, _____ has several allotropic forms. This element is the basis of the chemistry of all known life.
a. Thing
b. Carbon0
c. Undefined
d. Undefined

104. _____ are reptiles of the order Testudines most of whose body is shielded by a special bony or cartilagenous shell developed from their ribs.
a. Turtles0
b. Thing
c. Undefined
d. Undefined

105. _____ is the first period of the Mesozoic Era. Both the start and end of the _____ are marked by major extinction events. During the _____, both marine and continental life show an adaptive radiation beginning from the starkly impoverished biosphere that followed the Permian-_____ extinction. Corals of the hexacorallia group made their first appearance. The first flowering plants may have evolved during the _____, as did the first flying vertebrates, the pterosaurs.

Chapter 5. Rocks, Fossils, and Time-Making Sense of the Geologic Record

a. Triassic0
b. Event
c. Undefined
d. Undefined

106. The _____ is a geologic period of the Paleozoic era. During the _____ the first fish evolved legs and started to walk on land as tetrapods and the first insects and spiders also started to colonize terrestrial habitats. The first seed-bearing plants spread across dry land, forming huge forests. In the oceans, Primitive sharks became more numerous. The first ammonite mollusks appeared, and trilobites as well as great coral reefs were still common.

a. Thing
b. Devonian0
c. Undefined
d. Undefined

107. The _____ is the second of the six periods of the Paleozoic era. It follows the Cambrian period and is followed by the Silurian period. The _____ started at a major extinction called the Cambrian-_____ extinction and lasted for about 44.6 million years. It ended with another major extinction event that wiped out 60% of marine genera.

a. Ordovician0
b. Thing
c. Undefined
d. Undefined

108. The _____ holds that sedimentary rock strata are observed to contain fossilised flora and fauna, and that these fossil forms succeed each other in a specific, reliable order that can be identified over wide distances.

a. Thing
b. Faunal succession0
c. Undefined
d. Undefined

109. The _____ holds that sedimentary rock strata are observed to contain fossilised flora and fauna, and that these fossil forms succeed each other in a specific, reliable order that can be identified over wide distances.

a. Law of Faunal Succession0
b. Thing
c. Undefined
d. Undefined

110. The _____ is a major division of the geologic timescale that extends from the end of the Ordovician period to the beginning of the Devonian period. The base of the _____ is set at a major extinction event when 60% of marine species were wiped out.

a. Thing
b. Silurian0
c. Undefined
d. Undefined

111. _____ was one of the founders of modern geology. He proposed the Devonian period of the geological timescale and later the Cambrian period. The latter proposal was based on work which he did on Welsh rock strata.

a. Person
b. Adam Sedgwick0
c. Undefined
d. Undefined

112. The _____ is a major division of the geologic timescale that extends from the end of the Devonian period to the beginning of the Permian period. As with most older geologic periods, the rock beds that define the period's start and end are well identified, but the exact dates are uncertain. The first third of the _____ is called the Mississippian epoch, and the remainder is called the Pennsylvanian.

a. Carboniferous0
b. Thing
c. Undefined
d. Undefined

Chapter 5. Rocks, Fossils, and Time-Making Sense of the Geologic Record

113. The _____ was an epoch of the Carboniferous period lasting from roughly 360 to 325 Ma. As with most other geologic periods, the rock beds that define the period are well identified, but the exact start and end dates are uncertain by a few million years.
   a. Thing
   b. Mississippian0
   c. Undefined
   d. Undefined

114. _____ can refer to: a period of time; a distinctive historical period or era, a unit of the geologic time scale, less than a period and greater than an age, or a phase in the development of the universe with distinctive properties.
   a. Thing
   b. Epoch0
   c. Undefined
   d. Undefined

115. An _____ is a long period of time with different technical and colloquial meanings, and usages in language. It begins with some beginning event known as an epoch, epochal date, epochal event or epochal moment.
   a. Thing
   b. Era0
   c. Undefined
   d. Undefined

116. _____ is the substance of which physical objects are composed. _____ can be solid, liquid, plasma or gas. It constitutes the observable universe.
   a. Matter0
   b. Thing
   c. Undefined
   d. Undefined

117. An _____ is any piece of land that is completely surrounded by water, above high tide. There are two main types of islands: continental islands and oceanic islands. There are also artificial islands. A grouping of geographically and/or geologically related islands is called an archipelago.
   a. Island0
   b. Thing
   c. Undefined
   d. Undefined

118. _____ refers to intervals of geological strata that are defined on the basis of their characteristic fossil taxa.
   a. Biozone0
   b. Thing
   c. Undefined
   d. Undefined

119. The _____ is the last period of the Palaeozoic Era. As the _____ opened, the Earth was still in the grip of an ice age, so the polar regions were covered with deep layers of ice. During the _____, all the Earth's major land masses except portions of East Asia were collected into a single supercontinent known as Pangaea. The _____ ended with the most extensive extinction event recorded in paleontology: the _____-Triassic extinction event.
   a. Permian0
   b. Thing
   c. Undefined
   d. Undefined

120. _____ is a small island located in the middle of San Francisco Bay in California, United States. It served as a lighthouse, then a military fortification, then a military prison followed by a federal prison until 1963, when it became a national recreation area.
   a. Alcatraz Island0
   b. Place
   c. Undefined
   d. Undefined

Chapter 5. Rocks, Fossils, and Time-Making Sense of the Geologic Record

121. _____ is a phyllosilicate mineral. It crystallizes with monoclinic geometry. The name is derived from the Greek glaucos meaning 'gleaming' or 'silvery', to describe the appearance of the blue-green color, presumably relating to the sheen and blue-green color of the sea's surface. Its color ranges from olive green, black green to bluish green. It is probably the result of the iron content of the mineral.
   a. Thing
   b. Glauconite0
   c. Undefined
   d. Undefined

122. In nuclear physics, a decay product, also known as a _____, daughter isotope or daughter nuclide, is a nuclide resulting from the radioactive decay of a parent isotope or precursor nuclide. The _____ may be stable or it may decay to form a _____ of its own. The daughter of a _____ is sometimes called a granddaughter product.
   a. Thing
   b. Daughter product0
   c. Undefined
   d. Undefined

123. _____ is a chemical element. It is a soft silvery-white metallic alkali metal that occurs naturally bound to other elements in seawater and many minerals. It oxidizes rapidly in air and is very reactive, especially towards water. In many respects, it and sodium are chemically similar, although organisms in general, and animal cells in particular, treat them very differently.
   a. Potassium0
   b. Thing
   c. Undefined
   d. Undefined

124. A _____ is an intrusion into a cross-cutting fissure, meaning a _____ cuts across other pre-existing layers or bodies of rock, this means that a _____ is always younger than the rocks that contain it. The thickness is usually much smaller than the other two dimensions. Thickness can vary from sub-centimeter scale to many meters in thickness and the lateral dimensions can extend over many kilometers.
   a. Thing
   b. Dike0
   c. Undefined
   d. Undefined

125. A _____ in geology is an intrusive igneous rock body that crystallized from a magma below the surface of the Earth. Plutons include batholiths, dikes, sills, laccoliths, lopoliths, and other igneous bodies. In practice, "_____" usually refers to a distinctive mass of igneous rock, typically kilometers in dimension, without a tabular shape like those of dikes and sills.
   a. Pluton0
   b. Thing
   c. Undefined
   d. Undefined

126. _____ forms when rock cools and solidifies either below the surface as intrusive rocks or on the surface as extrusive rocks. This magma can be derived from partial melts of pre-existing rocks in either the Earth's mantle or crust. Typically, the melting is caused by one or more of the following processes -- an increase in temperature, a decrease in pressure, or a change in composition.
   a. Thing
   b. Igneous rock0
   c. Undefined
   d. Undefined

127. _____ is an igneous rock of volcanic origin. They often have a vesicular texture, which is the result voids left by volatiles escaping from the molten lava. Pumice is a rock, which is an example of explosive volcanic eruption. It is so vesicular that it floats in water.

Chapter 5. Rocks, Fossils, and Time-Making Sense of the Geologic Record

    a. Volcanic rock0
    b. Thing
    c. Undefined
    d. Undefined

128. The _____ is the earliest of three geologic eras of the Phanerozoic eon. The _____ is subdivided into six geologic periods; from oldest to youngest they are: the Cambrian, Ordovician, Silurian, Devonian, Carboniferous, and Permian.
    a. Paleozoic0
    b. Thing
    c. Undefined
    d. Undefined

129. The _____ is defined as the part of the land adjoining or near the ocean. A coastline is properly a line on a map indicating the disposition of a _____, but the word is often used to refer to the _____ itself. The adjective coastal describes something as being on, near to, or associated with a _____.
    a. Coast0
    b. Place
    c. Undefined
    d. Undefined

Chapter 6. Sedimentary Rocks-The Archives of Earth History

1. _____ is the geological process whereby material is added to a landform. This is the process by which wind and water create a sediment deposit, through the laying down of granular material that has been eroded and transported from another geographical location.
   - a. Thing
   - b. Deposition0
   - c. Undefined
   - d. Undefined

2. _____ rock is one of the three main rock groups. Rock formed from these covers 75% of the Earth's land area, and includes common types such as chalk, limestone, dolomite, sandstone, and shale.
   - a. Thing
   - b. Sedimentary0
   - c. Undefined
   - d. Undefined

3. _____ is one of the three main rock groups. _____ covers 75% of the Earth's land area. Four basic processes are involved in the formation of a clastic _____: weathering caused mainly by friction of waves, transportation where the sediment is carried along by a current, deposition and compaction where the sediment is squashed together to form a rock of this kind.
   - a. Sedimentary rock0
   - b. Thing
   - c. Undefined
   - d. Undefined

4. Fossils are the mineralized or otherwise preserved remains or traces of animals, plants, and other organisms. The totality of fossils, both discovered and undiscovered, and their placement in fossiliferous rock formations and sedimentary layers is known as the _____ record.
   - a. Thing
   - b. Fossil0
   - c. Undefined
   - d. Undefined

5. _____ is a part of mathematics concerned with questions of size, shape, and relative position of figures and with properties of space. _____ is one of the oldest sciences. Initially a body of practical knowledge concerning lengths, areas, and volumes, in the third century B.C. _____ was put into an axiomatic form by Euclid, whose treatment set a standard for many centuries to follow.
   - a. Thing
   - b. Geometry0
   - c. Undefined
   - d. Undefined

6. _____ is a geological term used to describe particles of rock derived from pre-existing rock through processes of weathering and erosion.
   - a. Detrital0
   - b. Thing
   - c. Undefined
   - d. Undefined

7. _____ is the substance of which physical objects are composed. _____ can be solid, liquid, plasma or gas. It constitutes the observable universe.
   - a. Matter0
   - b. Thing
   - c. Undefined
   - d. Undefined

8. A _____ should ideally be a distinctive rock that forms under certain conditions of sedimentation, reflecting a particular process or environment.
   - a. Thing
   - b. Facies0
   - c. Undefined
   - d. Undefined

Chapter 6. Sedimentary Rocks-The Archives of Earth History

9. The carbonate mineral _____ is a chemical or biochemical calcium carbonate and is one of the most widely distributed minerals on the Earth's surface. It is a common constituent of sedimentary rocks, limestone in particular. It is also the primary mineral in metamorphic marble
   a. Thing
   b. Calcite0
   c. Undefined
   d. Undefined

10. A _____ is a naturally occurring substance formed through geological processes that has a characteristic chemical composition, a highly ordered atomic structure and specific physical properties. A rock, by comparison, is an aggregate of minerals and need not have a specific chemical composition. Minerals range in composition from pure elements and simple salts to very complex silicates with thousands of known forms.
    a. Mineral0
    b. Thing
    c. Undefined
    d. Undefined

11. _____ is the second most common mineral in the Earth's continental crust. It is made up of a lattice of silica tetrahedra. _____ belongs to the rhombohedral crystal system. In nature _____ crystals are often twinned, distorted, or so intergrown with adjacent crystals of _____ or other minerals as to only show part of this shape, or to lack obvious crystal faces altogether and appear massive.
    a. Quartz0
    b. Thing
    c. Undefined
    d. Undefined

12. _____ is the name of a group of rock-forming minerals which make up as much as sixty percent of the Earth's crust. Feldspars crystallize from magma in both intrusive and extrusive rocks, and they can also occur as compact minerals, as veins, and are also present in many types of metamorphic rock.
    a. Feldspar0
    b. Thing
    c. Undefined
    d. Undefined

13. _____ is a sedimentary rock composed largely of the mineral calcite. _____ often contains variable amounts of silica in the form of chert or flint, as well as varying amounts of clay, silt and sand as disseminations, nodules, or layers within the rock. The primary source of the calcite in _____ is most commonly marine organisms. These organisms secrete shells that settle out of the water column and are deposited on ocean floors as pelagic ooze or alternatively is conglomerated in a coral reef.
    a. Thing
    b. Limestone0
    c. Undefined
    d. Undefined

14. _____ is a term used to describe a group of hydrous aluminium phyllosilicate minerals, that are typically less than 2 micrometres in diameter. _____ consists of a variety of phyllosilicate minerals rich in silicon and aluminium oxides and hydroxides which include variable amounts of structural water. Clays are generally formed by the chemical weathering of silicate-bearing rocks by carbonic acid but some are formed by hydrothermal activity.
    a. Thing
    b. Clay0
    c. Undefined
    d. Undefined

15. _____ are hydrous aluminium phyllosilicates, sometimes with variable amounts of iron, magnesium, alkali metals, alkaline earths and other cations. Clays have structures similar to the micas and therefore form flat hexagonal sheets. _____ are common weathering products and low temperature hydrothermal alteration products.

Chapter 6. Sedimentary Rocks-The Archives of Earth History

a. Clay minerals0
b. Thing
c. Undefined
d. Undefined

16. _____ is any particulate matter that can be transported by fluid flow and which eventually is deposited as a layer of solid particles on the bed or bottom of a body of water or other liquid.
a. Sediment0
b. Thing
c. Undefined
d. Undefined

17. _____ refers to the diameter of individual grains of sediment, or the lithified particles in clastic rocks. The term may also be applied to other granular materials. This is different from the crystallite size, which is the size of a single crystal inside the particles or grains.
a. Particle size0
b. Thing
c. Undefined
d. Undefined

18. _____ is rock that is of a certain particle size range. In geology, _____ is any loose rock that is at least two millimeters in its largest dimension and no more than 75 millimeters.
a. Gravel0
b. Thing
c. Undefined
d. Undefined

19. A _____ is a disturbance that propagates through space or spacetime, transferring energy and momentum and sometimes angular momentum.
a. Wave0
b. Thing
c. Undefined
d. Undefined

20. A _____ is a body of water with a current, confined within a bed and banks. Streams are important as conduits in the water cycle, instruments in aquifer recharge, and corridors for fish and wildlife migration.
a. Stream0
b. Thing
c. Undefined
d. Undefined

21. A _____ is a rock consisting of individual stones that have become cemented together. Conglomerates are sedimentary rocks consisting of rounded fragements and are thus differentiated from breccias, which consist of angular clasts. Both conglomerates and breccias are characterized by clasts larger than sand.
a. Thing
b. Conglomerate0
c. Undefined
d. Undefined

22. _____ is soil or rock derived granular material of a specific grain size. _____ may occur as a soil or alternatively as suspended sediment in a water column of any surface water body. It may also exist as deposition soil at the bottom of a water body.
a. Thing
b. Silt0
c. Undefined
d. Undefined

23. A _____ is a body of comparatively shallow salt or brackish water separated from the deeper sea by a shallow or exposed sandbank, coral reef, or similar feature. Thus, the enclosed body of water behind a barrier reef or barrier islands or enclosed by an atoll reef is called a _____.

Chapter 6. Sedimentary Rocks-The Archives of Earth History

a. Lagoon0
b. Place
c. Undefined
d. Undefined

24. A _____ is a body of water or other liquid of considerable size contained on a body of land. A vast majority are fresh water, and lie in the Northern Hemisphere at higher latitudes. Most have a natural outflow in the form of a river or stream, but some do not, and lose water solely by evaporation and/or underground seepage.
a. Lake0
b. Thing
c. Undefined
d. Undefined

25. Ocean _____ are any more or less continuous, directed movement of ocean water that flows in one of the Earth's oceans. They are rivers of hot or cold water within the ocean. They are generated from the forces acting upon the water like the earth's rotation, the wind, the temperature and salinity differences and the gravitation of the moon.
a. Currents0
b. Thing
c. Undefined
d. Undefined

26. A _____ is a hill of sand built by eolian processes. Dunes are subject to different forms and sizes based on their interaction with the wind. Most kinds of _____ are longer on the windward side where the sand is pushed up the _____, and a shorter in the lee of the wind. The trough between dunes is called a slack. A "_____ field" is an area covered by extensive sand dunes. Large _____ fields are known as ergs.
a. Thing
b. Dune0
c. Undefined
d. Undefined

27. A _____ is a large, slow moving river of ice, formed from compacted layers of snow, that slowly deforms and flows in response to gravity. _____ ice is the largest reservoir of fresh water on Earth, and second only to oceans as the largest reservoir of total water. Glaciers cover vast areas of polar regions but are restricted to the highest mountains in the tropics.
a. Glacier0
b. Thing
c. Undefined
d. Undefined

28. _____ is mechanical scraping of a rock surface by friction between rocks and moving particles during their transport in wind, glacier, waves, gravity or running water.
a. Thing
b. Abrasion0
c. Undefined
d. Undefined

29. _____ is a cloudiness or haziness of water caused by individual particles that are generally invisible to the naked eye, thus being much like smoke in air. _____ is generally caused by phytoplankton. Measurement of _____ is a key test of water quality.
a. Thing
b. Turbidity0
c. Undefined
d. Undefined

30. A _____ is a current of rapidly moving, sediment-laden water moving down a slope through air, water, or another fluid. The current moves because it has a higher density and turbidity than the fluid through which it flows.
a. Thing
b. Turbidity current0
c. Undefined
d. Undefined

Chapter 6. Sedimentary Rocks-The Archives of Earth History

31. The _____ is the extended perimeter of each continent and associated coastal plain, which is covered during interglacial periods such as the current epoch by relatively shallow seas and gulfs. The shelf usually ends at a point of increasing slope.
   a. Continental shelf0
   b. Thing
   c. Undefined
   d. Undefined

32. The _____ the bottom of the ocean. At the bottom of the continental slope is the continental rise, which is caused by sediment cascading down the continental slope.
   a. Thing
   b. Seafloor0
   c. Undefined
   d. Undefined

33. In physics, _____ is defined as the rate of change of displacement or the rate of displacement. Simply put, it is distance per units of time.
   a. Velocity0
   b. Thing
   c. Undefined
   d. Undefined

34. In geology, a _____ generally refers to a linear structural depression that extends laterally over a distance, while being less steep than a trench. It can be a narrow basin or a geologic rift. In meteorolology a _____ is an elongated region of relatively low atmospheric pressure, often associated with fronts.
   a. Thing
   b. Trough0
   c. Undefined
   d. Undefined

35. The _____ epoch is the period in the geologic timescale that extends from 5.332 million to 1.806 million years before present.
   a. Thing
   b. Pliocene0
   c. Undefined
   d. Undefined

36. A _____ is a geologic event during which sea level rises relative to the land and the shoreline moves toward higher ground, resulting in flooding. Transgressions can be caused either by the land sinking or the ocean basins filling with water.
   a. Thing
   b. Transgression0
   c. Undefined
   d. Undefined

37. A _____ is a rock, sandbar, or other feature lying beneath the surface of the water yet shallow enough to be a hazard to ships. They result from abiotic processes—deposition of sand, wave erosion planning down rock outcrops, and other natural processes.
   a. Thing
   b. Reef0
   c. Undefined
   d. Undefined

38. _____, a branch of geology, studies rock layers and layering. It is primarily used in the study of sedimentary and layered volcanic rocks. _____ includes two related subfields: lithologic or lithostratigraphy and biologic _____ or biostratigraphy.
   a. Stratigraphy0
   b. Thing
   c. Undefined
   d. Undefined

Chapter 6. Sedimentary Rocks-The Archives of Earth History

39. _____ is a small island located in the middle of San Francisco Bay in California, United States. It served as a lighthouse, then a military fortification, then a military prison followed by a federal prison until 1963, when it became a national recreation area.
   a. Alcatraz Island0
   b. Place
   c. Undefined
   d. Undefined

40. The term _____ is used in geology when one or a stack of originally flat and planar surfaces, such as sedimentary strata, are bent or curved as a result of plastic, i.e. permanent, deformation.
   a. Thing
   b. Fold0
   c. Undefined
   d. Undefined

41. In structural geology, a _____ is a downward-curving fold, with layers that dip toward the center of the structure. On a geologic map, synclines are recognized by a sequence of rock layers that grow progressively younger, followed by the youngest layer at the fold's center or hinge, and by a reverse sequence of the same rock layers on the opposite side of the hinge.
   a. Syncline0
   b. Thing
   c. Undefined
   d. Undefined

42. An _____ is a fold that is convex up or to the youngest beds. Anticlines are usually recognized by a sequence of rock layers that are progressively older toward the center of the fold because the uplifted core of the fold is preferentially eroded to a deeper stratigraphic level relative to the topographically lower flanks. If an _____ plunges, the surface strata will form Vs that point in the direction of the plunge.
   a. Anticline0
   b. Thing
   c. Undefined
   d. Undefined

43. In geology, _____ are sedimentary structures that indicate agitation by or wind.
   a. Thing
   b. Ripple marks0
   c. Undefined
   d. Undefined

44. _____ is water from a sea or ocean. On average, _____ in the world's oceans has a salinity of ~3.5%, or 35 parts per thousand. This means that every 1 kg of _____ has approximately 35 grams of dissolved salts.
   a. Thing
   b. Seawater0
   c. Undefined
   d. Undefined

45. _____ were vertebrate animals that dominated terrestrial ecosystems for over 160 million years, first appearing approximately 230 million years ago. At the end of the Cretaceous Period, approximately 65 million years ago, a catastrophic extinction event ended _____' dominance on land.
   a. Dinosaurs0
   b. Thing
   c. Undefined
   d. Undefined

46. _____ refer to marine animals from the class Anthozoa and exist as small sea anemone-like polyps, typically in colonies of many identical individuals. The group includes the important reef builders that are found in tropical oceans, which secrete calcium carbonate to form a hard skeleton.
   a. Coral0
   b. Thing
   c. Undefined
   d. Undefined

Chapter 6. Sedimentary Rocks-The Archives of Earth History

47. A _____ is flat or nearly flat land adjacent to a stream or river that experiences occasional or periodic flooding. It includes the floodway, which consists of the stream channel and adjacent areas that carry flood flows, and the flood fringe, which are areas covered by the flood, but which do not experience a strong current.
   a. Thing
   b. Floodplain0
   c. Undefined
   d. Undefined

48. _____ are marine animals that make up the class Crinoidea of the echinoderms. They are characterized by a mouth on the top surface that is surrounded by feeding arms. They have a U-shaped gut, and their anus is located next to the mouth. Although the basic echinoderm pattern of five-fold symmetry can be recognized, most _____ have many more than five arms.
   a. Crinoids0
   b. Thing
   c. Undefined
   d. Undefined

49. _____ is located in the U.S. state of Montana, bordering the Canadian provinces of Alberta and British Columbia. _____ contains two mountain ranges, over 130 named lakes, more than 1,000 different species of plants and hundreds of species of animals.
   a. Glacier National Park0
   b. Place
   c. Undefined
   d. Undefined

50. _____ generally, is the synthesis of triose phosphates from sunlight, carbon dioxide and water.
   a. Photosynthesis0
   b. Thing
   c. Undefined
   d. Undefined

51. _____ are unicellular microorganisms. They are typically a few micrometres long and have many shapes including curved rods, spheres, rods, and spirals.
   a. Bacteria0
   b. Thing
   c. Undefined
   d. Undefined

52. A _____ is a structure preserved in sedimentary rocks that record biological activity. While we are most familiar with relatively spectacular, fossilized hard-part remains such as shells and bones, a _____ is often less dramatic, but nonetheless very important.
   a. Trace fossil0
   b. Thing
   c. Undefined
   d. Undefined

53. _____ is a sedimentary rock composed mainly of sand-size mineral or rock grains. Most _____ is composed of quartz and/or feldspar because these are the most common minerals in the Earth's crust. Like sand, _____ may be any color, but the most common colors are tan, brown, yellow, red, gray and white.
   a. Sandstone0
   b. Thing
   c. Undefined
   d. Undefined

54. _____, both meaning "Earth", and graphein meaning "to describe" or "to write"or "to map", is the study of the earth and its features, inhabitants, and phenomena. A literal translation would be "to describe the Earth". The first person to use the word "_____" was Eratosthenes. Four historical traditions in geographical research are the spatial analysis of natural and human phenomena, area studies, study of man-land relationship, and research in earth sciences.

a. Geography0
b. Thing
c. Undefined
d. Undefined

55. _____ is the average and variations of weather over long periods of time. _____ zones can be defined using parameters such as temperature and rainfall.
   a. Climate0
   b. Thing
   c. Undefined
   d. Undefined

56. In geography, a _____ is a landscape form or region that receives very little precipitation. They are defined as areas that receive an average annual precipitation of less than 250 mm. A _____ where vegetation cover is exceedingly sparse correspond to the 'hyperarid' regions of the earth, where rainfall is exceedingly rare and infrequent.
   a. Place
   b. Desert0
   c. Undefined
   d. Undefined

57. A _____ is one of several large landmasses on Earth. They are generally identified by convention rather than any strict criteria, but seven areas are commonly reckoned as continents – they are: Asia, Africa, North America, South America, Antarctica, Europe, and Australia.
   a. Thing
   b. Continent0
   c. Undefined
   d. Undefined

58. A _____ is a landform that extends above the surrounding terrain in a limited area. A _____ is generally steeper than a hill, but there is no universally accepted standard definition for the height of a _____ or a hill although a _____ usually has an identifiable summit.
   a. Place
   b. Mountain0
   c. Undefined
   d. Undefined

59. In geology, a _____ is a depression with predominant extent in one direction. The terms U-shaped and V-shaped are descriptive terms of geography to characterize the form of valleys. Most valleys belong to one of these two main types or a mixture of them, at least with respect of the cross section of the slopes or hillsides.
   a. Valley0
   b. Thing
   c. Undefined
   d. Undefined

60. An _____ plain is a relatively flat and gently sloping landform found at the base of a range of hills or mountains, formed by the deposition of _____ soil over a long period of time by one or more rivers coming from the mountains.
   a. Alluvial0
   b. Thing
   c. Undefined
   d. Undefined

61. An alluvial fan is a fan-shaped deposit formed where a fast flowing stream flattens, slows, and spreads typically at the exit of a canyon onto a flatter plain. A convergence of neighboring _____ into a single apron of deposits against a slope is called a bajada, or compound alluvial fan.
   a. Thing
   b. Alluvial fans0
   c. Undefined
   d. Undefined

62. Playas are small, round depressions in the surface of the ground. A _____ is formed when rain fills this hole with water, creating a small lake. Playas are typically endorheic. Playas can also form when the water table intersects the surface and water seeps into them.

Chapter 6. Sedimentary Rocks-The Archives of Earth History

a. Playa0
c. Undefined
b. Thing
d. Undefined

63. _____ refers to water-soluble, mineral sediments that result from the evaporation of bodies of surficial water.
a. Thing
c. Undefined
b. Evaporite0
d. Undefined

64. _____ is the process of heating a solid substance to a point where it turns into a liquid. An object that has melted is molten.
a. Thing
c. Undefined
b. Melting0
d. Undefined

65. _____ refers to any glacially formed accumulation of unconsolidated debris which can occur in currently glaciated and formerly glaciated regions, such as those areas acted upon by a past ice age. This debris may have been plucked off the valley floor as a glacier advanced or fallen off the valley walls as a result of frost wedging. Moraines may be comprised of silt like glacial flour to large boulders. The debris is typically angular.
a. Moraine0
c. Undefined
b. Thing
d. Undefined

66. _____ occurs when snow falls on a glacier, is compressed, and becomes part of a glacier that winds its way toward a body of water.
a. Blue ice0
c. Undefined
b. Thing
d. Undefined

67. _____ is one of a number of channel types and has a channel that consists of a network of small channels separated by small and often temporary islands called braid bars or, in British usage, aits or eyots.
a. Braided stream0
c. Undefined
b. Thing
d. Undefined

68. _____ is the native consolidated rock underlying the Earth's surface. Above the _____ is usually an area of broken and weathered unconsolidated rock in the basal subsoil.
a. Bedrock0
c. Undefined
b. Thing
d. Undefined

69. A _____ is an annual layer of sediment or sedimentary rock. The word _____ is derived from the Swedish word varv whose meanings and connotations include revolution, in layers, and circle.
a. Varve0
c. Undefined
b. Thing
d. Undefined

70. A _____ is a lake with origins in a melted glacier. They can be green in color, the result of ground up minerals supporting a large population of algae.
a. Glacial Lake0
c. Undefined
b. Place
d. Undefined

Chapter 6. Sedimentary Rocks-The Archives of Earth History

71. A _____ is a landform where the mouth of a river flows into an ocean, sea, desert, estuary or lake. It builds up sediment outwards into the flat area which the river's flow encounters transported by the water and set down as the currents slow.
   a. Delta0
   b. Thing
   c. Undefined
   d. Undefined

72. _____ refers to the cyclic rizing and falling of Earth's ocean surface caused by the tidal forces of the Moon and the sun acting on the oceans. They cause changes in the depth of the marine and estuarine water bodies and produce oscillating currents known as tidal streams, making prediction of tides important for coastal navigation.
   a. Thing
   b. Tide0
   c. Undefined
   d. Undefined

73. _____ are the cyclic rizing and falling of Earth's ocean surface caused by the tidal forces of the Moon and the sun acting on the oceans. _____ cause changes in the depth of the marine and estuarine water bodies and produce oscillating currents known as tidal streams, making prediction of _____ important for coastal navigation.
   a. Tides0
   b. Thing
   c. Undefined
   d. Undefined

74. _____ are isolated fragments of rock found within finer-grained water-deposited sedimentary rocks. They range in size from small pebbles to boulders. The critical distinguishing feature is that there is evidence that they were not transported by normal water currents, but rather dropped in vertically through the water column.
   a. Thing
   b. Dropstones0
   c. Undefined
   d. Undefined

75. An _____ is a large piece of freshwater ice that has broken off from a snow-formed glacier or ice shelf and is floating in open water. Typically, only one ninth of the volume of an _____ is above water. The shape of the remainder under the water can be difficult to surmise from looking at what is visible above the surface.
   a. Iceberg0
   b. Thing
   c. Undefined
   d. Undefined

76. _____ is the displacement and mixing of sediment particles by benthic fauna or flora. Faunal activities, such as burrowing, ingestion and defecation of sediment grains, construction and maintenance of galleries, and infilling of abandoned dwellings, displace sediment grains and mix the sediment matrix. _____ is a diagenetic process and acts to alter the physical structure, as well as the chemical nature of the sediment.
   a. Bioturbation0
   b. Thing
   c. Undefined
   d. Undefined

77. _____ are coastal wetlands that form when mud is deposited by the tides or rivers, sea and oceans. They are found in sheltered areas such as bays, bayous, lagoons, and estuaries. _____ may be viewed geologically as exposed layers of bay mud, resulting from deposition of estuarine silts, clays and marine animal detritus.
   a. Thing
   b. Mudflats0
   c. Undefined
   d. Undefined

78. A _____ is the fringe of land at the edge of a large body of water, such as an ocean, sea, or lake. A strict definition is the strip of land along a water body that is alternately exposed and covered by waves and tides.

Chapter 6. Sedimentary Rocks-The Archives of Earth History 107

    a. Thing
    b. Shoreline0
    c. Undefined
    d. Undefined

79. The _____ is the last period of the Palaeozoic Era. As the _____ opened, the Earth was still in the grip of an ice age, so the polar regions were covered with deep layers of ice. During the _____, all the Earth's major land masses except portions of East Asia were collected into a single supercontinent known as Pangaea. The _____ ended with the most extensive extinction event recorded in paleontology: the _____-Triassic extinction event.
    a. Permian0
    b. Thing
    c. Undefined
    d. Undefined

80. In biology, _____ is non-living particulate organic material. It typically includes the bodies of dead organisms or fragments of organisms or faecal material. _____ is normally colonised by communities of microorganisms which act to decompose the material.
    a. Detritus0
    b. Thing
    c. Undefined
    d. Undefined

81. _____ is displacement of solids by the agents of ocean currents, wind, water, or ice by downward or down-slope movement in response to gravity or by living organisms.
    a. Thing
    b. Erosion0
    c. Undefined
    d. Undefined

82. _____ are where one sedimetary deposit ends and another one begins. The rock is prone to breakage at these points because of the weakness between the layers.
    a. Bedding planes0
    b. Thing
    c. Undefined
    d. Undefined

83. A _____ is a deep valley between cliffs often carved from the landscape by a river. Most were formed by a process of long-time erosion from a plateau level. The cliffs form because harder rock strata that are resistant to erosion and weathering remain exposed on the valley walls.
    a. Canyon0
    b. Thing
    c. Undefined
    d. Undefined

84. A _____ is a steep-sided valley on the sea floor of the continental slope. They are formed by powerful turbidity currents, volcanic and earthquake activity. Many continue as submarine channels across continental rise areas and may extend for hundreds of kilometers.
    a. Submarine canyon0
    b. Thing
    c. Undefined
    d. Undefined

85. _____ is a 16-ton, manned deep-ocean research submersible owned by the United States Navy and operated by the Woods Hole Oceanographic Institution in Woods Hole, Massachusetts. The three-person vessel allows for two scientists and one pilot to dive for up to nine hours at 4500 metersor 15,000 feet.
    a. Alvin0
    b. Thing
    c. Undefined
    d. Undefined

86. A _____ mark the maximum advance of the glacier. An is at the present boundary of the glacier. One famous is the Giant's Wall in Norway which, according to legend, was built by giants to keep intruders out of their realm.

Chapter 6. Sedimentary Rocks-The Archives of Earth History

a. Thing
b. Terminal moraines0
c. Undefined
d. Undefined

87. An _____ is a long, winding ridge of stratified sand and gravel which occur in glaciated and formerly glaciated regions of Europe and North America.
a. Esker0
b. Thing
c. Undefined
d. Undefined

88. A _____ is a geological feature, an irregularly shaped hill or mound composed of sorted or stratified sand and gravel that is deposited in contact with the glacial ice. It can have an irregular shape.
a. Place
b. Kame0
c. Undefined
d. Undefined

89. The _____ is a major river in the Indian subcontinent flowing east through the eponymous plains of northern India into Bangladesh. It is held sacred by Hindus and is worshipped in its personified form as the goddess Ganga.
a. Ganges0
b. Place
c. Undefined
d. Undefined

90. Water collecting on the ground or in a stream, river, lake, or wetland is called _____; as opposed to groundwater. _____ is naturally replenished by precipitation and naturally lost through discharge to the oceans, evaporation, and sub-surface seepage into the groundwater. _____ is the largest source of fresh water.
a. Thing
b. Surface water0
c. Undefined
d. Undefined

91. An _____ is any piece of land that is completely surrounded by water, above high tide. There are two main types of islands: continental islands and oceanic islands. There are also artificial islands. A grouping of geographically and/or geologically related islands is called an archipelago.
a. Island0
b. Thing
c. Undefined
d. Undefined

92. A _____ is an organism that is microscopic. They can be bacteria, fungi, archaea or protists, but not viruses and prions, which are generally classified as non-living. Micro-organisms are generally single-celled, or unicellular organisms.
a. Microorganism0
b. Thing
c. Undefined
d. Undefined

93. _____ consists of very fine rock and mineral particles less than 2 mm in diameter that are ejected from a volcanic vent. The very fine particles may be carried for many miles, settling out as a dust-like layer across the landscape
a. Thing
b. Ash fall0
c. Undefined
d. Undefined

94. The _____ is the part of the open sea or ocean that is not near the coast or sea floor. In contrast, the demersal zone comprises the water that is near to, and is significantly affected by, the coast or the sea floor.
a. Thing
b. Pelagic0
c. Undefined
d. Undefined

Chapter 6. Sedimentary Rocks-The Archives of Earth History

95. _____ refers to a sediment, sedimentary rock, or soil type which is formed from or contains a high proportion of calcium carbonate in the form of calcite or aragonite.
   a. Calcareous0
   b. Thing
   c. Undefined
   d. Undefined

96. In organic chemistry, a _____ is a salt of carbonic acid.
   a. Carbonate0
   b. Thing
   c. Undefined
   d. Undefined

97. _____ are a class of sedimentary rocks composed primarily of carbonate minerals. The two major types are limestone and dolomite, composed of calcite and the mineral dolomite respectively. Chalk and tufa are also minor sedimentary carbonates.
   a. Carbonate rocks0
   b. Thing
   c. Undefined
   d. Undefined

98. _____ is the name of a sedimentary carbonate rock and a mineral, both composed of calcium magnesium carbonate found in crystals. _____ rock is composed predominantly of the mineral _____. Limestone that is partially replaced by _____ is referred to as dolomitic limestone.
   a. Dolomite0
   b. Thing
   c. Undefined
   d. Undefined

99. _____ is a sedimentary carbonate rock that contains a high percentage of the mineral dolomite. It is usually referred to as dolomite rock. In old U.S.G.S. publications it was referred to as magnesian limestone.
   a. Thing
   b. Dolostone0
   c. Undefined
   d. Undefined

100. The character of the shelf changes dramatically at the _____, where the continental slope begins. With a few exceptions, it is located at a remarkably uniform depth of roughly 140 m; this is likely a hallmark of past ice ages, when sea level was lower than it is now.
   a. Thing
   b. Shelf break0
   c. Undefined
   d. Undefined

101. The _____ in the Southwest Asian region, is an extension of the Gulf of Oman located between Iran and the Arabian Peninsula. The _____ was the focus of the Iraq-Iran War that lasted from 1980 to 1988, with each side attacking the other's oil tankers.
   a. Place
   b. Persian Gulf0
   c. Undefined
   d. Undefined

102. An _____ is a sedimentary rock formed from ooids, spherical grains composed of concentric layers.
   a. Thing
   b. Oolite0
   c. Undefined
   d. Undefined

103. The _____ are members of the large and diverse phylum, which includes a variety of familiar animals well-known for their decorative shells or as seafood. These range from tiny snails, clams, and abalone to larger organisms such as squid, cuttlefish and the octopus

Chapter 6. Sedimentary Rocks-The Archives of Earth History

    a. Mollusks0
    b. Thing
    c. Undefined
    d. Undefined

104.   In inorganic chemistry, a _____ is a salt of sulfuric acid
    a. Sulfate0
    b. Thing
    c. Undefined
    d. Undefined

105.   _____ is a very soft mineral composed of calcium sulfate dihydrate, with the chemical formula CaSO4·2H2O. _____ occurs in nature as flattened and often twinned crystals and transparent cleavable masses. It may also occur silky and fibrous. Finally it may also be granular or quite compact.
    a. Thing
    b. Gypsum0
    c. Undefined
    d. Undefined

106.   _____ is the mineral form of sodium chloride. _____ forms isometric crystals. It commonly occurs with other evaporite deposit minerals such as several of the sulfates, halides and borates. _____ occurs in vast lakes of sedimentary evaporite minerals that result from the drying up of enclosed beds, playas, and seas.
    a. Halite0
    b. Thing
    c. Undefined
    d. Undefined

107.   _____ is a mineral - anhydrous calcium sulfate, $CaSO_4$. It is in the orthorhombic crystal system, with three directions of perfect cleavage parallel to the three planes of symmetry. It is not isomorphous with the orthorhombic barium and strontium sulfates, as might be expected from the chemical formulas.
    a. Anhydrite0
    b. Thing
    c. Undefined
    d. Undefined

108.   The _____ is defined as the part of the land adjoining or near the ocean. A coastline is properly a line on a map indicating the disposition of a _____, but the word is often used to refer to the _____ itself. The adjective coastal describes something as being on, near to, or associated with a _____.
    a. Place
    b. Coast0
    c. Undefined
    d. Undefined

109.   The _____ region of the United States comprises the coasts of states which border the Gulf of Mexico. The states of Texas, Louisiana, Mississippi, Alabama, and Florida are known as the Gulf States. All Gulf States are located in the Southern region of the United States.
    a. Place
    b. Gulf Coast0
    c. Undefined
    d. Undefined

110.   The _____ is a sea of the Atlantic Ocean almost completely enclosed by land: on the north by Europe, on the south by Africa, and on the east by Asia. It covers an approximate area of 2.5 million km², but its connection to the Atlantic is only 14 km wide.
    a. Mediterranean Sea0
    b. Place
    c. Undefined
    d. Undefined

111.   _____ is the saltiness or dissolved salt content of a body of water. In oceanography, it has been traditional to express halinity not as percent, but as parts per thousand, which is approximately grams of salt per liter of solution.

Chapter 6. Sedimentary Rocks-The Archives of Earth History

a. Thing
c. Undefined

b. Salinity0
d. Undefined

112. _____ is the process by which molecules in a liquid state become a gas.
a. Evaporation0
c. Undefined

b. Thing
d. Undefined

113. _____ is the use of the principles of geology to reconstruct and understand the history of the Earth. It focuses on geologic processes that change the Earth's surface and subsurface; and the use of stratigraphy, structural geology and paleontology to tell the sequence of these events. It also focuses on the evolution of plants and animals during different time periods in the geological timescale.
a. Thing
c. Undefined

b. Historical geology0
d. Undefined

114. _____ is the science and study of the solid matter that constitute the Earth. Encompassing such things as rocks, soil, and gemstones, _____ studies the composition, structure, physical properties, history, and the processes that shape Earth's components.
a. Geology0
c. Undefined

b. Thing
d. Undefined

115. Mean _____ is the average height of the sea, with reference to a suitable reference surface.
a. Thing
c. Undefined

b. Sea level0
d. Undefined

116. _____ is a geologic formation in the Glen Canyon Group that is spread across the U.S. states of northern Arizona, northwest Colorado, Nevada, and Utah. It is located in the Colorado Plateau province of the United States.
a. Navajo Sandstone0
c. Undefined

b. Place
d. Undefined

117. The _____ is a major unit of the geologic timescale that extends from the end of the Triassic to the beginning of the Cretaceous. The Jurassic constitutes the middle period of the Mesozoic era, also known as the "Age of Dinosaurs". The start of the period is marked by the major Triassic-Jurassic extinction event.
a. Jurassic Period0
c. Undefined

b. Thing
d. Undefined

118. _____ is the study of the ancient geologic environments of the Earth's surface as preserved in the stratigraphic record.
a. Thing
c. Undefined

b. Palaeogeography0
d. Undefined

119. _____ are underwater structures that look like deltas formed at the end of many large rivers, such as the Nile or Mississippi Rivers. They formed due to underwater currents. Close to land, a river deposits sediments onto the continental shelf. By then, the sediments are still suspended in the water, with some of the larger particles sinking to the floor of the continental shelf.

Chapter 6. Sedimentary Rocks-The Archives of Earth History

a. Thing
b. Submarine fans0
c. Undefined
d. Undefined

120. The sea floor below the break is the _____. Below the slope is the continental rise, which finally merges into the deep ocean floor, the abyssal plain. As the continental shelf and the slope are part of the continental margin, both are covered in this article.
a. Thing
b. Continental slope0
c. Undefined
d. Undefined

121. _____ have an extremely low yearly precipitation, receiving much less rain or snowfall annually than would satisfy the climatological demand for evaporation and transpiration.
a. Thing
b. Arid lands0
c. Undefined
d. Undefined

122. In horticulture, _____ is the process of pretreating seeds to simulate natural conditions that a seed must endure before germination.
a. Stratification0
b. Thing
c. Undefined
d. Undefined

123. Clastic sedimentary rocks are rocks composed predominantly of broken pieces or _____ of older weathered and eroded rocks.
a. Thing
b. Clasts0
c. Undefined
d. Undefined

124. _____ is a rock composed of angular fragments of rocks or minerals in a matrix, that is a cementing material, that may be similar or different in composition to the fragments.
a. Breccia0
b. Thing
c. Undefined
d. Undefined

Chapter 7. Evolution-The Theory and its Supporting Evidence

1. _____ is the process by which favorable traits that are heritable become more common in successive generations of a population of reproducing organisms, and unfavorable traits that are heritable become less common.
   a. Thing
   b. Natural selection0
   c. Undefined
   d. Undefined

2. _____ was already eminent as an English naturalist when he proposed and provided evidence for the theory that all species have evolved over time from one or a few common ancestors through the process of natural selection. The fact that evolution occurs became accepted by the scientific community and the general public in his lifetime, while his theory of natural selection came to be widely seen as the primary explanation of the process of evolution in the 1930s, and now forms the basis of modern evolutionary theory. In modified form, Darwin's theory remains a cornerstone of biology, as it provides a unifying explanation for the diversity of life.
   a. Person
   b. Charles Darwin0
   c. Undefined
   d. Undefined

3. _____ was a Moravian Augustinian priest and scientist often called the "father of modern genetics" for his study of the inheritance of traits in pea plants.
   a. Gregor Mendel0
   b. Person
   c. Undefined
   d. Undefined

4. Fossils are the mineralized or otherwise preserved remains or traces of animals, plants, and other organisms. The totality of fossils, both discovered and undiscovered, and their placement in fossiliferous rock formations and sedimentary layers is known as the _____ record.
   a. Fossil0
   b. Thing
   c. Undefined
   d. Undefined

5. The _____ is the largest of the Earth's oceanic divisions. It extends from the Arctic in the north to the Antarctic in the south, bounded by Asia and Australia on the west and the Americas on the east. At 169.2 million square kilometres in area, this largest division of the World Ocean – and, in turn, the hydrosphere – covers about 46% of the Earth's water surface and about 32% of its total surface area, making it larger than all of the Earth's land area combined.
   a. Pacific Ocean0
   b. Place
   c. Undefined
   d. Undefined

6. An _____ is any piece of land that is completely surrounded by water, above high tide. There are two main types of islands: continental islands and oceanic islands. There are also artificial islands. A grouping of geographically and/or geologically related islands is called an archipelago.
   a. Thing
   b. Island0
   c. Undefined
   d. Undefined

7. An _____ is a small island. A rock, sometimes a synonym for a type of _____, is a landform composed of rock, lying offshore, having no or minimal vegetation, and uninhabited. Also, an exposed sandbar is another type of _____.
   a. Place
   b. Islet0
   c. Undefined
   d. Undefined

8. An _____ is a chain or cluster of islands. It is now used to generally refer to any island group or, sometimes, to a sea containing a large number of scattered islands like the Aegean.

Chapter 7. Evolution-The Theory and its Supporting Evidence

a. Place
b. Archipelago0
c. Undefined
d. Undefined

9. The _____ are an archipelago of volcanic islands distributed around the equator, 965 kilometres west of continental Ecuador in the Pacific Ocean. They are famed for their vast number of endemic species and the studies by Charles Darwin during the voyage of the Beagle that contributed to the inception of Darwin's theory of evolution by natural selection.
   a. Galapagos Islands0
   b. Thing
   c. Undefined
   d. Undefined

10. _____ is a common gray to black extrusive volcanic rock. It is usually fine-grained due to rapid cooling of lava on the Earth's surface. It may be porphyritic containing larger crystals in a fine matrix, or vesicular, or frothy scoria.
    a. Thing
    b. Basalt0
    c. Undefined
    d. Undefined

11. _____ are reptiles of the order Testudines most of whose body is shielded by a special bony or cartilagenous shell developed from their ribs.
    a. Turtles0
    b. Thing
    c. Undefined
    d. Undefined

12. _____ are passerine birds, often seed-eating, found chiefly in the northern hemisphere and Africa. They are small to moderately large and have strong, stubby beaks, which in some species can be quite large. All have 12 tail feathers and 9 primaries. They have a bouncing flight, alternating bouts of flapping with gliding on closed wings, and most sing well.
    a. Thing
    b. Finches0
    c. Undefined
    d. Undefined

13. The _____ is defined as the part of the land adjoining or near the ocean. A coastline is properly a line on a map indicating the disposition of a _____, but the word is often used to refer to the _____ itself. The adjective coastal describes something as being on, near to, or associated with a _____.
    a. Place
    b. Coast0
    c. Undefined
    d. Undefined

14. _____ is the substance of which physical objects are composed. _____ can be solid, liquid, plasma or gas. It constitutes the observable universe.
    a. Thing
    b. Matter0
    c. Undefined
    d. Undefined

15. _____ is the average and variations of weather over long periods of time. _____ zones can be defined using parameters such as temperature and rainfall.
    a. Climate0
    b. Thing
    c. Undefined
    d. Undefined

16. The _____ is an African even-toed ungulate mammal, the tallest of all land-living animal species.
    a. Giraffe0
    b. Thing
    c. Undefined
    d. Undefined

Chapter 7. Evolution-The Theory and its Supporting Evidence

17. _____ is the intentional breeding of certain traits, or combinations of traits, over others.
    a. Artificial selection0
    b. Thing
    c. Undefined
    d. Undefined

18. _____ between members of a species is the driving force behind evolution and natural selection; especially for resources such as food, water, territory, and sunlight results in the ultimate survival and dominance of the variation of the species best suited for survival.
    a. Thing
    b. Competition0
    c. Undefined
    d. Undefined

19. _____ is the discipline concerned with the questions of how one should live ; what sorts of things exist and what are their essential natures ; what counts as genuine knowledge; and what are the correct principles of reasoning.
    a. Thing
    b. Philosophy0
    c. Undefined
    d. Undefined

20. _____ is the production of food, feed, fiber, fuel and other goods by the systematic raizing of plants and animals.
    a. Thing
    b. Agriculture0
    c. Undefined
    d. Undefined

21. _____ are proteins that accelerate chemical reactions. Almost all processes in a biological cell need them in order to occur at significant rates.
    a. Enzymes0
    b. Thing
    c. Undefined
    d. Undefined

22. A _____ is an organism that feeds on another living organism or organisms known as prey. A _____ may or may not kill their prey prior to or during the act of feeding on them.
    a. Thing
    b. Predator0
    c. Undefined
    d. Undefined

23. _____ is a phrase which is a shorthand for a concept relating to competition for survival or predominance.
    a. Thing
    b. Survival of the fittest0
    c. Undefined
    d. Undefined

24. _____ are any one of a number of viable DNA codings that occupies a given locus position on a chromosome. Usually _____ are DNA sequences that code for a gene.
    a. Alleles0
    b. Thing
    c. Undefined
    d. Undefined

25. _____ are people who study prehistoric life forms on Earth through the examination of plant and animal fossils. This includes the study of body fossils, tracks, burrows, cast-off parts, fossilised faeces, palynomorphs and chemical residues.
    a. Person
    b. Paleontologists0
    c. Undefined
    d. Undefined

Chapter 7. Evolution-The Theory and its Supporting Evidence

26. _____ generally denotes the integration of Charles Darwin's theory of the evolution of species by natural selection, Gregor Mendel's theory of genetics as the basis for biological inheritance, random genetic mutation as the source of variation, and mathematical population genetics.
   a. Thing
   b. Modern evolutionary synthesis0
   c. Undefined
   d. Undefined

27. _____ is a large organic compounds made of amino acids arranged in a linear chain and joined together by peptide bonds between the carboxyl and amino groups of adjacent amino acid residues. The sequence of amino acids in a _____ is defined by a gene and encoded in the genetic code.
   a. Protein0
   b. Thing
   c. Undefined
   d. Undefined

28. In chemistry, a _____ is defined as a sufficiently stable electrically neutral group of at least two atoms in a definite arrangement held together by strong chemical bonds.
   a. Molecule0
   b. Thing
   c. Undefined
   d. Undefined

29. _____ is a chemical element represented by the symbol H and an atomic number of 1. At standard temperature and pressure it is a colorless, odorless, nonmetallic, tasteless, highly flammable diatomic gas . With an atomic mass of 1.00794 g/mol, _____ is the lightest element. _____ is the most abundant of the chemical elements, constituting roughly 75% of the universe's elemental mass.
   a. Hydrogen0
   b. Thing
   c. Undefined
   d. Undefined

30. In chemistry, an _____ is a molecule that contains both amine and carboxyl functional groups.
   a. Amino acid0
   b. Thing
   c. Undefined
   d. Undefined

31. In biology, a _____ is a physical or chemical agent that changes the genetic information of an organism and thus increases the frequency of mutations above the natural background level.
   a. Thing
   b. Mutagen0
   c. Undefined
   d. Undefined

32. _____ light is electromagnetic radiation with a wavelength shorter than that of visible light, but longer than soft X-rays. The color violet has the shortest wavelength in the visible spectrum. UV light has a shorter wavelength than that of violet light.
   a. Thing
   b. Ultraviolet0
   c. Undefined
   d. Undefined

33. _____ as used in physics, is energy in the form of waves or moving subatomic particles.
   a. Thing
   b. Radiation0
   c. Undefined
   d. Undefined

34. _____ is the evolutionary process by which new biological species arise.

Chapter 7. Evolution-The Theory and its Supporting Evidence

a. Speciation0
b. Thing
c. Undefined
d. Undefined

35. The _____ is an imaginary line on the Earth's surface equidistant from the North Pole and South Pole. It thus divides the Earth into a Northern Hemisphere and a Southern Hemisphere.
a. Thing
b. Equator0
c. Undefined
d. Undefined

36. A _____ is a geologic event during which sea level rises relative to the land and the shoreline moves toward higher ground, resulting in flooding. Transgressions can be caused either by the land sinking or the ocean basins filling with water.
a. Thing
b. Transgression0
c. Undefined
d. Undefined

37. _____ occurs when huge populations physically isolated by an extrinsic barrier evolve intrinsic genetic reproductive isolation such that if the barrier between the populations breaks down, individuals of the two populations can no longer breed.
a. Thing
b. Allopatric speciation0
c. Undefined
d. Undefined

38. _____ is the condition of a system in which competing influences are balanced.
a. Thing
b. Equilibrium0
c. Undefined
d. Undefined

39. _____ occurs when two or more biological characteristics have a common evolutionary origin but have diverged over evolutionary time. These characters can be observable structures from different species or they can be molecular entities, such as genes or pathways. This is a kind of relationship observed in evolutionary biology.
a. Thing
b. Divergent evolution0
c. Undefined
d. Undefined

40. The term _____ is ambiguous: it can refer to all cetaceans, to just the larger ones, or only to members of particular families within the order Cetacea.
a. Thing
b. Whales0
c. Undefined
d. Undefined

41. The _____ is one of three geologic eras of the Phanerozoic eon. The _____ was a time of tectonic, climatic and evolutionary activity, shifting from a state of connectedness into their present configuration. The climate was exceptionally warm throughout the period, also playing an important role in the evolution and diversification of new animal species. By the end of the era, the basis of modern life was in place.
a. Thing
b. Mesozoic0
c. Undefined
d. Undefined

42. _____ is the process whereby organisms not closely related independently evolve similar traits as a result of having to adapt to similar environments or ecological niches. It is the opposite of divergent evolution, where related species evolve different traits. On a molecular level, this can happen due to random mutation unrelated to adaptive changes; see long branch attraction.

Chapter 7. Evolution-The Theory and its Supporting Evidence

a. Thing
b. Convergent evolution0
c. Undefined
d. Undefined

43. _____ in biology is an anatomical structure, physiological process or behavioral trait of an organism that has evolved over a short or long period of time by the process of natural selection such that it increases the expected long-term reproductive success of the organism. The term _____ is also sometimes used as a synonym for natural selection, but most biologists discourage this usage. Organisms that are adapted to their environment are able to:obtain air, water, food and nutrients, cope with physical conditions such as temperature, light and heat, defend themselves from their natural enemies, reproduce, and respond to changes around them
a. Thing
b. Adaptation0
c. Undefined
d. Undefined

44. The _____ Era meaning "new life", is the most recent of the three classic geological eras. It covers the 65.5 million years since the Cretaceous-Tertiary extinction event at the end of the Cretaceous that marked the demise of the last non-avian dinosaurs and the end of the Mesozoic Era. The _____ era is ongoing.
a. Cenozoic0
b. Thing
c. Undefined
d. Undefined

45. A _____ is one of several large landmasses on Earth. They are generally identified by convention rather than any strict criteria, but seven areas are commonly reckoned as continents – they are: Asia, Africa, North America, South America, Antarctica, Europe, and Australia.
a. Thing
b. Continent0
c. Undefined
d. Undefined

46. _____ is a collective term for animal life of any particular region or time. Paleontologists usually use _____ to refer to a typical collection of animals found in a specific time or place. Paleontologists sometimes refer to a sequence of 80 or so faunal stages, which are a series of rocks all containing similar fossils.
a. Thing
b. Fauna0
c. Undefined
d. Undefined

47. A _____ is a tree showing the evolutionary interrelationships among various species or other entities that are believed to have a common ancestor.
a. Thing
b. Phylogenetic tree0
c. Undefined
d. Undefined

48. A _____ is a marsupial from the family Macropodidae. In common use the term is used to describe the largest species from this family.
a. Kangaroo0
b. Thing
c. Undefined
d. Undefined

49. _____, genus Dipodomys, are small rodents native to North America. The name derives from their bipedal form: they hop like tiny kangaroos.
a. Kangaroo rats0
b. Thing
c. Undefined
d. Undefined

Chapter 7. Evolution-The Theory and its Supporting Evidence

50. _____ is a philosophy of classification that arranges organisms only by their order of branching in an evolutionary tree and not by their morphological similarity.
    a. Cladistics0
    b. Thing
    c. Undefined
    d. Undefined

51. A _____ is defined as a taxonomic group of organisms consisting of a single common ancestor and all the descendants of that ancestor. Any such group is considered to be a monophyletic group of organisms, and can be represented by both a phylogenetic analysis, as in a tree diagram, or by a cladogram, or simply as a taxonomic reference.
    a. Thing
    b. Clade0
    c. Undefined
    d. Undefined

52. A _____ is an animal with a diet consisting mainly of meat, whether it comes from animals living or dead. Some animals are considered a _____ even if their diets contain very little meat but involve preying on other animals. Animals that subsist on a diet consisting only of meat are referred to as an obligate _____. Plants that capture and digest insects are called carnivorous plants. Similarly fungi that capture microscopic animals are often called carnivorous fungi.
    a. Thing
    b. Carnivore0
    c. Undefined
    d. Undefined

53. _____ is the place where a particular species live and grow. It is essentially the environment—at least the physical environment—that surrounds a species population.
    a. Place
    b. Habitat0
    c. Undefined
    d. Undefined

54. The _____ is the second of the six periods of the Paleozoic era. It follows the Cambrian period and is followed by the Silurian period. The _____ started at a major extinction called the Cambrian-_____ extinction and lasted for about 44.6 million years. It ended with another major extinction event that wiped out 60% of marine genera.
    a. Ordovician0
    b. Thing
    c. Undefined
    d. Undefined

55. In biology and ecology, an _____ is a living complex adaptive system of organs that influence each other in such a way that they function in some way as a stable whole.
    a. Organism0
    b. Thing
    c. Undefined
    d. Undefined

56. _____ are decapod crustaceans of the infraorder Brachyura, which typically have a very short "tail" or where the abdomen is entirely hidden under the thorax. They are generally covered with a thick exoskeleton, and are armed with a single pair of claws. They are found in all of the world's oceans; there are also many freshwater and terrestrial _____, particularly in tropical regions.
    a. Thing
    b. Crabs0
    c. Undefined
    d. Undefined

57. An _____ is a long period of time with different technical and colloquial meanings, and usages in language. It begins with some beginning event known as an epoch, epochal date, epochal event or epochal moment.
    a. Era0
    b. Thing
    c. Undefined
    d. Undefined

Chapter 7. Evolution-The Theory and its Supporting Evidence

58. In biology and ecology, _____ is the cessation of existence of a species or group of taxa, reducing biodiversity. The moment of _____ is generally considered to be the death of the last individual of that species.
   a. Thing
   b. Extinction0
   c. Undefined
   d. Undefined

59. _____ are unicellular microorganisms. They are typically a few micrometres long and have many shapes including curved rods, spheres, rods, and spirals.
   a. Thing
   b. Bacteria0
   c. Undefined
   d. Undefined

60. In ecology, a _____ is a term describing the relational position of a species or population in an ecosystem.
   a. Niche0
   b. Thing
   c. Undefined
   d. Undefined

61. _____ were vertebrate animals that dominated terrestrial ecosystems for over 160 million years, first appearing approximately 230 million years ago. At the end of the Cretaceous Period, approximately 65 million years ago, a catastrophic extinction event ended _____' dominance on land.
   a. Thing
   b. Dinosaurs0
   c. Undefined
   d. Undefined

62. The _____ is the earliest of three geologic eras of the Phanerozoic eon. The _____ is subdivided into six geologic periods; from oldest to youngest they are: the Cambrian, Ordovician, Silurian, Devonian, Carboniferous, and Permian.
   a. Thing
   b. Paleozoic0
   c. Undefined
   d. Undefined

63. A _____ is a landform that extends above the surrounding terrain in a limited area. A _____ is generally steeper than a hill, but there is no universally accepted standard definition for the height of a _____ or a hill although a _____ usually has an identifiable summit.
   a. Place
   b. Mountain0
   c. Undefined
   d. Undefined

64. _____ is a field of study within geology concerned generally with the structures within the crust of the Earth, or other planets, and particularly with the forces and movements that have operated in a region to create these structures.
   a. Thing
   b. Tectonics0
   c. Undefined
   d. Undefined

65. _____ is the science and study of the solid matter that constitute the Earth. Encompassing such things as rocks, soil, and gemstones, _____ studies the composition, structure, physical properties, history, and the processes that shape Earth's components.
   a. Thing
   b. Geology0
   c. Undefined
   d. Undefined

66. A _____ is a largely obsolete term for a subsiding linear trough that was caused by the accumulation of sedimentary rock strata deposited in a basin and subsequently compressed, deformed, and uplifted into a mountain range, with attendant volcanism and plutonism.

Chapter 7. Evolution-The Theory and its Supporting Evidence

a. Thing
c. Undefined
b. Geosyncline0
d. Undefined

67. An _____ is a type of atom that is defined by its atomic number; that is, by the number of protons in its nucleus.
a. Element0
c. Undefined
b. Thing
d. Undefined

68. A _____ is a natural underground void large enough for a human to enter. Some people suggest that the term '_____' should only apply to cavities that have some part which does not receive daylight; however, in popular usage, the term includes smaller spaces like a sea _____, rock shelters, and grottos.
a. Cave0
c. Undefined
b. Place
d. Undefined

69. The _____ is a member of the Canidae family and a close relative of the Gray Wolf. They may occasionally assemble in small packs, but generally hunt alone.
a. Thing
c. Undefined
b. Coyote0
d. Undefined

70. _____ is the family of carnivorous and omnivorous mammals. It includes dogs, wolves, foxes, coyotes, dingoes and jackals. These animals are all digitigrades, meaning they walk on their toes.
a. Thing
c. Undefined
b. Canidae0
d. Undefined

71. The _____ is generally the most familiar of the species. It has the widest range not just of any fox but of any terrestrial carnivore. As its name suggests, its fur is predominantly reddish-brown, but there is a naturally occurring grey morph which is silver.
a. Red Fox0
c. Undefined
b. Thing
d. Undefined

72. _____ is a chemical element. An abundant nonmetallic, tetravalent element, _____ has several allotropic forms. This element is the basis of the chemistry of all known life.
a. Thing
c. Undefined
b. Carbon0
d. Undefined

73. _____ is a chemical element which has the symbol N and atomic number 7. Elemental _____ is a colorless, odourless, tasteless and mostly inert diatomic gas at standard conditions, constituting 78.1% by volume of Earth's atmosphere.
a. Thing
c. Undefined
b. Nitrogen0
d. Undefined

74. _____ are tetrapods and amniotes, animals whose embryos are surrounded by an amniotic membrane, and members of the class Sauropsida.They rely on gathering and losing heat from the environment to regulate their internal temperature, e.g, by moving between sun and shade, or by preferential circulation — moving warmed blood into the body core, while pushing cool blood to the periphery.

a. Thing
b. Reptiles0
c. Undefined
d. Undefined

75. _____ are a taxon of animals that include all living tetrapods or four-legged vertebrates, that do not have amniotic eggs, are ectothermic, term for the animals whose body heat is regulated by the external environment; previously known as cold-blooded, and generally spend part of their time on land.
a. Amphibians0
b. Thing
c. Undefined
d. Undefined

76. A _____ is a ruminant mammal belonging to the family Cervidae. A number of broadly similar animals from related families within the order Artiodactyla are often also called this.
a. Thing
b. Deer0
c. Undefined
d. Undefined

77. _____ make up the most species-rich order of insects. The order's scientific name, Coleoptera, means "sheathed wing", and contains more described species in it than in any other order in the animal kingdom.
a. Beetles0
b. Thing
c. Undefined
d. Undefined

78. _____ are a major group of arthropods and the most diverse group of animals on the Earth, with over a million described species—more than all other animal groups combined. They may be found in nearly all environments on the planet, although only a small number of species occur in the oceans where crustaceans tend to predominate instead.
a. Thing
b. Insects0
c. Undefined
d. Undefined

79. The U.S Environmental Protection Agency defines a _____ as "any substance or mixture of substances intended for preventing, destroying, repelling, or lessening the damage of any pest".
a. Thing
b. Pesticide0
c. Undefined
d. Undefined

80. _____ is an ecological concept referring to the relative representation of a species in a particular ecosystem. It is usually measured as the mean number of individuals found per sample.
a. Abundance0
b. Thing
c. Undefined
d. Undefined

81. _____ is the earliest and most primitive known bird to date. It lived in the late Jurassic Period around 155-150 million years ago in what is now southern Germany.
a. Thing
b. Archaeopteryx0
c. Undefined
d. Undefined

82. The term _____ refers to water and can be either a noun or an adjective. Dictionary definitions do not specify what kind of water, although in both general use and in the sciences, the implication is often that of fresh water.
a. Thing
b. Aquatic0
c. Undefined
d. Undefined

Chapter 7. Evolution-The Theory and its Supporting Evidence

83. _____ refers to a group of perissodactyl mammals that evolved in the mid Eocene around 40 million years ago from small, forest animals similar to the early horses. By the late Oligocene, they had divided into two groups: one that grazed in open areas and another that was more adapted to woodlands.
   a. Thing
   b. Chalicothere0
   c. Undefined
   d. Undefined

84. An _____ is a population of an organism which is at risk of becoming extinct because it is either few in number, or threatened by changing environmental or predation parameters. An _____ is usually a taxonomic species, but may be another evolutionary significant unit such as a subspecies.
   a. Thing
   b. Endangered species0
   c. Undefined
   d. Undefined

85. In geography, _____ latitudes of the globe lie between the tropics and the polar circles. The changes in these regions between summer and winter are generally subtle: warm or cool, rather than extreme hot or cold.
   a. Thing
   b. Temperate0
   c. Undefined
   d. Undefined

86. _____ contains low concentrations of dissolved salts and other total dissolved solids. It is an important renewable resource, necessary for the survival of most terrestrial organisms, and required by humans for drinking and agriculture, among many other uses.
   a. Fresh water0
   b. Thing
   c. Undefined
   d. Undefined

87. _____ is any particulate matter that can be transported by fluid flow and which eventually is deposited as a layer of solid particles on the bed or bottom of a body of water or other liquid.
   a. Thing
   b. Sediment0
   c. Undefined
   d. Undefined

88. In population genetics, _____ is the transfer of alleles of genes from one population to another.
   a. Gene flow0
   b. Thing
   c. Undefined
   d. Undefined

89. A _____ is an insect of the order Lepidoptera. They are notable for their unusual life cycle with a larval caterpillar stage, an inactive pupal stage and a spectacular metamorphosis into a familiar and colorful winged adult form, and most species being day-flying, they regularly attract attention.
   a. Butterfly0
   b. Thing
   c. Undefined
   d. Undefined

90. _____ represent the largest generally accepted groupings of animals and other living things with certain evolutionary traits.
   a. Thing
   b. Phyla0
   c. Undefined
   d. Undefined

91. _____ is an English word that describes any animal without a spinal column.

Chapter 7. Evolution-The Theory and its Supporting Evidence

a. Thing
b. Invertebrate0
c. Undefined
d. Undefined

92. _____ are fish with a full cartilaginous skeleton and a streamlined body. They respire with the use of five to seven gill slits.
a. Thing
b. Sharks0
c. Undefined
d. Undefined

93. _____ is a common and widely distributed type of rock formed by high-grade regional metamorphic processes from preexisting formations that were originally either igneous or sedimentary rocks. Gneissic rocks are usually medium to coarse foliated and largely recrystallized but do not carry large quantities of micas, chlorite or other platy minerals.
a. Gneiss0
b. Thing
c. Undefined
d. Undefined

94. _____ is the highest mountain within _____ National Park, and the second highest in the U.S. state of Wyoming. The origin of the name is controversial. The most common explanation is that "_____" means "large teat" in French, named by either French-Canadian or Iroquois members of an expedition led by Donald McKenzie of the Northwest Company.
a. Grand Teton0
b. Place
c. Undefined
d. Undefined

95. _____ is a United States National Park located in western Wyoming, south of Yellowstone National Park. It was established as a national park on February 26, 1929. The park covers 484 mi² of land and water.
a. Place
b. Grand Teton National Park0
c. Undefined
d. Undefined

96. _____ is a common and widely occurring type of intrusive, felsic, igneous rock. Granites are usually medium to coarsely crystalline, occasionally with some individual crystals larger than the groundmass forming a rock known as porphyry. Granites can be pink to dark gray or even black, depending on their chemistry and mineralogy.
a. Granite0
b. Thing
c. Undefined
d. Undefined

97. The _____ is a small but dramatic mountain range of the Rocky Mountains in North America. A north-south range, it is on the Wyoming side of the state's border with Idaho, just south of Yellowstone National Park.
a. Place
b. Teton Range0
c. Undefined
d. Undefined

98. The _____ refers to a group of medium-grade metamorphic rocks, chiefly notable for the preponderance of lamellar minerals such as micas, chlorite, talc, hornblende, graphite, and others. Quartz often occurs in drawn-out grains to such an extent that a particular form called quartz _____ is produced.
a. Thing
b. Schist0
c. Undefined
d. Undefined

99. The _____ is a geologic eon before the Proterozoic. Instead of being based on stratigraphy, this date is defined chronometrically. The lower boundary has not been officially recognized by the International Commission on Stratigraphy, but it is usually set at the end of the Hadean eon.

a. Archean0
b. Thing
c. Undefined
d. Undefined

Chapter 8. Precambrian Earth and Life History-The Hadean and Archean

1. The _____ is the geologic eon before the Archean. It extends back to the Earth's formation, and ended roughly 3.8 billion years ago, though the date varies according to different sources.
   a. Hadean0
   b. Thing
   c. Undefined
   d. Undefined

2. _____ can be defined as the solid state recrystallisation of pre-existing rocks due to changes in heat and/or pressure and/or introduction of fluids. There will be mineralogical, chemical and crystallographic changes. _____ produced with increasing pressure and temperature conditions is known as prograde _____. Conversely, decreasing temperatures and pressure characterize retrograde _____.
   a. Thing
   b. Metamorphism0
   c. Undefined
   d. Undefined

3. The _____ is a geologic eon before the Proterozoic. Instead of being based on stratigraphy, this date is defined chronometrically. The lower boundary has not been officially recognized by the International Commission on Stratigraphy, but it is usually set at the end of the Hadean eon.
   a. Thing
   b. Archean0
   c. Undefined
   d. Undefined

4. Fossils are the mineralized or otherwise preserved remains or traces of animals, plants, and other organisms. The totality of fossils, both discovered and undiscovered, and their placement in fossiliferous rock formations and sedimentary layers is known as the _____ record.
   a. Thing
   b. Fossil0
   c. Undefined
   d. Undefined

5. The _____ is an informal name for the eons of the geologic timescale that came before the current Phanerozoic eon. It spans from the formation of Earth around 4500 Ma to the evolution of abundant macroscopic hard-shelled animals, which marked the beginning of the Cambrian, the first period of the first era of the Phanerozoic eon, some 542 Ma.
   a. Thing
   b. Precambrian0
   c. Undefined
   d. Undefined

6. A _____ is one of several large landmasses on Earth. They are generally identified by convention rather than any strict criteria, but seven areas are commonly reckoned as continents – they are: Asia, Africa, North America, South America, Antarctica, Europe, and Australia.
   a. Continent0
   b. Thing
   c. Undefined
   d. Undefined

7. A _____ is an old and stable part of the continental crust that has survived the merging and splitting of continents and supercontinents. Cratons are generally found in the interiors of continents and are characteristically composed of ancient crystalline basement crust of lightweight felsic igneous rock such as granite. They have a thick crust and deep roots that extend into the mantle beneath to depths of 200 km.
   a. Thing
   b. Craton0
   c. Undefined
   d. Undefined

8. A _____ in geology is an intrusive igneous rock body that crystallized from a magma below the surface of the Earth. Plutons include batholiths, dikes, sills, laccoliths, lopoliths, and other igneous bodies. In practice, "_____" usually refers to a distinctive mass of igneous rock, typically kilometers in dimension, without a tabular shape like those of dikes and sills.

Chapter 8. Precambrian Earth and Life History-The Hadean and Archean

a. Pluton0
b. Thing
c. Undefined
d. Undefined

9. _____ is a common and widely occurring type of intrusive, felsic, igneous rock. Granites are usually medium to coarsely crystalline, occasionally with some individual crystals larger than the groundmass forming a rock known as porphyry. Granites can be pink to dark gray or even black, depending on their chemistry and mineralogy.
a. Thing
b. Granite0
c. Undefined
d. Undefined

10. _____ is a general field petrologic term applied to metamorphic and/or altered mafic volcanic rock. The green is due to abundant green chlorite, actinolite and epidote minerals that dominate the rock.
a. Greenschist0
b. Thing
c. Undefined
d. Undefined

11. _____ are zones of variably metamorphosed mafic to ultramafic volcanic sequences with associated sedimentary rocks that occur within Archaean and Proterozoic cratons between granite and gneiss bodies. The belts have been interpreted as having formed at ancient oceanic spreading centers and island arc terranes.
a. Greenstone belts0
b. Thing
c. Undefined
d. Undefined

12. _____ rock is one of the three main rock groups. Rock formed from these covers 75% of the Earth's land area, and includes common types such as chalk, limestone, dolomite, sandstone, and shale.
a. Sedimentary0
b. Thing
c. Undefined
d. Undefined

13. _____ is one of the three main rock groups. _____ covers 75% of the Earth's land area. Four basic processes are involved in the formation of a clastic _____: weathering caused mainly by friction of waves, transportation where the sediment is carried along by a current, deposition and compaction where the sediment is squashed together to form a rock of this kind.
a. Sedimentary rock0
b. Thing
c. Undefined
d. Undefined

14. _____ rocks form when molten rock, magma, cools and solidifies, with or without crystallization, either below the surface as intrusive, plutonic rocks or on the surface as extrusive, volcanic, rocks.
a. Thing
b. Igneous0
c. Undefined
d. Undefined

15. _____ is a field of study within geology concerned generally with the structures within the crust of the Earth, or other planets, and particularly with the forces and movements that have operated in a region to create these structures.
a. Tectonics0
b. Thing
c. Undefined
d. Undefined

16. The _____ is the current eon in the geologic timescale, and the one during which abundant animal life has existed. It covers roughly 545 million years and goes back to the time when diverse hard-shelled animals first appeared.

Chapter 8. Precambrian Earth and Life History-The Hadean and Archean

    a. Thing
    c. Undefined
    b. Phanerozoic0
    d. Undefined

17. _____ is a theory of geology that has been developed to explain the observed evidence for large scale motions of the Earth's lithosphere. The theory encompassed and superseded the older theory of continental drift.
    a. Plate tectonics0
    c. Undefined
    b. Thing
    d. Undefined

18. The _____ is a geological eon representing a period before the first abundant complex life on Earth. The _____ Eon extended from 2500 million years ago to 542.0 ± 1.0 million years ago. The _____ is the most recent part of the old informal Precambrian time.
    a. Proterozoic0
    c. Undefined
    b. Thing
    d. Undefined

19. A _____ is an opening, or rupture, in the Earth's surface or crust, which allows hot, molten rock, ash and gases to escape from deep below the surface.
    a. Volcano0
    c. Undefined
    b. Thing
    d. Undefined

20. A _____ in physical geography describes the collective mass of water found on, under, and over the surface of a planet.
    a. Hydrosphere0
    c. Undefined
    b. Thing
    d. Undefined

21. An _____ is a layer of gases that may surround a material body of sufficient mass. The gases are attracted by the gravity of the body, and are retained for a longer duration if gravity is high and the _____'s temperature is low. Some planets consist mainly of various gases, and thus have very deep atmospheres.
    a. Place
    c. Undefined
    b. Atmosphere0
    d. Undefined

22. _____ are unicellular microorganisms. They are typically a few micrometres long and have many shapes including curved rods, spheres, rods, and spirals.
    a. Bacteria0
    c. Undefined
    b. Thing
    d. Undefined

23. _____ is a highly sought-after precious metal which, for many centuries, has been used as money, a store of value and in jewelery. The metal occurs as nuggets or grains in rocks, underground "veins" and in alluvial deposits. It is one of the coinage metals. Itis dense, soft, shiny and the most malleable and ductile of the known metals.
    a. Gold0
    c. Undefined
    b. Thing
    d. Undefined

24. _____ is a chemical element in the periodic table that has the symbol Zn and atomic number 30. In some historical and sculptural contexts, it is known as spelter.
    a. Thing
    c. Undefined
    b. Zinc0
    d. Undefined

Chapter 8. Precambrian Earth and Life History-The Hadean and Archean

25. _____ is a chemical element. A heavy, malleable, ductile, precious, grey-white transition metal, it is resistant to corrosion and occurs in some nickel and copper ores along with some native deposits. It is used in jewelry, laboratory equipment, electrical contacts, dentistry, and automobile emissions control devices.
   a. Platinum0
   b. Thing
   c. Undefined
   d. Undefined

26. _____ is a ductile metal with excellent electrical conductivity, and finds extensive use as an electrical conductor, heat conductor, as a building material, and as a component of various alloys.
   a. Copper0
   b. Thing
   c. Undefined
   d. Undefined

27. The _____ is a major division of the geologic timescale. The _____ is the earliest period in whose rocks are found numerous large, distinctly fossilizable multicellular organisms that are more complex than sponges or medusoids. During this time, roughly fifty separate major groups of organisms or "phyla" emerged suddenly, in most cases without evident precursors. This radiation of animal phyla is referred to as the _____ explosion.
   a. Event
   b. Cambrian0
   c. Undefined
   d. Undefined

28. The _____ is the current eon in the geologic timescale, and the one during which abundant animal life has existed. It covers roughly 545 million years and goes back to the time when diverse hard-shelled animals first appeared.
   a. Thing
   b. Phanerozoic Eon0
   c. Undefined
   d. Undefined

29. The _____ is used by geologists and other scientists to describe the timing and relationships between events that have occurred during the history of Earth.
   a. Thing
   b. Geological time scale0
   c. Undefined
   d. Undefined

30. _____, a branch of geology, studies rock layers and layering. It is primarily used in the study of sedimentary and layered volcanic rocks. _____ includes two related subfields: lithologic or lithostratigraphy and biologic _____ or biostratigraphy.
   a. Stratigraphy0
   b. Thing
   c. Undefined
   d. Undefined

31. The _____ is the earliest of three geologic eras of the Phanerozoic eon. The _____ is subdivided into six geologic periods; from oldest to youngest they are: the Cambrian, Ordovician, Silurian, Devonian, Carboniferous, and Permian.
   a. Thing
   b. Paleozoic0
   c. Undefined
   d. Undefined

32. An _____ is a long period of time with different technical and colloquial meanings, and usages in language. It begins with some beginning event known as an epoch, epochal date, epochal event or epochal moment.
   a. Era0
   b. Thing
   c. Undefined
   d. Undefined

33. The _____ is one of three geologic eras of the Phanerozoic eon. The _____ was a time of tectonic, climatic and evolutionary activity, shifting from a state of connectedness into their present configuration. The climate was exceptionally warm throughout the period, also playing an important role in the evolution and diversification of new animal species. By the end of the era, the basis of modern life was in place.
   a. Thing
   b. Mesozoic0
   c. Undefined
   d. Undefined

34. The _____ Era meaning "new life", is the most recent of the three classic geological eras. It covers the 65.5 million years since the Cretaceous-Tertiary extinction event at the end of the Cretaceous that marked the demise of the last non-avian dinosaurs and the end of the Mesozoic Era. The _____ era is ongoing.
   a. Thing
   b. Cenozoic0
   c. Undefined
   d. Undefined

35. The _____ is the most recent of the three classic geological eras. It covers the 65.5 million years since the Cretaceous-Tertiary extinction event at the end of the Cretaceous that marked the demise of the last non-avian dinosaurs and the end of the Mesozoic Era.
   a. Thing
   b. Cenozoic era0
   c. Undefined
   d. Undefined

36. A _____ is a natural object originating in outer space that survives an impact with the Earth's surface without being destroyed. While in space it is called a meteoroid. When it enters the atmosphere, air resistance causes the body to heat up and emit light, thus forming a fireball.
   a. Thing
   b. Meteorite0
   c. Undefined
   d. Undefined

37. _____ refers to things having to do with the land or with the planet Earth.
   a. Thing
   b. Terrestrial0
   c. Undefined
   d. Undefined

38. A _____, telluric planet or rocky planet is a planet that is primarily composed of silicate rocks. Terrestrial planets are substantially different from gas giants, which might not have solid surfaces and are composed mostly of some combination of hydrogen, helium, and water existing in various physical states.
   a. Thing
   b. Terrestrial planet0
   c. Undefined
   d. Undefined

39. A _____, as defined by the International Astronomical Union, is a celestial body orbiting a star or stellar remnant that is massive enough to be rounded by its own gravity, not massive enough to cause thermonuclear fusion in its core, and has cleared its neighboring region of planetesimals.
   a. Thing
   b. Planet0
   c. Undefined
   d. Undefined

40. Water collecting on the ground or in a stream, river, lake, or wetland is called _____; as opposed to groundwater. _____ is naturally replenished by precipitation and naturally lost through discharge to the oceans, evaporation, and sub-surface seepage into the groundwater. _____ is the largest source of fresh water.

Chapter 8. Precambrian Earth and Life History-The Hadean and Archean 131

   a. Surface water0
   c. Undefined
   b. Thing
   d. Undefined

41. _____ is a common and widely distributed type of rock formed by high-grade regional metamorphic processes from preexisting formations that were originally either igneous or sedimentary rocks. Gneissic rocks are usually medium to coarse foliated and largely recrystallized but do not carry large quantities of micas, chlorite or other platy minerals.
   a. Gneiss0
   c. Undefined
   b. Thing
   d. Undefined

42. The _____ is the layer of granitic, sedimentary, and metamorphic rocks which form the continents and the areas of shallow seabed close to their shores, known as continental shelves. It is less dense than the material of the Earth's mantle and thus "floats" on top of it. _____ is also less dense than oceanic crust, though it is considerably thicker. About 40% of the Earth's surface is now underlain by _____.
   a. Continental crust0
   c. Undefined
   b. Thing
   d. Undefined

43. The _____ is a rock outcrop of Archaean tonalite gneiss in the Slave craton in Northwest Territories, Canada. It is the oldest known crustal rock outcrop in the world.
   a. Thing
   c. Undefined
   b. Acasta Gneiss0
   d. Undefined

44. In geology, a _____ is the outermost layer of a planet, part of its lithosphere. They are generally composed of a less dense material than its deeper layers. Earths' is composed mainly of basalt and granite. It is cooler and more rigid than the deeper layers of the mantle and core.
   a. Thing
   c. Undefined
   b. Crust0
   d. Undefined

45. _____ is the oxide of silicon, chemical formula SiO_2, and is known for its hardness as early as the 16th century. It is a principle component in most types of glass and substances such as concrete.
   a. Silica0
   c. Undefined
   b. Thing
   d. Undefined

46. _____ is a silvery and ductile member of the poor metal group of chemical elements. It has the symbol Al and atomic number 13.
   a. Thing
   c. Undefined
   b. Aluminum0
   d. Undefined

47. In geology, a _____ zone is an area on Earth where two tectonic plates meet and move towards one another, with one sliding underneath the other and moving down into the mantle, at rates typically measured in centimeters per year. An oceanic plate ordinarily slides underneath a continental plate; this often creates an orogenic zone with many volcanoes and earthquakes.
   a. Thing
   c. Undefined
   b. Subduction0
   d. Undefined

Chapter 8. Precambrian Earth and Life History-The Hadean and Archean

48. _____ is molten rock located beneath the surface of the Earth, and which often collects in a _____ chamber. _____ is a complex high-temperature fluid substance. Most are silicate solutions. It is capable of intrusion into adjacent rocks or of extrusion onto the surface as lava or ejected explosively as tephra to form pyroclastic rock. Environments of _____ formation include subduction zones, continental rift zones, mid-oceanic ridges, and hotspots, some of which are interpreted as mantle plumes.
   a. Thing
   b. Magma0
   c. Undefined
   d. Undefined

49. An _____ is any piece of land that is completely surrounded by water, above high tide. There are two main types of islands: continental islands and oceanic islands. There are also artificial islands. A grouping of geographically and/or geologically related islands is called an archipelago.
   a. Island0
   b. Thing
   c. Undefined
   d. Undefined

50. _____ is the process of heating a solid substance to a point where it turns into a liquid. An object that has melted is molten.
   a. Melting0
   b. Thing
   c. Undefined
   d. Undefined

51. _____ is an igneous, volcanic rock, of intermediate composition, with aphanitic to porphyritic texture.
   a. Thing
   b. Andesite0
   c. Undefined
   d. Undefined

52. Mean _____ is the average height of the sea, with reference to a suitable reference surface.
   a. Sea level0
   b. Thing
   c. Undefined
   d. Undefined

53. A _____ is a landform that extends above the surrounding terrain in a limited area. A _____ is generally steeper than a hill, but there is no universally accepted standard definition for the height of a _____ or a hill although a _____ usually has an identifiable summit.
   a. Mountain0
   b. Place
   c. Undefined
   d. Undefined

54. _____ is the process of building mountains, and may be studied as a tectonic structural event, as a geographical event and a chronological event, in that orogenic events cause distinctive structural phenomena and related tectonic activity, affect certain regions of rocks and crust and happen within a time frame.
   a. Thing
   b. Orogeny0
   c. Undefined
   d. Undefined

55. The _____ is a large shield covered by a thin layer of soil that forms the nucleus of the North American craton. It has a deep, common, joined bedrock region in eastern and central Canada and stretches North from the Great Lakes to the Arctic Ocean, covering half the country.
   a. Thing
   b. Canadian Shield0
   c. Undefined
   d. Undefined

Chapter 8. Precambrian Earth and Life History-The Hadean and Archean

56. _____ is a self-governed Danish territory lying between the Arctic and Atlantic Oceans. Though geographically and ethnically an Arctic island nation associated with the continent of North America, politically and historically _____ is closely tied to Europe. It is the largest island in the world that is not also considered a continent.
   a. Greenland0
   b. Place
   c. Undefined
   d. Undefined

57. A _____ is a body of water or other liquid of considerable size contained on a body of land. A vast majority are fresh water, and lie in the Northern Hemisphere at higher latitudes. Most have a natural outflow in the form of a river or stream, but some do not, and lose water solely by evaporation and/or underground seepage.
   a. Lake0
   b. Thing
   c. Undefined
   d. Undefined

58. _____, bounded by Ontario, Canada and Minnesota, USA, to the north and Wisconsin and Michigan, USA, to the south, is the largest of North America's Great Lakes. It is the largest freshwater lake in the world by surface area and is the world's third-largest freshwater lake by volume.
   a. Place
   b. Lake Superior0
   c. Undefined
   d. Undefined

59. _____ is located in the northeastern part of New York. The mountains are often included by geographers in the Appalachian Mountains, but they are geologically more similar to the Laurentian Mountains of Canada. The _____ are within the 6.1 million acres of Adirondack Park, which includes a constitutionally-protected Forest Preserve of approximately 2.3 million acres.
   a. Place
   b. Adirondack Mountains0
   c. Undefined
   d. Undefined

60. _____ is the study of Earth's surface features or those of other planets, moons, and asteroids
   a. Topography0
   b. Thing
   c. Undefined
   d. Undefined

61. The _____ on the geologic timescale had been intended to cover the world's recent period of repeated glaciations. The _____ follows the Pliocene and is followed by the Holocene. The _____ is the third epoch of the Neogene period or 6th epoch of the Cenozoic era. The end of the _____ corresponds with the end of the Paleolithic age used in archaeology. The _____ is divided into the Early _____, Middle _____ and Late _____, and numerous faunal stages.
   a. Thing
   b. Pleistocene0
   c. Undefined
   d. Undefined

62. _____ is displacement of solids by the agents of ocean currents, wind, water, or ice by downward or down-slope movement in response to gravity or by living organisms.
   a. Thing
   b. Erosion0
   c. Undefined
   d. Undefined

63. _____ is a common gray to black extrusive volcanic rock. It is usually fine-grained due to rapid cooling of lava on the Earth's surface. It may be porphyritic containing larger crystals in a fine matrix, or vesicular, or frothy scoria.

Chapter 8. Precambrian Earth and Life History-The Hadean and Archean

a. Thing
b. Basalt0
c. Undefined
d. Undefined

64. The _____ are a broad mountain range in western North America. The _____ stretch more than 4,800 kilometers from northernmost British Columbia, in Canada, to New Mexico, in the United States.
   a. Rocky Mountains0
   b. Place
   c. Undefined
   d. Undefined

65. _____ is the result of the transformation of a pre-existing rock type, the protolith, in a process called metamorphism, which means "change in form". The protolith is subjected to heat and extreme pressure causing profound physical and/or chemical change. The protolith may be sedimentary rock, igneous rock or another older rock.
   a. Thing
   b. Metamorphic rock0
   c. Undefined
   d. Undefined

66. Metamorphic rock is the result of the transformation of a pre-existing rock type, the protolith, in a process called metamorphism. The protolith is subjected to heat and extreme pressure causing profound physical and/or chemical change. _____ make up a large part of the Earth's crust. They are formed deep beneath the Earth's surface by great stresses from rocks above and high pressures and temperatures.
   a. Metamorphic rocks0
   b. Thing
   c. Undefined
   d. Undefined

67. A _____ is a deep valley between cliffs often carved from the landscape by a river. Most were formed by a process of long-time erosion from a plateau level. The cliffs form because harder rock strata that are resistant to erosion and weathering remain exposed on the valley walls.
   a. Canyon0
   b. Thing
   c. Undefined
   d. Undefined

68. The _____ is a very colorful, steep-sided gorge, carved by the Colorado River in the U.S. state of Arizona. It is one of the first national parks in the United States.
   a. Place
   b. Grand Canyon0
   c. Undefined
   d. Undefined

69. The _____ refers to a group of medium-grade metamorphic rocks, chiefly notable for the preponderance of lamellar minerals such as micas, chlorite, talc, hornblende, graphite, and others. Quartz often occurs in drawn-out grains to such an extent that a particular form called quartz _____ is produced.
   a. Schist0
   b. Thing
   c. Undefined
   d. Undefined

70. _____ is molten rock expelled by a volcano during an eruption. When first extruded from a volcanic vent, it is a liquid at temperatures from 700 °C to 1,200 °C.
   a. Lava0
   b. Thing
   c. Undefined
   d. Undefined

71. _____ is a dense, coarse-grained igneous rock, consisting mostly of the minerals olivine and pyroxene. _____ is ultramafic and ultrabasic, as the rock contains less than 45% silica. This type of rock is derived from the Earth's mantle, either as solid blocks and fragments, or as crystals accumulated from magmas that formed in the mantle.

Chapter 8. Precambrian Earth and Life History-The Hadean and Archean   135

a. Thing
b. Peridotite0
c. Undefined
d. Undefined

72. A _____ fault is a particular type of fault, or break in the fabric of the Earth's crust with resulting movement of each side against the other, in which a lower stratigraphic position is pushed up and over another. This is the result of compressional forces.
a. Thrust0
b. Thing
c. Undefined
d. Undefined

73. _____ is an igneous rock of volcanic origin. They often have a vesicular texture, which is the result voids left by volatiles escaping from the molten lava. Pumice is a rock, which is an example of explosive volcanic eruption. It is so vesicular that it floats in water.
a. Volcanic rock0
b. Thing
c. Undefined
d. Undefined

74. Faults are planar rock fractures, which show evidence of relative movement. Large faults within the Earth's crust are the result of shear motion and active _____ zones are the causal locations of most earthquakes. Earthquakes are caused by energy release during rapid slippage along faults. The largest examples are at tectonic plate boundaries but many faults occur far from active plate boundaries. Since faults do not usually consist of a single, clean fracture, the term _____ zone is used when referring to the zone of complex deformation that is associated with the _____ plane.
a. Thing
b. Fault0
c. Undefined
d. Undefined

75. _____ forms when rock cools and solidifies either below the surface as intrusive rocks or on the surface as extrusive rocks. This magma can be derived from partial melts of pre-existing rocks in either the Earth's mantle or crust. Typically, the melting is caused by one or more of the following processes -- an increase in temperature, a decrease in pressure, or a change in composition.
a. Igneous rock0
b. Thing
c. Undefined
d. Undefined

76. A _____ is a compound that contains this group, with chlorine in oxidation state +3. They are also known as salts of chlorous acid.
a. Thing
b. Chlorite0
c. Undefined
d. Undefined

77. _____ are clastic rocks composed solely or primarily of volcanic materials.
a. Pyroclastics0
b. Thing
c. Undefined
d. Undefined

78. Earth's _____ is a ~2,900 km thick rocky shell comprizing approximately 70% of Earth's volume. It is predominantly solid and overlies the Earth's iron-rich core, which occupies about 30% of Earth's volume. Past episodes of melting and volcanism at the shallower levels of the _____ have produced a very thin crust of crystallized melt products near the surface, upon which we live.
a. Mantle0
b. Thing
c. Undefined
d. Undefined

Chapter 8. Precambrian Earth and Life History-The Hadean and Archean

79. A _____ is a landform where the mouth of a river flows into an ocean, sea, desert, estuary or lake. It builds up sediment outwards into the flat area which the river's flow encounters transported by the water and set down as the currents slow.
   a. Thing
   b. Delta0
   c. Undefined
   d. Undefined

80. _____ is the geological process whereby material is added to a landform. This is the process by which wind and water create a sediment deposit, through the laying down of granular material that has been eroded and transported from another geographical location.
   a. Deposition0
   b. Thing
   c. Undefined
   d. Undefined

81. _____ is a fine-grained sedimentary rock whose original constituents were clays or muds. It is characterized by thin laminae breaking with an irregular curving fracture, often splintery and usually parallel to the often-indistinguishable bedding plane.
   a. Shale0
   b. Thing
   c. Undefined
   d. Undefined

82. _____ is a cloudiness or haziness of water caused by individual particles that are generally invisible to the naked eye, thus being much like smoke in air. _____ is generally caused by phytoplankton. Measurement of _____ is a key test of water quality.
   a. Turbidity0
   b. Thing
   c. Undefined
   d. Undefined

83. A _____ is a current of rapidly moving, sediment-laden water moving down a slope through air, water, or another fluid. The current moves because it has a higher density and turbidity than the fluid through which it flows.
   a. Turbidity current0
   b. Thing
   c. Undefined
   d. Undefined

84. _____ is a sedimentary rock composed mainly of sand-size mineral or rock grains. Most _____ is composed of quartz and/or feldspar because these are the most common minerals in the Earth's crust. Like sand, _____ may be any color, but the most common colors are tan, brown, yellow, red, gray and white.
   a. Sandstone0
   b. Thing
   c. Undefined
   d. Undefined

85. An _____ is a fine-grained sedimentary rock composed predominantly of indurated clay particles. Argillites are basically lithified muds and oozes. They contain variable amounts of silt-sized particles.
   a. Argillite0
   b. Thing
   c. Undefined
   d. Undefined

86. _____ is the second most common mineral in the Earth's continental crust. It is made up of a lattice of silica tetrahedra. _____ belongs to the rhombohedral crystal system. In nature _____ crystals are often twinned, distorted, or so intergrown with adjacent crystals of _____ or other minerals as to only show part of this shape, or to lack obvious crystal faces altogether and appear massive.

Chapter 8. Precambrian Earth and Life History-The Hadean and Archean

a. Quartz0
b. Thing
c. Undefined
d. Undefined

87. Ocean _____ are any more or less continuous, directed movement of ocean water that flows in one of the Earth's oceans.They are rivers of hot or cold water within the ocean. They are generated from the forces acting upon the water like the earth's rotation, the wind, the temperature and salinity differences and the gravitation of the moon.
    a. Thing
    b. Currents0
    c. Undefined
    d. Undefined

88. _____ is a term used to describe a group of hydrous aluminium phyllosilicate minerals, that are typically less than 2 micrometres in diameter. _____ consists of a variety of phyllosilicate minerals rich in silicon and aluminium oxides and hydroxides which include variable amounts of structural water. Clays are generally formed by the chemical weathering of silicate-bearing rocks by carbonic acid but some are formed by hydrothermal activity.
    a. Thing
    b. Clay0
    c. Undefined
    d. Undefined

89. In organic chemistry, a _____ is a salt of carbonic acid.
    a. Carbonate0
    b. Thing
    c. Undefined
    d. Undefined

90. A _____ is a rock consisting of individual stones that have become cemented together. Conglomerates are sedimentary rocks consisting of rounded fragements and are thus differentiated from breccias, which consist of angular clasts. Both conglomerates and breccias are characterized by clasts larger than sand.
    a. Thing
    b. Conglomerate0
    c. Undefined
    d. Undefined

91. _____ is a fine-grained silica-rich cryptocrystalline sedimentary rock that may contain small fossils. It varies greatly in color from white to black, but most often manifests as gray, brown, grayish brown and light green to rusty red; its color is an expression of trace elements present in the rock, and both red and green are most often related to traces of iron.
    a. Chert0
    b. Thing
    c. Undefined
    d. Undefined

92. _____ is a chemical element metal. It is a lustrous, silvery soft metal. It and nickel are notable for being the final elements produced by stellar nucleosynthesis, and thus are the heaviest elements which do not require a supernova or similarly cataclysmic event for formation.
    a. Thing
    b. Iron0
    c. Undefined
    d. Undefined

93. _____ are a distinctive type of rock often found in old sedimentary rocks. The structures consist of repeated thin layers of iron oxides, either magnetite or hematite, alternating with bands of iron-poor shale and chert. The conventional concept is that the banded iron layers were formed in water as the result of oxygen released by photosynthetic cyanobacteria, combining with dissolved iron in Earth's oceans to form insoluble iron oxides, which precipitated out, forming a thin layer on the substrate, which may have been anoxic mud.
    a. Banded iron formations0
    b. Thing
    c. Undefined
    d. Undefined

Chapter 8. Precambrian Earth and Life History-The Hadean and Archean

94. A _____ is a chain of volcanic islands or mountains formed by plate tectonics as an oceanic tectonic plate subducts under another tectonic plate and produces magma.
    a. Thing
    b. Volcanic arc0
    c. Undefined
    d. Undefined

95. _____ is any particulate matter that can be transported by fluid flow and which eventually is deposited as a layer of solid particles on the bed or bottom of a body of water or other liquid.
    a. Sediment0
    b. Thing
    c. Undefined
    d. Undefined

96. A _____ is an upwelling of abnormally hot rock within the Earth's mantle. As the heads of mantle plumes can partly melt when they reach shallow depths, they are thought to be the cause of volcanic centers known as hotspots and probably also to have caused flood basalts.
    a. Mantle plume0
    b. Event
    c. Undefined
    d. Undefined

97. In geology, a _____ is a place where the Earth's crust and lithosphere are being pulled apart.
    a. Rift0
    b. Thing
    c. Undefined
    d. Undefined

98. _____ are large geologic basins that are below sea level. Geologically, there are other undersea geomorphological features such as the continental shelves, the deep ocean trenches, and the undersea mountain rangeswhich are not considered to be part of the _____.
    a. Thing
    b. Ocean basins0
    c. Undefined
    d. Undefined

99. _____ refers to sections of the oceanic crust and the subjacent upper mantle that have been uplifted or emplaced to be exposed within continental crustal rocks.
    a. Ophiolite0
    b. Thing
    c. Undefined
    d. Undefined

100. _____ is a process by which sediment is added to a tectonic plate. When two tectonic plates collide, one of the plates may slide under the other. This process is called subduction. The plate which is being subducted, is floating on the asthenosphere and is pushed up and against the other plate, which will often be scraped by the subducted plate.
    a. Thing
    b. Accretion0
    c. Undefined
    d. Undefined

101. The _____ forms the core of both the North American continent and the Canadian Shield. It extends from Quebec in the east to eastern Manitoba in the west. The western margin extends from northern Minnesota through eastern Manitoba to northwestern Ontario.
    a. Superior Craton0
    b. Thing
    c. Undefined
    d. Undefined

102. _____ is the geologic theory proposed by James Hutton around the turn of the 19th century that volcanic activity was the source of rocks on the surface of the Earth.

Chapter 8. Precambrian Earth and Life History-The Hadean and Archean

a. Plutonic theory0
b. Thing
c. Undefined
d. Undefined

103. In geology, a _____ is a depression with predominant extent in one direction. The terms U-shaped and V-shaped are descriptive terms of geography to characterize the form of valleys. Most valleys belong to one of these two main types or a mixture of them, at least with respect of the cross section of the slopes or hillsides.
a. Thing
b. Valley0
c. Undefined
d. Undefined

104. The _____ is the second-longest named river in North America, with a length of 2320 miles from Lake Itasca to the Gulf of Mexico. It drains most of the area between the Rocky Mountains and the Appalachian Mountains, except for the areas drained by Hudson Bay via the Red River of the North, the Great Lakes and the Rio Grande.
a. Place
b. Mississippi River0
c. Undefined
d. Undefined

105. _____ is the part of Earth's lithosphere that surfaces in the ocean basins. _____ is primarily composed of mafic rocks, or sima. It is thinner than continental crust, or sial, generally less than 10 kilometers thick, however it is more dense, having a mean density of about 3.3 grams per cubic centimeter.
a. Thing
b. Oceanic crust0
c. Undefined
d. Undefined

106. In geology the term _____ refers to the system of forces that tend to decrease the volume of or shorten rocks. Compressive strength refers to the maximum compressive stress that can be applied to a material before failure occurs.
a. Compression0
b. Thing
c. Undefined
d. Undefined

107. _____ light is electromagnetic radiation with a wavelength shorter than that of visible light, but longer than soft X-rays. The color violet has the shortest wavelength in the visible spectrum. UV light has a shorter wavelength than that of violet light.
a. Ultraviolet0
b. Thing
c. Undefined
d. Undefined

108. _____ as used in physics, is energy in the form of waves or moving subatomic particles.
a. Radiation0
b. Thing
c. Undefined
d. Undefined

109. _____ in meteorology are large scale patterns in the atmospheric pressure field that are nearly stationary, effectively "blocking" or redirecting migratory cyclones. These _____ can remain in place for several days or even weeks, causing the areas affected by them to have the same kind of weather for an extended period of time.
a. Thing
b. Blocks0
c. Undefined
d. Undefined

110. The _____ is defined as the summation of all particles and energy that exist and the space-time in which all events occur.

a. Place
b. Universe0
c. Undefined
d. Undefined

111. _____ is a chemical element represented by the symbol H and an atomic number of 1. At standard temperature and pressure it is a colorless, odorless, nonmetallic, tasteless, highly flammable diatomic gas . With an atomic mass of 1.00794 g/mol, _____ is the lightest element. _____ is the most abundant of the chemical elements, constituting roughly 75% of the universe's elemental mass.
a. Hydrogen0
b. Thing
c. Undefined
d. Undefined

112. _____ is a chemical element. An abundant nonmetallic, tetravalent element, _____ has several allotropic forms. This element is the basis of the chemistry of all known life.
a. Carbon0
b. Thing
c. Undefined
d. Undefined

113. _____ is a chemical compound, normally in a gaseous state, and is composed of one carbon and two oxygen atoms. It is often referred to by its formula CO_2. It is present in the Earth's atmosphere at a concentration of approximately .000383 by volume and is an important greenhouse gas due to its ability to absorb many infrared wavelengths of sunlight, and due to the length of time it stays in the atmosphere.
a. Carbon dioxide0
b. Thing
c. Undefined
d. Undefined

114. _____, with the chemical formula CO, is a colorless, odorless, and tasteless gas. It is the product of the incomplete combustion of carbon-containing compounds, notably in internal-combustion engines. It has significant fuel value, burning in air with a characteristic blue flame, producing carbon dioxide.
a. Thing
b. Carbon monoxide0
c. Undefined
d. Undefined

115. _____ is the gas phase of water. _____ is one state of the water cycle within the hydrosphere. _____ can be produced from the evaporation of liquid water or from the sublimation of ice. Under normal atmospheric conditions, _____ is continuously evaporating and condensing.
a. Thing
b. Water vapor0
c. Undefined
d. Undefined

116. _____ is a chemical element which has the symbol N and atomic number 7. Elemental _____ is a colorless, odourless, tasteless and mostly inert diatomic gas at standard conditions, constituting 78.1% by volume of Earth's atmosphere.
a. Nitrogen0
b. Thing
c. Undefined
d. Undefined

117. _____ is the gas phase component of a another state of matter which does not completely fill its container. It is distinguished from the pure gas phase by the presence of the same substance in another state of matter. Hence when a liquid has completely evaporated, it is said that the system has been completely transformed to the gas phase.
a. Vapor0
b. Thing
c. Undefined
d. Undefined

Chapter 8. Precambrian Earth and Life History-The Hadean and Archean

118. A _____ is the region around an astronomical object in which phenomena are dominated or organized by its magnetic field. Earth is surrounded by a _____, as are the magnetized planets Jupiter, Saturn, Uranus and Neptune. The term _____ has also been used to describe regions dominated by the magnetic fields of celestial objects, e.g. pulsar magnetospheres.
   a. Magnetosphere0
   b. Thing
   c. Undefined
   d. Undefined

119. _____ or sulphur is the chemical element that has the symbol S and atomic number 16. It is an abundant, tasteless, multivalent non-metal. _____, in its native form, is a yellow crystalline solid. In nature, it can be found as the pure element or as sulfide and sulfate minerals. It is an essential element for life and is found in two amino acids, cysteine and methionine.
   a. Sulfur0
   b. Thing
   c. Undefined
   d. Undefined

120. _____ is a chemical compound with the formula SO2. This important gas is the main product from the combustion of sulfur compounds and is of significant environmental concern. Sulphur dioxide is produced by volcanoes and in various industrial processes.
   a. Sulfur dioxide0
   b. Thing
   c. Undefined
   d. Undefined

121. _____ is the slow release of a gas that was trapped, frozen, absorbed or adsorbed in some material. It can include sublimation and evaporation which are phase transitions of a substance into a gas, as well as desorption, seepage from cracks or internal volumes and gaseous products of slow chemical reactions.
   a. Thing
   b. Outgassing0
   c. Undefined
   d. Undefined

122. _____ is a chemical compound with the molecular formula CH_4. It is the simplest alkane, and the principal component of natural gas. Burning one molecule of _____ in the presence of oxygen releases one molecule. _____'s relative abundance and clean burning process makes it a very attractive fuel.
   a. Thing
   b. Methane0
   c. Undefined
   d. Undefined

123. A _____ is a process that results in the interconversion of chemical substances. The substance or substances initially involved in a _____ are called reactants. Chemical reactions are characterized by a chemical change, and they yield one or more products which are, in general, different from the reactants.
   a. Chemical reaction0
   b. Thing
   c. Undefined
   d. Undefined

124. _____ is a triatomic molecule, consisting of three oxygen atoms. It is an allotrope of oxygen that is much less stable than the diatomic species O2. Ground-level _____ is an air pollutant with harmful effects on the respiratory systems of animals. On the other hand, _____ in the upper atmosphere protects living organisms by preventing damaging ultraviolet light from reaching the Earth's surface.
   a. Thing
   b. Ozone0
   c. Undefined
   d. Undefined

Chapter 8. Precambrian Earth and Life History-The Hadean and Archean

125. The _____ is the part of the Earth's atmosphere which contains relatively high concentrations of ozone. "Relatively high" means a few parts per million—much higher than the concentrations in the lower atmosphere but still small compared to the main components of the atmosphere.
   a. Thing
   b. Ozone layer0
   c. Undefined
   d. Undefined

126. _____ is a geological term used to describe particles of rock derived from pre-existing rock through processes of weathering and erosion.
   a. Detrital0
   b. Thing
   c. Undefined
   d. Undefined

127. _____ is a uranium-rich mineral with a composition that is largely UO_2, but which also contains UO_3 and oxides of lead, thorium, and rare earths. _____ is a major ore of uranium. An important occurrence of pitchblende is at Great Bear Lake in the Northwest Territories of Canada, where it is found in large quantities associated with silver. Some of the highest grade uranium ores in the world have been found in the Athabasca Basin in northern Saskatchewan.
   a. Uraninite0
   b. Thing
   c. Undefined
   d. Undefined

128. A _____ is a naturally occurring substance formed through geological processes that has a characteristic chemical composition, a highly ordered atomic structure and specific physical properties. A rock, by comparison, is an aggregate of minerals and need not have a specific chemical composition. Minerals range in composition from pure elements and simple salts to very complex silicates with thousands of known forms.
   a. Mineral0
   b. Thing
   c. Undefined
   d. Undefined

129. The mineral _____ is iron disulfide, FeS2. It has isometric crystals that usually appear as cubes. Its metallic luster and pale-to-normal, brass-yellow hue have earned it a nickname due to many miners mistaking it for the real thing.
   a. Pyrite0
   b. Thing
   c. Undefined
   d. Undefined

130. _____ generally, is the synthesis of triose phosphates from sunlight, carbon dioxide and water.
   a. Thing
   b. Photosynthesis0
   c. Undefined
   d. Undefined

131. _____ is the complete set of chemical reactions that occur in living cells. These processes are the basis of life, allowing cells to grow and reproduce, maintain their structures, and respond to their environments.
   a. Thing
   b. Metabolism0
   c. Undefined
   d. Undefined

132. In biology and ecology, an _____ is a living complex adaptive system of organs that influence each other in such a way that they function in some way as a stable whole.
   a. Organism0
   b. Thing
   c. Undefined
   d. Undefined

133. In chemistry, a _____ is defined as a sufficiently stable electrically neutral group of at least two atoms in a definite arrangement held together by strong chemical bonds.

Chapter 8. Precambrian Earth and Life History-The Hadean and Archean

a. Thing
b. Molecule0
c. Undefined
d. Undefined

134. A _____ is a section of a river of relatively steep gradient causing an increase in water flow and turbulence. A _____ is a hydrological feature between a run and a cascade. It is characterized by the river becoming shallower and having some rocks exposed above the flow surface.
a. Rapid0
b. Thing
c. Undefined
d. Undefined

135. An _____ is a type of atom that is defined by its atomic number; that is, by the number of protons in its nucleus.
a. Thing
b. Element0
c. Undefined
d. Undefined

136. An _____ is any member of a large class of chemical compounds whose molecules contain carbon.
a. Organic compound0
b. Thing
c. Undefined
d. Undefined

137. A _____ is a chemical substance of two or more different chemically bonded chemical elements, with a fixed ratio determining the composition. The ratio of each element is usually expressed by chemical formula.
a. Thing
b. Chemical compound0
c. Undefined
d. Undefined

138. The _____ is the part of the earth, including air, land, surface rocks, and water, within which life occurs, and which biotic processes in turn alter or transform. From the broadest biophysiological point of view, the _____ is the global ecological system integrating all living beings and their relationships, including their interaction with the elements of the lithosphere, hydrosphere, and atmosphere. This _____ is postulated to have evolved, beginning through a process of biogenesis or biopoesis, at least some 3.5 billion years ago.
a. Biosphere0
b. Thing
c. Undefined
d. Undefined

139. _____ refers to small spherical units postulated by some scientists as a key stage in the origin of life. The term _____ is otherwise widely being used in various areas, such as, materials and pharmaceutical sciences, for spherical particles composed of various natural and synthetic materials with diameters in the micrometer range.
a. Microsphere0
b. Thing
c. Undefined
d. Undefined

140. _____ is the substance of which physical objects are composed. _____ can be solid, liquid, plasma or gas. It constitutes the observable universe.
a. Matter0
b. Thing
c. Undefined
d. Undefined

141. In chemistry, an _____ is a molecule that contains both amine and carboxyl functional groups.
a. Amino acid0
b. Thing
c. Undefined
d. Undefined

Chapter 8. Precambrian Earth and Life History-The Hadean and Archean

142. _____ is an atmospheric discharge of electricity, which usually, but not always, occurs during rain storms, and frequently during volcanic eruptions or dust storms.
    a. Lightning0
    b. Thing
    c. Undefined
    d. Undefined

143. _____, or DNA, is a nucleic acid molecule that contains the genetic instructions used in the development and functioning of all known living organisms. The main role of DNA is the long-term storage of information and it is often compared to a set of blueprints, since DNA contains the instructions needed to construct other components of cells, such as proteins and RNA molecules.
    a. Thing
    b. Deoxyribonucleic acid0
    c. Undefined
    d. Undefined

144. A _____ is a substance composed of molecules with large molecular mass composed of repeating structural units, or monomers, connected by covalent chemical bonds. The term is derived from the Greek words: polys meaning many, and meros meaning parts.
    a. Thing
    b. Polymer0
    c. Undefined
    d. Undefined

145. A _____ is a complex, high-molecular-weight biochemical macromolecule composed of nucleotide chains that convey genetic information.
    a. Nucleic acid0
    b. Thing
    c. Undefined
    d. Undefined

146. _____ is a large organic compounds made of amino acids arranged in a linear chain and joined together by peptide bonds between the carboxyl and amino groups of adjacent amino acid residues. The sequence of amino acids in a _____ is defined by a gene and encoded in the genetic code.
    a. Thing
    b. Protein0
    c. Undefined
    d. Undefined

147. _____ is the process by which molecules in a liquid state become a gas.
    a. Thing
    b. Evaporation0
    c. Undefined
    d. Undefined

148. A _____ is a fragment of cooled pyroclastic material, lava or magma.
    a. Cinder0
    b. Thing
    c. Undefined
    d. Undefined

149. _____ are steep, conical hills of volcanic fragments that accumulate around and downwind from a volcanic vent. The rock fragments, often called cinders are glassy and contain numerous gas bubbles "frozen" into place as magma exploded into the air and then cooled quickly.
    a. Thing
    b. Cinder cones0
    c. Undefined
    d. Undefined

150. _____ are proteins that accelerate chemical reactions. Almost all processes in a biological cell need them in order to occur at significant rates.

Chapter 8. Precambrian Earth and Life History-The Hadean and Archean

a. Thing
c. Undefined
b. Enzymes0
d. Undefined

151. _____ is a layer of gases surrounding the planet Earth and retained by the Earth's gravity. This mixture of gases is commonly known as air.
a. Thing
c. Undefined
b. Earths atmosphere0
d. Undefined

152. _____ was an eminent American invertebrate paleontologist. He has become well-known for his discovery in 1909 of well-preserved fossils in the Burgess shale formation of British Columbia, Canada.
a. Person
c. Undefined
b. Charles Walcott0
d. Undefined

153. The name _____ applies to most members of the molluscan class Gastropoda that have coiled shells. They are found in freshwater, marine, and terrestrial environments. Most are of herbivorous nature, though a few land species and many marine species may be omnivores or carnivores.
a. Snail0
c. Undefined
b. Thing
d. Undefined

154. A _____ is defined as "attached, lithified sedimentary growth structure, accretionary away from a point or limited surface of initiation." A variety of _____ morphologies exist including conical, stratiform, branching, domal, and columnar types. They're commonly thought to have been formed by the trapping, binding, and cementation of sedimentary grains by microorganisms, especially cyanobacteria.
a. Thing
c. Undefined
b. Stromatolite0
d. Undefined

155. _____ encompass several groups of relatively simple living aquatic organisms that capture light energy through photosynthesis, using it to convert inorganic substances into organic matter.
a. Algae0
c. Undefined
b. Thing
d. Undefined

156. The _____ is the largest of the Earth's oceanic divisions. It extends from the Arctic in the north to the Antarctic in the south, bounded by Asia and Australia on the west and the Americas on the east. At 169.2 million square kilometres in area, this largest division of the World Ocean – and, in turn, the hydrosphere – covers about 46% of the Earth's water surface and about 32% of its total surface area, making it larger than all of the Earth's land area combined.
a. Pacific Ocean0
c. Undefined
b. Place
d. Undefined

157. A _____ is a type of underwater vessel with limited mobility which is typically transported to its area of operation by a surface vessel or large submarine
a. Submersible0
c. Undefined
b. Thing
d. Undefined

158. The _____ the bottom of the ocean. At the bottom of the continental slope is the continental rise, which is caused by sediment cascading down the continental slope.

Chapter 8. Precambrian Earth and Life History-The Hadean and Archean

a. Thing
b. Seafloor0
c. Undefined
d. Undefined

159. A _____, is a fissure in a planet's surface from which geothermally heated water issues. Hydrothermal vents are commonly found near volcanically active places, tectonic plates that are moving apart, ocean basins, and hotspots.
a. Thing
b. Hydrothermal vent0
c. Undefined
d. Undefined

160. _____ is a 16-ton, manned deep-ocean research submersible owned by the United States Navy and operated by the Woods Hole Oceanographic Institution in Woods Hole, Massachusetts. The three-person vessel allows for two scientists and one pilot to dive for up to nine hours at 4500 metersor 15,000 feet.
a. Alvin0
b. Thing
c. Undefined
d. Undefined

161. The _____ is the third largest of the world's oceanic divisions, covering about 20% of the Earth's water surface. It is bounded on the north by Asia on the west by Africa; on the east by the Malay Peninsula, the Sunda Islands, and Australia; and on the south by the Southern Ocean.
a. Indian Ocean0
b. Place
c. Undefined
d. Undefined

162. The _____ is the second-largest of the world's oceanic divisions; with a total area of about 106.4 million square kilometres , it covers approximately one-fifth of the Earth's surface. The _____ occupies an elongated, S-shaped basin extending longitudinally between the Americas to the west, and Eurasia and Africa to the east.
a. Place
b. Atlantic Ocean0
c. Undefined
d. Undefined

163. An _____ is a volume of rock containing components or minerals in a mode of occurrence that renders it valuable for mining.
a. Ore0
h. Thing
c. Undefined
d. Undefined

164. _____ in the broad sense is the total spectrum of the electromagnetic radiation given off by the Sun. On Earth, it is filtered through the atmosphere, and the solar radiation is obvious as daylight when the Sun is above the horizon.
a. Thing
b. Sunlight0
c. Undefined
d. Undefined

165. _____ refers to describe the feeding relationships between species in an ecological community. Typically a _____ refers to a graph where only connections are recorded, and a _____ or ecosystem network refers to a network where the connections are given weights representing the quantity of nutrients or energy being transferred.
a. Food web0
b. Thing
c. Undefined
d. Undefined

166. _____ is water from a sea or ocean. On average, _____ in the world's oceans has a salinity of ~3.5%, or 35 parts per thousand. This means that every 1 kg of _____ has approximately 35 grams of dissolved salts.

Chapter 8. Precambrian Earth and Life History-The Hadean and Archean

a. Seawater0
b. Thing
c. Undefined
d. Undefined

167. _____ are hydrous aluminium phyllosilicates, sometimes with variable amounts of iron, magnesium, alkali metals, alkaline earths and other cations. Clays have structures similar to the micas and therefore form flat hexagonal sheets. _____ are common weathering products and low temperature hydrothermal alteration products.
a. Thing
b. Clay minerals0
c. Undefined
d. Undefined

168. The name _____ describes several groups of marine worms that secrete tubes which they then inhabit, emerging to filter feed.
a. Thing
b. Tubeworm0
c. Undefined
d. Undefined

169. _____ are organisms without a cell nucleus or any other membrane-bound organelles. Most are unicellular, but some are multicellular.
a. Thing
b. Prokaryotes0
c. Undefined
d. Undefined

170. A _____, in inorganic chemistry, is a salt of phosphoric acid. In organic chemistry it is an ester of phosphoric acid.
a. Phosphate0
b. Thing
c. Undefined
d. Undefined

171. _____ is an obsolete biological kingdom of the former five-kingdom system of scientific classification. It comprised most organisms with a prokaryotic cell organization.
a. Thing
b. Monera0
c. Undefined
d. Undefined

172. The _____ comprises the companies that produce industrial chemicals. It is central to modern world economy, converting raw materials into more than 70,000 different products. Polymers and plastics, especially polyethylene, polypropylene, polyvinyl chloride, polyethylene terephthalate, polystyrene and polycarbonate comprise about 80% of the industry's output worldwide.
a. Chemical industry0
b. Thing
c. Undefined
d. Undefined

173. _____ is a silvery white metal that takes on a high polish. It belongs to the transition metals, and is hard and ductile. It occurs most usually in combination with sulfur and iron in pentlandite, with sulfur in millerite, with arsenic in the mineral niccolite, and with arsenic and sulfur.
a. Thing
b. Nickel0
c. Undefined
d. Undefined

174. The term _____ refers to several types of chemical compounds containing sulfur in its lowest oxidation number of −2.

Chapter 8. Precambrian Earth and Life History-The Hadean and Archean

    a. Thing
    b. Sulfide0
    c. Undefined
    d. Undefined

175. _____ are a type of hydrothermal vent found on the ocean floor. The vents are formed in fields hundreds of meters wide when superheated water from below the Earth's crust comes through the ocean floor. It can also be known as a Sea Vent. The superheated water is rich in dissolved minerals from the crust, most notably sulfides, which crystallize to create a chimney-like structure around each vent. When the superheated water in the vent comes in contact with the cold ocean water, many minerals are precipitated, creating the distinctive black color.
    a. Black smokers0
    b. Thing
    c. Undefined
    d. Undefined

176. _____ ecology is the study of renewing a degraded, damaged, or destroyed ecosystem through active human intervention. It specifically refers to the scientific study that has evolved as recently as the 1980's.
    a. Thing
    b. Restoration0
    c. Undefined
    d. Undefined

177. _____ are rocks and minerals from which metallic iron can be extracted. The ores are usually rich in iron oxides and vary in color from dark grey to rusty red. The iron itself is usually found in the form of magnetite, hematite, limonite or siderite.
    a. Iron ores0
    b. Thing
    c. Undefined
    d. Undefined

178. _____ is a very coarse-grained igneous rock that has a grain size of 20 mm or more; such rocks are referred to as pegmatitic.
    a. Pegmatite0
    b. Thing
    c. Undefined
    d. Undefined

179. _____ is the chemical element that has the symbol Be and atomic number 4. A bivalent element, elemental _____ is a steel grey, strong, light-weight yet brittle, alkaline earth metal
    a. Beryllium0
    b. Thing
    c. Undefined
    d. Undefined

180. A _____ is a highly attractive and valuable piece of mineral, which, when cut and polished, is used in jewelry or other adornments.
    a. Gemstone0
    b. Thing
    c. Undefined
    d. Undefined

181. _____ like all craton land, was created as continents moved about the surface of the Earth, bumping into other continents and drifting away.
    a. Laurentia0
    b. Thing
    c. Undefined
    d. Undefined

182. _____ are any of the several different forms of an element each having different atomic mass. _____ of an element have nuclei with the same number of protons but different numbers of neutrons.

Chapter 8. Precambrian Earth and Life History-The Hadean and Archean

a. Thing
b. Isotopes0
c. Undefined
d. Undefined

183. _____, a sub-discipline of chemistry, is the study of the interactions between atoms, small molecules, and light.
a. Photochemistry0
b. Thing
c. Undefined
d. Undefined

184. The _____ is defined as the part of the land adjoining or near the ocean. A coastline is properly a line on a map indicating the disposition of a _____, but the word is often used to refer to the _____ itself. The adjective coastal describes something as being on, near to, or associated with a _____.
a. Place
b. Coast0
c. Undefined
d. Undefined

185. The _____ region of the United States comprises the coasts of states which border the Gulf of Mexico. The states of Texas, Louisiana, Mississippi, Alabama, and Florida are known as the Gulf States. All Gulf States are located in the Southern region of the United States.
a. Place
b. Gulf Coast0
c. Undefined
d. Undefined

186. The _____ is the extended perimeter of each continent and associated coastal plain, which is covered during interglacial periods such as the current epoch by relatively shallow seas and gulfs. The shelf usually ends at a point of increasing slope.
a. Continental shelf0
b. Thing
c. Undefined
d. Undefined

Chapter 9. Precambrian Earth and Life History-The Proterozoic Eon

1. The _____ is a geological eon representing a period before the first abundant complex life on Earth. The _____ Eon extended from 2500 million years ago to 542.0 ± 1.0 million years ago. The _____ is the most recent part of the old informal Precambrian time.
   a. Thing
   b. Proterozoic0
   c. Undefined
   d. Undefined

2. _____ is the process of building mountains, and may be studied as a tectonic structural event, as a geographical event and a chronological event, in that orogenic events cause distinctive structural phenomena and related tectonic activity, affect certain regions of rocks and crust and happen within a time frame.
   a. Orogeny0
   b. Thing
   c. Undefined
   d. Undefined

3. _____ like all craton land, was created as continents moved about the surface of the Earth, bumping into other continents and drifting away.
   a. Laurentia0
   b. Thing
   c. Undefined
   d. Undefined

4. _____ rocks form when molten rock, magma, cools and solidifies, with or without crystallization, either below the surface as intrusive, plutonic rocks or on the surface as extrusive, volcanic, rocks.
   a. Thing
   b. Igneous0
   c. Undefined
   d. Undefined

5. _____ rock is one of the three main rock groups. Rock formed from these covers 75% of the Earth's land area, and includes common types such as chalk, limestone, dolomite, sandstone, and shale.
   a. Sedimentary0
   b. Thing
   c. Undefined
   d. Undefined

6. _____ is one of the three main rock groups. _____ covers 75% of the Earth's land area. Four basic processes are involved in the formation of a clastic _____: weathering caused mainly by friction of waves, transportation where the sediment is carried along by a current, deposition and compaction where the sediment is squashed together to form a rock of this kind.
   a. Thing
   b. Sedimentary rock0
   c. Undefined
   d. Undefined

7. _____ is a field of study within geology concerned generally with the structures within the crust of the Earth, or other planets, and particularly with the forces and movements that have operated in a region to create these structures.
   a. Tectonics0
   b. Thing
   c. Undefined
   d. Undefined

8. _____ is a theory of geology that has been developed to explain the observed evidence for large scale motions of the Earth's lithosphere. The theory encompassed and superseded the older theory of continental drift.
   a. Thing
   b. Plate tectonics0
   c. Undefined
   d. Undefined

9. In geology, a _____ is a land mass comprizing more than one continental core, or craton.

a. Thing
b. Supercontinent0
c. Undefined
d. Undefined

10. _____ is the geological process whereby material is added to a landform. This is the process by which wind and water create a sediment deposit, through the laying down of granular material that has been eroded and transported from another geographical location.
   a. Thing
   b. Deposition0
   c. Undefined
   d. Undefined

11. _____ is a chemical element metal. It is a lustrous, silvery soft metal. It and nickel are notable for being the final elements produced by stellar nucleosynthesis, and thus are the heaviest elements which do not require a supernova or similarly cataclysmic event for formation.
   a. Thing
   b. Iron0
   c. Undefined
   d. Undefined

12. An _____ is a layer of gases that may surround a material body of sufficient mass. The gases are attracted by the gravity of the body, and are retained for a longer duration if gravity is high and the _____'s temperature is low. Some planets consist mainly of various gases, and thus have very deep atmospheres.
   a. Place
   b. Atmosphere0
   c. Undefined
   d. Undefined

13. _____ are a distinctive type of rock often found in old sedimentary rocks. The structures consist of repeated thin layers of iron oxides, either magnetite or hematite, alternating with bands of iron-poor shale and chert. The conventional concept is that the banded iron layers were formed in water as the result of oxygen released by photosynthetic cyanobacteria, combining with dissolved iron in Earth's oceans to form insoluble iron oxides, which precipitated out, forming a thin layer on the substrate, which may have been anoxic mud.
   a. Thing
   b. Banded iron formations0
   c. Undefined
   d. Undefined

14. _____ encompass several groups of relatively simple living aquatic organisms that capture light energy through photosynthesis, using it to convert inorganic substances into organic matter.
   a. Thing
   b. Algae0
   c. Undefined
   d. Undefined

15. A _____ is one of several large landmasses on Earth. They are generally identified by convention rather than any strict criteria, but seven areas are commonly reckoned as continents – they are: Asia, Africa, North America, South America, Antarctica, Europe, and Australia.
   a. Thing
   b. Continent0
   c. Undefined
   d. Undefined

16. _____ is a silvery white metal that takes on a high polish. It belongs to the transition metals, and is hard and ductile. It occurs most usually in combination with sulfur and iron in pentlandite, with sulfur in millerite, with arsenic in the mineral niccolite, and with arsenic and sulfur.
   a. Nickel0
   b. Thing
   c. Undefined
   d. Undefined

Chapter 9. Precambrian Earth and Life History-The Proterozoic Eon

17. _____ is a chemical element. A heavy, malleable, ductile, precious, grey-white transition metal, it is resistant to corrosion and occurs in some nickel and copper ores along with some native deposits. It is used in jewelry, laboratory equipment, electrical contacts, dentistry, and automobile emissions control devices.
   a. Thing
   b. Platinum0
   c. Undefined
   d. Undefined

18. _____ are rocks and minerals from which metallic iron can be extracted. The ores are usually rich in iron oxides and vary in color from dark grey to rusty red. The iron itself is usually found in the form of magnetite, hematite, limonite or siderite.
   a. Iron ores0
   b. Thing
   c. Undefined
   d. Undefined

19. An _____ is a volume of rock containing components or minerals in a mode of occurrence that renders it valuable for mining.
   a. Thing
   b. Ore0
   c. Undefined
   d. Undefined

20. _____ is a ductile metal with excellent electrical conductivity, and finds extensive use as an electrical conductor, heat conductor, as a building material, and as a component of various alloys.
   a. Thing
   b. Copper0
   c. Undefined
   d. Undefined

21. The _____ is used by geologists and other scientists to describe the timing and relationships between events that have occurred during the history of Earth.
   a. Thing
   b. Geological time scale0
   c. Undefined
   d. Undefined

22. The _____ is the current eon in the geologic timescale, and the one during which abundant animal life has existed. It covers roughly 545 million years and goes back to the time when diverse hard-shelled animals first appeared.
   a. Thing
   b. Phanerozoic0
   c. Undefined
   d. Undefined

23. The _____ is an informal name for the eons of the geologic timescale that came before the current Phanerozoic eon. It spans from the formation of Earth around 4500 Ma to the evolution of abundant macroscopic hard-shelled animals, which marked the beginning of the Cambrian, the first period of the first era of the Phanerozoic eon, some 542 Ma.
   a. Precambrian0
   b. Thing
   c. Undefined
   d. Undefined

24. The _____ is a geologic eon before the Proterozoic. Instead of being based on stratigraphy, this date is defined chronometrically. The lower boundary has not been officially recognized by the International Commission on Stratigraphy, but it is usually set at the end of the Hadean eon.
   a. Thing
   b. Archean0
   c. Undefined
   d. Undefined

Chapter 9. Precambrian Earth and Life History-The Proterozoic Eon

25. _____ is a common and widely occurring type of intrusive, felsic, igneous rock. Granites are usually medium to coarsely crystalline, occasionally with some individual crystals larger than the groundmass forming a rock known as porphyry. Granites can be pink to dark gray or even black, depending on their chemistry and mineralogy.
   a. Thing
   b. Granite0
   c. Undefined
   d. Undefined

26. _____ is a general field petrologic term applied to metamorphic and/or altered mafic volcanic rock. The green is due to abundant green chlorite, actinolite and epidote minerals that dominate the rock.
   a. Thing
   b. Greenschist0
   c. Undefined
   d. Undefined

27. _____ are zones of variably metamorphosed mafic to ultramafic volcanic sequences with associated sedimentary rocks that occur within Archaean and Proterozoic cratons between granite and gneiss bodies. The belts have been interpreted as having formed at ancient oceanic spreading centers and island arc terranes.
   a. Thing
   b. Greenstone belts0
   c. Undefined
   d. Undefined

28. A _____ is an old and stable part of the continental crust that has survived the merging and splitting of continents and supercontinents. Cratons are generally found in the interiors of continents and are characteristically composed of ancient crystalline basement crust of lightweight felsic igneous rock such as granite. They have a thick crust and deep roots that extend into the mantle beneath to depths of 200 km.
   a. Craton0
   b. Thing
   c. Undefined
   d. Undefined

29. In geology, a _____ is the outermost layer of a planet, part of its lithosphere. They are generally composed of a less dense material than its deeper layers. Earths' is composed mainly of basalt and granite. It is cooler and more rigid than the deeper layers of the mantle and core.
   a. Thing
   b. Crust0
   c. Undefined
   d. Undefined

30. _____ can be defined as the solid state recrystallisation of pre-existing rocks due to changes in heat and/or pressure and/or introduction of fluids. There will be mineralogical, chemical and crystallographic changes. _____ produced with increasing pressure and temperature conditions is known as prograde _____. Conversely, decreasing temperatures and pressure characterize retrograde _____.
   a. Metamorphism0
   b. Thing
   c. Undefined
   d. Undefined

31. An _____ is a buried erosion surface separating two rock masses or strata of different ages, indicating that sediment deposition was not continuous. In general, the older layer was exposed to erosion for an interval of time before deposition of the younger, but the term is used to describe any break in the sedimentary geologic record.
   a. Thing
   b. Unconformity0
   c. Undefined
   d. Undefined

Chapter 9. Precambrian Earth and Life History-The Proterozoic Eon

32. A _____ is a naturally occurring substance formed through geological processes that has a characteristic chemical composition, a highly ordered atomic structure and specific physical properties. A rock, by comparison, is an aggregate of minerals and need not have a specific chemical composition. Minerals range in composition from pure elements and simple salts to very complex silicates with thousands of known forms.
   a. Mineral0
   b. Thing
   c. Undefined
   d. Undefined

33. The _____ is the part of the earth, including air, land, surface rocks, and water, within which life occurs, and which biotic processes in turn alter or transform. From the broadest biophysiological point of view, the _____ is the global ecological system integrating all living beings and their relationships, including their interaction with the elements of the lithosphere, hydrosphere, and atmosphere. This _____ is postulated to have evolved, beginning through a process of biogenesis or biopoesis, at least some 3.5 billion years ago.
   a. Thing
   b. Biosphere0
   c. Undefined
   d. Undefined

34. An _____ is any piece of land that is completely surrounded by water, above high tide. There are two main types of islands: continental islands and oceanic islands. There are also artificial islands. A grouping of geographically and/or geologically related islands is called an archipelago.
   a. Island0
   b. Thing
   c. Undefined
   d. Undefined

35. _____ is a process by which sediment is added to a tectonic plate. When two tectonic plates collide, one of the plates may slide under the other. This process is called subduction. The plate which is being subducted, is floating on the asthenosphere and is pushed up and against the other plate, which will often be scraped by the subducted plate.
   a. Accretion0
   b. Thing
   c. Undefined
   d. Undefined

36. The _____ is a major division of the geologic timescale. The _____ is the earliest period in whose rocks are found numerous large, distinctly fossilizable multicellular organisms that are more complex than sponges or medusoids. During this time, roughly fifty separate major groups of organisms or "phyla" emerged suddenly, in most cases without evident precursors. This radiation of animal phyla is referred to as the _____ explosion.
   a. Cambrian0
   b. Event
   c. Undefined
   d. Undefined

37. _____ are large emplacements of igneous intrusive rock that forms from cooled magma deep in the Earth's crust. They are almost always made mostly of felsic or intermediate rock-types, such as granite, quartz monzonite, or diorite.
   a. Thing
   b. Batholiths0
   c. Undefined
   d. Undefined

38. _____ is molten rock located beneath the surface of the Earth, and which often collects in a _____ chamber. _____ is a complex high-temperature fluid substance. Most are silicate solutions. It is capable of intrusion into adjacent rocks or of extrusion onto the surface as lava or ejected explosively as tephra to form pyroclastic rock. Environments of _____ formation include subduction zones, continental rift zones, mid-oceanic ridges, and hotspots, some of which are interpreted as mantle plumes.

Chapter 9. Precambrian Earth and Life History-The Proterozoic Eon

a. Thing
b. Magma0
c. Undefined
d. Undefined

39. A _____ in geology is an intrusive igneous rock body that crystallized from a magma below the surface of the Earth. Plutons include batholiths, dikes, sills, laccoliths, lopoliths, and other igneous bodies. In practice, "_____" usually refers to a distinctive mass of igneous rock, typically kilometers in dimension, without a tabular shape like those of dikes and sills.
a. Thing
b. Pluton0
c. Undefined
d. Undefined

40. The _____ describes the periodic opening and closing of ocean basins.
a. Wilson cycle0
b. Thing
c. Undefined
d. Undefined

41. _____ is a sedimentary rock composed mainly of sand-size mineral or rock grains. Most _____ is composed of quartz and/or feldspar because these are the most common minerals in the Earth's crust. Like sand, _____ may be any color, but the most common colors are tan, brown, yellow, red, gray and white.
a. Sandstone0
b. Thing
c. Undefined
d. Undefined

42. In organic chemistry, a _____ is a salt of carbonic acid.
a. Thing
b. Carbonate0
c. Undefined
d. Undefined

43. _____ are a class of sedimentary rocks composed primarily of carbonate minerals. The two major types are limestone and dolomite, composed of calcite and the mineral dolomite respectively. Chalk and tufa are also minor sedimentary carbonates.
a. Thing
b. Carbonate rocks0
c. Undefined
d. Undefined

44. In geology, _____ are sedimentary structures that indicate agitation by or wind.
a. Ripple marks0
b. Thing
c. Undefined
d. Undefined

45. The Laurentian _____ are a group of five large lakes in North America on or near the Canada-United States border. They are the largest group of fresh water lakes on Earth.
a. Great Lakes0
b. Place
c. Undefined
d. Undefined

46. A _____ is defined as "attached, lithified sedimentary growth structure, accretionary away from a point or limited surface of initiation." A variety of _____ morphologies exist including conical, stratiform, branching, domal, and columnar types. They're commonly thought to have been formed by the trapping, binding, and cementation of sedimentary grains by microorganisms, especially cyanobacteria.
a. Thing
b. Stromatolite0
c. Undefined
d. Undefined

47. A _____ is a body of water or other liquid of considerable size contained on a body of land. A vast majority are fresh water, and lie in the Northern Hemisphere at higher latitudes. Most have a natural outflow in the form of a river or stream, but some do not, and lose water solely by evaporation and/or underground seepage.
   a. Lake0
   b. Thing
   c. Undefined
   d. Undefined

48. _____ is a sedimentary carbonate rock that contains a high percentage of the mineral dolomite. It is usually referred to as dolomite rock. In old U.S.G.S. publications it was referred to as magnesian limestone.
   a. Dolostone0
   b. Thing
   c. Undefined
   d. Undefined

49. _____ are volcanic features formed by the collapse of land following a volcanic eruption. They are often confused with volcanic craters.
   a. Thing
   b. Calderas0
   c. Undefined
   d. Undefined

50. _____ is an igneous, volcanic rock, of felsic composition. It may have any texture from aphanitic to porphyritic. The mineral assemblage is usually quartz, alkali feldspar and plagioclase. Biotite and pyroxene are common accessory minerals.
   a. Thing
   b. Rhyolite0
   c. Undefined
   d. Undefined

51. _____ is a very important series of tectosilicate minerals within the feldspar family. Rather than referring to a particular mineral with a specific chemical composition, it is a solid solution series.
   a. Plagioclase0
   b. Thing
   c. Undefined
   d. Undefined

52. _____ is the name of a group of rock-forming minerals which make up as much as sixty percent of the Earth's crust. Feldspars crystallize from magma in both intrusive and extrusive rocks, and they can also occur as compact minerals, as veins, and are also present in many types of metamorphic rock.
   a. Thing
   b. Feldspar0
   c. Undefined
   d. Undefined

53. _____ is an oceanographic phenomenon that involves wind-driven motion of dense, cooler, and usually nutrient-rich water towards the ocean surface, replacing the warmer, usually nutrient-deplete surface water.
   a. Thing
   b. Upwelling0
   c. Undefined
   d. Undefined

54. A _____ is a landform that extends above the surrounding terrain in a limited area. A _____ is generally steeper than a hill, but there is no universally accepted standard definition for the height of a _____ or a hill although a _____ usually has an identifiable summit.
   a. Mountain0
   b. Place
   c. Undefined
   d. Undefined

Chapter 9. Precambrian Earth and Life History-The Proterozoic Eon

55. _____ is a historical and geographical region centered on the Scandinavian Peninsula in Northern Europe and includes the three kingdoms of Denmark, Norway and Sweden. The other Nordic countries, Finland, Iceland and the Faroe Islands, are also sometimes included because of their close historic and cultural relations to Norway, Sweden, and Denmark.
   a. Scandinavia0
   b. Place
   c. Undefined
   d. Undefined

56. The _____ are a vast system of mountains in eastern North America.
   a. Place
   b. Appalachian Mountains0
   c. Undefined
   d. Undefined

57. The _____ is the current eon in the geologic timescale, and the one during which abundant animal life has existed. It covers roughly 545 million years and goes back to the time when diverse hard-shelled animals first appeared.
   a. Phanerozoic Eon0
   b. Thing
   c. Undefined
   d. Undefined

58. In geology, a _____ generally refers to a linear structural depression that extends laterally over a distance, while being less steep than a trench. It can be a narrow basin or a geologic rift. In meteorolology a _____ is an elongated region of relatively low atmospheric pressure, often associated with fronts.
   a. Thing
   b. Trough0
   c. Undefined
   d. Undefined

59. In geology, a _____ is a place where the Earth's crust and lithosphere are being pulled apart.
   a. Thing
   b. Rift0
   c. Undefined
   d. Undefined

60. _____, bounded by Ontario, Canada and Minnesota, USA, to the north and Wisconsin and Michigan, USA, to the south, is the largest of North America's Great Lakes. It is the largest freshwater lake in the world by surface area and is the world's third-largest freshwater lake by volume.
   a. Lake Superior0
   b. Place
   c. Undefined
   d. Undefined

61. Faults are planar rock fractures, which show evidence of relative movement. Large faults within the Earth's crust are the result of shear motion and active _____ zones are the causal locations of most earthquakes. Earthquakes are caused by energy release during rapid slippage along faults. The largest examples are at tectonic plate boundaries but many faults occur far from active plate boundaries. Since faults do not usually consist of a single, clean fracture, the term _____ zone is used when referring to the zone of complex deformation that is associated with the _____ plane.
   a. Thing
   b. Fault0
   c. Undefined
   d. Undefined

62. _____ is molten rock expelled by a volcano during an eruption. When first extruded from a volcanic vent, it is a liquid at temperatures from 700 °C to 1,200 °C.
   a. Lava0
   b. Thing
   c. Undefined
   d. Undefined

Chapter 9. Precambrian Earth and Life History-The Proterozoic Eon

63. _____ is a common gray to black extrusive volcanic rock. It is usually fine-grained due to rapid cooling of lava on the Earth's surface. It may be porphyritic containing larger crystals in a fine matrix, or vesicular, or frothy scoria.
   a. Basalt0
   b. Thing
   c. Undefined
   d. Undefined

64. A _____ is a rock consisting of individual stones that have become cemented together. Conglomerates are sedimentary rocks consisting of rounded fragements and are thus differentiated from breccias, which consist of angular clasts. Both conglomerates and breccias are characterized by clasts larger than sand.
   a. Thing
   b. Conglomerate0
   c. Undefined
   d. Undefined

65. _____ is a fine-grained sedimentary rock whose original constituents were clays or muds. It is characterized by thin laminae breaking with an irregular curving fracture, often splintery and usually parallel to the often-indistinguishable bedding plane.
   a. Thing
   b. Shale0
   c. Undefined
   d. Undefined

66. _____ is any particulate matter that can be transported by fluid flow and which eventually is deposited as a layer of solid particles on the bed or bottom of a body of water or other liquid.
   a. Sediment0
   b. Thing
   c. Undefined
   d. Undefined

67. The _____ Era meaning "new life", is the most recent of the three classic geological eras. It covers the 65.5 million years since the Cretaceous-Tertiary extinction event at the end of the Cretaceous that marked the demise of the last non-avian dinosaurs and the end of the Mesozoic Era. The _____ era is ongoing.
   a. Thing
   b. Cenozoic0
   c. Undefined
   d. Undefined

68. An _____ plain is a relatively flat and gently sloping landform found at the base of a range of hills or mountains, formed by the deposition of _____ soil over a long period of time by one or more rivers coming from the mountains.
   a. Alluvial0
   b. Thing
   c. Undefined
   d. Undefined

69. An alluvial fan is a fan-shaped deposit formed where a fast flowing stream flattens, slows, and spreads typically at the exit of a canyon onto a flatter plain. A convergence of neighboring _____ into a single apron of deposits against a slope is called a bajada, or compound alluvial fan.
   a. Thing
   b. Alluvial fans0
   c. Undefined
   d. Undefined

70. _____ is a sedimentary rock composed largely of the mineral calcite. _____ often contains variable amounts of silica in the form of chert or flint, as well as varying amounts of clay, silt and sand as disseminations, nodules, or layers within the rock. The primary source of the calcite in _____ is most commonly marine organisms. These organisms secrete shells that settle out of the water column and are deposited on ocean floors as pelagic ooze or alternatively is conglomerated in a coral reef.

Chapter 9. Precambrian Earth and Life History-The Proterozoic Eon

a. Limestone0
b. Thing
c. Undefined
d. Undefined

71. A _____ is a large, slow moving river of ice, formed from compacted layers of snow, that slowly deforms and flows in response to gravity. _____ ice is the largest reservoir of fresh water on Earth, and second only to oceans as the largest reservoir of total water. Glaciers cover vast areas of polar regions but are restricted to the highest mountains in the tropics.
a. Thing
b. Glacier0
c. Undefined
d. Undefined

72. _____ is located in the U.S. state of Montana, bordering the Canadian provinces of Alberta and British Columbia. _____ contains two mountain ranges, over 130 named lakes, more than 1,000 different species of plants and hundreds of species of animals.
a. Glacier National Park0
b. Place
c. Undefined
d. Undefined

73. A _____ is a deep valley between cliffs often carved from the landscape by a river. Most were formed by a process of long-time erosion from a plateau level. The cliffs form because harder rock strata that are resistant to erosion and weathering remain exposed on the valley walls.
a. Canyon0
b. Thing
c. Undefined
d. Undefined

74. The _____ is a very colorful, steep-sided gorge, carved by the Colorado River in the U.S. state of Arizona. It is one of the first national parks in the United States.
a. Grand Canyon0
b. Place
c. Undefined
d. Undefined

75. _____ is a valley in the U.S. state of California, and is the location of the lowest elevation in North America at –282 feet. Located southeast of the Sierra Nevada range in the Great Basin and the Mojave Desert, it constitutes much of _____ National Park. It runs north-south between the Amargosa Range to the east and the Panamint Range to the west; the Sylvania Mountains and the Owlshead Mountains form its northern and southern boundaries, respectively.
a. Death Valley0
b. Place
c. Undefined
d. Undefined

76. The _____ on the geologic timescale had been intended to cover the world's recent period of repeated glaciations. The _____ follows the Pliocene and is followed by the Holocene. The _____ is the third epoch of the Neogene period or 6th epoch of the Cenozoic era. The end of the _____ corresponds with the end of the Paleolithic age used in archaeology. The _____ is divided into the Early _____, Middle _____ and Late _____, and numerous faunal stages.
a. Pleistocene0
b. Thing
c. Undefined
d. Undefined

77. The _____ are a broad mountain range in western North America. The _____ stretch more than 4,800 kilometers from northernmost British Columbia, in Canada, to New Mexico, in the United States.

a. Place
b. Rocky Mountains0
c. Undefined
d. Undefined

78. In geology, a _____ is a depression with predominant extent in one direction. The terms U-shaped and V-shaped are descriptive terms of geography to characterize the form of valleys. Most valleys belong to one of these two main types or a mixture of them, at least with respect of the cross section of the slopes or hillsides.
   a. Thing
   b. Valley0
   c. Undefined
   d. Undefined

79. _____ is displacement of solids by the agents of ocean currents, wind, water, or ice by downward or down-slope movement in response to gravity or by living organisms.
   a. Erosion0
   b. Thing
   c. Undefined
   d. Undefined

80. A glacier is a large, slow moving river of ice, formed from compacted layers of snow, that slowly deforms and flows in response to gravity. Glacier ice is the largest reservoir of fresh water on Earth, and second only to oceans as the largest reservoir of total water. _____ cover vast areas of polar regions but are restricted to the highest mountains in the tropics.
   a. Glaciers0
   b. Thing
   c. Undefined
   d. Undefined

81. Mean _____ is the average height of the sea, with reference to a suitable reference surface.
   a. Thing
   b. Sea level0
   c. Undefined
   d. Undefined

82. The _____ is the earliest of three geologic eras of the Phanerozoic eon. The _____ is subdivided into six geologic periods; from oldest to youngest they are: the Cambrian, Ordovician, Silurian, Devonian, Carboniferous, and Permian.
   a. Thing
   b. Paleozoic0
   c. Undefined
   d. Undefined

83. _____ is the supercontinent that existed during the Paleozoic and Mesozoic eras before each of the component continents were separated into their current configuration.
   a. Pangaea0
   b. Event
   c. Undefined
   d. Undefined

84. An _____ is a long period of time with different technical and colloquial meanings, and usages in language. It begins with some beginning event known as an epoch, epochal date, epochal event or epochal moment.
   a. Era0
   b. Thing
   c. Undefined
   d. Undefined

85. _____ are large geologic basins that are below sea level. Geologically, there are other undersea geomorphological features such as the continental shelves, the deep ocean trenches, and the undersea mountain rangeswhich are not considered to be part of the _____.
   a. Ocean basins0
   b. Thing
   c. Undefined
   d. Undefined

Chapter 9. Precambrian Earth and Life History-The Proterozoic Eon

86. _____ is a hypothetical supercontinent that existed from the Pan-African orogeny about 600 million years ago to the end of the Precambrian about 540 million years ago.
   a. Place
   b. Pannotia0
   c. Undefined
   d. Undefined

87. In geology, _____ refers to one of the oldest known supercontinents, which contained most or all of Earth's then-current landmass. Paleomagnetic evidence provides clues to the paleolatitude of individual formations, but not to their longitude, which geologists have pieced together by comparing similar strata, often now widely dispersed.
   a. Thing
   b. Rodinia0
   c. Undefined
   d. Undefined

88. The _____ is an epoch of the Carboniferous period lasting from roughly 325 Ma to 299 Ma. As with most other geologic periods, the rock beds that define the period are well identified, but the exact date of the start and end are uncertain by a few million years.
   a. Pennsylvanian0
   b. Thing
   c. Undefined
   d. Undefined

89. An _____ is a mass of glacier ice that covers surrounding terrain and is greater than 19,305 mile². The only current ice sheets are in Antarctica and Greenland. Ice sheets are bigger than ice shelves or glaciers. Masses of ice covering less than 50,000 km² are termed an ice cap. An ice cap will typically feed a series of glaciers around its periphery. Although the surface is cold, the base of an _____ is generally warmer. This process produces fast-flowing channels in the _____.
   a. Ice sheet0
   b. Thing
   c. Undefined
   d. Undefined

90. _____ is a chemical element. An abundant nonmetallic, tetravalent element, _____ has several allotropic forms. This element is the basis of the chemistry of all known life.
   a. Thing
   b. Carbon0
   c. Undefined
   d. Undefined

91. _____ is a chemical compound, normally in a gaseous state, and is composed of one carbon and two oxygen atoms. It is often referred to by its formula CO_2. It is present in the Earth's atmosphere at a concentration of approximately .000383 by volume and is an important greenhouse gas due to its ability to absorb many infrared wavelengths of sunlight, and due to the length of time it stays in the atmosphere.
   a. Thing
   b. Carbon dioxide0
   c. Undefined
   d. Undefined

92. In geology, _____ minerals and rocks are silicate minerals, magmas, and volcanic and intrusive igneous rocks that have relatively high concentrations of the heavier elements. The term is a combination of "magnesium" and ferrum.
   a. Thing
   b. Mafic0
   c. Undefined
   d. Undefined

93. A _____ is an intrusion into a cross-cutting fissure, meaning a _____ cuts across other pre-existing layers or bodies of rock, this means that a _____ is always younger than the rocks that contain it. The thickness is usually much smaller than the other two dimensions. Thickness can vary from sub-centimeter scale to many meters in thickness and the lateral dimensions can extend over many kilometers.

a. Thing
b. Dike0
c. Undefined
d. Undefined

94. _____ is a dark, coarse-grained, intrusive igneous rock chemically equivalent to basalt. It is a plutonic rock, formed when molten magma is trapped beneath the Earth's surface and cools into a crystalline mass.
a. Gabbro0
b. Thing
c. Undefined
d. Undefined

95. _____ is the native consolidated rock underlying the Earth's surface. Above the _____ is usually an area of broken and weathered unconsolidated rock in the basal subsoil.
a. Bedrock0
b. Thing
c. Undefined
d. Undefined

96. _____ is a fine-grained silica-rich cryptocrystalline sedimentary rock that may contain small fossils. It varies greatly in color from white to black, but most often manifests as gray, brown, grayish brown and light green to rusty red; its color is an expression of trace elements present in the rock, and both red and green are most often related to traces of iron.
a. Thing
b. Chert0
c. Undefined
d. Undefined

97. An _____ is a chemical compound containing an oxygen atom and other elements. Most of the earth's crust consists of them. They result when elements are oxidized by air.
a. Oxide0
b. Thing
c. Undefined
d. Undefined

98. _____ is a ferrimagnetic mineral one of several iron oxides and a member of the spinel group. The chemical IUPAC name is iron oxide and the common chemical name ferrous-ferric oxide.
a. Magnetite0
b. Thing
c. Undefined
d. Undefined

99. _____ is a very common mineral, colored black to steel or silver-gray, brown to reddish brown, or red. It is mined as the main ore of iron. Varieties include kidney ore, martite iron rose and specularite. While the forms of it vary, they all have a rust-red streak. it is harder than pure iron, but much more brittle.
a. Hematite0
b. Thing
c. Undefined
d. Undefined

100. An _____ is a type of atom that is defined by its atomic number; that is, by the number of protons in its nucleus.
a. Element0
b. Thing
c. Undefined
d. Undefined

101. _____ is water from a sea or ocean. On average, _____ in the world's oceans has a salinity of ~3.5%, or 35 parts per thousand. This means that every 1 kg of _____ has approximately 35 grams of dissolved salts.
a. Seawater0
b. Thing
c. Undefined
d. Undefined

102. _____ is the oxide of silicon, chemical formula SiO_2, and is known for its hardness as early as the 16th century. It is a principle component in most types of glass and substances such as concrete.

Chapter 9. Precambrian Earth and Life History-The Proterozoic Eon   163

a. Silica0
b. Thing
c. Undefined
d. Undefined

103. A _____ is a geological feature that is also known as a Rip in the earth causing magma to flow out and forming an undersea volcano, it also has geological features, a continuous elevational crest for some distance. Ridges are usually termed hills or mountains as well, depending on size.
a. Thing
b. Ridge0
c. Undefined
d. Undefined

104. A _____ is an opening, or rupture, in the Earth's surface or crust, which allows hot, molten rock, ash and gases to escape from deep below the surface.
a. Volcano0
b. Thing
c. Undefined
d. Undefined

105. _____ are underwater fissures in the earth's surface from which magma can erupt. They estimated to account for 75% of annual magma output. The vast majority are located near areas of tectonic plate movement, known as mid-ocean ridges.
a. Thing
b. Submarine volcanoes0
c. Undefined
d. Undefined

106. The _____ is the extended perimeter of each continent and associated coastal plain, which is covered during interglacial periods such as the current epoch by relatively shallow seas and gulfs. The shelf usually ends at a point of increasing slope.
a. Thing
b. Continental shelf0
c. Undefined
d. Undefined

107. _____ is a 16-ton, manned deep-ocean research submersible owned by the United States Navy and operated by the Woods Hole Oceanographic Institution in Woods Hole, Massachusetts. The three-person vessel allows for two scientists and one pilot to dive for up to nine hours at 4500 metersor 15,000 feet.
a. Thing
b. Alvin0
c. Undefined
d. Undefined

108. _____ is an ecological concept referring to the relative representation of a species in a particular ecosystem. It is usually measured as the mean number of individuals found per sample.
a. Thing
b. Abundance0
c. Undefined
d. Undefined

109. _____ is a triatomic molecule, consisting of three oxygen atoms. It is an allotrope of oxygen that is much less stable than the diatomic species O2. Ground-level _____ is an air pollutant with harmful effects on the respiratory systems of animals. On the other hand, _____ in the upper atmosphere protects living organisms by preventing damaging ultraviolet light from reaching the Earth's surface.
a. Thing
b. Ozone0
c. Undefined
d. Undefined

Chapter 9. Precambrian Earth and Life History-The Proterozoic Eon

110. The _____ is the part of the Earth's atmosphere which contains relatively high concentrations of ozone . "Relatively high" means a few parts per million—much higher than the concentrations in the lower atmosphere but still small compared to the main components of the atmosphere.
   a. Ozone layer0
   b. Thing
   c. Undefined
   d. Undefined

111. _____ light is electromagnetic radiation with a wavelength shorter than that of visible light, but longer than soft X-rays. The color violet has the shortest wavelength in the visible spectrum. UV light has a shorter wavelength than that of violet light.
   a. Thing
   b. Ultraviolet0
   c. Undefined
   d. Undefined

112. _____ as used in physics, is energy in the form of waves or moving subatomic particles.
   a. Radiation0
   b. Thing
   c. Undefined
   d. Undefined

113. Fossils are the mineralized or otherwise preserved remains or traces of animals, plants, and other organisms. The totality of fossils, both discovered and undiscovered, and their placement in fossiliferous rock formations and sedimentary layers is known as the _____ record.
   a. Fossil0
   b. Thing
   c. Undefined
   d. Undefined

114. _____ are unicellular microorganisms. They are typically a few micrometres long and have many shapes including curved rods, spheres, rods, and spirals.
   a. Thing
   b. Bacteria0
   c. Undefined
   d. Undefined

115. _____ are organisms without a cell nucleus or any other membrane-bound organelles. Most are unicellular, but some are multicellular.
   a. Prokaryotes0
   b. Thing
   c. Undefined
   d. Undefined

116. Animals, plants, fungi, and protists are _____, organisms with a complex cell or cells, where the genetic material is organized into a membrane-bound nucleus or nuclei.
   a. Thing
   b. Eukaryotes0
   c. Undefined
   d. Undefined

117. In biology and ecology, an _____ is a living complex adaptive system of organs that influence each other in such a way that they function in some way as a stable whole.
   a. Thing
   b. Organism0
   c. Undefined
   d. Undefined

118. _____ are any one of a number of viable DNA codings that occupies a given locus position on a chromosome. Usually _____ are DNA sequences that code for a gene.

a. Alleles0
b. Thing
c. Undefined
d. Undefined

119. _____ is a membrane-enclosed organelle, found in most eukaryotic cells. _____ are sometimes described as "cellular power plants," because they generate most of the cell's supply of ATP, used as a source of chemical energy.
a. Thing
b. Mitochondria0
c. Undefined
d. Undefined

120. _____ are organelles found in plant cells and eukaryotic algae that conduct photosynthesis. _____ absorb sunlight and use it in conjunction with water and carbon dioxide to produce sugars. _____ capture light energy from the sun to conserve free energy in the form of ATP and reduce NADP to NADPH through a complex set of processes called photosynthesis.
a. Chloroplasts0
b. Thing
c. Undefined
d. Undefined

121. _____ generally, is the synthesis of triose phosphates from sunlight, carbon dioxide and water.
a. Thing
b. Photosynthesis0
c. Undefined
d. Undefined

122. _____ is the complete set of chemical reactions that occur in living cells. These processes are the basis of life, allowing cells to grow and reproduce, maintain their structures, and respond to their environments.
a. Thing
b. Metabolism0
c. Undefined
d. Undefined

123. _____ are small organic structures found as fossils. In general, any small, non-acid soluble organic structure that can not otherwise be accounted for is an acritarch. Most _____ are likely the remains of single-celled organisms, especially the planktonic algae. They are found in sedimentary rocks from the present back into the Precambrian. They are typically isolated from siliciclastic sedimentary rocks using hydrofluoric acid but are occasionally extracted from carbonate-rich rocks.
a. Acritarchs0
b. Thing
c. Undefined
d. Undefined

124. An _____ organism is an organism that has an oxygen based metabolism
a. Aerobic0
b. Thing
c. Undefined
d. Undefined

125. The _____ refers to plants that have specialized tissues for conducting water, minerals, and photosynthetic products through the plant. They include the ferns, clubmosses, horsetails, flowering plants, conifers and other gymnosperms.
a. Thing
b. Vascular plant0
c. Undefined
d. Undefined

126. _____ is a close association between two different types of organisms in a community. It can be defined as:The living together in permanent or prolonged close association of members of usually two different species, with beneficial or deleterious consequences for at least one of the parties.

a. Symbiosis0
b. Thing
c. Undefined
d. Undefined

127. _____ is a large organic compounds made of amino acids arranged in a linear chain and joined together by peptide bonds between the carboxyl and amino groups of adjacent amino acid residues. The sequence of amino acids in a _____ is defined by a gene and encoded in the genetic code.
a. Protein0
b. Thing
c. Undefined
d. Undefined

128. _____ is a hard, metamorphic rock which was originally sandstone. Sandstone is converted into _____ through heating and pressure usually related to tectonic compression within orogenic belts.
a. Thing
b. Quartzite0
c. Undefined
d. Undefined

129. _____ is a collective term for animal life of any particular region or time. Paleontologists usually use _____ to refer to a typical collection of animals found in a specific time or place. Paleontologists sometimes refer to a sequence of 80 or so faunal stages, which are a series of rocks all containing similar fossils.
a. Thing
b. Fauna0
c. Undefined
d. Undefined

130. _____ are a major group of arthropods and the most diverse group of animals on the Earth, with over a million described species—more than all other animal groups combined. They may be found in nearly all environments on the planet, although only a small number of species occur in the oceans where crustaceans tend to predominate instead.
a. Insects0
b. Thing
c. Undefined
d. Undefined

131. _____ are extinct arthropods. They appeared in the second Epoch of the Cambrian period and flourished throughout the lower Paleozoic era before beginning a drawn-out decline to extinction when all _____, with the sole exception of Proetida, died out. The last of the _____ disappeared in the mass extinction at the end of the Permian.
a. Trilobites0
b. Thing
c. Undefined
d. Undefined

132. _____ represent the largest generally accepted groupings of animals and other living things with certain evolutionary traits.
a. Phyla0
b. Thing
c. Undefined
d. Undefined

133. _____ are decapod crustaceans of the infraorder Brachyura, which typically have a very short "tail" or where the abdomen is entirely hidden under the thorax. They are generally covered with a thick exoskeleton, and are armed with a single pair of claws. They are found in all of the world's oceans; there are also many freshwater and terrestrial _____, particularly in tropical regions.
a. Crabs0
b. Thing
c. Undefined
d. Undefined

Chapter 9. Precambrian Earth and Life History-The Proterozoic Eon

134. The _____ are a large phylum of animals, comprizing the segmented worms, with about 15,000 modern species including the well-known earthworms and leeches. They are found in most wet environments, and include many terrestrial, freshwater, and especially marine species, as well as some which are parasitic or mutualistic. They range in length from under a millimeter to over 3 meters.
   a. Thing
   b. Annelids0
   c. Undefined
   d. Undefined

135. _____ is a fossil animal from the Ediacaran or Vendian fauna. This fossil varies from 3 mm to 10 cm in size. It is oval in shape with larger ones being elongated more.
   a. Kimberella quadrata0
   b. Thing
   c. Undefined
   d. Undefined

136. _____ is the extraction of valuable minerals or other geological materials from the earth, usually from an ore body, vein, or seam. Any material that cannot be grown from agricultural processes, or created artificially in a laboratory or factory, is usually extracted from the earth by this method.
   a. Mining0
   b. Thing
   c. Undefined
   d. Undefined

137. _____ is deterioration of essential properties in a material due to reactions with its surroundings. In the most common use of the word, this means a loss of an electron of metals reacting with water or oxygen.
   a. Corrosion0
   b. Thing
   c. Undefined
   d. Undefined

138. A _____ is a natural object originating in outer space that survives an impact with the Earth's surface without being destroyed. While in space it is called a meteoroid. When it enters the atmosphere, air resistance causes the body to heat up and emit light, thus forming a fireball.
   a. Thing
   b. Meteorite0
   c. Undefined
   d. Undefined

139. _____ forms when rock cools and solidifies either below the surface as intrusive rocks or on the surface as extrusive rocks. This magma can be derived from partial melts of pre-existing rocks in either the Earth's mantle or crust. Typically, the melting is caused by one or more of the following processes -- an increase in temperature, a decrease in pressure, or a change in composition.
   a. Thing
   b. Igneous rock0
   c. Undefined
   d. Undefined

140. _____ is a steel-gray, lustrous, hard metal that takes a high polish and has a high melting point. It is also odourless, tasteless, and malleable
   a. Chromium0
   b. Thing
   c. Undefined
   d. Undefined

141. In organic chemistry, a _____ is an organic compound consisting entirely of hydrogen and carbon. With relation to chemical terminology, aromatic hydrocarbons or arenes, alkanes, alkenes and alkyne-based compounds composed entirely of carbon or hydrogen are referred to as "Pure" hydrocarbons, whereas other hydrocarbons with bonded compounds or impurities of sulphur or nitrogen, are referred to as "impure", and remain somewhat erroneously referred to as hydrocarbons.

a. Hydrocarbon0   b. Thing
c. Undefined   d. Undefined

142. _____ is a very coarse-grained igneous rock that has a grain size of 20 mm or more; such rocks are referred to as pegmatitic.
a. Pegmatite0   b. Thing
c. Undefined   d. Undefined

143. _____ is the chemical element that has the symbol Be and atomic number 4. A bivalent element, elemental _____ is a steel grey, strong, light-weight yet brittle, alkaline earth metal
a. Thing   b. Beryllium0
c. Undefined   d. Undefined

144. _____ is a chemical element in the periodic table that has the symbol Sn. This silvery, malleable poor metal that is not easily oxidized in air and resists corrosion is found in many alloys and is used to coat other metals to prevent corrosion. It is obtained chiefly from the mineral cassiterite, where it occurs as an oxide. It is the classic alloying metal to make bronze.
a. Tin0   b. Thing
c. Undefined   d. Undefined

145. The _____ mineral group is chemically one of the most complicated groups of silicate minerals. It is a complex silicate of aluminium and boron, but because of isomorphous replacement, its composition varies widely with sodium, calcium, iron, magnesium, lithium and other elements entering into the structure.
a. Tourmaline0   b. Thing
c. Undefined   d. Undefined

146. The _____ group of sheet silicate minerals includes several closely related materials having highly perfect basal cleavage. All are monoclinic with a tendency towards pseudo-hexagonal crystals and are similar in chemical composition. The highly perfect cleavage, which is the most prominent characteristic of _____, is explained by the hexagonal sheet-like arrangement of its atoms.
a. Thing   b. Mica0
c. Undefined   d. Undefined

147. _____ is the second most common mineral in the Earth's continental crust. It is made up of a lattice of silica tetrahedra. _____ belongs to the rhombohedral crystal system. In nature _____ crystals are often twinned, distorted, or so intergrown with adjacent crystals of _____ or other minerals as to only show part of this shape, or to lack obvious crystal faces altogether and appear massive.
a. Thing   b. Quartz0
c. Undefined   d. Undefined

148. A _____ is a highly attractive and valuable piece of mineral, which, when cut and polished, is used in jewelry or other adornments.
a. Gemstone0   b. Thing
c. Undefined   d. Undefined

Chapter 9. Precambrian Earth and Life History-The Proterozoic Eon 169

149. The _____ are a small, isolated mountain range rizing from the Great Plains of North America in western South Dakota and extending into Wyoming, USA. Set off from the main body of the Rocky Mountains, the region is somewhat of a geological anomaly—accurately described as an "island of trees in a sea of grass.
- a. Place
- b. Black Hills0
- c. Undefined
- d. Undefined

150. A _____ is a solid in which the constituent atoms, molecules, or ions are packed in a regularly ordered, repeating pattern extending in all three spatial dimensions. Most metals encountered in everyday life are polycrystals. Crystals are often symmetrically intergrown to form _____ twins.
- a. Thing
- b. Crystal0
- c. Undefined
- d. Undefined

151. _____ are naturally occurring substances that are considered valuable in their relatively unmodified or natural form. Its value rests in the amount of the material available and the demand for the certain material.
- a. Thing
- b. Natural resources0
- c. Undefined
- d. Undefined

152. _____ is an opaque, impure variety of quartz, usually red, yellow or brown in color. This mineral breaks with a smooth surface, and is used for ornamentation or as a gemstone.
- a. Thing
- b. Jasper0
- c. Undefined
- d. Undefined

153. A _____, is a site for the disposal of waste materials by burial and is the oldest form of waste treatment.
- a. Landfill0
- b. Thing
- c. Undefined
- d. Undefined

154. _____ is one of the phenomena by which materials exert attractive or repulsive forces on other materials. Some well known materials that exhibit easily detectable magnetic properties are nickel, iron, some steels, and the mineral magnetite; however, all materials are influenced to greater or lesser degree by the presence of a magnetic field.
- a. Magnetism0
- b. Thing
- c. Undefined
- d. Undefined

155. _____ is a self-governed Danish territory lying between the Arctic and Atlantic Oceans. Though geographically and ethnically an Arctic island nation associated with the continent of North America, politically and historically _____ is closely tied to Europe. It is the largest island in the world that is not also considered a continent.
- a. Place
- b. Greenland0
- c. Undefined
- d. Undefined

156. _____ refers to sections of the oceanic crust and the subjacent upper mantle that have been uplifted or emplaced to be exposed within continental crustal rocks.
- a. Ophiolite0
- b. Thing
- c. Undefined
- d. Undefined

157. A _____ is a chemical substance of two or more different chemically bonded chemical elements, with a fixed ratio determining the composition. The ratio of each element is usually expressed by chemical formula.

Chapter 9. Precambrian Earth and Life History-The Proterozoic Eon

a. Chemical compound0
b. Thing
c. Undefined
d. Undefined

158. _____ is rock that is of a certain particle size range. In geology, _____ is any loose rock that is at least two millimeters in its largest dimension and no more than 75 millimeters.
   a. Gravel0
   b. Thing
   c. Undefined
   d. Undefined

159. Earth's _____ is a ~2,900 km thick rocky shell comprizing approximately 70% of Earth's volume. It is predominantly solid and overlies the Earth's iron-rich core, which occupies about 30% of Earth's volume. Past episodes of melting and volcanism at the shallower levels of the _____ have produced a very thin crust of crystallized melt products near the surface, upon which we live.
   a. Thing
   b. Mantle0
   c. Undefined
   d. Undefined

160. The _____ the bottom of the ocean. At the bottom of the continental slope is the continental rise, which is caused by sediment cascading down the continental slope.
   a. Seafloor0
   b. Thing
   c. Undefined
   d. Undefined

161. _____ is the part of Earth's lithosphere that surfaces in the ocean basins. _____ is primarily composed of mafic rocks, or sima. It is thinner than continental crust, or sial, generally less than 10 kilometers thick, however it is more dense, having a mean density of about 3.3 grams per cubic centimeter.
   a. Thing
   b. Oceanic crust0
   c. Undefined
   d. Undefined

162. _____ refers to things having to do with the land or with the planet Earth.
   a. Terrestrial0
   b. Thing
   c. Undefined
   d. Undefined

163. _____ is the result of the transformation of a pre-existing rock type, the protolith, in a process called metamorphism, which means "change in form". The protolith is subjected to heat and extreme pressure causing profound physical and/or chemical change. The protolith may be sedimentary rock, igneous rock or another older rock.
   a. Metamorphic rock0
   b. Thing
   c. Undefined
   d. Undefined

164. Metamorphic rock is the result of the transformation of a pre-existing rock type, the protolith, in a process called metamorphism. The protolith is subjected to heat and extreme pressure causing profound physical and/or chemical change. _____ make up a large part of the Earth's crust. They are formed deep beneath the Earth's surface by great stresses from rocks above and high pressures and temperatures.
   a. Thing
   b. Metamorphic rocks0
   c. Undefined
   d. Undefined

165. The _____ is a large shield covered by a thin layer of soil that forms the nucleus of the North American craton. It has a deep, common, joined bedrock region in eastern and central Canada and stretches North from the Great Lakes to the Arctic Ocean, covering half the country.

Chapter 9. Precambrian Earth and Life History-The Proterozoic Eon

a. Canadian Shield0
c. Undefined
b. Thing
d. Undefined

166. A _____ is a geologic event during which sea level rises relative to the land and the shoreline moves toward higher ground, resulting in flooding. Transgressions can be caused either by the land sinking or the ocean basins filling with water.
a. Transgression0
c. Undefined
b. Thing
d. Undefined

167. _____ refers to water-soluble, mineral sediments that result from the evaporation of bodies of surficial water.
a. Thing
c. Undefined
b. Evaporite0
d. Undefined

168. The _____ was a great mountain building period that perhaps had the greatest overall effect on the geologic structure of basement rocks within the New York Bight region. The effects of this orogeny are most apparent throughout New England, but the sediments derived from mountainous areas formed in the northeast can be traced throughout the Appalachians and midcontinental North America.
a. Thing
c. Undefined
b. Taconic orogeny0
d. Undefined

169. In plate tectonics, a _____ is an actively deforming region where two tectonic plates or fragments of lithosphere move towards one another. When two plates move toward one another, they form either a subduction zone or a continental collision.
a. Thing
c. Undefined
b. Convergent boundary0
d. Undefined

170. _____ is the science and study of the solid matter that constitute the Earth. Encompassing such things as rocks, soil, and gemstones, _____ studies the composition, structure, physical properties, history, and the processes that shape Earth's components.
a. Thing
c. Undefined
b. Geology0
d. Undefined

171. _____ are artificial channels for water. There are two main types of _____: irrigation _____, which are used for the delivery of water, and waterways, which are transportation _____ used for passage of goods and people, often connected to existing lakes, rivers, or oceans.
a. Thing
c. Undefined
b. Canals0
d. Undefined

172. The _____ is a major division of the geologic timescale that extends from the end of the Ordovician period to the beginning of the Devonian period. The base of the _____ is set at a major extinction event when 60% of marine species were wiped out.
a. Silurian0
c. Undefined
b. Thing
d. Undefined

173. The _____ is a geologic period of the Paleozoic era. During the _____ the first fish evolved legs and started to walk on land as tetrapods and the first insects and spiders also started to colonize terrestrial habitats. The first seed-bearing plants spread across dry land, forming huge forests. In the oceans, Primitive sharks became more numerous. The first ammonite mollusks appeared, and trilobites as well as great coral reefs were still common.
- a. Thing
- b. Devonian0
- c. Undefined
- d. Undefined

174. The _____ is a major division of the geologic timescale that extends from the end of the Devonian period to the beginning of the Permian period. As with most older geologic periods, the rock beds that define the period's start and end are well identified, but the exact dates are uncertain. The first third of the _____ is called the Mississippian epoch, and the remainder is called the Pennsylvanian.
- a. Thing
- b. Carboniferous0
- c. Undefined
- d. Undefined

175. _____ is a fossil fuel formed in swamp ecosystems where plant remains were saved by water and mud from oxidization and biodegradation. It is a sedimentary rock, but the harder forms, such as anthracite _____, can be regarded as metamorphic rocks because of later exposure to elevated temperature and pressure. It is composed primarily of carbon along with assorted other elements, including sulfur.
- a. Coal0
- b. Thing
- c. Undefined
- d. Undefined

176. The _____ is the second of the six periods of the Paleozoic era. It follows the Cambrian period and is followed by the Silurian period. The _____ started at a major extinction called the Cambrian-_____ extinction and lasted for about 44.6 million years. It ended with another major extinction event that wiped out 60% of marine genera.
- a. Thing
- b. Ordovician0
- c. Undefined
- d. Undefined

177. The _____ was a major shift of technological, socioeconomic, and cultural conditions that occurred in the late 18th century and early 19th century in some Western countries. It began in Britain and spread throughout the world, a process that continues.
- a. Thing
- b. Industrial Revolution0
- c. Undefined
- d. Undefined

178. _____ was an English geologist, credited with creating the first nationwide geologic map. He is known as the "Father of English Geology", however recognition was slow in coming. His work was plagiarised, he was financially ruined, and he spent time in debtors' prison. It was only much later in his life that Smith received recognition for his accomplishments.
- a. Person
- b. William Smith0
- c. Undefined
- d. Undefined

179. _____ is a geological term used to describe particles of rock derived from pre-existing rock through processes of weathering and erosion.
- a. Detrital0
- b. Thing
- c. Undefined
- d. Undefined

Chapter 9. Precambrian Earth and Life History-The Proterozoic Eon

180. A _____ is a group of mountains bordered by lowlands or separated from other mountain ranges by passes or rivers. Individual mountains within the same _____ do not necessarily have the same geology; they may be a mix of different orogeny, for example volcanoes, uplifted mountains or fold mountains and may, therefore, be of different rock.
  a. Mountain range0
  b. Thing
  c. Undefined
  d. Undefined

181. _____ is the study of the ancient geologic environments of the Earth's surface as preserved in the stratigraphic record.
  a. Thing
  b. Palaeogeography0
  c. Undefined
  d. Undefined

182. _____, both meaning "Earth", and graphein meaning "to describe" or "to write"or "to map", is the study of the earth and its features, inhabitants, and phenomena. A literal translation would be "to describe the Earth". The first person to use the word "_____" was Eratosthenes. Four historical traditions in geographical research are the spatial analysis of natural and human phenomena, area studies, study of man-land relationship, and research in earth sciences.
  a. Thing
  b. Geography0
  c. Undefined
  d. Undefined

183. _____ is the use of the principles of geology to reconstruct and understand the history of the Earth. It focuses on geologic processes that change the Earth's surface and subsurface; and the use of stratigraphy, structural geology and paleontology to tell the sequence of these events. It also focuses on the evolution of plants and animals during different time periods in the geological timescale.
  a. Thing
  b. Historical geology0
  c. Undefined
  d. Undefined

184. _____ refers to the study of the record of the Earth's magnetic field preserved in various magnetic minerals through time. The study of _____ has demonstrated that the Earth's magnetic field varies substantially in both orientation and intensity through time.
  a. Paleomagnetism0
  b. Thing
  c. Undefined
  d. Undefined

185. _____ are maps of continents and mountain ranges in the distant past or future.
  a. Thing
  b. Paleomaps0
  c. Undefined
  d. Undefined

186. _____, a branch of geology, studies rock layers and layering. It is primarily used in the study of sedimentary and layered volcanic rocks. _____ includes two related subfields: lithologic or lithostratigraphy and biologic _____ or biostratigraphy.
  a. Thing
  b. Stratigraphy0
  c. Undefined
  d. Undefined

187. A _____ is a wetland that features temporary or permanent inundation of large areas of land by shallow bodies of water, generally with a substantial number of hummocks, or dry-land protrusions, and covered by aquatic vegetation, or vegetation that tolerates periodical inundation.

a. Thing
b. Swamp0
c. Undefined
d. Undefined

188. The _____ is one of three geologic eras of the Phanerozoic eon. The _____ was a time of tectonic, climatic and evolutionary activity, shifting from a state of connectedness into their present configuration. The climate was exceptionally warm throughout the period, also playing an important role in the evolution and diversification of new animal species. By the end of the era, the basis of modern life was in place.

a. Thing
b. Mesozoic0
c. Undefined
d. Undefined

189. The _____ is the most recent of the three classic geological eras. It covers the 65.5 million years since the Cretaceous-Tertiary extinction event at the end of the Cretaceous that marked the demise of the last non-avian dinosaurs and the end of the Mesozoic Era.

a. Thing
b. Cenozoic era0
c. Undefined
d. Undefined

190. An _____ phenomenon is an observed event which deviates from what is expected according to existing rules or scientific theory.

a. Thing
b. Anomalous0
c. Undefined
d. Undefined

191. _____ is the average and variations of weather over long periods of time. _____ zones can be defined using parameters such as temperature and rainfall.

a. Climate0
b. Thing
c. Undefined
d. Undefined

Chapter 10. Early Paleozoic Earth History

1. The scientific study of the Earth, its origins and evolution, the materials that make it up, and the processes that act on it is called _____.
   a. 1509 Istanbul earthquake
   b. Geology10
   c. Undefined
   d. Undefined

2. A member of a group of easily combustible, organic sedimentary rocks composed mostly of plant remains and containing a high proportion of carbon is called _____.
   a. Coal10
   b. 1509 Istanbul earthquake
   c. Undefined
   d. Undefined

3. A period of time in the Paleozoic Era that covered the time span between 400 and 345 million years is referred to as _____.
   a. Devonian10
   b. 1509 Istanbul earthquake
   c. Undefined
   d. Undefined

4. Aggregates of minerals or rock fragments are called _____.
   a. Rocks10
   b. 1509 Istanbul earthquake
   c. Undefined
   d. Undefined

5. _____ refers to the mechanism by which the earth is believed to have formed from a small nucleus by additions of solid bodies, such as meteorites, asteroids, or planetesimals. Also used in plate tectonics to indicate the addition of terranes to a continent.
   a. Accretion10
   b. AASHTO Soil Classification System
   c. Undefined
   d. Undefined

6. A body of rock identified by lithic characteristics and stratigraphic position and is mappable at the earth's surface or traceable in the subsurface is a _____.
   a. 1509 Istanbul earthquake
   b. Formation10
   c. Undefined
   d. Undefined

7. _____ refers to all geologic time from the beginning of Earth history to 570 million years ago. Also refers to the rocks that formed in that epoch.
   a. Precambrian10
   b. 1509 Istanbul earthquake
   c. Undefined
   d. Undefined

8. _____ refers to a major division on the geologic time scale; eras are divided into shorter units called periods.
   a. AASHTO Soil Classification System
   b. Era10
   c. Undefined
   d. Undefined

9. The segment of the Earth's continents that have remained tectonically stable and relatively earthquake-free for a vast period of time is a _____. The _____ is composed of the continental shield and the surrounding continental platform.
   a. Craton10
   b. 1509 Istanbul earthquake
   c. Undefined
   d. Undefined

10. _____ refers to eon of geologic time. Includes all time following the Precambrian.

176 Chapter 10. Early Paleozoic Earth History

    a. 1509 Istanbul earthquake
    c. Undefined
    b. Phanerozoic10
    d. Undefined

11. A design carved or chipped out on the slabs of Breton tombs is a _____. It is a highly version of an antropomorphic figure.
    a. Shield10
    c. Undefined
    b. 1509 Istanbul earthquake
    d. Undefined

12. Describing a mineral that will not react with or convert to a new mineral or substance, given enough time is referred to as _____.
    a. Stable10
    c. Undefined
    b. 1509 Istanbul earthquake
    d. Undefined

13. Rock resulting from precipitation of chemical compounds from a water solution is referred to as _____.
    a. 1509 Istanbul earthquake
    c. Undefined
    b. Chemical sedimentary rocks10
    d. Undefined

14. The covering of a large region of a continent by a sheet of glacial ice is referred to as _____.
    a. 1509 Istanbul earthquake
    c. Undefined
    b. Continental glaciation10
    d. Undefined

15. _____ refers to rigid parts of the Earth's crust and part of the Earth's upper mantle that moves and adjoins each other along zones of seismic activity.
    a. 1509 Istanbul earthquake
    c. Undefined
    b. Plate10
    d. Undefined

16. The top of the ocean, where the water meets the atmosphere is called _____.
    a. Sea level10
    o. Undefined
    b. 1509 Istanbul earthquake
    d. Undefined

17. A hole dug into the ground in the attempt to intersect water or other subsurface fluids is referred to as a _____.
    a. Well10
    c. Undefined
    b. 1509 Istanbul earthquake
    d. Undefined

18. _____ refers to the coming together of two lithospheric plates. _____ causes subduction when one or both plates are oceanic and mountain formation when both plates are continental.
    a. 1509 Istanbul earthquake
    c. Undefined
    b. Convergence10
    d. Undefined

19. Molten rock that forms naturally within the Earth is _____. _____ may be either a liquid or a fluid mixture of liquid, crystals, and dissolved gases.
    a. Magma10
    c. Undefined
    b. 1509 Istanbul earthquake
    d. Undefined

20. A large mass of rock projecting above surrounding terrain is called a _____.

a. 1509 Istanbul earthquake
b. Mountain10
c. Undefined
d. Undefined

21. _____ refers to a boundary in which two plates move together, resulting in oceanic lithosphere being thrust beneath an overriding plate, eventually to be reabsorbed into the mantle. It can also involve the collision of two continental plates to create a mountain system.
   a. Convergent plate boundary10
   b. 1509 Istanbul earthquake
   c. Undefined
   d. Undefined

22. _____ refers to the theory that the Earth's lithosphere consists of large, rigid plates that move horizontally in response to the flow of the asthenosphere beneath them, and that interactions among the plates at their borders cause most major geologic activity, including the creation of oceans, continents, mountains, volcanoes, and earthquakes.
   a. 1509 Istanbul earthquake
   b. Plate tectonics10
   c. Undefined
   d. Undefined

23. _____ refers to a major division of geology that deals with the origin of Earth and its development through time. Usually involves the study of fossils and their sequence in rock beds.
   a. 1509 Istanbul earthquake
   b. Historical geology10
   c. Undefined
   d. Undefined

24. The study of rock strata, especially of their distribution, deposition, and age is called _____.
   a. 1509 Istanbul earthquake
   b. Stratigraphic10
   c. Undefined
   d. Undefined

25. A deviation from the average or expected value is an _____. In paleomagnetism, a 'positive' _____ is a stronger-than-average magnetic field at the earth's surface.
   a. AASHTO Soil Classification System
   b. Anomaly10
   c. Undefined
   d. Undefined

26. The outermost layer of the Earth, consisting of relatively low-density rock is called _____.
   a. Crust10
   b. 1509 Istanbul earthquake
   c. Undefined
   d. Undefined

27. _____ refers to earth's crust, which is formed at mid-oceanic ridges, typically 5 to 10 kilometers thick with a density of 3.0 grams per centimeter cubed.
   a. AASHTO Soil Classification System
   b. Oceanic crust10
   c. Undefined
   d. Undefined

28. _____ refers to the earliest era of the Phanerozoic Eon, marked by the presence of marine invertebrates, fish, amphibians, insects, and land plants.
   a. Paleozoic era10
   b. 1509 Istanbul earthquake
   c. Undefined
   d. Undefined

29. _____ refers to the proposed supercontinent that 200 million years ago began to break apart and form the present landmasses.

Chapter 10. Early Paleozoic Earth History

  a. 1509 Istanbul earthquake
  c. Undefined

  b. Pangaea10
  d. Undefined

30. Strain involving an increase in length is an _____. _____ can cause crustal thinning and faulting.
  a. AASHTO Soil Classification System
  c. Undefined

  b. Extension10
  d. Undefined

31. The southern part of the Permo-Triassic drift landmass of Pangaea is called _____.
  a. 1509 Istanbul earthquake
  c. Undefined

  b. Gondwana10
  d. Undefined

32. Low latitude areas characterized by high temperatures and high precipitation are referred to as _____. At high elevations, however, _____ mountains may be both cold and relatively dry.
  a. 1509 Istanbul earthquake
  c. Undefined

  b. Tropical10
  d. Undefined

33. _____ refers to a basic unit of the geologic time scale that is a subdivision of an era. Periods may be divided into smaller units called epochs.
  a. 1509 Istanbul earthquake
  c. Undefined

  b. Period10
  d. Undefined

34. _____ refers to the northern portion of Pangaea consisting of North America and Eurasia.
  a. 1509 Istanbul earthquake
  c. Undefined

  b. Laurasia10
  d. Undefined

35. An imaginary line that separates the drainage of two streams, often found along a ridge is referred to as the _____.
  a. 1509 Istanbul earthquake
  c. Undefined

  b. Divide10
  d. Undefined

36. _____ refers to the theory that living organisms mutate and change, generally from simple to increasingly complex forms.
  a. AASHTO Soil Classification System
  c. Undefined

  b. Evolution10
  d. Undefined

37. _____ refers to a naturally formed aggregate of usually inorganic materials from within the Earth.
  a. Rock10
  c. Undefined

  b. 1509 Istanbul earthquake
  d. Undefined

38. A boundary separating two or more rocks of markedly different ages, marking a gap in the geologic record is referred to as _____.
  a. Unconformity10
  c. Undefined

  b. AASHTO Soil Classification System
  d. Undefined

39. _____ refers to a portion of a rock unit that possesses a distinctive set of characteristics that distinguishes it from other parts of the same unit.

Chapter 10. Early Paleozoic Earth History

a. 1509 Istanbul earthquake
b. Facies10
c. Undefined
d. Undefined

40. Rocks formed by solidification of sediments formed and transported at the Earth's surface are referred to as _____.
a. 1509 Istanbul earthquake
b. Sedimentary rocks10
c. Undefined
d. Undefined

41. _____ refers to the description, correlation, and classification of unconformity-bounded sequences of sedimentary strata. The unconformities that define sequences represent fluctuations in sea level that allowed land erosion to take place.
a. 1509 Istanbul earthquake
b. Sequence stratigraphy10
c. Undefined
d. Undefined

42. A descriptive term applied to igneous rocks with silica between 44% and 52% is _____.
a. Basic10
b. 1509 Istanbul earthquake
c. Undefined
d. Undefined

43. Parallel layers of sedimentary rock are called _____.
a. Strata10
b. 1509 Istanbul earthquake
c. Undefined
d. Undefined

44. _____ refers to the description, correlation, and classification of strata in sedimentary rocks.
a. 1509 Istanbul earthquake
b. Stratigraphy10
c. Undefined
d. Undefined

45. The process of determining that two or more geographically distant rocks or rock strata originated in the same time period is referred to as _____.
a. 1509 Istanbul earthquake
b. Correlation10
c. Undefined
d. Undefined

46. Any accumulation of material, by mechanical settling from water or air, chemical precipitation, evaporation from solution, etc is referred to as _____.
a. 1509 Istanbul earthquake
b. Deposition10
c. Undefined
d. Undefined

47. The process by which particles of rock and soil are loosened, as by weathering, and then transported elsewhere, as by wind, water, ice, or gravity is _____.
a. AASHTO Soil Classification System
b. Erosion10
c. Undefined
d. Undefined

48. The process by which exposure to atmospheric agents, such as air or moisture, causes rocks and minerals to break down is called _____. This process takes place at or near the Earth's surface. _____ entails little or no movement of the material that it loosens from the rocks and minerals.

a. 1509 Istanbul earthquake b. Weathering10
c. Undefined d. Undefined

49. The undifferentiated rocks that underlie the rocks of interest in an area are referred to as _____.
a. Basement10 b. 1509 Istanbul earthquake
c. Undefined d. Undefined

50. _____ refers to the structure in which relatively thin layers are inclined at an angle to the main bedding. Formed by currents of wind or water.
a. 1509 Istanbul earthquake b. Cross-bedding10
c. Undefined d. Undefined

51. A sedimentary structure consisting of a very small dune of sand or silt whose long dimension is at right angles to the current is a _____.
a. Ripple10 b. 1509 Istanbul earthquake
c. Undefined d. Undefined

52. A pattern of wavy lines formed along the top of a bed by wind, water currents, or waves are _____.
a. Ripple marks10 b. 1509 Istanbul earthquake
c. Undefined d. Undefined

53. One of several minerals containing one central carbon atom with strong covalent bonds to three oxygen atoms and typically having ionic bonds to one or more positive ions is _____.
a. Carbonate10 b. 1509 Istanbul earthquake
c. Undefined d. Undefined

54. The part of a coast that is washed by waves or tides, which cover it with sediments of various sizes and composition, such as sand or pebbles is called a _____.
a. Beach10 b. 1509 Istanbul earthquake
c. Undefined d. Undefined

55. _____ refers to a clastic rock composed of particles that range in diameter from 1/16 millimeter to 2 millimeters in diameter. Sandstones make up about 25% of all sedimentary rocks.
a. 1509 Istanbul earthquake b. Sandstone10
c. Undefined d. Undefined

56. _____ refers to the boundary between a body of water and dry land.
a. 1509 Istanbul earthquake b. Shoreline10
c. Undefined d. Undefined

57. _____ refers to a sedimentary rock composed of detrital sediment particles less than 0.004 millimeters in diameter. _____ tends to be red, brown, black, or gray, and usually originate in relatively still waters.
a. Shale10 b. 1509 Istanbul earthquake
c. Undefined d. Undefined

Chapter 10. Early Paleozoic Earth History

58. A sedimentary rock composed primarily of calcium carbonate is _____. Some 10% to 15% of all sedimentary rocks are limestones. _____ is usually organic, but it may also be inorganic.
    a. 1509 Istanbul earthquake
    b. Limestone10
    c. Undefined
    d. Undefined

59. The vertical difference between the summit of a mountain and the adjacent valley or plain is referred to as a _____.
    a. Relief10
    b. 1509 Istanbul earthquake
    c. Undefined
    d. Undefined

60. The locality that eroded to provide sediment to form a sedimentary rock is called _____.
    a. Source area10
    b. 1509 Istanbul earthquake
    c. Undefined
    d. Undefined

61. Mineral with the formula SiO is referred to as _____.
    a. Quartz10
    b. 1509 Istanbul earthquake
    c. Undefined
    d. Undefined

62. The epoch of the Quaternary Period of geologic time, following the Pliocene Epoch and preceding the Holocene is referred to as the _____.
    a. Pleistocene10
    b. 1509 Istanbul earthquake
    c. Undefined
    d. Undefined

63. Boundary surface between two different rock types or ages of rocks is called _____.
    a. 1509 Istanbul earthquake
    b. Contact10
    c. Undefined
    d. Undefined

64. Angular chunk of solid rock ejected during an eruption is referred to as a _____.
    a. Block10
    b. 1509 Istanbul earthquake
    c. Undefined
    d. Undefined

65. A sandstone in which more than 90% of the grains are quartz is the _____.
    a. 1509 Istanbul earthquake
    b. Quartz sandstone10
    c. Undefined
    d. Undefined

66. Any place where bedrock is visible on the surface of the Earth is referred to as _____.
    a. Outcrop10
    b. AASHTO Soil Classification System
    c. Undefined
    d. Undefined

67. Refers to substances containing or composed of calcium carbonate is called _____.
    a. Calcareous10
    b. 1509 Istanbul earthquake
    c. Undefined
    d. Undefined

68. _____ refers to a ridge-like or mound-like structure, layered or massive, built by sedentary calcareous organisms; it is wave resistant and stands above the surrounding contemporaneously deposited sediment.

Chapter 10. Early Paleozoic Earth History

a. 1509 Istanbul earthquake
b. Reef10
c. Undefined
d. Undefined

69. The proportion of dissolved salts to pure water, usually expressed in parts per thousand is referred to as _____.
a. 1509 Istanbul earthquake
b. Salinity10
c. Undefined
d. Undefined

70. The innermost layer of the Earth, consisting primarily of pure metals such as iron and nickel is the _____. The _____ is the densest layer of the Earth, and is divided into the outer _____, which is believed to be liquid, and the inner _____, which is believed to be solid.
a. 1509 Istanbul earthquake
b. Core10
c. Undefined
d. Undefined

71. The lowering of the Earth's surface, caused by such factors as compaction, a decrease in groundwater, or the pumping of oil is called _____.
a. Subsidence10
b. 1509 Istanbul earthquake
c. Undefined
d. Undefined

72. _____ refers to the set of physical features, such as mountains, valleys, and the shapes of landforms, that characterizes a given landscape.
a. Topography10
b. 1509 Istanbul earthquake
c. Undefined
d. Undefined

73. The movement of air from a region of high pressure to a region of low pressure is _____.
a. Wind10
b. 1509 Istanbul earthquake
c. Undefined
d. Undefined

74. A round or oval depression in the Earth's surface, containing the youngest section of rock in its lowest, central part is a _____.
a. Basin10
b. 1509 Istanbul earthquake
c. Undefined
d. Undefined

75. The largest time unit on the geologic time scale, next in order of magnitude above era is an _____.
a. Eon10
b. AASHTO Soil Classification System
c. Undefined
d. Undefined

76. Inorganic chemical sediment that precipitates when the salty water in which it had dissolved evaporates is called _____.
a. AASHTO Soil Classification System
b. Evaporite10
c. Undefined
d. Undefined

77. _____ refers to any condensed water falling from the atmosphere to the surface of the earth. Common types include rain, snow, sleet, and hail.
a. 1509 Istanbul earthquake
b. Precipitation10
c. Undefined
d. Undefined

Chapter 10. Early Paleozoic Earth History 183

78. _____ refers to the change of state of water from the liquid to vapor phase. Requires the addition of 80 calories per cubic centimeter.
    a. AASHTO Soil Classification System
    b. Evaporation10
    c. Undefined
    d. Undefined

79. _____ refers to a concordant pluton that is substantially wider than it is thick. Sills form within a few kilometers of the Earth's surface.
    a. 1509 Istanbul earthquake
    b. Sill10
    c. Undefined
    d. Undefined

80. _____ refers to drop out of a saturated solution as crystals. The crystals that drop out of a saturated solution.
    a. 1509 Istanbul earthquake
    b. Precipitate10
    c. Undefined
    d. Undefined

81. General term for the processes of folding, faulting, shearing, compression, or extension of rocks as the result of various natural forces is called _____.
    a. 1509 Istanbul earthquake
    b. Deformation10
    c. Undefined
    d. Undefined

82. An episode of mountain building is called _____.
    a. AASHTO Soil Classification System
    b. Orogeny10
    c. Undefined
    d. Undefined

83. The ocean floor from the shore of continents to the abyssal plain is called _____.
    a. Continental margin10
    b. 1509 Istanbul earthquake
    c. Undefined
    d. Undefined

84. _____ refers to a boundary in which two plates move apart, resulting in upwelling of material from the mantle to create new seafloor.
    a. Divergent plate boundary10
    b. 1509 Istanbul earthquake
    c. Undefined
    d. Undefined

85. The sinking of an oceanic plate edge as a result of convergence with a plate of lesser density is called _____. _____ often causes earthquakes and creates volcano chains.
    a. 1509 Istanbul earthquake
    b. Subduction10
    c. Undefined
    d. Undefined

86. A reef separated from the shoreline by the deeper water of a lagoon is called a _____.
    a. Barrier reef10
    b. 1509 Istanbul earthquake
    c. Undefined
    d. Undefined

87. An evaporite composed of halite is referred to as _____.
    a. Rock salt10
    b. 1509 Istanbul earthquake
    c. Undefined
    d. Undefined

88. Term loosely used for silt and clay, usually wet is referred to as _____.

Chapter 10. Early Paleozoic Earth History

a. Mud10
c. Undefined
b. 1509 Istanbul earthquake
d. Undefined

89. A shallow, extensive flat area where both biological and nonbiological carbonates are deposited is a _____.
a. Carbonate platform10
c. Undefined
b. 1509 Istanbul earthquake
d. Undefined

90. The set of geological processes that result in the expulsion of lava, pyroclastics, and gases at the Earth's surface is referred to as _____.
a. 1509 Istanbul earthquake
c. Undefined
b. Volcanism10
d. Undefined

91. A continental margin far from a plate margin, with no volcanoes and few earthquakes is a _____.
a. 1509 Istanbul earthquake
c. Undefined
b. Passive margin10
d. Undefined

92. _____ refers to the area of dry land that borders on a body of water.
a. Coast10
c. Undefined
b. 1509 Istanbul earthquake
d. Undefined

93. Being or pertaining to a sedimentary rock composed primarily from fragments of preexisting rocks or fossils is called _____.
a. Clastic10
c. Undefined
b. 1509 Istanbul earthquake
d. Undefined

94. An alluvial fan having its apex at the mouth of a stream is a _____.
a. Delta10
c. Undefined
b. 1509 Istanbul earthquake
d. Undefined

95. The solid material that precipitates in the pore space of sediments, binding the grains together to form solid rock is referred to as _____.
a. 1509 Istanbul earthquake
c. Undefined
b. Cement10
d. Undefined

96. Rounded particles coarser than 2 mm in diameter are called _____.
a. 1509 Istanbul earthquake
c. Undefined
b. Gravel10
d. Undefined

97. A naturally occurring, usually inorganic, solid consisting of either a single element or a compound, and having a definite chemical composition and a systematic internal arrangement of atoms is referred to as a _____.
a. Mineral10
c. Undefined
b. 1509 Istanbul earthquake
d. Undefined

98. _____ refer to the valuable minerals of an area that are presently legally recoverable or that may be so in the future; includes both the known ore bodies and the potential ores of a region.

Chapter 10. Early Paleozoic Earth History

a. 1509 Istanbul earthquake
c. Undefined
b. Mineral resources10
d. Undefined

99. The total amount of a geologic material in all its deposits, discovered and undiscovered are _____.
a. Resources10
c. Undefined
b. 1509 Istanbul earthquake
d. Undefined

100. _____ refers to a chemical combination of silicon and oxygen.
a. 1509 Istanbul earthquake
c. Undefined
b. Silica10
d. Undefined

101. A non-crystaline rock that results from very rapid cooling of magma is _____.
a. Glass10
c. Undefined
b. 1509 Istanbul earthquake
d. Undefined

102. _____ refers to a crack or break in a rock. To break in random places instead of cleaving.
a. Fracture10
c. Undefined
b. 1509 Istanbul earthquake
d. Undefined

103. Cracking or rupturing of a body under stress is referred to as _____.
a. Fracturing10
c. Undefined
b. 1509 Istanbul earthquake
d. Undefined

104. Fluid organic sediment formed by the diagenesis of organic material in the pores of sedimentary rocks, mainly sandstones and limestones is referred to as _____.
a. 1509 Istanbul earthquake
c. Undefined
b. Gas10
d. Undefined

105. _____ refers to a fluid organic sediment formed by the diagenesis of organic material in the pores of sedimentary rocks, mainly sandstones and limestones.
a. AASHTO Soil Classification System
c. Undefined
b. Oil10
d. Undefined

106. _____ refers to an evaporite composed of gypsum.
a. 1509 Istanbul earthquake
c. Undefined
b. Rock gypsum10
d. Undefined

107. A mineral deposit that can be mined for a profit is called _____.
a. AASHTO Soil Classification System
c. Undefined
b. Ore10
d. Undefined

108. Bridge of rock left above an opening eroded in a headland by waves is an _____.
a. Arch10
c. Undefined
b. AASHTO Soil Classification System
d. Undefined

109. _____ refers to any evidence of past life, including remains, traces, imprints as well as life history artifacts.

a. 1509 Istanbul earthquake
b. Fossil10
c. Undefined
d. Undefined

Chapter 11. Late Paleozoic Earth History

1. A body of rock identified by lithic characteristics and stratigraphic position and is mappable at the earth's surface or traceable in the subsurface is a _____.
   a. Formation11
   b. 1509 Istanbul earthquake
   c. Undefined
   d. Undefined

2. An alluvial fan having its apex at the mouth of a stream is a _____.
   a. 1509 Istanbul earthquake
   b. Delta11
   c. Undefined
   d. Undefined

3. A hole dug into the ground in the attempt to intersect water or other subsurface fluids is referred to as a _____.
   a. 1509 Istanbul earthquake
   b. Well11
   c. Undefined
   d. Undefined

4. _____ refers to a basic unit of the geologic time scale that is a subdivision of an era. Periods may be divided into smaller units called epochs.
   a. Period11
   b. 1509 Istanbul earthquake
   c. Undefined
   d. Undefined

5. _____ refers to any evidence of past life, including remains, traces, imprints as well as life history artifacts.
   a. Fossil11
   b. 1509 Istanbul earthquake
   c. Undefined
   d. Undefined

6. _____ refers to a major division on the geologic time scale; eras are divided into shorter units called periods.
   a. AASHTO Soil Classification System
   b. Era11
   c. Undefined
   d. Undefined

7. _____ refers to rigid parts of the Earth's crust and part of the Earth's upper mantle that moves and adjoins each other along zones of seismic activity.
   a. Plate11
   b. 1509 Istanbul earthquake
   c. Undefined
   d. Undefined

8. A large mass of rock projecting above surrounding terrain is called a _____.
   a. 1509 Istanbul earthquake
   b. Mountain11
   c. Undefined
   d. Undefined

9. The southern part of the Permo-Triassic drift landmass of Pangaea is called _____.
   a. 1509 Istanbul earthquake
   b. Gondwana11
   c. Undefined
   d. Undefined

10. The top of the ocean, where the water meets the atmosphere is called _____.
    a. Sea level11
    b. 1509 Istanbul earthquake
    c. Undefined
    d. Undefined

11. _____ refers to the proposed supercontinent that 200 million years ago began to break apart and form the present landmasses.

a. 1509 Istanbul earthquake
b. Pangaea11
c. Undefined
d. Undefined

12. _____ refers to a boundary in which two plates move together, resulting in oceanic lithosphere being thrust beneath an overriding plate, eventually to be reabsorbed into the mantle. It can also involve the collision of two continental plates to create a mountain system.
a. Convergent plate boundary11
b. 1509 Istanbul earthquake
c. Undefined
d. Undefined

13. A period of time in the Paleozoic Era that covered the time span between 400 and 345 million years is referred to as _____.
a. 1509 Istanbul earthquake
b. Devonian11
c. Undefined
d. Undefined

14. _____ refers to the northern portion of Pangaea consisting of North America and Eurasia.
a. Laurasia11
b. 1509 Istanbul earthquake
c. Undefined
d. Undefined

15. The ocean floor from the shore of continents to the abyssal plain is called _____.
a. 1509 Istanbul earthquake
b. Continental margin11
c. Undefined
d. Undefined

16. The process by which particles of rock and soil are loosened, as by weathering, and then transported elsewhere, as by wind, water, ice, or gravity is _____.
a. Erosion11
b. AASHTO Soil Classification System
c. Undefined
d. Undefined

17. _____ refers to of or pertaining to rivers; produced by river action.
a. Fluvial11
b. 1509 Istanbul earthquake
c. Undefined
d. Undefined

18. An episode of mountain building is called _____.
a. AASHTO Soil Classification System
b. Orogeny11
c. Undefined
d. Undefined

19. The covering of a large region of a continent by a sheet of glacial ice is referred to as _____.
a. Continental glaciation11
b. 1509 Istanbul earthquake
c. Undefined
d. Undefined

20. General term for the processes of folding, faulting, shearing, compression, or extension of rocks as the result of various natural forces is called _____.
a. 1509 Istanbul earthquake
b. Deformation11
c. Undefined
d. Undefined

21. A round or oval depression in the Earth's surface, containing the youngest section of rock in its lowest, central part is a _____.

Chapter 11. Late Paleozoic Earth History

a. 1509 Istanbul earthquake
b. Basin11
c. Undefined
d. Undefined

22. A member of a group of easily combustible, organic sedimentary rocks composed mostly of plant remains and containing a high proportion of carbon is called _____.
a. Coal11
b. 1509 Istanbul earthquake
c. Undefined
d. Undefined

23. _____ refer to multiple scratches or minute lines, generally parallel but occasionally cross-cutting, inscribed on a rock surface by a geologic agent. Common indicators of direction of glacier flow.
a. 1509 Istanbul earthquake
b. Striations11
c. Undefined
d. Undefined

24. The sinking of an oceanic plate edge as a result of convergence with a plate of lesser density is called _____. _____ often causes earthquakes and creates volcano chains.
a. Subduction11
b. 1509 Istanbul earthquake
c. Undefined
d. Undefined

25. One of several minerals containing one central carbon atom with strong covalent bonds to three oxygen atoms and typically having ionic bonds to one or more positive ions is _____.
a. Carbonate11
b. 1509 Istanbul earthquake
c. Undefined
d. Undefined

26. _____ refers to the theory that living organisms mutate and change, generally from simple to increasingly complex forms.
a. Evolution11
b. AASHTO Soil Classification System
c. Undefined
d. Undefined

27. _____ refers to the formation, movement, and recession of glaciers or ice sheet; geologic processes of glacial activity.
a. 1509 Istanbul earthquake
b. Glaciation11
c. Undefined
d. Undefined

28. A boundary separating two or more rocks of markedly different ages, marking a gap in the geologic record is referred to as _____.
a. AASHTO Soil Classification System
b. Unconformity11
c. Undefined
d. Undefined

29. The segment of the Earth's continents that have remained tectonically stable and relatively earthquake-free for a vast period of time is a _____. The _____ is composed of the continental shield and the surrounding continental platform.
a. 1509 Istanbul earthquake
b. Craton11
c. Undefined
d. Undefined

30. Mineral with the formula SiO is referred to as _____.

a. 1509 Istanbul earthquake
b. Quartz11
c. Undefined
d. Undefined

31. A non-crystaline rock that results from very rapid cooling of magma is _____.
   a. Glass11
   b. 1509 Istanbul earthquake
   c. Undefined
   d. Undefined

32. _____ refers to a naturally formed aggregate of usually inorganic materials from within the Earth.
   a. 1509 Istanbul earthquake
   b. Rock11
   c. Undefined
   d. Undefined

33. _____ refers to a clastic rock composed of particles that range in diameter from 1/16 millimeter to 2 millimeters in diameter. Sandstones make up about 25% of all sedimentary rocks.
   a. 1509 Istanbul earthquake
   b. Sandstone11
   c. Undefined
   d. Undefined

34. Aggregates of minerals or rock fragments are called _____.
   a. 1509 Istanbul earthquake
   b. Rocks11
   c. Undefined
   d. Undefined

35. The study of rock strata, especially of their distribution, deposition, and age is called _____.
   a. 1509 Istanbul earthquake
   b. Stratigraphic11
   c. Undefined
   d. Undefined

36. Inorganic chemical sediment that precipitates when the salty water in which it had dissolved evaporates is called _____.
   a. AASHTO Soil Classification System
   b. Evaporite11
   c. Undefined
   d. Undefined

37. _____ refers to any of a group of naturally occurring substances made up of hydrocarbons. These substances may be gaseous, liquid, or semi-solid.
   a. 1509 Istanbul earthquake
   b. Petroleum11
   c. Undefined
   d. Undefined

38. _____ refers to a ridge-like or mound-like structure, layered or massive, built by sedentary calcareous organisms; it is wave resistant and stands above the surrounding contemporaneously deposited sediment.
   a. 1509 Istanbul earthquake
   b. Reef11
   c. Undefined
   d. Undefined

39. The discovered deposits of a geologic material that are economically and legally feasible to recover under present circumstances are referred to as _____.
   a. Reserves11
   b. 1509 Istanbul earthquake
   c. Undefined
   d. Undefined

40. A reef separated from the shoreline by the deeper water of a lagoon is called a _____.

Chapter 11. Late Paleozoic Earth History

a. Barrier reef11
b. 1509 Istanbul earthquake
c. Undefined
d. Undefined

41. _____ refers to any condensed water falling from the atmosphere to the surface of the earth. Common types include rain, snow, sleet, and hail.
a. Precipitation11
b. 1509 Istanbul earthquake
c. Undefined
d. Undefined

42. A group of interacting or interdependent parts that form a complex whole is called a _____.
a. 1509 Istanbul earthquake
b. System11
c. Undefined
d. Undefined

43. Any accumulation of material, by mechanical settling from water or air, chemical precipitation, evaporation from solution, etc is referred to as _____.
a. Deposition11
b. 1509 Istanbul earthquake
c. Undefined
d. Undefined

44. Pertaining to the absence of free oxygen is referred to as _____.
a. AASHTO Soil Classification System
b. Anaerobic11
c. Undefined
d. Undefined

45. Sediment that is composed of transported solid fragments of preexisting igneous, sedimentary, or metamorphic rocks is called _____.
a. Detrital sediment11
b. 1509 Istanbul earthquake
c. Undefined
d. Undefined

46. _____ refers to a collection of transported fragments or precipitated materials that accumulate, typically in loose layers, as of sand or mud.
a. Sediment11
b. 1509 Istanbul earthquake
c. Undefined
d. Undefined

47. The process by which exposure to atmospheric agents, such as air or moisture, causes rocks and minerals to break down is called _____. This process takes place at or near the Earth's surface. _____ entails little or no movement of the material that it loosens from the rocks and minerals.
a. 1509 Istanbul earthquake
b. Weathering11
c. Undefined
d. Undefined

48. The innermost layer of the Earth, consisting primarily of pure metals such as iron and nickel is the _____. The _____ is the densest layer of the Earth, and is divided into the outer _____, which is believed to be liquid, and the inner _____, which is believed to be solid.
a. Core11
b. 1509 Istanbul earthquake
c. Undefined
d. Undefined

49. _____ refers to a portion of a rock unit that possesses a distinctive set of characteristics that distinguishes it from other parts of the same unit.

a. 1509 Istanbul earthquake
c. Undefined
b. Facies11
d. Undefined

50. Refers to substances containing or composed of calcium carbonate is called _____.
   a. 1509 Istanbul earthquake
   b. Calcareous11
   c. Undefined
   d. Undefined

51. Any place where bedrock is visible on the surface of the Earth is referred to as _____.
   a. Outcrop11
   b. AASHTO Soil Classification System
   c. Undefined
   d. Undefined

52. _____ refers to a pile of rock fragments lying at the bottom of the cliff or steep slope from which they have broken off.
   a. Talus11
   b. 1509 Istanbul earthquake
   c. Undefined
   d. Undefined

53. Parallel layers of sedimentary rock are called _____.
   a. 1509 Istanbul earthquake
   b. Strata11
   c. Undefined
   d. Undefined

54. A design carved or chipped out on the slabs of Breton tombs is a _____. It is a highly version of an antropomorphic figure.
   a. 1509 Istanbul earthquake
   b. Shield11
   c. Undefined
   d. Undefined

55. _____ refers to a sedimentary rock composed of detrital sediment particles less than 0.004 millimeters in diameter. _____ tends to be red, brown, black, or gray, and usually originate in relatively still waters.
   a. 1509 Istanbul earthquake
   b. Shale11
   c. Undefined
   d. Undefined

56. The situation in mass wasting that occurs when material free-falls or bounces down a cliff is called a _____.
   a. Fall11
   b. 1509 Istanbul earthquake
   c. Undefined
   d. Undefined

57. _____ refers to a tentative explanation of a given set of data that is expected to remain valid after future observation and experimentation.
   a. 1509 Istanbul earthquake
   b. Hypothesis11
   c. Undefined
   d. Undefined

58. Describing a mineral that will not react with or convert to a new mineral or substance, given enough time is referred to as _____.
   a. Stable11
   b. 1509 Istanbul earthquake
   c. Undefined
   d. Undefined

59. The undifferentiated rocks that underlie the rocks of interest in an area are referred to as _____.

Chapter 11. Late Paleozoic Earth History

a. Basement11
b. 1509 Istanbul earthquake
c. Undefined
d. Undefined

60. A numerical expression of the amount of energy released by an earthquake, determined by measuring earthquake waves on standardized recording instruments is called a _____. The number scale for magnitudes is logarithmic rather than arithmetic. Therefore, deflections on a seismograph for a _____ 5 earthquake, for example, are 10 times greater than those for a _____ 4 earthquake, 100 times greater than for a _____ 3 earthquake, and so on.
   a. 1509 Istanbul earthquake
   b. Magnitude11
   c. Undefined
   d. Undefined

61. _____ refers to all geologic time from the beginning of Earth history to 570 million years ago. Also refers to the rocks that formed in that epoch.
   a. Precambrian11
   b. 1509 Istanbul earthquake
   c. Undefined
   d. Undefined

62. _____ refers to a rugged region of the lunar surface representing an early period in lunar history when intense meteorite bombardment formed craters.
   a. Highland11
   b. 1509 Istanbul earthquake
   c. Undefined
   d. Undefined

63. Angular chunk of solid rock ejected during an eruption is referred to as a _____.
   a. Block11
   b. 1509 Istanbul earthquake
   c. Undefined
   d. Undefined

64. The processes by which crustal forces cause a rock formation to break and slip along a fault are called _____.
   a. 1509 Istanbul earthquake
   b. Faulting11
   c. Undefined
   d. Undefined

65. An igneous pluton that is not tabular in shape is _____.
   a. Massive11
   b. 1509 Istanbul earthquake
   c. Undefined
   d. Undefined

66. An impermeable stratum that caps an oil reservoir and prevents oil and gas from escaping to the ground surface is called _____.
   a. 1509 Istanbul earthquake
   b. Caprock11
   c. Undefined
   d. Undefined

67. _____ refers to a fluid organic sediment formed by the diagenesis of organic material in the pores of sedimentary rocks, mainly sandstones and limestones.
   a. Oil11
   b. AASHTO Soil Classification System
   c. Undefined
   d. Undefined

68. Fine particles of pulverized rock blown from an explosion vent are called _____. Measuring less than 1/10 inch in diameter, _____ may be either solid or molten when first erupted.

Chapter 11. Late Paleozoic Earth History

a. AASHTO Soil Classification System
b. Ash11
c. Undefined
d. Undefined

69. A sedimentary rock composed primarily of calcium carbonate is _____. Some 10% to 15% of all sedimentary rocks are limestones. _____ is usually organic, but it may also be inorganic.
a. 1509 Istanbul earthquake
b. Limestone11
c. Undefined
d. Undefined

70. _____ refers to igneous rocks that cool on the surface of the Earth, including beneath water; typically with small crystals due to the rapidity of cooling.
a. 1509 Istanbul earthquake
b. Volcanic11
c. Undefined
d. Undefined

71. A chain of volcanoes fueled by magma that rises from an underlying subducting plate is called a _____.
a. Volcanic arc11
b. 1509 Istanbul earthquake
c. Undefined
d. Undefined

72. Part of the continental margin, the ocean floor from the coastal shore of continents to the continental slope, usually to a depth of about 200 meters is the _____. The _____ usually has a very slight slope, roughly 0.1 degrees.
a. Continental shelf11
b. 1509 Istanbul earthquake
c. Undefined
d. Undefined

73. _____ refers to a border that lies between continental and oceanic lithosphere, but is not a plate margin. It is marked by lack of seismic and volcanic activity.
a. 1509 Istanbul earthquake
b. Passive continental margin11
c. Undefined
d. Undefined

74. _____ refers to the mechanism by which the earth is believed to have formed from a small nucleus by additions of solid bodies, such as meteorites, asteroids, or planetesimals. Also used in plate tectonics to indicate the addition of terranes to a continent.
a. AASHTO Soil Classification System
b. Accretion11
c. Undefined
d. Undefined

75. _____ refers to the coming together of two lithospheric plates. _____ causes subduction when one or both plates are oceanic and mountain formation when both plates are continental.
a. Convergence11
b. 1509 Istanbul earthquake
c. Undefined
d. Undefined

76. Earth's crust that includes both the continents and the continental shelves is the _____.
a. 1509 Istanbul earthquake
b. Continental crust11
c. Undefined
d. Undefined

77. _____ refers to a group of closely spaced mountains or parallel ridges.
a. Mountain range11
b. 1509 Istanbul earthquake
c. Undefined
d. Undefined

Chapter 11. Late Paleozoic Earth History

78. _____ refers to the area of dry land that borders on a body of water.
   a. Coast11
   b. 1509 Istanbul earthquake
   c. Undefined
   d. Undefined

79. _____ refers to elongate trenched or crack like valley on the lunar surface.
   a. Rile11
   b. 1509 Istanbul earthquake
   c. Undefined
   d. Undefined

80. The outermost layer of the Earth, consisting of relatively low-density rock is called _____.
   a. Crust11
   b. 1509 Istanbul earthquake
   c. Undefined
   d. Undefined

81. _____ refers to earth's crust, which is formed at mid-oceanic ridges, typically 5 to 10 kilometers thick with a density of 3.0 grams per centimeter cubed.
   a. Oceanic crust11
   b. AASHTO Soil Classification System
   c. Undefined
   d. Undefined

82. The convergence of two continental plates, resulting in the formation of mountain ranges is called _____.
   a. Continental collision11
   b. 1509 Istanbul earthquake
   c. Undefined
   d. Undefined

83. The scientific study of the Earth, its origins and evolution, the materials that make it up, and the processes that act on it is called _____.
   a. Geology11
   b. 1509 Istanbul earthquake
   c. Undefined
   d. Undefined

84. _____ refers to the theory that the Earth's lithosphere consists of large, rigid plates that move horizontally in response to the flow of the asthenosphere beneath them, and that interactions among the plates at their borders cause most major geologic activity, including the creation of oceans, continents, mountains, volcanoes, and earthquakes.
   a. Plate tectonics11
   b. 1509 Istanbul earthquake
   c. Undefined
   d. Undefined

85. _____ refers to the study of the large-scale processes that collectively deform Earth's crust.
   a. 1509 Istanbul earthquake
   b. Tectonics11
   c. Undefined
   d. Undefined

86. A comprehensive explanation of a given set of data that has been repeatedly confirmed by observation and experimentation and has gained general acceptance within the scientific community but has not yet been decisively proven is referred to as _____.
   a. Theory11
   b. 1509 Istanbul earthquake
   c. Undefined
   d. Undefined

87. _____ refers to the term from the Greek 'meta' and 'morph', commonly occurs to rocks which are subjected to increased heat and/or pressure. Also applies to the conversion of snow into glacial ice.

Chapter 11. Late Paleozoic Earth History

    a. Metamorphic11
    b. 1509 Istanbul earthquake
    c. Undefined
    d. Undefined

88. Rocks that crystallize from molten material at the surface of the earth or within the earth are called _____.
    a. AASHTO Soil Classification System
    b. Igneous rocks11
    c. Undefined
    d. Undefined

89. Being or pertaining to a sedimentary rock composed primarily from fragments of preexisting rocks or fossils is called _____.
    a. Clastic11
    b. 1509 Istanbul earthquake
    c. Undefined
    d. Undefined

90. _____ refers to a property of a mineral imparted by light-either transmitted through or reflected by crystals, irregular masses, or a streak.
    a. Color11
    b. 1509 Istanbul earthquake
    c. Undefined
    d. Undefined

91. _____ refers to a type of iron oxide that has a brick-red color when powdered.
    a. Hematite11
    b. 1509 Istanbul earthquake
    c. Undefined
    d. Undefined

92. The process of combining with oxygen ions is _____. A mineral that is exposed to air may undergo _____ as a form of chemical weathering.
    a. Oxidation11
    b. AASHTO Soil Classification System
    c. Undefined
    d. Undefined

93. A naturally occurring, usually inorganic, solid consisting of either a single element or a compound, and having a definite chemical composition and a systematic internal arrangement of atoms is referred to as a _____.
    a. Mineral11
    b. 1509 Istanbul earthquake
    c. Undefined
    d. Undefined

94. Ability to do work is referred to as _____. Most evident in glacial systems as radiant _____ from the sun and as latent _____ required to melt ice to water.
    a. AASHTO Soil Classification System
    b. Energy11
    c. Undefined
    d. Undefined

95. _____ refer to the valuable minerals of an area that are presently legally recoverable or that may be so in the future; includes both the known ore bodies and the potential ores of a region.
    a. 1509 Istanbul earthquake
    b. Mineral resources11
    c. Undefined
    d. Undefined

96. The total amount of a geologic material in all its deposits, discovered and undiscovered are _____.
    a. Resources11
    b. 1509 Istanbul earthquake
    c. Undefined
    d. Undefined

Chapter 11. Late Paleozoic Earth History

97. Fluid organic sediment formed by the diagenesis of organic material in the pores of sedimentary rocks, mainly sandstones and limestones is referred to as _____.
   a. 1509 Istanbul earthquake
   b. Gas11
   c. Undefined
   d. Undefined

98. A shiny black coal that develops from deeply buried lignite through heat and pressure, and that has a carbon content of 80% to 93%, which makes it a more efficient heating fuel than lignite is _____.
   a. 1509 Istanbul earthquake
   b. Bituminous coal11
   c. Undefined
   d. Undefined

99. _____ refers to a transitional material between snow and glacial ice, being older and denser than snow, but not yet transformed into glacial ice.
   a. 1509 Istanbul earthquake
   b. Fire11
   c. Undefined
   d. Undefined

100. A hard, jet-black coal that develops from lignite and bituminous coal through metamorphism, has a carbon content of 92% to 98%, and contains little or no gas is called _____. _____ burns with an extremely hot, blue flame and very little smoke, but it is difficult to ignite and both difficult and dangerous to mine.
   a. Anthracite11
   b. AASHTO Soil Classification System
   c. Undefined
   d. Undefined

101. A major branch of a stream system is referred to as a _____.
   a. River11
   b. 1509 Istanbul earthquake
   c. Undefined
   d. Undefined

102. _____ refers to a chemical combination of silicon and oxygen.
   a. Silica11
   b. 1509 Istanbul earthquake
   c. Undefined
   d. Undefined

103. The solid material that precipitates in the pore space of sediments, binding the grains together to form solid rock is referred to as _____.
   a. Cement11
   b. 1509 Istanbul earthquake
   c. Undefined
   d. Undefined

104. _____ refers to the earliest era of the Phanerozoic Eon, marked by the presence of marine invertebrates, fish, amphibians, insects, and land plants.
   a. Paleozoic era11
   b. 1509 Istanbul earthquake
   c. Undefined
   d. Undefined

Chapter 12. Paleozoic Life History: Invertebrates

1. _____ refers to the beginning or source area for a stream. Also called the headwaters.
   a. Head12
   b. 1509 Istanbul earthquake
   c. Undefined
   d. Undefined

2. _____ refers to a sedimentary rock composed of detrital sediment particles less than 0.004 millimeters in diameter. _____ tends to be red, brown, black, or gray, and usually originate in relatively still waters.
   a. Shale12
   b. 1509 Istanbul earthquake
   c. Undefined
   d. Undefined

3. The accumulation of precipitation into surface and underground areas, including lakes, rivers, and aquifers is a _____.
   a. 1509 Istanbul earthquake
   b. Collection12
   c. Undefined
   d. Undefined

4. Any accumulation of material, by mechanical settling from water or air, chemical precipitation, evaporation from solution, etc is referred to as _____.
   a. Deposition12
   b. 1509 Istanbul earthquake
   c. Undefined
   d. Undefined

5. _____ refers to any evidence of past life, including remains, traces, imprints as well as life history artifacts.
   a. Fossil12
   b. 1509 Istanbul earthquake
   c. Undefined
   d. Undefined

6. Term loosely used for silt and clay, usually wet is referred to as _____.
   a. 1509 Istanbul earthquake
   b. Mud12
   c. Undefined
   d. Undefined

7. The mass movement of a single, intact mass of rock, soil, or unconsolidated material along a weak plane, such as a fault, fracture, or bedding plane is a _____. A _____ may involve as little as a minor displacement of soil or as much as the displacement of an entire mountainside.
   a. Slide12
   b. 1509 Istanbul earthquake
   c. Undefined
   d. Undefined

8. _____ refers to a downward and outward slide occurring along a concave slip plane. The material that breaks off in such a slide.
   a. Slump12
   b. 1509 Istanbul earthquake
   c. Undefined
   d. Undefined

9. _____ refers to a downslope movement of dense, sediment-laden water created when sand and mud on the continental shelf and slope are dislodged and thrown into suspension.
   a. 1509 Istanbul earthquake
   b. Turbidity current12
   c. Undefined
   d. Undefined

10. Pertaining to the absence of free oxygen is referred to as _____.
    a. AASHTO Soil Classification System
    b. Anaerobic12
    c. Undefined
    d. Undefined

Chapter 12. Paleozoic Life History: Invertebrates

11. _____ refers to the process by which a stream's gradient becomes less steep, due to the erosion of sediment from the stream bed. Such erosion generally follows a sharp reduction in the amount of sediment entering the stream.
   a. 1509 Istanbul earthquake
   b. Degradation12
   c. Undefined
   d. Undefined

12. _____ refers to the theory that living organisms mutate and change, generally from simple to increasingly complex forms.
   a. Evolution12
   b. AASHTO Soil Classification System
   c. Undefined
   d. Undefined

13. _____ refers to rigid parts of the Earth's crust and part of the Earth's upper mantle that moves and adjoins each other along zones of seismic activity.
   a. 1509 Istanbul earthquake
   b. Plate12
   c. Undefined
   d. Undefined

14. _____ refers to the theory that the Earth's lithosphere consists of large, rigid plates that move horizontally in response to the flow of the asthenosphere beneath them, and that interactions among the plates at their borders cause most major geologic activity, including the creation of oceans, continents, mountains, volcanoes, and earthquakes.
   a. Plate tectonics12
   b. 1509 Istanbul earthquake
   c. Undefined
   d. Undefined

15. A group of interacting or interdependent parts that form a complex whole is called a _____.
   a. 1509 Istanbul earthquake
   b. System12
   c. Undefined
   d. Undefined

16. _____ refers to the study of the large-scale processes that collectively deform Earth's crust.
   a. 1509 Istanbul earthquake
   b. Tectonics12
   c. Undefined
   d. Undefined

17. A body of rock identified by lithic characteristics and stratigraphic position and is mappable at the earth's surface or traceable in the subsurface is a _____.
   a. Formation12
   b. 1509 Istanbul earthquake
   c. Undefined
   d. Undefined

18. A large mass of rock projecting above surrounding terrain is called a _____.
   a. 1509 Istanbul earthquake
   b. Mountain12
   c. Undefined
   d. Undefined

19. _____ refers to all geologic time from the beginning of Earth history to 570 million years ago. Also refers to the rocks that formed in that epoch.
   a. Precambrian12
   b. 1509 Istanbul earthquake
   c. Undefined
   d. Undefined

20. _____ refers to a basic unit of the geologic time scale that is a subdivision of an era. Periods may be divided into smaller units called epochs.

Chapter 12. Paleozoic Life History: Invertebrates

a. Period12
b. 1509 Istanbul earthquake
c. Undefined
d. Undefined

21. _____ refers to a major division on the geologic time scale; eras are divided into shorter units called periods.
a. AASHTO Soil Classification System
b. Era12
c. Undefined
d. Undefined

22. A situation, which is generally uncomfortable, or otherwise undesirable is a _____.
a. Problem12
b. 1509 Istanbul earthquake
c. Undefined
d. Undefined

23. A comprehensive explanation of a given set of data that has been repeatedly confirmed by observation and experimentation and has gained general acceptance within the scientific community but has not yet been decisively proven is referred to as _____.
a. Theory12
b. 1509 Istanbul earthquake
c. Undefined
d. Undefined

24. The largest time unit on the geologic time scale, next in order of magnitude above era is an _____.
a. AASHTO Soil Classification System
b. Eon12
c. Undefined
d. Undefined

25. Refers to substances containing or composed of calcium carbonate is called _____.
a. Calcareous12
b. 1509 Istanbul earthquake
c. Undefined
d. Undefined

26. A descriptive term applied to igneous rocks with silica between 44% and 52% is _____.
a. 1509 Istanbul earthquake
b. Basic12
c. Undefined
d. Undefined

27. A hole dug into the ground in the attempt to intersect water or other subsurface fluids is referred to as a _____.
a. Well12
b. 1509 Istanbul earthquake
c. Undefined
d. Undefined

28. The point downstream where a river empties into another stream or water body is called _____.
a. Mouth12
b. 1509 Istanbul earthquake
c. Undefined
d. Undefined

29. _____ refers to a collection of transported fragments or precipitated materials that accumulate, typically in loose layers, as of sand or mud.
a. Sediment12
b. 1509 Istanbul earthquake
c. Undefined
d. Undefined

30. A group of tiny single-celled organisms that live in surface waters and whose secretions and calcite shells account for most of the oceans carbonate sediments is called _____.

Chapter 12. Paleozoic Life History: Invertebrates

    a. 1509 Istanbul earthquake   b. Foraminifera12
    c. Undefined   d. Undefined

31. A mode of sediment transport in which the upward currents in eddies of turbulent flow are capable of supporting the weight of sediment particles and keeping them held indefinitely in the surrounding fluid is called _____.
    a. Suspension12   b. 1509 Istanbul earthquake
    c. Undefined   d. Undefined

32. Ability to do work is referred to as _____. Most evident in glacial systems as radiant _____ from the sun and as latent _____ required to melt ice to water.
    a. AASHTO Soil Classification System   b. Energy12
    c. Undefined   d. Undefined

33. The study of the history of ancient life from the fossil record is _____.
    a. Paleontology12   b. 1509 Istanbul earthquake
    c. Undefined   d. Undefined

34. The segment of the Earth's continents that have remained tectonically stable and relatively earthquake-free for a vast period of time is a _____. The _____ is composed of the continental shield and the surrounding continental platform.
    a. 1509 Istanbul earthquake   b. Craton12
    c. Undefined   d. Undefined

35. _____ refers to line about which a fold appears to be hinged. Line of maximum curvature of a folded surface.
    a. Hinge line12   b. 1509 Istanbul earthquake
    c. Undefined   d. Undefined

36. An igneous pluton that is not tabular in shape is _____.
    a. Massive12   b. 1509 Istanbul earthquake
    c. Undefined   d. Undefined

37. _____ refers to the earliest era of the Phanerozoic Eon, marked by the presence of marine invertebrates, fish, amphibians, insects, and land plants.
    a. Paleozoic era12   b. 1509 Istanbul earthquake
    c. Undefined   d. Undefined

38. _____ refers to a form of matter that cannot be broken down into a chemically simpler form by heating, cooling, or chemical reactions. There are 115 known elements, 92 of them natural and 23 man-made. Elements are represented by one or two-letter abbreviations.
    a. Element12   b. AASHTO Soil Classification System
    c. Undefined   d. Undefined

39. The process of determining that two or more geographically distant rocks or rock strata originated in the same time period is referred to as _____.

Chapter 12. Paleozoic Life History: Invertebrates

a. Correlation12
b. 1509 Istanbul earthquake
c. Undefined
d. Undefined

40. The study of rock strata, especially of their distribution, deposition, and age is called _____.
a. 1509 Istanbul earthquake
b. Stratigraphic12
c. Undefined
d. Undefined

41. A period of time in the Paleozoic Era that covered the time span between 400 and 345 million years is referred to as _____.
a. 1509 Istanbul earthquake
b. Devonian12
c. Undefined
d. Undefined

42. The initial point within the Earth that ruptures in an earthquake, directly below the epicenter is called the _____.
a. Focus12
b. 1509 Istanbul earthquake
c. Undefined
d. Undefined

43. _____ refers to a timeline based on a stratigraphic succession that provides a chronological record of the history of a region. The entire span of time since the Earth formed.
a. 1509 Istanbul earthquake
b. Geologic time12
c. Undefined
d. Undefined

44. _____ refers to the formation, movement, and recession of glaciers or ice sheet; geologic processes of glacial activity.
a. Glaciation12
b. 1509 Istanbul earthquake
c. Undefined
d. Undefined

45. The southern part of the Permo-Triassic drift landmass of Pangaea is called _____.
a. Gondwana12
b. 1509 Istanbul earthquake
c. Undefined
d. Undefined

46. A numerical expression of the amount of energy released by an earthquake, determined by measuring earthquake waves on standardized recording instruments is called a _____. The number scale for magnitudes is logarithmic rather than arithmetic. Therefore, deflections on a seismograph for a _____ 5 earthquake, for example, are 10 times greater than those for a _____ 4 earthquake, 100 times greater than for a _____ 3 earthquake, and so on.
a. 1509 Istanbul earthquake
b. Magnitude12
c. Undefined
d. Undefined

47. The relationship between distance on a map and the distance on the terrain being represented by that map is a _____.
a. Scale12
b. 1509 Istanbul earthquake
c. Undefined
d. Undefined

48. The intermediate era of the Phanerozoic Eon, following the Paleozoic Era and preceding the Cenozoic Era, and marked by the dominance of marine and terrestrial reptiles, and the appearance of birds, mammals, and flowering plants is a _____.

Chapter 12. Paleozoic Life History: Invertebrates

a. Mesozoic Era12
b. 1509 Istanbul earthquake
c. Undefined
d. Undefined

49. Any portion of a meteoroid that survives its traverse through Earth's atmosphere and strikes the surface is referred to as a _____.
a. Meteorite12
b. 1509 Istanbul earthquake
c. Undefined
d. Undefined

50. The latest era of the Phanerozoic Eon, following the Mesozoic Era and continuing to the present time, and marked by the presence of a wide variety of mammals, including the first hominids is referred to as _____.
a. Cenozoic Era12
b. 1509 Istanbul earthquake
c. Undefined
d. Undefined

51. A unit of the geologic time scale that is a subdivision of a period is referred to as an _____.
a. AASHTO Soil Classification System
b. Epoch12
c. Undefined
d. Undefined

52. _____ refers to the general term for the steady rise in the average global temperatures over the last 100 years.
a. Global warming12
b. 1509 Istanbul earthquake
c. Undefined
d. Undefined

53. A sedimentary rock composed primarily of calcium carbonate is _____. Some 10% to 15% of all sedimentary rocks are limestones. _____ is usually organic, but it may also be inorganic.
a. Limestone12
b. 1509 Istanbul earthquake
c. Undefined
d. Undefined

54. _____ refers to a ridge-like or mound-like structure, layered or massive, built by sedentary calcareous organisms; it is wave resistant and stands above the surrounding contemporaneously deposited sediment.
a. Reef12
b. 1509 Istanbul earthquake
c. Undefined
d. Undefined

55. Low latitude areas characterized by high temperatures and high precipitation are referred to as _____. At high elevations, however, _____ mountains may be both cold and relatively dry.
a. Tropical12
b. 1509 Istanbul earthquake
c. Undefined
d. Undefined

56. Parallel layers of sedimentary rock are called _____.
a. 1509 Istanbul earthquake
b. Strata12
c. Undefined
d. Undefined

57. _____ refers to the proposed supercontinent that 200 million years ago began to break apart and form the present landmasses.
a. 1509 Istanbul earthquake
b. Pangaea12
c. Undefined
d. Undefined

58. The proportion of dissolved salts to pure water, usually expressed in parts per thousand is referred to as _____.

Chapter 12. Paleozoic Life History: Invertebrates

a. Salinity12
b. 1509 Istanbul earthquake
c. Undefined
d. Undefined

59. The process by which particles of rock and soil are loosened, as by weathering, and then transported elsewhere, as by wind, water, ice, or gravity is _____.
   a. AASHTO Soil Classification System
   b. Erosion12
   c. Undefined
   d. Undefined

60. The top of the ocean, where the water meets the atmosphere is called _____.
   a. Sea level12
   b. 1509 Istanbul earthquake
   c. Undefined
   d. Undefined

61. _____ refers to the gaseous portion of a planet, the planet's envelope of air. One of the traditional subdivisions of Earth's physical environment.
   a. AASHTO Soil Classification System
   b. Atmosphere12
   c. Undefined
   d. Undefined

62. The process of combining with oxygen ions is _____. A mineral that is exposed to air may undergo _____ as a form of chemical weathering.
   a. AASHTO Soil Classification System
   b. Oxidation12
   c. Undefined
   d. Undefined

63. _____ refers to eon of geologic time. Includes all time following the Precambrian.
   a. 1509 Istanbul earthquake
   b. Phanerozoic12
   c. Undefined
   d. Undefined

64. _____ refers to igneous rocks that cool on the surface of the Earth, including beneath water; typically with small crystals due to the rapidity of cooling.
   a. 1509 Istanbul earthquake
   b. Volcanic12
   c. Undefined
   d. Undefined

65. An episode of mountain building is called _____.
   a. AASHTO Soil Classification System
   b. Orogeny12
   c. Undefined
   d. Undefined

Chapter 13. Paleozoic Lfte History: Vertebrates and Plants

1. _____ refers to the area of dry land that borders on a body of water.
   a. 1509 Istanbul earthquake
   b. Coast13
   c. Undefined
   d. Undefined

2. _____ refers to the theory that living organisms mutate and change, generally from simple to increasingly complex forms.
   a. AASHTO Soil Classification System
   b. Evolution13
   c. Undefined
   d. Undefined

3. _____ refers to any evidence of past life, including remains, traces, imprints as well as life history artifacts.
   a. Fossil13
   b. 1509 Istanbul earthquake
   c. Undefined
   d. Undefined

4. _____ refers to a tentative explanation of a given set of data that is expected to remain valid after future observation and experimentation.
   a. 1509 Istanbul earthquake
   b. Hypothesis13
   c. Undefined
   d. Undefined

5. Aggregates of minerals or rock fragments are called _____.
   a. 1509 Istanbul earthquake
   b. Rocks13
   c. Undefined
   d. Undefined

6. A comprehensive explanation of a given set of data that has been repeatedly confirmed by observation and experimentation and has gained general acceptance within the scientific community but has not yet been decisively proven is referred to as _____.
   a. Theory13
   b. 1509 Istanbul earthquake
   c. Undefined
   d. Undefined

7. The initial point within the Earth that ruptures in an earthquake, directly below the epicenter is called the _____.
   a. 1509 Istanbul earthquake
   b. Focus13
   c. Undefined
   d. Undefined

8. A descriptive term applied to igneous rocks with silica between 44% and 52% is _____.
   a. 1509 Istanbul earthquake
   b. Basic13
   c. Undefined
   d. Undefined

9. The tendency of certain minerals to break along distinct planes in their crystal structures where the bonds are weakest is called _____. _____ is tested by striking or hammering a mineral, and is classified by the number of surfaces it produces and the angles between adjacent surfaces.
   a. 1509 Istanbul earthquake
   b. Cleavage13
   c. Undefined
   d. Undefined

10. A body of rock identified by lithic characteristics and stratigraphic position and is mappable at the earth's surface or traceable in the subsurface is a _____.
    a. 1509 Istanbul earthquake
    b. Formation13
    c. Undefined
    d. Undefined

Chapter 13. Paleozoic Lfte History: Vertebrates and Plants

11. _____ refers to rigid parts of the Earth's crust and part of the Earth's upper mantle that moves and adjoins each other along zones of seismic activity.
   a. Plate13
   b. 1509 Istanbul earthquake
   c. Undefined
   d. Undefined

12. A period of time in the Paleozoic Era that covered the time span between 400 and 345 million years is referred to as _____.
   a. Devonian13
   b. 1509 Istanbul earthquake
   c. Undefined
   d. Undefined

13. The point downstream where a river empties into another stream or water body is called _____.
   a. Mouth13
   b. 1509 Istanbul earthquake
   c. Undefined
   d. Undefined

14. Bright streaks that appear to radiate from certain craters on the lunar surface are _____. The _____ consist of fine debris ejected from the primary crater.
   a. 1509 Istanbul earthquake
   b. Rays13
   c. Undefined
   d. Undefined

15. Bridge of rock left above an opening eroded in a headland by waves is an _____.
   a. AASHTO Soil Classification System
   b. Arch13
   c. Undefined
   d. Undefined

16. A hole dug into the ground in the attempt to intersect water or other subsurface fluids is referred to as a _____.
   a. 1509 Istanbul earthquake
   b. Well13
   c. Undefined
   d. Undefined

17. _____ refers to the beginning or source area for a stream. Also called the headwaters.
   a. Head13
   b. 1509 Istanbul earthquake
   c. Undefined
   d. Undefined

18. _____ refers to a basic unit of the geologic time scale that is a subdivision of an era. Periods may be divided into smaller units called epochs.
   a. Period13
   b. 1509 Istanbul earthquake
   c. Undefined
   d. Undefined

19. _____ refers to a collection of transported fragments or precipitated materials that accumulate, typically in loose layers, as of sand or mud.
   a. 1509 Istanbul earthquake
   b. Sediment13
   c. Undefined
   d. Undefined

20. _____ refers to a major division on the geologic time scale; eras are divided into shorter units called periods.
   a. Era13
   b. AASHTO Soil Classification System
   c. Undefined
   d. Undefined

Chapter 13. Paleozoic Lfte History: Vertebrates and Plants   207

21. _____ refers to the gaseous portion of a planet, the planet's envelope of air. One of the traditional subdivisions of Earth's physical environment.
   a. AASHTO Soil Classification System   b. Atmosphere13
   c. Undefined   d. Undefined

22. The force of attraction exerted by one body in the universe on another is _____. _____ is directly proportional to the product of the masses of the two attracted bodies. The force of attraction exerted by the Earth on bodies on or near its surface, tending to pull them toward the Earth's center.
   a. Gravity13   b. 1509 Istanbul earthquake
   c. Undefined   d. Undefined

23. _____ refers to a property of a mineral imparted by light-either transmitted through or reflected by crystals, irregular masses, or a streak.
   a. Color13   b. 1509 Istanbul earthquake
   c. Undefined   d. Undefined

24. Portion of a fold shared by an anticline and a syncline is referred to as a _____.
   a. Limb13   b. 1509 Istanbul earthquake
   c. Undefined   d. Undefined

25. _____ refers to a clastic rock composed of particles that range in diameter from 1/16 millimeter to 2 millimeters in diameter. Sandstones make up about 25% of all sedimentary rocks.
   a. Sandstone13   b. 1509 Istanbul earthquake
   c. Undefined   d. Undefined

26. Vesicular ejecta that are the product of basaltic magma are called _____.
   a. 1509 Istanbul earthquake   b. Scotia13
   c. Undefined   d. Undefined

27. Horn-like projections formed upon a lava dome are called _____.
   a. Spines13   b. 1509 Istanbul earthquake
   c. Undefined   d. Undefined

28. The movement of air from a region of high pressure to a region of low pressure is _____.
   a. Wind13   b. 1509 Istanbul earthquake
   c. Undefined   d. Undefined

29. _____ refers to separation of different ingredients from an originally homogeneous mixture.
   a. 1509 Istanbul earthquake   b. Differentiation13
   c. Undefined   d. Undefined

30. _____ refers to the earliest era of the Phanerozoic Eon, marked by the presence of marine invertebrates, fish, amphibians, insects, and land plants.
   a. Paleozoic era13   b. 1509 Istanbul earthquake
   c. Undefined   d. Undefined

Chapter 13. Paleozoic Lfte History: Vertebrates and Plants

31. A group of interacting or interdependent parts that form a complex whole is called a _____.
   a. 1509 Istanbul earthquake
   b. System13
   c. Undefined
   d. Undefined

32. The scientific study of the Earth, its origins and evolution, the materials that make it up, and the processes that act on it is called _____.
   a. 1509 Istanbul earthquake
   b. Geology13
   c. Undefined
   d. Undefined

33. Rocks formed by solidification of sediments formed and transported at the Earth's surface are referred to as _____.
   a. Sedimentary rocks13
   b. 1509 Istanbul earthquake
   c. Undefined
   d. Undefined

34. The process by which particles of rock and soil are loosened, as by weathering, and then transported elsewhere, as by wind, water, ice, or gravity is _____.
   a. AASHTO Soil Classification System
   b. Erosion13
   c. Undefined
   d. Undefined

35. _____ refers to the top few meters of regolith, generally including some organic matter derived from plants.
   a. Soil13
   b. 1509 Istanbul earthquake
   c. Undefined
   d. Undefined

36. The process by which exposure to atmospheric agents, such as air or moisture, causes rocks and minerals to break down is called _____. This process takes place at or near the Earth's surface. _____ entails little or no movement of the material that it loosens from the rocks and minerals.
   a. Weathering13
   b. 1509 Istanbul earthquake
   c. Undefined
   d. Undefined

37. An electrically neutral substance that consists of two or more elements combined in specific, constant proportions is a _____. A _____ typically has physical characteristics different from those of its constituent elements.
   a. Compound13
   b. 1509 Istanbul earthquake
   c. Undefined
   d. Undefined

38. A situation, which is generally uncomfortable, or otherwise undesirable is a _____.
   a. 1509 Istanbul earthquake
   b. Problem13
   c. Undefined
   d. Undefined

39. The process of combining with oxygen ions is _____. A mineral that is exposed to air may undergo _____ as a form of chemical weathering.
   a. AASHTO Soil Classification System
   b. Oxidation13
   c. Undefined
   d. Undefined

40. _____ refers to a descriptive term applied to igneous rocks that are transitional between basic and acidic with silica between 54% and 65%.

Chapter 13. Paleozoic Lfte History: Vertebrates and Plants

a. AASHTO Soil Classification System
c. Undefined
b. Intermediate13
d. Undefined

41. _____ refers to a form of matter that cannot be broken down into a chemically simpler form by heating, cooling, or chemical reactions. There are 115 known elements, 92 of them natural and 23 man-made. Elements are represented by one or two-letter abbreviations.
a. Element13
c. Undefined
b. AASHTO Soil Classification System
d. Undefined

42. The relationship between distance on a map and the distance on the terrain being represented by that map is a _____.
a. 1509 Istanbul earthquake
c. Undefined
b. Scale13
d. Undefined

43. A member of a group of easily combustible, organic sedimentary rocks composed mostly of plant remains and containing a high proportion of carbon is called _____.
a. 1509 Istanbul earthquake
c. Undefined
b. Coal13
d. Undefined

44. The southern part of the Permo-Triassic drift landmass of Pangaea is called _____.
a. Gondwana13
c. Undefined
b. 1509 Istanbul earthquake
d. Undefined

45. The segment of the Earth's continents that have remained tectonically stable and relatively earthquake-free for a vast period of time is a _____. The _____ is composed of the continental shield and the surrounding continental platform.
a. 1509 Istanbul earthquake
c. Undefined
b. Craton13
d. Undefined

46. An episode of mountain building is called _____.
a. AASHTO Soil Classification System
c. Undefined
b. Orogeny13
d. Undefined

47. _____ refers to eon of geologic time. Includes all time following the Precambrian.
a. Phanerozoic13
c. Undefined
b. 1509 Istanbul earthquake
d. Undefined

48. A mode of sediment transport in which the upward currents in eddies of turbulent flow are capable of supporting the weight of sediment particles and keeping them held indefinitely in the surrounding fluid is called _____.
a. 1509 Istanbul earthquake
c. Undefined
b. Suspension13
d. Undefined

Chapter 14. Mesozoic Earth History

1. _____ refers to the area of dry land that borders on a body of water.
   a. Coast14
   b. 1509 Istanbul earthquake
   c. Undefined
   d. Undefined

2. _____ refers to a deposit formed when heavy minerals are mechanically concentrated by currents, most commonly streams and waves. Placers are sources of gold, tin, platinum, diamonds, and other valuable minerals.
   a. 1509 Istanbul earthquake
   b. Placer14
   c. Undefined
   d. Undefined

3. A measure of how tightly packed the atoms of a substance is _____. Measured in grams per cubic centimeter and varies by the mineral or substance.
   a. Density14
   b. 1509 Istanbul earthquake
   c. Undefined
   d. Undefined

4. Rocks that crystallize from molten material at the surface of the earth or within the earth are called _____.
   a. AASHTO Soil Classification System
   b. Igneous rocks14
   c. Undefined
   d. Undefined

5. Aggregates of minerals or rock fragments are called _____.
   a. Rocks14
   b. 1509 Istanbul earthquake
   c. Undefined
   d. Undefined

6. _____ refers to a body of water found on the Earth's surface and confined to a narrow topographic depression, down which it flows and transports rock particles, sediment, and dissolved particles. Rivers, creeks, brooks, and runs are all streams.
   a. 1509 Istanbul earthquake
   b. Stream14
   c. Undefined
   d. Undefined

7. The process by which exposure to atmospheric agents, such as air or moisture, causes rocks and minerals to break down is called _____. This process takes place at or near the Earth's surface. _____ entails little or no movement of the material that it loosens from the rocks and minerals.
   a. 1509 Istanbul earthquake
   b. Weathering14
   c. Undefined
   d. Undefined

8. Rounded particles coarser than 2 mm in diameter are called _____.
   a. 1509 Istanbul earthquake
   b. Gravel14
   c. Undefined
   d. Undefined

9. A mineral deposit consisting of a zone of veins in consolidated rock, as opposed to a placer deposit is called _____.
   a. 1509 Istanbul earthquake
   b. Lode14
   c. Undefined
   d. Undefined

10. A main mineralized unit that may not be economically valuable in itself but to which workable deposits are related is the _____. An ore deposit from which a placer is derived; the mother rock of a placer.

Chapter 14. Mesozoic Earth History

a. 1509 Istanbul earthquake
b. Mother Lode14
c. Undefined
d. Undefined

11. _____ refers to a naturally formed aggregate of usually inorganic materials from within the Earth.
a. 1509 Istanbul earthquake
b. Rock14
c. Undefined
d. Undefined

12. _____ refers to a major division on the geologic time scale; eras are divided into shorter units called periods.
a. Era14
b. AASHTO Soil Classification System
c. Undefined
d. Undefined

13. _____ refers to the theory that living organisms mutate and change, generally from simple to increasingly complex forms.
a. Evolution14
b. AASHTO Soil Classification System
c. Undefined
d. Undefined

14. _____ refers to the proposed supercontinent that 200 million years ago began to break apart and form the present landmasses.
a. Pangaea14
b. 1509 Istanbul earthquake
c. Undefined
d. Undefined

15. A body of rock identified by lithic characteristics and stratigraphic position and is mappable at the earth's surface or traceable in the subsurface is a _____.
a. 1509 Istanbul earthquake
b. Formation14
c. Undefined
d. Undefined

16. A hole dug into the ground in the attempt to intersect water or other subsurface fluids is referred to as a _____.
a. 1509 Istanbul earthquake
b. Well14
c. Undefined
d. Undefined

17. Boundary surface between two different rock types or ages of rocks is called _____.
a. 1509 Istanbul earthquake
b. Contact14
c. Undefined
d. Undefined

18. The southern part of the Permo-Triassic drift landmass of Pangaea is called _____.
a. 1509 Istanbul earthquake
b. Gondwana14
c. Undefined
d. Undefined

19. _____ refers to the northern portion of Pangaea consisting of North America and Eurasia.
a. Laurasia14
b. 1509 Istanbul earthquake
c. Undefined
d. Undefined

20. _____ refers to the tearing apart of a plate to form a depression in the Earth's crust and often eventually separating the plate into two or more smaller plates.

a. Rifting14
b. 1509 Istanbul earthquake
c. Undefined
d. Undefined

21. _____ refers to the change of state of water from the liquid to vapor phase. Requires the addition of 80 calories per cubic centimeter.
a. AASHTO Soil Classification System
b. Evaporation14
c. Undefined
d. Undefined

22. Inorganic chemical sediment that precipitates when the salty water in which it had dissolved evaporates is called _____.
a. AASHTO Soil Classification System
b. Evaporite14
c. Undefined
d. Undefined

23. Low latitude areas characterized by high temperatures and high precipitation are referred to as _____. At high elevations, however, _____ mountains may be both cold and relatively dry.
a. Tropical14
b. 1509 Istanbul earthquake
c. Undefined
d. Undefined

24. A round or oval depression in the Earth's surface, containing the youngest section of rock in its lowest, central part is a _____.
a. 1509 Istanbul earthquake
b. Basin14
c. Undefined
d. Undefined

25. The top of the ocean, where the water meets the atmosphere is called _____.
a. 1509 Istanbul earthquake
b. Sea level14
c. Undefined
d. Undefined

26. _____ refers to the height of floodwaters in feet or meters above an established datum plane.
a. 1509 Istanbul earthquake
b. Stage14
c. Undefined
d. Undefined

27. _____ refers to a basic unit of the geologic time scale that is a subdivision of an era. Periods may be divided into smaller units called epochs.
a. Period14
b. 1509 Istanbul earthquake
c. Undefined
d. Undefined

28. _____ refers to the set of physical features, such as mountains, valleys, and the shapes of landforms, that characterizes a given landscape.
a. Topography14
b. 1509 Istanbul earthquake
c. Undefined
d. Undefined

29. The movement of air from a region of high pressure to a region of low pressure is _____.
a. 1509 Istanbul earthquake
b. Wind14
c. Undefined
d. Undefined

30. A large mass of rock projecting above surrounding terrain is called a _____.

Chapter 14. Mesozoic Earth History

a. Mountain14
c. Undefined

b. 1509 Istanbul earthquake
d. Undefined

31. _____ refers to any condensed water falling from the atmosphere to the surface of the earth. Common types include rain, snow, sleet, and hail.

a. Precipitation14
c. Undefined

b. 1509 Istanbul earthquake
d. Undefined

32. A region with an average annual rainfall of 10 inches or less and sparse vegetation, typically having thin, dry, and crumbly soil is a _____. A _____ has an aridity index greater than 4.0.

a. 1509 Istanbul earthquake
c. Undefined

b. Desert14
d. Undefined

33. A member of a group of easily combustible, organic sedimentary rocks composed mostly of plant remains and containing a high proportion of carbon is called _____.

a. 1509 Istanbul earthquake
c. Undefined

b. Coal14
d. Undefined

34. The vertical drop in a stream's elevation over a given horizontal distance, expressed as an angle is referred to as a _____.

a. Gradient14
c. Undefined

b. 1509 Istanbul earthquake
d. Undefined

35. _____ refers to the gaseous portion of a planet, the planet's envelope of air. One of the traditional subdivisions of Earth's physical environment.

a. AASHTO Soil Classification System
c. Undefined

b. Atmosphere14
d. Undefined

36. Distinct crystals of ice are called _____. Commonly accumulates with a density of 50 - 200 kg·m, although wind-abraded and packed _____ may have a higher initial density.

a. Snow14
c. Undefined

b. 1509 Istanbul earthquake
d. Undefined

37. The segment of the Earth's continents that have remained tectonically stable and relatively earthquake-free for a vast period of time is a _____. The _____ is composed of the continental shield and the surrounding continental platform.

a. Craton14
c. Undefined

b. 1509 Istanbul earthquake
d. Undefined

38. The process by which particles of rock and soil are loosened, as by weathering, and then transported elsewhere, as by wind, water, ice, or gravity is _____.

a. AASHTO Soil Classification System
c. Undefined

b. Erosion14
d. Undefined

39. A group of interacting or interdependent parts that form a complex whole is called a _____.

Chapter 14. Mesozoic Earth History

    a. System14
    b. 1509 Istanbul earthquake
    c. Undefined
    d. Undefined

40. Molten rock that forms naturally within the Earth is _____. _____ may be either a liquid or a fluid mixture of liquid, crystals, and dissolved gases.
    a. Magma14
    b. 1509 Istanbul earthquake
    c. Undefined
    d. Undefined

41. Vesicular ejecta that are the product of basaltic magma are called _____.
    a. Scotia14
    b. 1509 Istanbul earthquake
    c. Undefined
    d. Undefined

42. A process whereby cold, nutrient-rich water is brought to the surface is called _____. Coastal _____ occurs mostly in trade-wind belts.
    a. AASHTO Soil Classification System
    b. Upwelling14
    c. Undefined
    d. Undefined

43. Magma that comes to the Earth's surface through a volcano or fissure is referred to as _____.
    a. 1509 Istanbul earthquake
    b. Lava14
    c. Undefined
    d. Undefined

44. _____ refers to the process of emplacement of magma in pre-existing rock. Also, the term refers to igneous rock mass so formed within the surrounding rock.
    a. AASHTO Soil Classification System
    b. Intrusion14
    c. Undefined
    d. Undefined

45. _____ refers to rigid parts of the Earth's crust and part of the Earth's upper mantle that moves and adjoins each other along zones of seismic activity.
    a. Plate14
    b. 1509 Istanbul earthquake
    c. Undefined
    d. Undefined

46. A major branch of a stream system is referred to as a _____.
    a. River14
    b. 1509 Istanbul earthquake
    c. Undefined
    d. Undefined

47. _____ refers to a concordant pluton that is substantially wider than it is thick. Sills form within a few kilometers of the Earth's surface.
    a. Sill14
    b. 1509 Istanbul earthquake
    c. Undefined
    d. Undefined

48. Part of the continental margin, the ocean floor from the coastal shore of continents to the continental slope, usually to a depth of about 200 meters is the _____. The _____ usually has a very slight slope, roughly 0.1 degrees.
    a. 1509 Istanbul earthquake
    b. Continental shelf14
    c. Undefined
    d. Undefined

Chapter 14. Mesozoic Earth History

49. The capability of a given substance to allow the passage of a fluid is called _____. _____ depends on the size of and the degree of connection among a substance's pores.
    a. Permeability14
    b. 1509 Istanbul earthquake
    c. Undefined
    d. Undefined

50. _____ refers to any of a group of naturally occurring substances made up of hydrocarbons. These substances may be gaseous, liquid, or semi-solid.
    a. Petroleum14
    b. 1509 Istanbul earthquake
    c. Undefined
    d. Undefined

51. The percentage of a soil, rock, or sediment's volume that is made up of pores is _____.
    a. Porosity14
    b. 1509 Istanbul earthquake
    c. Undefined
    d. Undefined

52. Any accumulation of material, by mechanical settling from water or air, chemical precipitation, evaporation from solution, etc is referred to as _____.
    a. 1509 Istanbul earthquake
    b. Deposition14
    c. Undefined
    d. Undefined

53. _____ refers to a ridge-like or mound-like structure, layered or massive, built by sedentary calcareous organisms; it is wave resistant and stands above the surrounding contemporaneously deposited sediment.
    a. 1509 Istanbul earthquake
    b. Reef14
    c. Undefined
    d. Undefined

54. One of several minerals containing one central carbon atom with strong covalent bonds to three oxygen atoms and typically having ionic bonds to one or more positive ions is _____.
    a. Carbonate14
    b. 1509 Istanbul earthquake
    c. Undefined
    d. Undefined

55. _____ refers to a portion of a rock unit that possesses a distinctive set of characteristics that distinguishes it from other parts of the same unit.
    a. Facies14
    b. 1509 Istanbul earthquake
    c. Undefined
    d. Undefined

56. _____ refers to the earliest era of the Phanerozoic Eon, marked by the presence of marine invertebrates, fish, amphibians, insects, and land plants.
    a. 1509 Istanbul earthquake
    b. Paleozoic era14
    c. Undefined
    d. Undefined

57. The sinking of an oceanic plate edge as a result of convergence with a plate of lesser density is called _____. _____ often causes earthquakes and creates volcano chains.
    a. Subduction14
    b. 1509 Istanbul earthquake
    c. Undefined
    d. Undefined

58. _____ refers to the study of the large-scale processes that collectively deform Earth's crust.

a. Tectonics14
b. 1509 Istanbul earthquake
c. Undefined
d. Undefined

59. _____ refers to a boundary in which two plates move together, resulting in oceanic lithosphere being thrust beneath an overriding plate, eventually to be reabsorbed into the mantle. It can also involve the collision of two continental plates to create a mountain system.
a. 1509 Istanbul earthquake
b. Convergent plate boundary14
c. Undefined
d. Undefined

60. General term for the processes of folding, faulting, shearing, compression, or extension of rocks as the result of various natural forces is called _____.
a. 1509 Istanbul earthquake
b. Deformation14
c. Undefined
d. Undefined

61. An episode of mountain building is called _____.
a. Orogeny14
b. AASHTO Soil Classification System
c. Undefined
d. Undefined

62. Earth's crust that includes both the continents and the continental shelves is the _____.
a. Continental crust14
b. 1509 Istanbul earthquake
c. Undefined
d. Undefined

63. The outermost layer of the Earth, consisting of relatively low-density rock is called _____.
a. 1509 Istanbul earthquake
b. Crust14
c. Undefined
d. Undefined

64. The middle layer of the Earth, lying just below the crust and consisting of relatively dense rocks is called the _____. The _____ is divided into two sections, the upper _____ and the lower _____; the lower _____ has greater density than the upper _____.
a. Mantle14
b. 1509 Istanbul earthquake
c. Undefined
d. Undefined

65. _____ refers to earth's crust, which is formed at mid-oceanic ridges, typically 5 to 10 kilometers thick with a density of 3.0 grams per centimeter cubed.
a. Oceanic crust14
b. AASHTO Soil Classification System
c. Undefined
d. Undefined

66. _____ refers to a range of mountains all formed in the same orogeny.
a. Orogenic belt14
b. AASHTO Soil Classification System
c. Undefined
d. Undefined

67. Deformation of the earth's crust by natural processes leading to the formation of ocean basins, continents, mountain systems, and other earth features is called _____.
a. Tectonism14
b. 1509 Istanbul earthquake
c. Undefined
d. Undefined

Chapter 14. Mesozoic Earth History

68. _____ refers to the upper portion of the mantle extending from the Moho to a depth of 400km.
    a. AASHTO Soil Classification System
    b. Upper mantle14
    c. Undefined
    d. Undefined

69. _____ refers to igneous rocks that cool on the surface of the Earth, including beneath water; typically with small crystals due to the rapidity of cooling.
    a. Volcanic14
    b. 1509 Istanbul earthquake
    c. Undefined
    d. Undefined

70. The zone of convergence of two tectonic plates, one of which usually overrides the other is referred to as the _____.
    a. Subduction zone14
    b. 1509 Istanbul earthquake
    c. Undefined
    d. Undefined

71. The intermediate era of the Phanerozoic Eon, following the Paleozoic Era and preceding the Cenozoic Era, and marked by the dominance of marine and terrestrial reptiles, and the appearance of birds, mammals, and flowering plants is a _____.
    a. 1509 Istanbul earthquake
    b. Mesozoic Era14
    c. Undefined
    d. Undefined

72. The dark, dense, aphanitic, extrusive rock that has a silica content of 40% to 50% and makes up most of the ocean floor is _____. _____ is the most abundant volcanic rock in the Earth's crust.
    a. 1509 Istanbul earthquake
    b. Basalt14
    c. Undefined
    d. Undefined

73. Metamorphic rock formed under great pressures, but not so great temperatures is _____.
    a. Blueschist14
    b. 1509 Istanbul earthquake
    c. Undefined
    d. Undefined

74. A member of a group of sedimentary rocks that consist primarily of microscopic silica crystals is _____. _____ may be either organic or inorganic, but the most common forms are inorganic.
    a. 1509 Istanbul earthquake
    b. Chert14
    c. Undefined
    d. Undefined

75. A fracture dividing a rock into two sections that have visibly moved relative to each other is a _____.
    a. 1509 Istanbul earthquake
    b. Fault14
    c. Undefined
    d. Undefined

76. _____ refers to the term from the Greek 'meta' and 'morph', commonly occurs to rocks which are subjected to increased heat and/or pressure. Also applies to the conversion of snow into glacial ice.
    a. 1509 Istanbul earthquake
    b. Metamorphic14
    c. Undefined
    d. Undefined

77. _____ refers to a sedimentary rock composed of detrital sediment particles less than 0.004 millimeters in diameter. _____ tends to be red, brown, black, or gray, and usually originate in relatively still waters.

a. 1509 Istanbul earthquake   b. Shale14
c. Undefined   d. Undefined

78. A sedimentary rock consisting mostly of silt grains is called _____.
a. 1509 Istanbul earthquake   b. Siltstone14
c. Undefined   d. Undefined

79. A reverse fault marked by a dip of 45° or less is called _____.
a. 1509 Istanbul earthquake   b. Thrust fault14
c. Undefined   d. Undefined

80. An elongated depression in the seafloor produced by bending of oceanic crust during subduction is a _____.
a. 1509 Istanbul earthquake   b. Trench14
c. Undefined   d. Undefined

81. The entire area between the tops of the slopes on both sides of a stream is a _____.
a. 1509 Istanbul earthquake   b. Valley14
c. Undefined   d. Undefined

82. _____ refers to any evidence of past life, including remains, traces, imprints as well as life history artifacts.
a. Fossil14   b. 1509 Istanbul earthquake
c. Undefined   d. Undefined

83. A sedimentary structure consisting of a very small dune of sand or silt whose long dimension is at right angles to the current is a _____.
a. 1509 Istanbul earthquake   b. Ripple14
c. Undefined   d. Undefined

84. A pattern of wavy lines formed along the top of a bed by wind, water currents, or waves are _____.
a. Ripple marks14   b. 1509 Istanbul earthquake
c. Undefined   d. Undefined

85. A mineral in which the systematic internal arrangement of atoms is outwardly reflected as a latticework of repeated three-dimensional units that form a geometric solid with a surface consisting of symmetrical planes is called _____.
a. Crystal14   b. 1509 Istanbul earthquake
c. Undefined   d. Undefined

86. _____ refers to a clastic rock composed of particles more than 2 millimeters in diameter and marked by the roundness of its component grains and rock fragments.
a. Conglomerate14   b. 1509 Istanbul earthquake
c. Undefined   d. Undefined

87. A material that forms as the organic matter of buried wood is either filled in or replaced by inorganic silica carried in by ground water is called _____.

Chapter 14. Mesozoic Earth History

a. Petrified wood14
b. 1509 Istanbul earthquake
c. Undefined
d. Undefined

88. Mineral with the formula SiO is referred to as _____.
a. Quartz14
b. 1509 Istanbul earthquake
c. Undefined
d. Undefined

89. Fine particles of pulverized rock blown from an explosion vent are called _____. Measuring less than 1/10 inch in diameter, _____ may be either solid or molten when first erupted.
a. AASHTO Soil Classification System
b. Ash14
c. Undefined
d. Undefined

90. Water stored beneath the surface in open pore spaces and fractures in rock is called _____.
a. Groundwater14
b. 1509 Istanbul earthquake
c. Undefined
d. Undefined

91. _____ refers to a chemical combination of silicon and oxygen.
a. Silica14
b. 1509 Istanbul earthquake
c. Undefined
d. Undefined

92. An elevated area with relatively little internal relief is called a _____.
a. Plateau14
b. 1509 Istanbul earthquake
c. Undefined
d. Undefined

93. _____ refers to of or pertaining to rivers; produced by river action.
a. 1509 Istanbul earthquake
b. Fluvial14
c. Undefined
d. Undefined

94. _____ refers to a process whereby silica replaces the original material of a substance.
a. Silicification14
b. 1509 Istanbul earthquake
c. Undefined
d. Undefined

95. _____ refers to extremely small fragments, usually of glass, that forms when escaping gases force a fine spray of magma from a volcano.
a. 1509 Istanbul earthquake
b. Volcanic ash14
c. Undefined
d. Undefined

96. _____ refers to a usually asymmetrical mound or ridge of sand that has been transported and deposited by wind. Dunes form in both arid and humid climates.
a. Dune14
b. 1509 Istanbul earthquake
c. Undefined
d. Undefined

97. _____ refers to a clastic rock composed of particles that range in diameter from 1/16 millimeter to 2 millimeters in diameter. Sandstones make up about 25% of all sedimentary rocks.

a. 1509 Istanbul earthquake
b. Sandstone14
c. Undefined
d. Undefined

98. _____ refers to the boundary between a body of water and dry land.
a. Shoreline14
b. 1509 Istanbul earthquake
c. Undefined
d. Undefined

99. The study of rock strata, especially of their distribution, deposition, and age is called _____.
a. Stratigraphic14
b. 1509 Istanbul earthquake
c. Undefined
d. Undefined

100. An igneous pluton that is not tabular in shape is _____.
a. 1509 Istanbul earthquake
b. Massive14
c. Undefined
d. Undefined

101. The mechanism by which new seafloor crust is created at oceanic ridges and slowly spreads away as plates are separating is referred to as _____.
a. 1509 Istanbul earthquake
b. Seafloor spreading14
c. Undefined
d. Undefined

102. _____ refers to a collection of transported fragments or precipitated materials that accumulate, typically in loose layers, as of sand or mud.
a. Sediment14
b. 1509 Istanbul earthquake
c. Undefined
d. Undefined

103. Being or pertaining to a sedimentary rock composed primarily from fragments of preexisting rocks or fossils is called _____.
a. Clastic14
b. 1509 Istanbul earthquake
c. Undefined
d. Undefined

104. The vertical difference between the summit of a mountain and the adjacent valley or plain is referred to as a _____.
a. Relief14
b. 1509 Istanbul earthquake
c. Undefined
d. Undefined

105. _____ refers to the mechanism by which the earth is believed to have formed from a small nucleus by additions of solid bodies, such as meteorites, asteroids, or planetesimals. Also used in plate tectonics to indicate the addition of terranes to a continent.
a. Accretion14
b. AASHTO Soil Classification System
c. Undefined
d. Undefined

106. _____ refers to mountain formation, as caused by volcanism, subduction, plate divergence, folding, or the movement of fault blocks.
a. AASHTO Soil Classification System
b. Orogenesis14
c. Undefined
d. Undefined

Chapter 14. Mesozoic Earth History

107. An area in the upper mantle, ranging from 100 to 200 kilometers in width, from which magma rises in a plume to form volcanoes. A _____ may endure for 10 million years or more.
  a. 1509 Istanbul earthquake
  b. Hot spot14
  c. Undefined
  d. Undefined

108. A descriptive term applied to igneous rocks with silica between 44% and 52% is _____.
  a. Basic14
  b. 1509 Istanbul earthquake
  c. Undefined
  d. Undefined

109. _____ refers to a particular region or locale.
  a. Terrane14
  b. 1509 Istanbul earthquake
  c. Undefined
  d. Undefined

110. _____ refers to a fluid organic sediment formed by the diagenesis of organic material in the pores of sedimentary rocks, mainly sandstones and limestones.
  a. Oil14
  b. AASHTO Soil Classification System
  c. Undefined
  d. Undefined

111. A naturally occurring, usually inorganic, solid consisting of either a single element or a compound, and having a definite chemical composition and a systematic internal arrangement of atoms is referred to as a _____.
  a. 1509 Istanbul earthquake
  b. Mineral14
  c. Undefined
  d. Undefined

112. The total amount of a geologic material in all its deposits, discovered and undiscovered are _____.
  a. 1509 Istanbul earthquake
  b. Resources14
  c. Undefined
  d. Undefined

113. The ocean floor from the shore of continents to the abyssal plain is called _____.
  a. 1509 Istanbul earthquake
  b. Continental margin14
  c. Undefined
  d. Undefined

114. Fluid organic sediment formed by the diagenesis of organic material in the pores of sedimentary rocks, mainly sandstones and limestones is referred to as _____.
  a. 1509 Istanbul earthquake
  b. Gas14
  c. Undefined
  d. Undefined

115. _____ refers to, also called ironstone, a concretion of iron carbonate. Common in the Mazon Creek fossil beds.
  a. 1509 Istanbul earthquake
  b. Siderite14
  c. Undefined
  d. Undefined

116. A rock made from molten or partly molten material that has cooled and solidified is referred to as _____.
  a. Igneous rock14
  b. AASHTO Soil Classification System
  c. Undefined
  d. Undefined

117. The set of geological processes that result in the expulsion of lava, pyroclastics, and gases at the Earth's surface is referred to as _____.

a. Volcanism14
b. 1509 Istanbul earthquake
c. Undefined
d. Undefined

118. An _____ is a volcanic event that is distinguished by its duration or style.
a. Episode14
b. AASHTO Soil Classification System
c. Undefined
d. Undefined

119. _____ refers to a timeline based on a stratigraphic succession that provides a chronological record of the history of a region. The entire span of time since the Earth formed.
a. 1509 Istanbul earthquake
b. Geologic time14
c. Undefined
d. Undefined

120. _____ refers to igneous plutonic rock, less felsic than granite, typically light in color; rough plutonic equivalent of dacite.
a. 1509 Istanbul earthquake
b. Granodiorite14
c. Undefined
d. Undefined

121. An igneous rock with a porphyritic texture is referred to as _____.
a. 1509 Istanbul earthquake
b. Porphyry14
c. Undefined
d. Undefined

122. A copper deposit, usually of low grade, in which the copper-bearing minerals occur in disseminated grains and/or in veinlets through a large volume of rock, is called _____.
a. Porphyry copper14
b. 1509 Istanbul earthquake
c. Undefined
d. Undefined

123. The incomplete melting of a rock composed of minerals with differing melting points is called _____ When _____ occurs, the minerals with higher melting points remain solid while the minerals whose melting points have been reached turn to magma.
a. 1509 Istanbul earthquake
b. Partial melting14
c. Undefined
d. Undefined

124. The processes by which crustal forces cause a rock formation to break and slip along a fault are called _____.
a. 1509 Istanbul earthquake
b. Faulting14
c. Undefined
d. Undefined

125. The processes by which crustal forces deform an area of crust so that layers of rock are pushed into folds are called _____.
a. Folding14
b. 1509 Istanbul earthquake
c. Undefined
d. Undefined

126. _____ refer to the valuable minerals of an area that are presently legally recoverable or that may be so in the future; includes both the known ore bodies and the potential ores of a region.
a. Mineral resources14
b. 1509 Istanbul earthquake
c. Undefined
d. Undefined

Chapter 14. Mesozoic Earth History

127. _____ refers to the coming together of two lithospheric plates. _____ causes subduction when one or both plates are oceanic and mountain formation when both plates are continental.
    a. Convergence14
    b. 1509 Istanbul earthquake
    c. Undefined
    d. Undefined

128. _____ refers to a long, narrow trough bounded by normal faults. It represents a region where divergence is taking place.
    a. 1509 Istanbul earthquake
    b. Rift14
    c. Undefined
    d. Undefined

Chapter 15. Life of the Mesozoic Era

1. _____ refers to a major division on the geologic time scale; eras are divided into shorter units called periods.
   a. Era15
   b. AASHTO Soil Classification System
   c. Undefined
   d. Undefined

2. _____ refers to the proposed supercontinent that 200 million years ago began to break apart and form the present landmasses.
   a. 1509 Istanbul earthquake
   b. Pangaea15
   c. Undefined
   d. Undefined

3. The totality of life forms on Earth is referred to as the _____.
   a. 1509 Istanbul earthquake
   b. Biosphere15
   c. Undefined
   d. Undefined

4. A numerical expression of the amount of energy released by an earthquake, determined by measuring earthquake waves on standardized recording instruments is called a _____. The number scale for magnitudes is logarithmic rather than arithmetic. Therefore, deflections on a seismograph for a _____ 5 earthquake, for example, are 10 times greater than those for a _____ 4 earthquake, 100 times greater than for a _____ 3 earthquake, and so on.
   a. Magnitude15
   b. 1509 Istanbul earthquake
   c. Undefined
   d. Undefined

5. A group of tiny single-celled organisms that live in surface waters and whose secretions and calcite shells account for most of the oceans carbonate sediments is called _____.
   a. 1509 Istanbul earthquake
   b. Foraminifera15
   c. Undefined
   d. Undefined

6. A hole dug into the ground in the attempt to intersect water or other subsurface fluids is referred to as a _____.
   a. Well15
   b. 1509 Istanbul earthquake
   c. Undefined
   d. Undefined

7. A mode of sediment transport in which the upward currents in eddies of turbulent flow are capable of supporting the weight of sediment particles and keeping them held indefinitely in the surrounding fluid is called _____.
   a. 1509 Istanbul earthquake
   b. Suspension15
   c. Undefined
   d. Undefined

8. _____ refers to a ridge-like or mound-like structure, layered or massive, built by sedentary calcareous organisms; it is wave resistant and stands above the surrounding contemporaneously deposited sediment.
   a. Reef15
   b. 1509 Istanbul earthquake
   c. Undefined
   d. Undefined

9. _____ refers to any evidence of past life, including remains, traces, imprints as well as life history artifacts.
   a. Fossil15
   b. 1509 Istanbul earthquake
   c. Undefined
   d. Undefined

10. _____ refers to a chemical combination of silicon and oxygen.
    a. 1509 Istanbul earthquake
    b. Silica15
    c. Undefined
    d. Undefined

Chapter 15. Life of the Mesozoic Era 225

11. _____ refers to an epoch in Earth's history from about 24 to 5 million years ago. Also refers to the rocks that formed in that epoch.
   a. 1509 Istanbul earthquake
   b. Miocene15
   c. Undefined
   d. Undefined

12. Aggregates of minerals or rock fragments are called _____.
   a. 1509 Istanbul earthquake
   b. Rocks15
   c. Undefined
   d. Undefined

13. _____ refers to a descriptive term applied to igneous rocks that are transitional between basic and acidic with silica between 54% and 65%.
   a. Intermediate15
   b. AASHTO Soil Classification System
   c. Undefined
   d. Undefined

14. _____ refers to a basic unit of the geologic time scale that is a subdivision of an era. Periods may be divided into smaller units called epochs.
   a. 1509 Istanbul earthquake
   b. Period15
   c. Undefined
   d. Undefined

15. _____ refers to the theory that living organisms mutate and change, generally from simple to increasingly complex forms.
   a. AASHTO Soil Classification System
   b. Evolution15
   c. Undefined
   d. Undefined

16. A descriptive term applied to igneous rocks with silica between 44% and 52% is _____.
   a. Basic15
   b. 1509 Istanbul earthquake
   c. Undefined
   d. Undefined

17. The intermediate era of the Phanerozoic Eon, following the Paleozoic Era and preceding the Cenozoic Era, and marked by the dominance of marine and terrestrial reptiles, and the appearance of birds, mammals, and flowering plants is a _____.
   a. 1509 Istanbul earthquake
   b. Mesozoic Era15
   c. Undefined
   d. Undefined

18. A high mountain peak that forms when the walls of three or more cirques intersect is called a _____.
   a. Horn15
   b. 1509 Istanbul earthquake
   c. Undefined
   d. Undefined

19. _____ refers to the beginning or source area for a stream. Also called the headwaters.
   a. Head15
   b. 1509 Istanbul earthquake
   c. Undefined
   d. Undefined

20. The point downstream where a river empties into another stream or water body is called _____.
   a. 1509 Istanbul earthquake
   b. Mouth15
   c. Undefined
   d. Undefined

21. A hole or opening, as at the bed of a glacier is a _____. When the rate of deformation into a space behind an obstacle is less the rate of movement past the obstacle, a _____ will form.
   a. 1509 Istanbul earthquake
   b. Cavity15
   c. Undefined
   d. Undefined

22. The study of the history of ancient life from the fossil record is _____.
   a. 1509 Istanbul earthquake
   b. Paleontology15
   c. Undefined
   d. Undefined

23. Parallel layers of sedimentary rock are called _____.
   a. Strata15
   b. 1509 Istanbul earthquake
   c. Undefined
   d. Undefined

24. A sedimentary rock composed primarily of calcium carbonate is _____. Some 10% to 15% of all sedimentary rocks are limestones. _____ is usually organic, but it may also be inorganic.
   a. 1509 Istanbul earthquake
   b. Limestone15
   c. Undefined
   d. Undefined

25. The angle formed by the inclined plane of a geological structure and the horizontal plane of the Earth's surface is referred to as a _____.
   a. 1509 Istanbul earthquake
   b. Dip15
   c. Undefined
   d. Undefined

26. _____ refers to a clastic rock composed of particles that range in diameter from 1/16 millimeter to 2 millimeters in diameter. Sandstones make up about 25% of all sedimentary rocks.
   a. Sandstone15
   b. 1509 Istanbul earthquake
   c. Undefined
   d. Undefined

27. The scientific study of the Earth, its origins and evolution, the materials that make it up, and the processes that act on it is called _____.
   a. 1509 Istanbul earthquake
   b. Geology15
   c. Undefined
   d. Undefined

28. Many megalithic mounds in the southern Iberian peninsula, Sardinia and the British Isles present a concave façade with its two extremities ending in extensions known as _____ or horns are called _____. They define a partly enclosed space described as the forecourt of a horned cairn.
   a. 1509 Istanbul earthquake
   b. Wings15
   c. Undefined
   d. Undefined

29. _____ refers to pyroclastic material derived directly from magma reaching the surface.
   a. 1509 Istanbul earthquake
   b. Juvenile15
   c. Undefined
   d. Undefined

30. _____ refers to a tentative explanation of a given set of data that is expected to remain valid after future observation and experimentation.

Chapter 15. Life of the Mesozoic Era

a. 1509 Istanbul earthquake
b. Hypothesis15
c. Undefined
d. Undefined

31. The process by which two lithospheric plates separated by rifting move farther apart, with soft mantle rock rising between them and forming new oceanic lithospheres is called _____.
a. Divergence15
b. 1509 Istanbul earthquake
c. Undefined
d. Undefined

32. Low latitude areas characterized by high temperatures and high precipitation are referred to as _____. At high elevations, however, _____ mountains may be both cold and relatively dry.
a. Tropical15
b. 1509 Istanbul earthquake
c. Undefined
d. Undefined

33. The southern part of the Permo-Triassic drift landmass of Pangaea is called _____.
a. Gondwana15
b. 1509 Istanbul earthquake
c. Undefined
d. Undefined

34. _____ refers to the northern portion of Pangaea consisting of North America and Eurasia.
a. Laurasia15
b. 1509 Istanbul earthquake
c. Undefined
d. Undefined

35. Angular distance of a point on the earth's surface north or south of the equator, measured along a meridian, the equator being _____ 0°, the north pole _____ 90°N, and the south pole _____ 90°S.
a. Latitude15
b. 1509 Istanbul earthquake
c. Undefined
d. Undefined

36. _____ refers to the earliest era of the Phanerozoic Eon, marked by the presence of marine invertebrates, fish, amphibians, insects, and land plants.
a. 1509 Istanbul earthquake
b. Paleozoic era15
c. Undefined
d. Undefined

37. _____ refers to a form of matter that cannot be broken down into a chemically simpler form by heating, cooling, or chemical reactions. There are 115 known elements, 92 of them natural and 23 man-made. Elements are represented by one or two-letter abbreviations.
a. Element15
b. AASHTO Soil Classification System
c. Undefined
d. Undefined

38. A deviation from the average or expected value is an _____. In paleomagnetism, a 'positive' _____ is a stronger-than-average magnetic field at the earth's surface.
a. Anomaly15
b. AASHTO Soil Classification System
c. Undefined
d. Undefined

39. Mineral with the formula SiO is referred to as _____.
a. 1509 Istanbul earthquake
b. Quartz15
c. Undefined
d. Undefined

Chapter 15. Life of the Mesozoic Era

40. _____ refers to the gaseous portion of a planet, the planet's envelope of air. One of the traditional subdivisions of Earth's physical environment.
    a. Atmosphere15
    b. AASHTO Soil Classification System
    c. Undefined
    d. Undefined

41. The outermost layer of the Earth, consisting of relatively low-density rock is called _____.
    a. 1509 Istanbul earthquake
    b. Crust15
    c. Undefined
    d. Undefined

42. Any portion of a meteoroid that survives its traverse through Earth's atmosphere and strikes the surface is referred to as a _____.
    a. Meteorite15
    b. 1509 Istanbul earthquake
    c. Undefined
    d. Undefined

43. _____ refers to a descriptive term applied to igneous rocks with more than 60% silica.
    a. Acid15
    b. AASHTO Soil Classification System
    c. Undefined
    d. Undefined

44. Rain that contains such acidic compounds as sulfuric acid and nitric acid, which are produced by the combination of atmospheric water with oxides released when hydrocarbons are burned, is _____. _____ is widely considered responsible for damaging forests, crops, and human-made structures, and for killing aquatic life.
    a. Acid rain15
    b. AASHTO Soil Classification System
    c. Undefined
    d. Undefined

45. _____ refers to a naturally formed aggregate of usually inorganic materials from within the Earth.
    a. 1509 Istanbul earthquake
    b. Rock15
    c. Undefined
    d. Undefined

46. The set of geological processes that result in the expulsion of lava, pyroclastics, and gases at the Earth's surface is referred to as _____.
    a. Volcanism15
    b. 1509 Istanbul earthquake
    c. Undefined
    d. Undefined

47. _____ refers to a rock made from the consolidation of solid fragments, as of other rocks or organic remains, or by precipitation of minerals from solution.
    a. 1509 Istanbul earthquake
    b. Sedimentary rock15
    c. Undefined
    d. Undefined

48. A steep-sided, usually circular depression formed by either explosion or collapse at a volcanic vent is a _____.
    a. 1509 Istanbul earthquake
    b. Crater15
    c. Undefined
    d. Undefined

49. A situation, which is generally uncomfortable, or otherwise undesirable is a _____.
    a. 1509 Istanbul earthquake
    b. Problem15
    c. Undefined
    d. Undefined

Chapter 15. Life of the Mesozoic Era

50. A round or oval depression in the Earth's surface, containing the youngest section of rock in its lowest, central part is a _____.
    a. 1509 Istanbul earthquake
    b. Basin15
    c. Undefined
    d. Undefined

51. An _____ is a volcanic event that is distinguished by its duration or style.
    a. Episode15
    b. AASHTO Soil Classification System
    c. Undefined
    d. Undefined

52. A large mass of rock projecting above surrounding terrain is called a _____.
    a. 1509 Istanbul earthquake
    b. Mountain15
    c. Undefined
    d. Undefined

Chapter 16. Cenozoic Geologic History: The Tertiary Period

1. _____ refers to the set of physical features, such as mountains, valleys, and the shapes of landforms, that characterizes a given landscape.
   a. 1509 Istanbul earthquake
   b. Topography16
   c. Undefined
   d. Undefined

2. A hole dug into the ground in the attempt to intersect water or other subsurface fluids is referred to as a _____.
   a. Well16
   b. 1509 Istanbul earthquake
   c. Undefined
   d. Undefined

3. _____ refers to igneous rocks that cool on the surface of the Earth, including beneath water; typically with small crystals due to the rapidity of cooling.
   a. Volcanic16
   b. 1509 Istanbul earthquake
   c. Undefined
   d. Undefined

4. The latest era of the Phanerozoic Eon, following the Mesozoic Era and continuing to the present time, and marked by the presence of a wide variety of mammals, including the first hominids is referred to as _____.
   a. Cenozoic Era16
   b. 1509 Istanbul earthquake
   c. Undefined
   d. Undefined

5. An imaginary line that separates the drainage of two streams, often found along a ridge is referred to as the _____.
   a. Divide16
   b. 1509 Istanbul earthquake
   c. Undefined
   d. Undefined

6. _____ refers to a timeline based on a stratigraphic succession that provides a chronological record of the history of a region. The entire span of time since the Earth formed.
   a. Geologic time16
   b. 1509 Istanbul earthquake
   c. Undefined
   d. Undefined

7. _____ refers to a basic unit of the geologic time scale that is a subdivision of an era. Periods may be divided into smaller units called epochs.
   a. Period16
   b. 1509 Istanbul earthquake
   c. Undefined
   d. Undefined

8. _____ refers to the period of Earth's history from about 2 million years ago to the present; also, the rocks and deposits of that age.
   a. Quaternary16
   b. 1509 Istanbul earthquake
   c. Undefined
   d. Undefined

9. Aggregates of minerals or rock fragments are called _____.
   a. Rocks16
   b. 1509 Istanbul earthquake
   c. Undefined
   d. Undefined

10. _____ refers to a major division on the geologic time scale; eras are divided into shorter units called periods.
    a. Era16
    b. AASHTO Soil Classification System
    c. Undefined
    d. Undefined

Chapter 16. Cenozoic Geologic History: The Tertiary Period

11. _____ refers to the theory that living organisms mutate and change, generally from simple to increasingly complex forms.
    a. AASHTO Soil Classification System
    b. Evolution16
    c. Undefined
    d. Undefined

12. _____ refers to the division of all of Earth history into blocks of time distinguished by geologic and evolutionary events, ordered sequentially and arranged into eons made up of eras, which are in turn made up of periods, which are in turn made up of epochs.
    a. Geologic time scale16
    b. 1509 Istanbul earthquake
    c. Undefined
    d. Undefined

13. _____ refers to the proposed supercontinent that 200 million years ago began to break apart and form the present landmasses.
    a. 1509 Istanbul earthquake
    b. Pangaea16
    c. Undefined
    d. Undefined

14. The relationship between distance on a map and the distance on the terrain being represented by that map is a _____.
    a. Scale16
    b. 1509 Istanbul earthquake
    c. Undefined
    d. Undefined

15. A member of a group of easily combustible, organic sedimentary rocks composed mostly of plant remains and containing a high proportion of carbon is called _____.
    a. 1509 Istanbul earthquake
    b. Coal16
    c. Undefined
    d. Undefined

16. A round or oval depression in the Earth's surface, containing the youngest section of rock in its lowest, central part is a _____.
    a. 1509 Istanbul earthquake
    b. Basin16
    c. Undefined
    d. Undefined

17. The outermost layer of the Earth, consisting of relatively low-density rock is called _____.
    a. Crust16
    b. 1509 Istanbul earthquake
    c. Undefined
    d. Undefined

18. _____ refers to rigid parts of the Earth's crust and part of the Earth's upper mantle that moves and adjoins each other along zones of seismic activity.
    a. Plate16
    b. 1509 Istanbul earthquake
    c. Undefined
    d. Undefined

19. _____ refers to the tearing apart of a plate to form a depression in the Earth's crust and often eventually separating the plate into two or more smaller plates.
    a. Rifting16
    b. 1509 Istanbul earthquake
    c. Undefined
    d. Undefined

Chapter 16. Cenozoic Geologic History: The Tertiary Period

20. The dark, dense, aphanitic, extrusive rock that has a silica content of 40% to 50% and makes up most of the ocean floor is _____. _____ is the most abundant volcanic rock in the Earth's crust.
    a. Basalt16
    b. 1509 Istanbul earthquake
    c. Undefined
    d. Undefined

21. Molten rock that forms naturally within the Earth is _____. _____ may be either a liquid or a fluid mixture of liquid, crystals, and dissolved gases.
    a. 1509 Istanbul earthquake
    b. Magma16
    c. Undefined
    d. Undefined

22. _____ refers to an epoch in Earth's history from about 24 to 5 million years ago. Also refers to the rocks that formed in that epoch.
    a. 1509 Istanbul earthquake
    b. Miocene16
    c. Undefined
    d. Undefined

23. _____ refers to earth's crust, which is formed at mid-oceanic ridges, typically 5 to 10 kilometers thick with a density of 3.0 grams per centimeter cubed.
    a. Oceanic crust16
    b. AASHTO Soil Classification System
    c. Undefined
    d. Undefined

24. A process whereby cold, nutrient-rich water is brought to the surface is called _____. Coastal _____ occurs mostly in trade-wind belts.
    a. Upwelling16
    b. AASHTO Soil Classification System
    c. Undefined
    d. Undefined

25. General term for the processes of folding, faulting, shearing, compression, or extension of rocks as the result of various natural forces is called _____.
    a. 1509 Istanbul earthquake
    b. Deformation16
    c. Undefined
    d. Undefined

26. An _____ is a volcanic event that is distinguished by its duration or style.
    a. AASHTO Soil Classification System
    b. Episode16
    c. Undefined
    d. Undefined

27. A large mass of rock projecting above surrounding terrain is called a _____.
    a. 1509 Istanbul earthquake
    b. Mountain16
    c. Undefined
    d. Undefined

28. An episode of mountain building is called _____.
    a. Orogeny16
    b. AASHTO Soil Classification System
    c. Undefined
    d. Undefined

29. A unit of the geologic time scale that is a subdivision of a period is referred to as an _____.
    a. AASHTO Soil Classification System
    b. Epoch16
    c. Undefined
    d. Undefined

Chapter 16. Cenozoic Geologic History: The Tertiary Period 233

30. _____ refers to the theory that the Earth's lithosphere consists of large, rigid plates that move horizontally in response to the flow of the asthenosphere beneath them, and that interactions among the plates at their borders cause most major geologic activity, including the creation of oceans, continents, mountains, volcanoes, and earthquakes.
  a. Plate tectonics16
  b. 1509 Istanbul earthquake
  c. Undefined
  d. Undefined

31. _____ refers to the study of the large-scale processes that collectively deform Earth's crust.
  a. Tectonics16
  b. 1509 Istanbul earthquake
  c. Undefined
  d. Undefined

32. _____ refers to a long, narrow trough bounded by normal faults. It represents a region where divergence is taking place.
  a. Rift16
  b. 1509 Istanbul earthquake
  c. Undefined
  d. Undefined

33. A group of interacting or interdependent parts that form a complex whole is called a _____.
  a. 1509 Istanbul earthquake
  b. System16
  c. Undefined
  d. Undefined

34. Earth's crust that includes both the continents and the continental shelves is the _____.
  a. 1509 Istanbul earthquake
  b. Continental crust16
  c. Undefined
  d. Undefined

35. _____ refers to a range of mountains all formed in the same orogeny.
  a. Orogenic belt16
  b. AASHTO Soil Classification System
  c. Undefined
  d. Undefined

36. The set of geological processes that result in the expulsion of lava, pyroclastics, and gases at the Earth's surface is referred to as _____.
  a. 1509 Istanbul earthquake
  b. Volcanism16
  c. Undefined
  d. Undefined

37. The southern part of the Permo-Triassic drift landmass of Pangaea is called _____.
  a. 1509 Istanbul earthquake
  b. Gondwana16
  c. Undefined
  d. Undefined

38. Stress that reduces the volume or length of a rock, as that produced by the convergence of plate margins is called _____.
  a. Compression16
  b. 1509 Istanbul earthquake
  c. Undefined
  d. Undefined

39. The scientific study of the Earth, its origins and evolution, the materials that make it up, and the processes that act on it is called _____.
  a. Geology16
  b. 1509 Istanbul earthquake
  c. Undefined
  d. Undefined

Chapter 16. Cenozoic Geologic History: The Tertiary Period

40. _____ refers to the coming together of two lithospheric plates. _____ causes subduction when one or both plates are oceanic and mountain formation when both plates are continental.
    a. 1509 Istanbul earthquake
    b. Convergence16
    c. Undefined
    d. Undefined

41. Inorganic chemical sediment that precipitates when the salty water in which it had dissolved evaporates is called _____.
    a. Evaporite16
    b. AASHTO Soil Classification System
    c. Undefined
    d. Undefined

42. That which tends to put stationary objects in motion or change motions of moving bodies is referred to as _____.
    a. Force16
    b. 1509 Istanbul earthquake
    c. Undefined
    d. Undefined

43. _____ refers to a layer of solid, brittle rock making up the outer 100 kilometers of the Earth, encompassing both the crust and the outermost part of the upper mantle.
    a. 1509 Istanbul earthquake
    b. Lithosphere16
    c. Undefined
    d. Undefined

44. A movement within the Earth's crust or mantle, caused by the sudden rupture or repositioning of underground rocks as they release stress is an _____.
    a. AASHTO Soil Classification System
    b. Earthquake16
    c. Undefined
    d. Undefined

45. A numerical expression of the amount of energy released by an earthquake, determined by measuring earthquake waves on standardized recording instruments is called a _____. The number scale for magnitudes is logarithmic rather than arithmetic. Therefore, deflections on a seismograph for a _____ 5 earthquake, for example, are 10 times greater than those for a _____ 4 earthquake, 100 times greater than for a _____ 3 earthquake, and so on.
    a. 1509 Istanbul earthquake
    b. Magnitude16
    c. Undefined
    d. Undefined

46. A logarithmic scale that measures the amount of energy released during an earthquake on the basis of the amplitude of the highest peak recorded on a seismogram is a _____. Each unit increase in the _____ represents a 10-fold increase in the amplitude recorded on the seismogram and a 30-fold increase in energy released by the earthquake. Theoretically the _____ has no upper limit, but the yield point of the Earth's rocks imposes an effective limit between 9.0 and 9.5.
    a. 1509 Istanbul earthquake
    b. Richter scale16
    c. Undefined
    d. Undefined

47. The sinking of an oceanic plate edge as a result of convergence with a plate of lesser density is called _____. _____ often causes earthquakes and creates volcano chains.
    a. 1509 Istanbul earthquake
    b. Subduction16
    c. Undefined
    d. Undefined

48. The zone of convergence of two tectonic plates, one of which usually overrides the other is referred to as the _____.

Chapter 16. Cenozoic Geologic History: The Tertiary Period

a. 1509 Istanbul earthquake
b. Subduction zone16
c. Undefined
d. Undefined

49. _____ refers to a general term applied to all mineral material transported by a glacier and deposited directly by or from the ice, or by running water emanating from the glacier. Generally applies to Pleistocene glacial deposits.
a. Drift16
b. 1509 Istanbul earthquake
c. Undefined
d. Undefined

50. A measure of how tightly packed the atoms of a substance is _____. Measured in grams per cubic centimeter and varies by the mineral or substance.
a. 1509 Istanbul earthquake
b. Density16
c. Undefined
d. Undefined

51. A fracture dividing a rock into two sections that have visibly moved relative to each other is a _____.
a. 1509 Istanbul earthquake
b. Fault16
c. Undefined
d. Undefined

52. Rocks formed by solidification of sediments formed and transported at the Earth's surface are referred to as _____.
a. Sedimentary rocks16
b. 1509 Istanbul earthquake
c. Undefined
d. Undefined

53. An elongated depression in the seafloor produced by bending of oceanic crust during subduction is a _____.
a. Trench16
b. 1509 Istanbul earthquake
c. Undefined
d. Undefined

54. A comprehensive explanation of a given set of data that has been repeatedly confirmed by observation and experimentation and has gained general acceptance within the scientific community but has not yet been decisively proven is referred to as _____.
a. Theory16
b. 1509 Istanbul earthquake
c. Undefined
d. Undefined

55. The process by which conditions within the Earth, below the zone of diagenesis, alter the mineral content, chemical composition, and structure of solid rock without melting it is called _____. Igneous, sedimentary, and metamorphic rocks may all undergo _____.
a. Metamorphism16
b. 1509 Istanbul earthquake
c. Undefined
d. Undefined

56. _____ refers to the area of dry land that borders on a body of water.
a. Coast16
b. 1509 Istanbul earthquake
c. Undefined
d. Undefined

57. The ocean floor from the shore of continents to the abyssal plain is called _____.
a. Continental margin16
b. 1509 Istanbul earthquake
c. Undefined
d. Undefined

Chapter 16. Cenozoic Geologic History: The Tertiary Period

58. _____ refers to a border that lies between continental and oceanic lithosphere, but is not a plate margin. It is marked by lack of seismic and volcanic activity.
   a. 1509 Istanbul earthquake
   b. Passive continental margin16
   c. Undefined
   d. Undefined

59. _____ refers to a collection of transported fragments or precipitated materials that accumulate, typically in loose layers, as of sand or mud.
   a. 1509 Istanbul earthquake
   b. Sediment16
   c. Undefined
   d. Undefined

60. A margin consisting of a continental shelf, a continental slope, and an oceanic trench is referred to as _____.
   a. AASHTO Soil Classification System
   b. Active continental margin16
   c. Undefined
   d. Undefined

61. The process by which particles of rock and soil are loosened, as by weathering, and then transported elsewhere, as by wind, water, ice, or gravity is _____.
   a. AASHTO Soil Classification System
   b. Erosion16
   c. Undefined
   d. Undefined

62. _____ refers to the beginning or source area for a stream. Also called the headwaters.
   a. Head16
   b. 1509 Istanbul earthquake
   c. Undefined
   d. Undefined

63. The middle layer of the Earth, lying just below the crust and consisting of relatively dense rocks is called the _____. The _____ is divided into two sections, the upper _____ and the lower _____; the lower _____ has greater density than the upper _____.
   a. 1509 Istanbul earthquake
   b. Mantle16
   c. Undefined
   d. Undefined

64. _____ refers to a mass of hotter-than-normal mantle material that ascends toward the surface, where it may lead to igneous activity. These plumes of solid yet mobile material may originate as deep as the core-mantle boundary.
   a. 1509 Istanbul earthquake
   b. Mantle plume16
   c. Undefined
   d. Undefined

65. Deep steep-sided depression in the ocean floor caused by the subduction of oceanic crust beneath either other oceanic crust or continental crust is an _____.
   a. Oceanic trench16
   b. AASHTO Soil Classification System
   c. Undefined
   d. Undefined

66. A moving body of ice that forms on land from the accumulation and compaction of snow, and that flows downslope or outward due to gravity and the pressure of its own weight is a _____.
   a. Glacier16
   b. 1509 Istanbul earthquake
   c. Undefined
   d. Undefined

67. _____ refers to a naturally formed aggregate of usually inorganic materials from within the Earth.

Chapter 16. Cenozoic Geologic History: The Tertiary Period

    a. Rock16
    b. 1509 Istanbul earthquake
    c. Undefined
    d. Undefined

68. _____ refers to a flat thinnish dressed stone.
    a. Slab16
    b. 1509 Istanbul earthquake
    c. Undefined
    d. Undefined

69. An elongated mountain belt arrayed around a continental craton and formed by a later episode of compressive deformation is an _____.
    a. AASHTO Soil Classification System
    b. Orogen16
    c. Undefined
    d. Undefined

70. Parallel layers of sedimentary rock are called _____.
    a. 1509 Istanbul earthquake
    b. Strata16
    c. Undefined
    d. Undefined

71. A reverse fault marked by a dip of 45° or less is called _____.
    a. Thrust fault16
    b. 1509 Istanbul earthquake
    c. Undefined
    d. Undefined

72. Any unconsolidated material at Earth's surface is _____.
    a. 1509 Istanbul earthquake
    b. Debris16
    c. Undefined
    d. Undefined

73. The intermediate era of the Phanerozoic Eon, following the Paleozoic Era and preceding the Cenozoic Era, and marked by the dominance of marine and terrestrial reptiles, and the appearance of birds, mammals, and flowering plants is a _____.
    a. 1509 Istanbul earthquake
    b. Mesozoic Era16
    c. Undefined
    d. Undefined

74. The top of the ocean, where the water meets the atmosphere is called _____.
    a. 1509 Istanbul earthquake
    b. Sea level16
    c. Undefined
    d. Undefined

75. The entire area between the tops of the slopes on both sides of a stream is a _____.
    a. Valley16
    b. 1509 Istanbul earthquake
    c. Undefined
    d. Undefined

76. All processes that adds snow or ice to a glacier or to floating ice or snow cove are referred to as _____.
    a. AASHTO Soil Classification System
    b. Accumulation16
    c. Undefined
    d. Undefined

77. _____ refers to the term from the Greek 'meta' and 'morph', commonly occurs to rocks which are subjected to increased heat and/or pressure. Also applies to the conversion of snow into glacial ice.

Chapter 16. Cenozoic Geologic History: The Tertiary Period

a. 1509 Istanbul earthquake
b. Metamorphic16
c. Undefined
d. Undefined

78. Angular chunk of solid rock ejected during an eruption is referred to as a _____.
a. Block16
b. 1509 Istanbul earthquake
c. Undefined
d. Undefined

79. _____ refers to igneous rocks formed beneath the surface of the Earth; typically with large crystals due to the slowness of cooling.
a. 1509 Istanbul earthquake
b. Plutonic16
c. Undefined
d. Undefined

80. The processes by which crustal forces cause a rock formation to break and slip along a fault are called _____.
a. Faulting16
b. 1509 Istanbul earthquake
c. Undefined
d. Undefined

81. The epoch of the Quaternary Period of geologic time, following the Pliocene Epoch and preceding the Holocene is referred to as the _____.
a. 1509 Istanbul earthquake
b. Pleistocene16
c. Undefined
d. Undefined

82. A high mountain peak that forms when the walls of three or more cirques intersect is called a _____.
a. Horn16
b. 1509 Istanbul earthquake
c. Undefined
d. Undefined

83. Any accumulation of material, by mechanical settling from water or air, chemical precipitation, evaporation from solution, etc is referred to as _____.
a. Deposition16
b. 1509 Istanbul earthquake
c. Undefined
d. Undefined

84. _____ refers to a group of closely spaced mountains or parallel ridges.
a. Mountain range16
b. 1509 Istanbul earthquake
c. Undefined
d. Undefined

85. The process by which exposure to atmospheric agents, such as air or moisture, causes rocks and minerals to break down is called _____. This process takes place at or near the Earth's surface. _____ entails little or no movement of the material that it loosens from the rocks and minerals.
a. Weathering16
b. 1509 Istanbul earthquake
c. Undefined
d. Undefined

86. _____ refers to a coarse-grained, foliated metamorphic rock marked by bands of light-colored minerals such as quartz and feldspar that alternate with bands of dark-colored minerals. This alternation develops through metamorphic differentiation.
a. 1509 Istanbul earthquake
b. Gneiss16
c. Undefined
d. Undefined

Chapter 16. Cenozoic Geologic History: The Tertiary Period

87. A pink-colored, felsic, plutonic rock that contains potassium and usually sodium feldspars, and has quartz content of about 10% is _____. _____ is commonly found on continents but virtually absent from the ocean basins.
   a. Granite16
   b. 1509 Istanbul earthquake
   c. Undefined
   d. Undefined

88. _____ refers to all geologic time from the beginning of Earth history to 570 million years ago. Also refers to the rocks that formed in that epoch.
   a. Precambrian16
   b. 1509 Istanbul earthquake
   c. Undefined
   d. Undefined

89. A coarse-grained, strongly foliated metamorphic rock that develops from phyllite and splits easily into flat, parallel slabs is _____.
   a. Schist16
   b. 1509 Istanbul earthquake
   c. Undefined
   d. Undefined

90. Fine particles of pulverized rock blown from an explosion vent are called _____. Measuring less than 1/10 inch in diameter, _____ may be either solid or molten when first erupted.
   a. AASHTO Soil Classification System
   b. Ash16
   c. Undefined
   d. Undefined

91. Magma that comes to the Earth's surface through a volcano or fissure is referred to as _____.
   a. Lava16
   b. 1509 Istanbul earthquake
   c. Undefined
   d. Undefined

92. An elevated area with relatively little internal relief is called a _____.
   a. 1509 Istanbul earthquake
   b. Plateau16
   c. Undefined
   d. Undefined

93. Any relatively sunken part of the Earth's surface, especially a low-lying area surrounded by higher ground is called a _____.
   a. Depression16
   b. 1509 Istanbul earthquake
   c. Undefined
   d. Undefined

94. _____ refers to any of a group of felsic igneous rocks that are the extrusive equivalents of granite.
   a. Rhyolite16
   b. 1509 Istanbul earthquake
   c. Undefined
   d. Undefined

95. A major branch of a stream system is referred to as a _____.
   a. 1509 Istanbul earthquake
   b. River16
   c. Undefined
   d. Undefined

96. _____ refers to a natural spring marked by the intermittent escape of hot water and steam.
   a. Geyser16
   b. 1509 Istanbul earthquake
   c. Undefined
   d. Undefined

97. The circulation of water through hot volcanic rocks and magmas, producing hot springs and geysers on the surface is called _____.
- a. 1509 Istanbul earthquake
- b. Hydrothermal activity16
- c. Undefined
- d. Undefined

98. _____ refers to a round or oval bulge on the Earth's surface, containing the oldest section of rock in its raised, central part.
- a. Dome16
- b. 1509 Istanbul earthquake
- c. Undefined
- d. Undefined

99. The angle formed by the inclined plane of a geological structure and the horizontal plane of the Earth's surface is referred to as a _____.
- a. Dip16
- b. 1509 Istanbul earthquake
- c. Undefined
- d. Undefined

100. _____ refers to pertaining to material or processes associated with transportation and or subaerial deposition by concentrated running water.
- a. AASHTO Soil Classification System
- b. Alluvial16
- c. Undefined
- d. Undefined

101. A dry lake basin found in a desert is called a _____.
- a. Playa16
- b. 1509 Istanbul earthquake
- c. Undefined
- d. Undefined

102. A shallow temporary lake on a flat valley floor in a dry region is referred to as a _____.
- a. 1509 Istanbul earthquake
- b. Playa lake16
- c. Undefined
- d. Undefined

103. A region on the downwind side of a mountain range that receives less rain because of the mountains is referred to as _____.
- a. 1509 Istanbul earthquake
- b. Rain shadow16
- c. Undefined
- d. Undefined

104. Low latitude areas characterized by high temperatures and high precipitation are referred to as _____. At high elevations, however, _____ mountains may be both cold and relatively dry.
- a. Tropical16
- b. 1509 Istanbul earthquake
- c. Undefined
- d. Undefined

105. _____ refers to a boundary in which two plates move together, resulting in oceanic lithosphere being thrust beneath an overriding plate, eventually to be reabsorbed into the mantle. It can also involve the collision of two continental plates to create a mountain system.
- a. 1509 Istanbul earthquake
- b. Convergent plate boundary16
- c. Undefined
- d. Undefined

106. A major strike-slip fault that cuts through the lithosphere and accommodates motion between two plates is a _____.

Chapter 16. Cenozoic Geologic History: The Tertiary Period

a. Transform fault16
b. 1509 Istanbul earthquake
c. Undefined
d. Undefined

107. _____ refer to plate boundaries with mostly horizontal movement that connect spreading centers to each other or to subduction zones.
a. 1509 Istanbul earthquake
b. Transform faults16
c. Undefined
d. Undefined

108. Fluid organic sediment formed by the diagenesis of organic material in the pores of sedimentary rocks, mainly sandstones and limestones is referred to as _____.
a. 1509 Istanbul earthquake
b. Gas16
c. Undefined
d. Undefined

109. _____ refers to a fluid organic sediment formed by the diagenesis of organic material in the pores of sedimentary rocks, mainly sandstones and limestones.
a. Oil16
b. AASHTO Soil Classification System
c. Undefined
d. Undefined

110. A body of rock identified by lithic characteristics and stratigraphic position and is mappable at the earth's surface or traceable in the subsurface is a _____.
a. 1509 Istanbul earthquake
b. Formation16
c. Undefined
d. Undefined

111. _____ refers to of or pertaining to rivers; produced by river action.
a. Fluvial16
b. 1509 Istanbul earthquake
c. Undefined
d. Undefined

112. Part of the continental margin, the ocean floor from the coastal shore of continents to the continental slope, usually to a depth of about 200 meters is the _____. The _____ usually has a very slight slope, roughly 0.1 degrees.
a. Continental shelf16
b. 1509 Istanbul earthquake
c. Undefined
d. Undefined

113. _____ refers to a clastic rock composed of particles that range in diameter from 1/16 millimeter to 2 millimeters in diameter. Sandstones make up about 25% of all sedimentary rocks.
a. Sandstone16
b. 1509 Istanbul earthquake
c. Undefined
d. Undefined

114. A sedimentary rock consisting mostly of silt grains is called _____.
a. Siltstone16
b. 1509 Istanbul earthquake
c. Undefined
d. Undefined

115. _____ refers to extremely small fragments, usually of glass, that forms when escaping gases force a fine spray of magma from a volcano.
a. 1509 Istanbul earthquake
b. Volcanic ash16
c. Undefined
d. Undefined

Chapter 16. Cenozoic Geologic History: The Tertiary Period

116. An intrusive rock, as distinguished from the preexisting country rock that surrounds it is called _____.
   a. Pluton16
   b. 1509 Istanbul earthquake
   c. Undefined
   d. Undefined

117. _____ refers to a portion of a rock unit that possesses a distinctive set of characteristics that distinguishes it from other parts of the same unit.
   a. 1509 Istanbul earthquake
   b. Facies16
   c. Undefined
   d. Undefined

118. _____ refer to a set of characteristics that distinguish a given section of sedimentary rock from nearby sections. Such characteristics include mineral content, grain size, shape, and density.
   a. 1509 Istanbul earthquake
   b. Sedimentary facies16
   c. Undefined
   d. Undefined

119. One of several minerals containing one central carbon atom with strong covalent bonds to three oxygen atoms and typically having ionic bonds to one or more positive ions is _____.
   a. Carbonate16
   b. 1509 Istanbul earthquake
   c. Undefined
   d. Undefined

120. A shallow, extensive flat area where both biological and nonbiological carbonates are deposited is a _____.
   a. Carbonate platform16
   b. 1509 Istanbul earthquake
   c. Undefined
   d. Undefined

121. An electrically neutral substance that consists of two or more elements combined in specific, constant proportions is a _____. A _____ typically has physical characteristics different from those of its constituent elements.
   a. Compound16
   b. 1509 Istanbul earthquake
   c. Undefined
   d. Undefined

122. A solid, waxy, organic substance that forms when pressure and heat from the Earth act on the remains of plants and animals is _____. _____ converts to various liquid and gaseous hydrocarbons at a depth of 7 or more kilometers and a temperature between 50° and 100°C.
   a. 1509 Istanbul earthquake
   b. Kerogen16
   c. Undefined
   d. Undefined

123. A brown or black clastic source rock containing kerogen is called _____.
   a. AASHTO Soil Classification System
   b. Oil shale16
   c. Undefined
   d. Undefined

124. _____ refers to a sedimentary rock composed of detrital sediment particles less than 0.004 millimeters in diameter. _____ tends to be red, brown, black, or gray, and usually originate in relatively still waters.
   a. 1509 Istanbul earthquake
   b. Shale16
   c. Undefined
   d. Undefined

125. A naturally occurring, usually inorganic, solid consisting of either a single element or a compound, and having a definite chemical composition and a systematic internal arrangement of atoms is referred to as a _____.

Chapter 16. Cenozoic Geologic History: The Tertiary Period 243

a. 1509 Istanbul earthquake
b. Mineral16
c. Undefined
d. Undefined

126. _____, or diatomaceous earth, is a siliceous sedimentary rock formed from the accumulations of diatoms or other nanoplankton.
a. 1509 Istanbul earthquake
b. Diatomite16
c. Undefined
d. Undefined

127. _____ refers to any evidence of past life, including remains, traces, imprints as well as life history artifacts.
a. 1509 Istanbul earthquake
b. Fossil16
c. Undefined
d. Undefined

128. _____ refers to a rock made from the consolidation of solid fragments, as of other rocks or organic remains, or by precipitation of minerals from solution.
a. Sedimentary rock16
b. 1509 Istanbul earthquake
c. Undefined
d. Undefined

129. A shiny black coal that develops from deeply buried lignite through heat and pressure, and that has a carbon content of 80% to 93%, which makes it a more efficient heating fuel than lignite is _____.
a. 1509 Istanbul earthquake
b. Bituminous coal16
c. Undefined
d. Undefined

130. _____ refers to a soft, brownish coal that develops from peat through bacterial action, is rich in kerogen, and has a carbon content of 70%, which makes it a more efficient heating fuel than peat.
a. Lignite16
b. 1509 Istanbul earthquake
c. Undefined
d. Undefined

131. The total amount of a geologic material in all its deposits, discovered and undiscovered are _____.
a. Resources16
b. 1509 Istanbul earthquake
c. Undefined
d. Undefined

132. Rounded particles coarser than 2 mm in diameter are called _____.
a. 1509 Istanbul earthquake
b. Gravel16
c. Undefined
d. Undefined

133. _____ refers to a deposit formed when heavy minerals are mechanically concentrated by currents, most commonly streams and waves. Placers are sources of gold, tin, platinum, diamonds, and other valuable minerals.
a. 1509 Istanbul earthquake
b. Placer16
c. Undefined
d. Undefined

134. _____ refers to a body of water found on the Earth's surface and confined to a narrow topographic depression, down which it flows and transports rock particles, sediment, and dissolved particles. Rivers, creeks, brooks, and runs are all streams.
a. Stream16
b. 1509 Istanbul earthquake
c. Undefined
d. Undefined

Chapter 16. Cenozoic Geologic History: The Tertiary Period

135. _____ refers to a massive discordant pluton with a surface area greater than 100 square kilometers, typically having a depth of about 30 kilometers. Batholiths are generally found in elongated mountain ranges after the country rock above them has eroded.
   a. 1509 Istanbul earthquake
   b. Batholith16
   c. Undefined
   d. Undefined

136. Mineral with the formula SiO is referred to as _____.
   a. Quartz16
   b. 1509 Istanbul earthquake
   c. Undefined
   d. Undefined

137. A gaseous mixture of naturally occurring hydrocarbons is _____.
   a. 1509 Istanbul earthquake
   b. Natural gas16
   c. Undefined
   d. Undefined

138. _____ refers to any of a group of naturally occurring substances made up of hydrocarbons. These substances may be gaseous, liquid, or semi-solid.
   a. 1509 Istanbul earthquake
   b. Petroleum16
   c. Undefined
   d. Undefined

139. The study of rock strata, especially of their distribution, deposition, and age is called _____.
   a. Stratigraphic16
   b. 1509 Istanbul earthquake
   c. Undefined
   d. Undefined

140. Strain involving an increase in length is an _____. _____ can cause crustal thinning and faulting.
   a. AASHTO Soil Classification System
   b. Extension16
   c. Undefined
   d. Undefined

141. _____ refer to the valuable minerals of an area that are presently legally recoverable or that may be so in the future; includes both the known ore bodies and the potential ores of a region.
   a. Mineral resources16
   b. 1509 Istanbul earthquake
   c. Undefined
   d. Undefined

142. A high mountain pass that forms when part of an arête erodes is referred to as a _____.
   a. Col16
   b. 1509 Istanbul earthquake
   c. Undefined
   d. Undefined

143. Being or pertaining to rock fragments formed in a volcanic eruption is referred to as _____.
   a. 1509 Istanbul earthquake
   b. Pyroclastic16
   c. Undefined
   d. Undefined

144. A design carved or chipped out on the slabs of Breton tombs is a _____. It is a highly version of an antropomorphic figure.
   a. Shield16
   b. 1509 Istanbul earthquake
   c. Undefined
   d. Undefined

Chapter 16. Cenozoic Geologic History: The Tertiary Period

145. The vertical difference between the summit of a mountain and the adjacent valley or plain is referred to as a _____.
    a. Relief16
    b. 1509 Istanbul earthquake
    c. Undefined
    d. Undefined

146. A deep, semi-circular basin eroded out of a mountain by an alpine glacier is referred to as a _____.
    a. Cirque16
    b. 1509 Istanbul earthquake
    c. Undefined
    d. Undefined

147. _____ refers to any physical, recognizable form or feature on the earth's surface, having a characteristic shape and range in composition, and produced by natural causes.
    a. 1509 Istanbul earthquake
    b. Landform16
    c. Undefined
    d. Undefined

Chapter 17. Cenozoic Geologic History: The Quaternary Period

1. _____ refers to a timeline based on a stratigraphic succession that provides a chronological record of the history of a region. The entire span of time since the Earth formed.
   a. Geologic time17
   b. 1509 Istanbul earthquake
   c. Undefined
   d. Undefined

2. The epoch of the Quaternary Period of geologic time, following the Pliocene Epoch and preceding the Holocene is referred to as the _____.
   a. 1509 Istanbul earthquake
   b. Pleistocene17
   c. Undefined
   d. Undefined

3. _____ refers to the period of Earth's history from about 2 million years ago to the present; also, the rocks and deposits of that age.
   a. Quaternary17
   b. 1509 Istanbul earthquake
   c. Undefined
   d. Undefined

4. _____ refers to the formation, movement, and recession of glaciers or ice sheet; geologic processes of glacial activity.
   a. Glaciation17
   b. 1509 Istanbul earthquake
   c. Undefined
   d. Undefined

5. _____ refers to the general term for the steady rise in the average global temperatures over the last 100 years.
   a. 1509 Istanbul earthquake
   b. Global warming17
   c. Undefined
   d. Undefined

6. _____ refers to a period during which the Earth is substantially cooler than usual and a significant portion of its land surface is covered by glaciers. Ice ages generally last tens of millions of years.
   a. AASHTO Soil Classification System
   b. Ice age17
   c. Undefined
   d. Undefined

7. A region with an average annual rainfall of 10 inches or less and sparse vegetation, typically having thin, dry, and crumbly soil is a _____. A _____ has an aridity index greater than 4.0.
   a. Desert17
   b. 1509 Istanbul earthquake
   c. Undefined
   d. Undefined

8. _____ refers to any condensed water falling from the atmosphere to the surface of the earth. Common types include rain, snow, sleet, and hail.
   a. Precipitation17
   b. 1509 Istanbul earthquake
   c. Undefined
   d. Undefined

9. The entire area between the tops of the slopes on both sides of a stream is a _____.
   a. 1509 Istanbul earthquake
   b. Valley17
   c. Undefined
   d. Undefined

10. A large mass of rock projecting above surrounding terrain is called a _____.
    a. 1509 Istanbul earthquake
    b. Mountain17
    c. Undefined
    d. Undefined

Chapter 17. Cenozoic Geologic History: The Quaternary Period

11. A hole dug into the ground in the attempt to intersect water or other subsurface fluids is referred to as a _____.
    a. 1509 Istanbul earthquake
    b. Well17
    c. Undefined
    d. Undefined

12. Aggregates of minerals or rock fragments are called _____.
    a. 1509 Istanbul earthquake
    b. Rocks17
    c. Undefined
    d. Undefined

13. _____ refers to the top few meters of regolith, generally including some organic matter derived from plants.
    a. 1509 Istanbul earthquake
    b. Soil17
    c. Undefined
    d. Undefined

14. A unit of the geologic time scale that is a subdivision of a period is referred to as an _____.
    a. AASHTO Soil Classification System
    b. Epoch17
    c. Undefined
    d. Undefined

15. _____ refers to the time period from 10,000 years ago to the present.
    a. Holocene17
    b. 1509 Istanbul earthquake
    c. Undefined
    d. Undefined

16. The set of geological processes that result in the expulsion of lava, pyroclastics, and gases at the Earth's surface is referred to as _____.
    a. 1509 Istanbul earthquake
    b. Volcanism17
    c. Undefined
    d. Undefined

17. The processes by which crustal forces cause a rock formation to break and slip along a fault are called _____.
    a. 1509 Istanbul earthquake
    b. Faulting17
    c. Undefined
    d. Undefined

18. The processes by which crustal forces deform an area of crust so that layers of rock are pushed into folds are called _____.
    a. 1509 Istanbul earthquake
    b. Folding17
    c. Undefined
    d. Undefined

19. _____ refers to rigid parts of the Earth's crust and part of the Earth's upper mantle that moves and adjoins each other along zones of seismic activity.
    a. Plate17
    b. 1509 Istanbul earthquake
    c. Undefined
    d. Undefined

20. _____ refers to a boundary between two plates that are sliding past each other.
    a. Transform plate boundary17
    b. 1509 Istanbul earthquake
    c. Undefined
    d. Undefined

21. A moving body of ice that forms on land from the accumulation and compaction of snow, and that flows downslope or outward due to gravity and the pressure of its own weight is a _____.

Chapter 17. Cenozoic Geologic History: The Quaternary Period

a. 1509 Istanbul earthquake
b. Glacier17
c. Undefined
d. Undefined

22. _____ refers to a collection of transported fragments or precipitated materials that accumulate, typically in loose layers, as of sand or mud.
a. Sediment17
b. 1509 Istanbul earthquake
c. Undefined
d. Undefined

23. The sinking of an oceanic plate edge as a result of convergence with a plate of lesser density is called _____. _____ often causes earthquakes and creates volcano chains.
a. 1509 Istanbul earthquake
b. Subduction17
c. Undefined
d. Undefined

24. Deformation of the earth's crust by natural processes leading to the formation of ocean basins, continents, mountain systems, and other earth features is called _____.
a. Tectonism17
b. 1509 Istanbul earthquake
c. Undefined
d. Undefined

25. A steep-sided, usually circular depression formed by either explosion or collapse at a volcanic vent is a _____.
a. Crater17
b. 1509 Istanbul earthquake
c. Undefined
d. Undefined

26. Magma that comes to the Earth's surface through a volcano or fissure is referred to as _____.
a. Lava17
b. 1509 Istanbul earthquake
c. Undefined
d. Undefined

27. The first epoch of the Quaternary Period, beginning 2 to 3 million years ago and ending approximately 10,000 years ago is referred to as the _____.
a. 1509 Istanbul earthquake
b. Pleistocene epoch17
c. Undefined
d. Undefined

28. _____ refers to the description, correlation, and classification of strata in sedimentary rocks.
a. 1509 Istanbul earthquake
b. Stratigraphy17
c. Undefined
d. Undefined

29. The study of rock strata, especially of their distribution, deposition, and age is called _____.
a. 1509 Istanbul earthquake
b. Stratigraphic17
c. Undefined
d. Undefined

30. A group of interacting or interdependent parts that form a complex whole is called a _____.
a. System17
b. 1509 Istanbul earthquake
c. Undefined
d. Undefined

31. One of two or more forms of a single element is an _____; the atoms of each _____ have the same number of protons but different numbers of neutrons in their nuclei. Thus isotopes have the same atomic number but differ in atomic mass.

Chapter 17. Cenozoic Geologic History: The Quaternary Period 249

a. AASHTO Soil Classification System
b. Isotope17
c. Undefined
d. Undefined

32. A comprehensive explanation of a given set of data that has been repeatedly confirmed by observation and experimentation and has gained general acceptance within the scientific community but has not yet been decisively proven is referred to as _____.
   a. Theory17
   b. 1509 Istanbul earthquake
   c. Undefined
   d. Undefined

33. _____ refers to a naturally formed aggregate of usually inorganic materials from within the Earth.
   a. Rock17
   b. 1509 Istanbul earthquake
   c. Undefined
   d. Undefined

34. The outer margin of a glacier is called _____.
   a. 1509 Istanbul earthquake
   b. Terminus17
   c. Undefined
   d. Undefined

35. _____ refers to a basic unit of the geologic time scale that is a subdivision of an era. Periods may be divided into smaller units called epochs.
   a. 1509 Istanbul earthquake
   b. Period17
   c. Undefined
   d. Undefined

36. The top of the ocean, where the water meets the atmosphere is called _____.
   a. 1509 Istanbul earthquake
   b. Sea level17
   c. Undefined
   d. Undefined

37. A flat, steplike surface that lines a stream above the floodplain, often paired one on each side of the stream, marking a former floodplain that existed at a higher level before regional uplift or an increase in discharge caused the stream to erode into it is called the _____.
   a. 1509 Istanbul earthquake
   b. Terrace17
   c. Undefined
   d. Undefined

38. _____ refers to a rock fragment carried by glacial ice, or by floating ice, and subsequently deposited at some distance from the outcrop of which it was derived.
   a. Erratic17
   b. AASHTO Soil Classification System
   c. Undefined
   d. Undefined

39. _____ refer to multiple scratches or minute lines, generally parallel but occasionally cross-cutting, inscribed on a rock surface by a geologic agent. Common indicators of direction of glacier flow.
   a. 1509 Istanbul earthquake
   b. Striations17
   c. Undefined
   d. Undefined

40. A steep volcanic cone built by both lava flows and pyroclastic eruptions is called a _____.
   a. Composite volcano17
   b. 1509 Istanbul earthquake
   c. Undefined
   d. Undefined

Chapter 17. Cenozoic Geologic History: The Quaternary Period

41. The process of determining that two or more geographically distant rocks or rock strata originated in the same time period is referred to as _____.
   a. Correlation17
   b. 1509 Istanbul earthquake
   c. Undefined
   d. Undefined

42. _____ refers to a round or oval bulge on the Earth's surface, containing the oldest section of rock in its raised, central part.
   a. 1509 Istanbul earthquake
   b. Dome17
   c. Undefined
   d. Undefined

43. Mass of lava, created by many individual flows, that has built a dome-shaped pile of lava is called a _____.
   a. 1509 Istanbul earthquake
   b. Lava dome17
   c. Undefined
   d. Undefined

44. A situation, which is generally uncomfortable, or otherwise undesirable is a _____.
   a. Problem17
   b. 1509 Istanbul earthquake
   c. Undefined
   d. Undefined

45. A vast depression at the top of a volcanic cone, formed when an eruption substantially empties the reservoir of magma beneath the cone's summit is a _____. A _____ may be more than 15 kilometers in diameter and more than 1000 meters deep.
   a. 1509 Istanbul earthquake
   b. Caldera17
   c. Undefined
   d. Undefined

46. The circulation of water through hot volcanic rocks and magmas, producing hot springs and geysers on the surface is called _____.
   a. 1509 Istanbul earthquake
   b. Hydrothermal activity17
   c. Undefined
   d. Undefined

47. Molten rock that forms naturally within the Earth is _____. _____ may be either a liquid or a fluid mixture of liquid, crystals, and dissolved gases.
   a. 1509 Istanbul earthquake
   b. Magma17
   c. Undefined
   d. Undefined

48. All processes that adds snow or ice to a glacier or to floating ice or snow cove are referred to as _____.
   a. AASHTO Soil Classification System
   b. Accumulation17
   c. Undefined
   d. Undefined

49. Fine particles of pulverized rock blown from an explosion vent are called _____. Measuring less than 1/10 inch in diameter, _____ may be either solid or molten when first erupted.
   a. Ash17
   b. AASHTO Soil Classification System
   c. Undefined
   d. Undefined

50. _____ refers to the process by which solid, liquid, and gaseous materials are ejected into the earth's atmosphere and onto the earth's surface by volcanic activity. Eruptions range from the quiet overflow of liquid rock to the tremendously violent expulsion of pyroclastics.

Chapter 17. Cenozoic Geologic History: The Quaternary Period

a. AASHTO Soil Classification System
b. Eruption17
c. Undefined
d. Undefined

51. Light-colored, frothy volcanic rock, usually of dacite or rhyolite composition, formed by the expansion of gas in erupting lava is _____. Commonly seen as lumps or fragments of pea-size and larger, but can also occur abundantly as ash-sized particles.
a. Pumice17
b. 1509 Istanbul earthquake
c. Undefined
d. Undefined

52. _____ refers to igneous rocks that cool on the surface of the Earth, including beneath water; typically with small crystals due to the rapidity of cooling.
a. Volcanic17
b. 1509 Istanbul earthquake
c. Undefined
d. Undefined

53. _____ refers to extremely small fragments, usually of glass, that forms when escaping gases force a fine spray of magma from a volcano.
a. Volcanic ash17
b. 1509 Istanbul earthquake
c. Undefined
d. Undefined

54. Being or pertaining to rock fragments formed in a volcanic eruption is referred to as _____.
a. 1509 Istanbul earthquake
b. Pyroclastic17
c. Undefined
d. Undefined

55. The middle layer of the Earth, lying just below the crust and consisting of relatively dense rocks is called the _____. The _____ is divided into two sections, the upper _____ and the lower _____; the lower _____ has greater density than the upper _____.
a. Mantle17
b. 1509 Istanbul earthquake
c. Undefined
d. Undefined

56. _____ refers to a mass of hotter-than-normal mantle material that ascends toward the surface, where it may lead to igneous activity. These plumes of solid yet mobile material may originate as deep as the core-mantle boundary.
a. Mantle plume17
b. 1509 Istanbul earthquake
c. Undefined
d. Undefined

57. A major branch of a stream system is referred to as a _____.
a. River17
b. 1509 Istanbul earthquake
c. Undefined
d. Undefined

58. _____ refers to rock formed of pyroclastic material.
a. Tuff17
b. 1509 Istanbul earthquake
c. Undefined
d. Undefined

59. An area in the upper mantle, ranging from 100 to 200 kilometers in width, from which magma rises in a plume to form volcanoes. A _____ may endure for 10 million years or more.

252 Chapter 17. Cenozoic Geologic History: The Quaternary Period

    a. Hot spot17
    b. 1509 Istanbul earthquake
    c. Undefined
    d. Undefined

60. _____ refers to ice, which covers an ocean or sea; includes mostly continuous pack ice, broken only by narrow open water 'leads' or wider 'polynas', and discrete ice floes.
    a. Sea ice17
    b. 1509 Istanbul earthquake
    c. Undefined
    d. Undefined

61. A group of tiny single-celled organisms that live in surface waters and whose secretions and calcite shells account for most of the oceans carbonate sediments is called _____.
    a. 1509 Istanbul earthquake
    b. Foraminifera17
    c. Undefined
    d. Undefined

62. Refers to substances containing or composed of calcium carbonate is called _____.
    a. 1509 Istanbul earthquake
    b. Calcareous17
    c. Undefined
    d. Undefined

63. _____ refer to varieties of the same element that have different mass numbers; their nuclei contain the same number of protons but different numbers of neutrons.
    a. AASHTO Soil Classification System
    b. Isotopes17
    c. Undefined
    d. Undefined

64. Compacted and intergrown mass of crystalline ice with a density is _____.
    a. 1509 Istanbul earthquake
    b. Glacial ice17
    c. Undefined
    d. Undefined

65. A body of rock identified by lithic characteristics and stratigraphic position and is mappable at the earth's surface or traceable in the subsurface is a _____.
    a. 1509 Istanbul earthquake
    b. Formation17
    c. Undefined
    d. Undefined

66. _____ refers to a glacier of considerable thickness and more than 50,000 square kilometers in area, forming a continuous cover of snow and ice over a land surface, spreading outward in all directions and not confined by the underlying topography. Ice sheets are now confined to Polar Regions, but during the Pleistocene Epoch they covered large parts of North America and northern Europe.
    a. Ice sheet17
    b. AASHTO Soil Classification System
    c. Undefined
    d. Undefined

67. _____ refers to an epoch in Earth's history from about 24 to 5 million years ago. Also refers to the rocks that formed in that epoch.
    a. 1509 Istanbul earthquake
    b. Miocene17
    c. Undefined
    d. Undefined

68. _____ refers to the change of state of water from the liquid to vapor phase. Requires the addition of 80 calories per cubic centimeter.

Chapter 17. Cenozoic Geologic History: The Quaternary Period

   a. Evaporation17
   c. Undefined
   b. AASHTO Soil Classification System
   d. Undefined

69. _____ refers to any evidence of past life, including remains, traces, imprints as well as life history artifacts.
   a. Fossil17
   b. 1509 Istanbul earthquake
   c. Undefined
   d. Undefined

70. The movement of air from a region of high pressure to a region of low pressure is _____.
   a. Wind17
   b. 1509 Istanbul earthquake
   c. Undefined
   d. Undefined

71. A mechanism of glacial movement in which the ice mass slides over the surface below is referred to as a _____.
   a. Basal slip17
   b. 1509 Istanbul earthquake
   c. Undefined
   d. Undefined

72. General term for the processes of folding, faulting, shearing, compression, or extension of rocks as the result of various natural forces is called _____.
   a. 1509 Istanbul earthquake
   b. Deformation17
   c. Undefined
   d. Undefined

73. Any accumulation of material, by mechanical settling from water or air, chemical precipitation, evaporation from solution, etc is referred to as _____.
   a. Deposition17
   b. 1509 Istanbul earthquake
   c. Undefined
   d. Undefined

74. The process by which particles of rock and soil are loosened, as by weathering, and then transported elsewhere, as by wind, water, ice, or gravity is _____.
   a. Erosion17
   b. AASHTO Soil Classification System
   c. Undefined
   d. Undefined

75. _____ refers to capable of being molded into any form, which is retained.
   a. Plastic17
   b. 1509 Istanbul earthquake
   c. Undefined
   d. Undefined

76. A type of glacial movement that occurs within the glacier, below a depth of approximately 50 meters, in which the ice is not fractured, is referred to as _____.
   a. 1509 Istanbul earthquake
   b. Plastic flow17
   c. Undefined
   d. Undefined

77. A negatively charged particle that orbits rapidly around the nucleus of an atom is referred to as an _____.
   a. Electron17
   b. AASHTO Soil Classification System
   c. Undefined
   d. Undefined

78. _____ refers to waterlogged, spongy ground, consisting of mosses containing acidic, decaying vegetation such as spaghnum, sedges, and heaths that may develop into peat.

a. 1509 Istanbul earthquake
b. Bog17
c. Undefined
d. Undefined

79. An extremely slow moving, thick sheet of ice that covers a large part of a continent is a _____.
a. Continental glacier17
b. 1509 Istanbul earthquake
c. Undefined
d. Undefined

80. _____ refers to an alpine glacier that flows through a preexisting stream valley.
a. Valley glacier17
b. 1509 Istanbul earthquake
c. Undefined
d. Undefined

81. Distinct crystals of ice are called _____. Commonly accumulates with a density of 50 - 200 kg·m, although wind-abraded and packed _____ may have a higher initial density.
a. Snow17
b. 1509 Istanbul earthquake
c. Undefined
d. Undefined

82. The part of a glacier in which there is greater overall gain than loss in volume is the _____. A _____ can be identified by a blanket of snow that survives summer melting.
a. 1509 Istanbul earthquake
b. Zone of accumulation17
c. Undefined
d. Undefined

83. _____ refers to the set of physical features, such as mountains, valleys, and the shapes of landforms, that characterizes a given landscape.
a. 1509 Istanbul earthquake
b. Topography17
c. Undefined
d. Undefined

84. Uplift of the crust of the earth that results from unloading such as results from the melting of ice sheets is an _____.
a. AASHTO Soil Classification System
b. Isostatic rebound17
c. Undefined
d. Undefined

85. _____ refers to general term referring to the rock underlying other unconsolidated material, i.e. soil.
a. Bedrock17
b. 1509 Istanbul earthquake
c. Undefined
d. Undefined

86. A ridge-like accumulation that is being or was produced at the outer margin of an actively flowing glacier at any given time is referred to as the _____.
a. AASHTO Soil Classification System
b. End moraine17
c. Undefined
d. Undefined

87. Rounded particles coarser than 2 mm in diameter are called _____.
a. 1509 Istanbul earthquake
b. Gravel17
c. Undefined
d. Undefined

88. A single, large mass of glacial till that accumulates, typically at the edge of a glacier is referred to as a _____.

Chapter 17. Cenozoic Geologic History: The Quaternary Period

a. 1509 Istanbul earthquake
b. Moraine17
c. Undefined
d. Undefined

89. A load of sediment, consisting of sand and gravel that is deposited by meltwater in front of a glacier is called _____.
a. Outwash17
b. AASHTO Soil Classification System
c. Undefined
d. Undefined

90. _____ refers to the water portion of our planet; one of the traditional subdivisions of Earth's physical environment.
a. Hydrosphere17
b. 1509 Istanbul earthquake
c. Undefined
d. Undefined

91. _____ refers to any physical, recognizable form or feature on the earth's surface, having a characteristic shape and range in composition, and produced by natural causes.
a. 1509 Istanbul earthquake
b. Landform17
c. Undefined
d. Undefined

92. The lowest level to which a stream can erode the channel through which it flows, generally equal to the prevailing global sea level is referred to as the _____.
a. Base level17
b. 1509 Istanbul earthquake
c. Undefined
d. Undefined

93. _____ refers to the area of dry land that borders on a body of water.
a. 1509 Istanbul earthquake
b. Coast17
c. Undefined
d. Undefined

94. The equilibrium maintained between the gravity tending to depress and the buoyancy tending to raise a given segment of the lithosphere as it floats above the asthenosphere is called _____.
a. Isostasy17
b. AASHTO Soil Classification System
c. Undefined
d. Undefined

95. The vertical difference between the summit of a mountain and the adjacent valley or plain is referred to as a _____.
a. Relief17
b. 1509 Istanbul earthquake
c. Undefined
d. Undefined

96. _____ refers to the steep-walled, broad-floored shape considered diagnostic of former mountain glaciation. Often contrasted to the 'V' shape typical of mass wasting slopes feeding river systems.
a. 1509 Istanbul earthquake
b. Trough17
c. Undefined
d. Undefined

97. The outermost layer of the Earth, consisting of relatively low-density rock is called _____.
a. Crust17
b. 1509 Istanbul earthquake
c. Undefined
d. Undefined

Chapter 17. Cenozoic Geologic History: The Quaternary Period

98. Material is in _____ if it is adjusted to the physical and chemical conditions of its environment so that it does not change or alter with time.
    a. Equilibrium17
    b. AASHTO Soil Classification System
    c. Undefined
    d. Undefined

99. The liquid portion of magma excluding the solid crystals is called _____.
    a. 1509 Istanbul earthquake
    b. Melt17
    c. Undefined
    d. Undefined

100. An end or lateral moraine, built during a temporary but significant halt in the final retreat of a glacier is called the _____.
    a. Recessional moraine17
    b. 1509 Istanbul earthquake
    c. Undefined
    d. Undefined

101. An end moraine that marks the farthest advance of a glacier and usually has the form of a massive concentric ridge or complex of ridges, underlain by till and other types of drift is a _____.
    a. 1509 Istanbul earthquake
    b. Terminal moraine17
    c. Undefined
    d. Undefined

102. _____ refers to the boundary between a body of water and dry land.
    a. 1509 Istanbul earthquake
    b. Shoreline17
    c. Undefined
    d. Undefined

103. _____ refers to the area immediately adjacent to a glacier, often affected by outwash and by ice or moraine-dammed lakes.
    a. Proglacial17
    b. 1509 Istanbul earthquake
    c. Undefined
    d. Undefined

104. _____ refers to the height of floodwaters in feet or meters above an established datum plane.
    a. Stage17
    b. 1509 Istanbul earthquake
    c. Undefined
    d. Undefined

105. A lake that formed from rainwater falling into a landlocked basin during a glacial period marked by greater precipitation than is found in the region in prior or subsequent periods is a _____.
    a. Pluvial lake17
    b. 1509 Istanbul earthquake
    c. Undefined
    d. Undefined

106. A non-crystaline rock that results from very rapid cooling of magma is _____.
    a. Glass17
    b. 1509 Istanbul earthquake
    c. Undefined
    d. Undefined

107. Term loosely used for silt and clay, usually wet is referred to as _____.
    a. 1509 Istanbul earthquake
    b. Mud17
    c. Undefined
    d. Undefined

108. The time between winter and summer is _____.

Chapter 17. Cenozoic Geologic History: The Quaternary Period

a. 1509 Istanbul earthquake
b. Spring17
c. Undefined
d. Undefined

109. _____ refers to a glacial lake in northwest Montana during Pleistocene times, which was formed by an ice dam of the Cordilleran ice sheet; this dam broke periodically, flooding a portion of current-day northern Idaho and Washington.
a. 1509 Istanbul earthquake
b. Lake Missoula17
c. Undefined
d. Undefined

110. _____ refers to an ice-marginal lake formed just beyond the frontal moraine of a retreating glacier and generally in direct contact with the ice.
a. Proglacial lake17
b. 1509 Istanbul earthquake
c. Undefined
d. Undefined

111. _____ refers to a body of water found on the Earth's surface and confined to a narrow topographic depression, down which it flows and transports rock particles, sediment, and dissolved particles. Rivers, creeks, brooks, and runs are all streams.
a. Stream17
b. 1509 Istanbul earthquake
c. Undefined
d. Undefined

112. Any unconsolidated material at Earth's surface is _____.
a. Debris17
b. 1509 Istanbul earthquake
c. Undefined
d. Undefined

113. _____ refers to the overflow of a stream channel that occurs when discharge exceeds the channel's capacity. The most common and destructive geologic hazard.
a. 1509 Istanbul earthquake
b. Flood17
c. Undefined
d. Undefined

114. _____ refer to lakes formed in closed basins as a result of climates, which also encouraged glaciation.
a. 1509 Istanbul earthquake
b. Pluvial lakes17
c. Undefined
d. Undefined

115. A lake that derives much or all of its water from the melting of glacier ice, fed by meltwater, and lying outside the glaciers margin is called the _____.
a. 1509 Istanbul earthquake
b. Glacial lake17
c. Undefined
d. Undefined

116. A sedimentary structure consisting of a very small dune of sand or silt whose long dimension is at right angles to the current is a _____.
a. 1509 Istanbul earthquake
b. Ripple17
c. Undefined
d. Undefined

117. _____ refers to the gaseous portion of a planet, the planet's envelope of air. One of the traditional subdivisions of Earth's physical environment.

a. Atmosphere17
b. AASHTO Soil Classification System
c. Undefined
d. Undefined

118. Fluid organic sediment formed by the diagenesis of organic material in the pores of sedimentary rocks, mainly sandstones and limestones is referred to as _____.
a. 1509 Istanbul earthquake
b. Gas17
c. Undefined
d. Undefined

119. _____ refers to a descriptive term applied to igneous rocks that are transitional between basic and acidic with silica between 54% and 65%.
a. Intermediate17
b. AASHTO Soil Classification System
c. Undefined
d. Undefined

120. _____ refers to a tentative explanation of a given set of data that is expected to remain valid after future observation and experimentation.
a. Hypothesis17
b. 1509 Istanbul earthquake
c. Undefined
d. Undefined

121. The degree to which the Earth's orbit around the sun varies from a perfect circle - it ranges between about 1% and 5% across a 100,000 year cycle is called _____.
a. Eccentricity17
b. AASHTO Soil Classification System
c. Undefined
d. Undefined

122. Angular distance of a point on the earth's surface north or south of the equator, measured along a meridian, the equator being _____ 0°, the north pole _____ 90°N, and the south pole _____ 90°S.
a. Latitude17
b. 1509 Istanbul earthquake
c. Undefined
d. Undefined

123. _____ refers to the theory that the Earth's lithosphere consists of large, rigid plates that move horizontally in response to the flow of the asthenosphere beneath them, and that interactions among the plates at their borders cause most major geologic activity, including the creation of oceans, continents, mountains, volcanoes, and earthquakes.
a. 1509 Istanbul earthquake
b. Plate tectonics17
c. Undefined
d. Undefined

124. Ability to do work is referred to as _____. Most evident in glacial systems as radiant _____ from the sun and as latent _____ required to melt ice to water.
a. Energy17
b. AASHTO Soil Classification System
c. Undefined
d. Undefined

125. Energy derived from the Sun, including energy from solar generating systems, hydroelectric systems, and wind power is called _____.
a. Solar energy17
b. 1509 Istanbul earthquake
c. Undefined
d. Undefined

Chapter 17. Cenozoic Geologic History: The Quaternary Period

126. The slow gyration of the Earth's axis, analogous to that of a spinning top, which causes the slow change in the orientation of the Earth's axis relative to the sun that accounts for the reversal of the seasons of winter and summer in the Northern and Southern Hemisphere is referred to as _____.
    a. Precession17
    b. 1509 Istanbul earthquake
    c. Undefined
    d. Undefined

127. A naturally occurring, usually inorganic, solid consisting of either a single element or a compound, and having a definite chemical composition and a systematic internal arrangement of atoms is referred to as a _____.
    a. 1509 Istanbul earthquake
    b. Mineral17
    c. Undefined
    d. Undefined

128. The total amount of a geologic material in all its deposits, discovered and undiscovered are _____.
    a. Resources17
    b. 1509 Istanbul earthquake
    c. Undefined
    d. Undefined

129. _____ refers to a chemical combination of silicon and oxygen.
    a. 1509 Istanbul earthquake
    b. Silica17
    c. Undefined
    d. Undefined

130. _____ refers to a deposit formed when heavy minerals are mechanically concentrated by currents, most commonly streams and waves. Placers are sources of gold, tin, platinum, diamonds, and other valuable minerals.
    a. 1509 Istanbul earthquake
    b. Placer17
    c. Undefined
    d. Undefined

131. _____ occurs when the applied load of a structure's foundation is greater than the bearing strength of the foundation material.
    a. 1509 Istanbul earthquake
    b. Settlement17
    c. Undefined
    d. Undefined

132. A soft brown mass of compressed, partially decomposed vegetation that forms in a water-saturated environment and has a carbon content of 50% is _____. Dried _____ can be burned as fuel.
    a. Peat17
    b. 1509 Istanbul earthquake
    c. Undefined
    d. Undefined

133. A mineral or fuel deposit, known or not yet discovered, that may be or become available for human exploitation is called a _____.
    a. Resource17
    b. 1509 Istanbul earthquake
    c. Undefined
    d. Undefined

134. The lowering of the Earth's surface, caused by such factors as compaction, a decrease in groundwater, or the pumping of oil is called _____.
    a. Subsidence17
    b. 1509 Istanbul earthquake
    c. Undefined
    d. Undefined

135. Inorganic chemical sediment that precipitates when the salty water in which it had dissolved evaporates is called _____.

a. Evaporite17
c. Undefined

b. AASHTO Soil Classification System
d. Undefined

136. _____ refer to the valuable minerals of an area that are presently legally recoverable or that may be so in the future; includes both the known ore bodies and the potential ores of a region.

a. Mineral resources17
c. Undefined

b. 1509 Istanbul earthquake
d. Undefined

Chapter 18. Life of the Cenozoic Era

1. _____ refers to the gaseous portion of a planet, the planet's envelope of air. One of the traditional subdivisions of Earth's physical environment.
   a. AASHTO Soil Classification System
   b. Atmosphere18
   c. Undefined
   d. Undefined

2. Observable phenomena that occur before an earthquake and indicate that an event is soon to occur are referred to as _____.
   a. Precursors18
   b. 1509 Istanbul earthquake
   c. Undefined
   d. Undefined

3. _____ refers to a major division on the geologic time scale; eras are divided into shorter units called periods.
   a. Era18
   b. AASHTO Soil Classification System
   c. Undefined
   d. Undefined

4. Aggregates of minerals or rock fragments are called _____.
   a. Rocks18
   b. 1509 Istanbul earthquake
   c. Undefined
   d. Undefined

5. Rocks formed by solidification of sediments formed and transported at the Earth's surface are referred to as _____.
   a. Sedimentary rocks18
   b. 1509 Istanbul earthquake
   c. Undefined
   d. Undefined

6. A hole dug into the ground in the attempt to intersect water or other subsurface fluids is referred to as a _____.
   a. 1509 Istanbul earthquake
   b. Well18
   c. Undefined
   d. Undefined

7. _____ refers to any evidence of past life, including remains, traces, imprints as well as life history artifacts.
   a. Fossil18
   b. 1509 Istanbul earthquake
   c. Undefined
   d. Undefined

8. A body of rock identified by lithic characteristics and stratigraphic position and is mappable at the earth's surface or traceable in the subsurface is a _____.
   a. Formation18
   b. 1509 Istanbul earthquake
   c. Undefined
   d. Undefined

9. A group of tiny single-celled organisms that live in surface waters and whose secretions and calcite shells account for most of the oceans carbonate sediments is called _____.
   a. Foraminifera18
   b. 1509 Istanbul earthquake
   c. Undefined
   d. Undefined

10. _____ refers to an epoch in Earth's history from about 24 to 5 million years ago. Also refers to the rocks that formed in that epoch.
    a. Miocene18
    b. 1509 Istanbul earthquake
    c. Undefined
    d. Undefined

Chapter 18. Life of the Cenozoic Era

11. The set of geological processes that result in the expulsion of lava, pyroclastics, and gases at the Earth's surface is referred to as _____.
   a. 1509 Istanbul earthquake
   b. Volcanism18
   c. Undefined
   d. Undefined

12. Fine particles of pulverized rock blown from an explosion vent are called _____. Measuring less than 1/10 inch in diameter, _____ may be either solid or molten when first erupted.
   a. Ash18
   b. AASHTO Soil Classification System
   c. Undefined
   d. Undefined

13. _____ refers to a chemical combination of silicon and oxygen.
   a. 1509 Istanbul earthquake
   b. Silica18
   c. Undefined
   d. Undefined

14. _____ refers to igneous rocks that cool on the surface of the Earth, including beneath water; typically with small crystals due to the rapidity of cooling.
   a. Volcanic18
   b. 1509 Istanbul earthquake
   c. Undefined
   d. Undefined

15. _____, or diatomaceous earth, is a siliceous sedimentary rock formed from the accumulations of diatoms or other nanoplankton.
   a. 1509 Istanbul earthquake
   b. Diatomite18
   c. Undefined
   d. Undefined

16. An igneous pluton that is not tabular in shape is _____.
   a. Massive18
   b. 1509 Istanbul earthquake
   c. Undefined
   d. Undefined

17. Any place where bedrock is visible on the surface of the Earth is referred to as _____.
   a. AASHTO Soil Classification System
   b. Outcrop18
   c. Undefined
   d. Undefined

18. _____ refers to a ridge-like or mound-like structure, layered or massive, built by sedentary calcareous organisms; it is wave resistant and stands above the surrounding contemporaneously deposited sediment.
   a. 1509 Istanbul earthquake
   b. Reef18
   c. Undefined
   d. Undefined

19. The epoch of the Quaternary Period of geologic time, following the Pliocene Epoch and preceding the Holocene is referred to as the _____.
   a. Pleistocene18
   b. 1509 Istanbul earthquake
   c. Undefined
   d. Undefined

20. _____ refers to a basic unit of the geologic time scale that is a subdivision of an era. Periods may be divided into smaller units called epochs.

a. Period18
b. 1509 Istanbul earthquake
c. Undefined
d. Undefined

21. _____ refers to any condensed water falling from the atmosphere to the surface of the earth. Common types include rain, snow, sleet, and hail.
a. 1509 Istanbul earthquake
b. Precipitation18
c. Undefined
d. Undefined

22. Low latitude areas characterized by high temperatures and high precipitation are referred to as _____. At high elevations, however, _____ mountains may be both cold and relatively dry.
a. Tropical18
b. 1509 Istanbul earthquake
c. Undefined
d. Undefined

23. Movement of heat from one place to another is a _____.
a. Heat transfer18
b. 1509 Istanbul earthquake
c. Undefined
d. Undefined

24. Fluid organic sediment formed by the diagenesis of organic material in the pores of sedimentary rocks, mainly sandstones and limestones is referred to as _____.
a. Gas18
b. 1509 Istanbul earthquake
c. Undefined
d. Undefined

25. _____ refers to a climate typical of the mid-latitudes, with neither exceptionally high nor low temperatures and precipitation.
a. 1509 Istanbul earthquake
b. Temperate climate18
c. Undefined
d. Undefined

26. A region with an average annual rainfall of 10 inches or less and sparse vegetation, typically having thin, dry, and crumbly soil is a _____. A _____ has an aridity index greater than 4.0.
a. Desert18
b. 1509 Istanbul earthquake
c. Undefined
d. Undefined

27. _____ refers to one of the two types of dry climate. A marginal and more humid variant of the desert that separates it from bordering humid climates.
a. Steppe18
b. 1509 Istanbul earthquake
c. Undefined
d. Undefined

28. The latest era of the Phanerozoic Eon, following the Mesozoic Era and continuing to the present time, and marked by the presence of a wide variety of mammals, including the first hominids is referred to as _____.
a. 1509 Istanbul earthquake
b. Cenozoic Era18
c. Undefined
d. Undefined

29. _____ refers to the proposed supercontinent that 200 million years ago began to break apart and form the present landmasses.

Chapter 18. Life of the Cenozoic Era

a. Pangaea18
b. 1509 Istanbul earthquake
c. Undefined
d. Undefined

30. _____ refers to the theory that living organisms mutate and change, generally from simple to increasingly complex forms.
a. AASHTO Soil Classification System
b. Evolution18
c. Undefined
d. Undefined

31. _____ refers to the beginning or source area for a stream. Also called the headwaters.
a. 1509 Istanbul earthquake
b. Head18
c. Undefined
d. Undefined

32. A high mountain peak that forms when the walls of three or more cirques intersect is called a _____.
a. Horn18
b. 1509 Istanbul earthquake
c. Undefined
d. Undefined

33. A major branch of a stream system is referred to as a _____.
a. River18
b. 1509 Istanbul earthquake
c. Undefined
d. Undefined

34. Many megalithic mounds in the southern Iberian peninsula, Sardinia and the British Isles present a concave façade with its two extremities ending in extensions known as _____ or horns are called _____. They define a partly enclosed space described as the forecourt of a horned cairn.
a. 1509 Istanbul earthquake
b. Wings18
c. Undefined
d. Undefined

35. The motion of surfaces sliding past one another is called _____.
a. 1509 Istanbul earthquake
b. Shearing18
c. Undefined
d. Undefined

36. _____ refers to the top few meters of regolith, generally including some organic matter derived from plants.
a. 1509 Istanbul earthquake
b. Soil18
c. Undefined
d. Undefined

37. A unit of the geologic time scale that is a subdivision of a period is referred to as an _____.
a. Epoch18
b. AASHTO Soil Classification System
c. Undefined
d. Undefined

38. A large mass of rock projecting above surrounding terrain is called a _____.
a. Mountain18
b. 1509 Istanbul earthquake
c. Undefined
d. Undefined

39. A group of interacting or interdependent parts that form a complex whole is called a _____.
a. System18
b. 1509 Istanbul earthquake
c. Undefined
d. Undefined

Chapter 18. Life of the Cenozoic Era

40. The total amount of a geologic material in all its deposits, discovered and undiscovered are _____.
    a. Resources18
    b. 1509 Istanbul earthquake
    c. Undefined
    d. Undefined

41. _____ refers to a descriptive term applied to igneous rocks that are transitional between basic and acidic with silica between 54% and 65%.
    a. AASHTO Soil Classification System
    b. Intermediate18
    c. Undefined
    d. Undefined

42. The solid material that precipitates in the pore space of sediments, binding the grains together to form solid rock is referred to as _____.
    a. Cement18
    b. 1509 Istanbul earthquake
    c. Undefined
    d. Undefined

43. A spit that curves sharply at its coastal end is referred to as a _____.
    a. 1509 Istanbul earthquake
    b. Hook18
    c. Undefined
    d. Undefined

44. _____ refers to the period of Earth's history from about 2 million years ago to the present; also, the rocks and deposits of that age.
    a. Quaternary18
    b. 1509 Istanbul earthquake
    c. Undefined
    d. Undefined

45. _____ refers to a period during which the Earth is substantially cooler than usual and a significant portion of its land surface is covered by glaciers. Ice ages generally last tens of millions of years.
    a. Ice age18
    b. AASHTO Soil Classification System
    c. Undefined
    d. Undefined

46. _____ refers to a naturally formed opening beneath the surface of the Earth, generally formed by dissolution of carbonate bedrock. Caves may also form by erosion of coastal bedrock, partial melting of glaciers, or solidification of lava into hollow tubes.
    a. Cave18
    b. 1509 Istanbul earthquake
    c. Undefined
    d. Undefined

47. Permanently frozen regolith, ranging in thickness from 30 centimeters to over 1000 meters is _____.
    a. 1509 Istanbul earthquake
    b. Permafrost18
    c. Undefined
    d. Undefined

48. _____ refers to any of a group of naturally occurring substances made up of hydrocarbons. These substances may be gaseous, liquid, or semi-solid.
    a. 1509 Istanbul earthquake
    b. Petroleum18
    c. Undefined
    d. Undefined

49. A treeless plain characteristic of arctic regions with organically rich, poorly drained _____ soils and permanently frozen ground is called a _____.

Chapter 18. Life of the Cenozoic Era

a. 1509 Istanbul earthquake
c. Undefined
b. Tundra18
d. Undefined

50. _____ refers to a tentative explanation of a given set of data that is expected to remain valid after future observation and experimentation.
a. Hypothesis18
c. Undefined
b. 1509 Istanbul earthquake
d. Undefined

51. A situation, which is generally uncomfortable, or otherwise undesirable is a _____.
a. Problem18
c. Undefined
b. 1509 Istanbul earthquake
d. Undefined

52. Enriched ore, often obtained by flotation, produced at a mill is _____.
a. 1509 Istanbul earthquake
c. Undefined
b. Concentrate18
d. Undefined

53. The force acting on a rock or another solid to deform it, measured in kilograms per square centimeter or pounds per square inch is _____.
a. 1509 Istanbul earthquake
c. Undefined
b. Stress18
d. Undefined

54. The southern part of the Permo-Triassic drift landmass of Pangaea is called _____.
a. Gondwana18
c. Undefined
b. 1509 Istanbul earthquake
d. Undefined

Chapter 19. Primate and Human Evolution

1. _____ refers to the theory that living organisms mutate and change, generally from simple to increasingly complex forms.
   a. AASHTO Soil Classification System
   b. Evolution19
   c. Undefined
   d. Undefined

2. Low latitude areas characterized by high temperatures and high precipitation are referred to as _____. At high elevations, however, _____ mountains may be both cold and relatively dry.
   a. Tropical19
   b. 1509 Istanbul earthquake
   c. Undefined
   d. Undefined

3. A hole dug into the ground in the attempt to intersect water or other subsurface fluids is referred to as a _____.
   a. 1509 Istanbul earthquake
   b. Well19
   c. Undefined
   d. Undefined

4. A region with an average annual rainfall of 10 inches or less and sparse vegetation, typically having thin, dry, and crumbly soil is a _____. A _____ has an aridity index greater than 4.0.
   a. 1509 Istanbul earthquake
   b. Desert19
   c. Undefined
   d. Undefined

5. Boundary surface between two different rock types or ages of rocks is called _____.
   a. 1509 Istanbul earthquake
   b. Contact19
   c. Undefined
   d. Undefined

6. _____ refers to an epoch in Earth's history from about 24 to 5 million years ago. Also refers to the rocks that formed in that epoch.
   a. Miocene19
   b. 1509 Istanbul earthquake
   c. Undefined
   d. Undefined

7. _____ refers to any evidence of past life, including remains, traces, imprints as well as life history artifacts.
   a. 1509 Istanbul earthquake
   b. Fossil19
   c. Undefined
   d. Undefined

8. Fine particles of pulverized rock blown from an explosion vent are called _____. Measuring less than 1/10 inch in diameter, _____ may be either solid or molten when first erupted.
   a. Ash19
   b. AASHTO Soil Classification System
   c. Undefined
   d. Undefined

9. _____ refers to igneous rocks that cool on the surface of the Earth, including beneath water; typically with small crystals due to the rapidity of cooling.
   a. Volcanic19
   b. 1509 Istanbul earthquake
   c. Undefined
   d. Undefined

10. _____ refers to extremely small fragments, usually of glass, that forms when escaping gases force a fine spray of magma from a volcano.
    a. 1509 Istanbul earthquake
    b. Volcanic ash19
    c. Undefined
    d. Undefined

11. _____ refers to rock formed of pyroclastic material.
    a. 1509 Istanbul earthquake
    b. Tuff19
    c. Undefined
    d. Undefined

12. A plate boundary at which the plates are moving apart as a result of spreading is referred to as _____.
    a. 1509 Istanbul earthquake
    b. Divergent boundary19
    c. Undefined
    d. Undefined

13. A unit of the geologic time scale that is a subdivision of a period is referred to as an _____.
    a. Epoch19
    b. AASHTO Soil Classification System
    c. Undefined
    d. Undefined

14. _____ refers to a long, narrow trough bounded by normal faults. It represents a region where divergence is taking place.
    a. 1509 Istanbul earthquake
    b. Rift19
    c. Undefined
    d. Undefined

15. Rift is a _____.
    a. Rift valley19
    b. 1509 Istanbul earthquake
    c. Undefined
    d. Undefined

16. The entire area between the tops of the slopes on both sides of a stream is a _____.
    a. Valley19
    b. 1509 Istanbul earthquake
    c. Undefined
    d. Undefined

17. The solid structure created when lava, gases, and hot particles escape to the Earth's surface through vents is called a _____. Volcanoes are usually conical. A _____ is 'active' when it is erupting or has erupted recently. Volcanoes that have not erupted recently but are considered likely to erupt in the future are said to be 'dormant.' A _____ that has not erupted for a long time and is not expected to erupt in the future is 'extinct'.
    a. Volcano19
    b. 1509 Istanbul earthquake
    c. Undefined
    d. Undefined

18. The solid material that precipitates in the pore space of sediments, binding the grains together to form solid rock is referred to as _____.
    a. 1509 Istanbul earthquake
    b. Cement19
    c. Undefined
    d. Undefined

19. _____ refers to the top few meters of regolith, generally including some organic matter derived from plants.
    a. 1509 Istanbul earthquake
    b. Soil19
    c. Undefined
    d. Undefined

20. The process by which particles of rock and soil are loosened, as by weathering, and then transported elsewhere, as by wind, water, ice, or gravity is _____.
    a. AASHTO Soil Classification System
    b. Erosion19
    c. Undefined
    d. Undefined

Chapter 19. Primate and Human Evolution

21. Magma that comes to the Earth's surface through a volcano or fissure is referred to as _____.
    a. Lava19
    b. 1509 Istanbul earthquake
    c. Undefined
    d. Undefined

22. A comprehensive explanation of a given set of data that has been repeatedly confirmed by observation and experimentation and has gained general acceptance within the scientific community but has not yet been decisively proven is referred to as _____.
    a. 1509 Istanbul earthquake
    b. Theory19
    c. Undefined
    d. Undefined

23. The epoch of the Quaternary Period of geologic time, following the Pliocene Epoch and preceding the Holocene is referred to as the _____.
    a. Pleistocene19
    b. 1509 Istanbul earthquake
    c. Undefined
    d. Undefined

24. An igneous pluton that is not tabular in shape is _____.
    a. 1509 Istanbul earthquake
    b. Massive19
    c. Undefined
    d. Undefined

25. _____ refers to a tentative explanation of a given set of data that is expected to remain valid after future observation and experimentation.
    a. 1509 Istanbul earthquake
    b. Hypothesis19
    c. Undefined
    d. Undefined

26. The point downstream where a river empties into another stream or water body is called _____.
    a. 1509 Istanbul earthquake
    b. Mouth19
    c. Undefined
    d. Undefined

27. _____ refers to a transitional material between snow and glacial ice, being older and denser than snow, but not yet transformed into glacial ice.
    a. Fire19
    b. 1509 Istanbul earthquake
    c. Undefined
    d. Undefined

28. _____ refers to a naturally formed aggregate of usually inorganic materials from within the Earth.
    a. 1509 Istanbul earthquake
    b. Rock19
    c. Undefined
    d. Undefined

29. A treeless plain characteristic of arctic regions with organically rich, poorly drained _____ soils and permanently frozen ground is called a _____.
    a. Tundra19
    b. 1509 Istanbul earthquake
    c. Undefined
    d. Undefined

30. _____ refers to a basic unit of the geologic time scale that is a subdivision of an era. Periods may be divided into smaller units called epochs.

a. 1509 Istanbul earthquake
b. Period19
c. Undefined
d. Undefined

31. _____ refers to a naturally formed opening beneath the surface of the Earth, generally formed by dissolution of carbonate bedrock. Caves may also form by erosion of coastal bedrock, partial melting of glaciers, or solidification of lava into hollow tubes.
   a. 1509 Istanbul earthquake
   b. Cave19
   c. Undefined
   d. Undefined

32. A series of events through which a rock changes, over time, between igneous, sedimentary, and metamorphic forms is the _____.
   a. Rock cycle19
   b. 1509 Istanbul earthquake
   c. Undefined
   d. Undefined

33. _____ refers to the gaseous portion of a planet, the planet's envelope of air. One of the traditional subdivisions of Earth's physical environment.
   a. Atmosphere19
   b. AASHTO Soil Classification System
   c. Undefined
   d. Undefined

34. The perpetual movement of water among the mantle, oceans, land, and atmosphere of the Earth is the _____.
   a. Hydrologic cycle19
   b. 1509 Istanbul earthquake
   c. Undefined
   d. Undefined

35. _____ refers to the set of physical features, such as mountains, valleys, and the shapes of landforms, that characterizes a given landscape.
   a. 1509 Istanbul earthquake
   b. Topography19
   c. Undefined
   d. Undefined

36. A body of rock identified by lithic characteristics and stratigraphic position and is mappable at the earth's surface or traceable in the subsurface is a _____.
   a. 1509 Istanbul earthquake
   b. Formation19
   c. Undefined
   d. Undefined

37. A naturally occurring, usually inorganic, solid consisting of either a single element or a compound, and having a definite chemical composition and a systematic internal arrangement of atoms is referred to as a _____.
   a. 1509 Istanbul earthquake
   b. Mineral19
   c. Undefined
   d. Undefined

38. _____ refer to the valuable minerals of an area that are presently legally recoverable or that may be so in the future; includes both the known ore bodies and the potential ores of a region.
   a. Mineral resources19
   b. 1509 Istanbul earthquake
   c. Undefined
   d. Undefined

39. _____ refers to rigid parts of the Earth's crust and part of the Earth's upper mantle that moves and adjoins each other along zones of seismic activity.

Chapter 19. Primate and Human Evolution

a. Plate19
b. 1509 Istanbul earthquake
c. Undefined
d. Undefined

40. The total amount of a geologic material in all its deposits, discovered and undiscovered are _____.
a. Resources19
b. 1509 Istanbul earthquake
c. Undefined
d. Undefined

41. The relationship between distance on a map and the distance on the terrain being represented by that map is a _____.
a. Scale19
b. 1509 Istanbul earthquake
c. Undefined
d. Undefined

42. The totality of life forms on Earth is referred to as the _____.
a. Biosphere19
b. 1509 Istanbul earthquake
c. Undefined
d. Undefined

43. _____ refers to a descriptive term applied to igneous rocks with more than 60% silica.
a. AASHTO Soil Classification System
b. Acid19
c. Undefined
d. Undefined

44. _____ refers to the general term for the steady rise in the average global temperatures over the last 100 years.
a. 1509 Istanbul earthquake
b. Global warming19
c. Undefined
d. Undefined

45. Warming of global climate by retention of outgoing radiation - inferred to be happening at present because of increasing atmospheric carbon dioxide content driven by combustion of fossil fuels is referred to as _____.
a. Greenhouse effect19
b. 1509 Istanbul earthquake
c. Undefined
d. Undefined

46. A group of interacting or interdependent parts that form a complex whole is called a _____.
a. System19
b. 1509 Istanbul earthquake
c. Undefined
d. Undefined

47. The top of the ocean, where the water meets the atmosphere is called _____.
a. 1509 Istanbul earthquake
b. Sea level19
c. Undefined
d. Undefined

48. The geosystem that describes the continual movement of carbon between the atmosphere and its other principal reservoirs-the lithosphere, hydrosphere, and biosphere is called the _____.
a. Carbon cycle19
b. 1509 Istanbul earthquake
c. Undefined
d. Undefined

49. _____ refers to a group of compounds that, on escape to the atmosphere, break down, releasing chlorine atoms that destroy ozone molecules.

a. 1509 Istanbul earthquake
b. Chlorofluorocarbons19
c. Undefined
d. Undefined

50. The outermost layer of the Earth, consisting of relatively low-density rock is called _____.
a. 1509 Istanbul earthquake
b. Crust19
c. Undefined
d. Undefined

51. One of several minerals containing negative oxygen ions bonded to one or more positive metallic ions are called _____.
a. Oxide19
b. AASHTO Soil Classification System
c. Undefined
d. Undefined

52. _____ refers to water in the gaseous state.
a. 1509 Istanbul earthquake
b. Vapor19
c. Undefined
d. Undefined

ANSWER KEY

Chapter 1

1. a	2. b	3. b	4. a	5. b	6. a	7. a	8. b	9. b	10. b
11. b	12. b	13. a	14. b	15. b	16. a	17. b	18. a	19. a	20. b
21. a	22. b	23. a	24. a	25. b	26. b	27. a	28. a	29. a	30. a
31. a	32. b	33. a	34. a	35. a	36. b	37. b	38. b	39. a	40. b
41. b	42. a	43. b	44. a	45. a	46. a	47. b	48. a	49. a	50. b
51. b	52. a	53. a	54. b	55. a	56. b	57. a	58. b	59. b	60. a
61. b	62. a	63. b	64. a	65. b	66. a	67. b	68. a	69. b	70. a
71. b	72. a	73. a	74. a	75. b	76. b	77. b	78. a	79. a	80. b
81. b	82. a	83. a	84. b	85. a	86. a	87. b	88. a	89. a	90. b
91. b	92. b	93. b	94. b	95. b	96. a	97. b	98. b	99. b	100. b
101. b	102. b	103. a	104. b	105. b	106. a	107. a	108. b	109. b	110. a
111. b	112. b	113. b	114. a	115. b	116. a	117. a	118. a	119. b	120. b
121. b	122. b	123. a	124. a	125. b	126. b	127. b	128. b	129. b	130. a
131. b	132. b	133. a	134. a	135. a	136. b	137. a	138. a	139. a	140. a
141. a	142. a	143. b	144. b						

Chapter 2

1. b	2. a	3. b	4. a	5. a	6. a	7. b	8. a	9. a	10. a
11. b	12. b	13. b	14. a	15. b	16. b	17. b	18. b	19. b	20. a
21. a	22. b	23. a	24. b	25. b	26. b	27. b	28. a	29. a	30. b
31. b	32. b	33. a	34. a	35. a	36. b	37. b	38. b	39. b	40. a
41. a	42. a	43. a	44. a	45. b	46. a	47. a	48. b	49. b	50. b
51. a	52. b	53. a	54. b	55. a	56. a	57. b	58. b	59. b	60. a
61. b	62. a	63. b	64. b	65. a	66. b	67. b	68. b	69. a	70. a
71. b	72. b	73. b	74. b	75. a	76. a	77. b	78. b	79. a	80. b
81. b	82. a	83. b	84. a	85. b	86. a	87. b	88. b	89. a	90. a
91. a	92. b	93. b	94. a	95. b	96. b	97. a	98. b	99. b	100. a
101. b	102. a	103. b	104. a	105. b	106. a	107. a	108. b	109. b	110. a
111. b	112. b	113. b	114. a	115. a	116. a	117. b	118. a	119. b	120. b
121. a	122. b	123. a	124. b	125. a	126. a	127. b	128. b	129. b	130. b
131. b	132. a	133. b	134. a	135. b	136. a	137. b	138. b	139. a	140. a
141. a	142. a	143. a	144. a	145. b	146. a	147. b	148. b	149. b	150. a
151. b	152. a	153. a	154. a	155. a	156. b	157. a	158. a		

Chapter 3

1. b	2. b	3. b	4. b	5. b	6. a	7. a	8. b	9. b	10. a
11. b	12. a	13. b	14. a	15. b	16. a	17. a	18. b	19. b	20. b
21. b	22. b	23. a	24. b	25. b	26. b	27. b	28. b	29. a	30. b
31. b	32. b	33. b	34. b	35. b	36. b	37. b	38. b	39. a	40. b
41. a	42. b	43. a	44. b	45. b	46. a	47. a	48. a	49. a	50. a
51. b	52. a	53. b	54. a	55. b	56. b	57. a	58. b	59. a	60. a
61. a	62. b	63. a	64. a	65. a	66. a	67. b	68. a	69. a	70. a
71. b	72. b	73. b	74. b	75. a	76. b	77. a	78. a	79. b	80. a
81. a	82. b	83. a	84. a	85. a	86. a	87. b	88. a	89. a	90. a
91. b	92. b	93. b	94. b	95. a	96. a	97. b	98. a	99. b	100. b
101. a	102. a	103. a	104. b	105. a	106. a	107. b	108. a	109. a	110. b
111. a	112. a	113. a	114. b	115. b	116. a	117. a	118. a	119. b	120. a
121. b	122. b	123. b	124. b	125. a	126. a	127. a	128. b	129. b	130. a
131. a	132. a	133. b	134. b	135. b	136. b	137. a	138. b	139. b	140. a
141. b	142. b	143. a	144. b	145. b	146. b	147. a	148. b	149. b	150. a
151. a	152. b	153. a	154. a	155. a	156. b	157. b	158. b	159. a	160. a
161. a	162. a	163. b	164. a	165. a	166. b	167. a	168. a	169. a	170. a
171. a	172. a	173. a	174. b	175. a	176. b	177. a	178. b	179. a	180. b
181. b	182. b	183. b	184. b	185. a	186. a	187. a			

Chapter 4

1. a	2. a	3. a	4. a	5. a	6. a	7. b	8. a	9. a	10. a
11. a	12. a	13. a	14. b	15. a	16. a	17. b	18. a	19. b	20. a
21. b	22. b	23. b	24. b	25. b	26. b	27. a	28. b	29. a	30. a
31. a	32. a	33. a	34. a	35. b	36. b	37. b	38. b	39. b	40. b
41. b	42. a	43. b	44. b	45. a	46. a	47. a	48. b	49. b	50. b
51. a	52. a	53. b	54. b	55. a	56. b	57. b	58. a	59. b	60. a
61. a	62. b	63. b	64. b	65. b	66. a	67. a	68. a	69. b	70. a
71. b	72. b	73. a	74. a	75. b	76. a	77. a	78. b	79. b	80. a
81. a	82. a	83. b	84. a	85. b	86. b	87. b	88. b	89. b	90. b
91. a	92. a	93. a	94. a	95. b	96. b	97. b	98. a	99. b	100. b
101. b	102. a	103. b	104. b	105. a	106. b	107. a	108. a	109. b	110. a
111. b	112. a	113. b	114. b	115. b	116. a	117. b	118. a	119. a	120. b
121. b	122. a	123. a	124. a	125. b	126. b				

ANSWER KEY

Chapter 5

1. a	2. b	3. a	4. a	5. b	6. b	7. b	8. a	9. a	10. a
11. a	12. a	13. b	14. a	15. b	16. b	17. a	18. a	19. a	20. b
21. a	22. a	23. a	24. b	25. b	26. a	27. b	28. a	29. a	30. b
31. b	32. a	33. a	34. a	35. a	36. b	37. a	38. b	39. a	40. b
41. b	42. b	43. a	44. a	45. b	46. a	47. b	48. a	49. b	50. a
51. b	52. b	53. a	54. b	55. b	56. a	57. a	58. b	59. b	60. a
61. a	62. a	63. b	64. a	65. b	66. b	67. a	68. a	69. a	70. b
71. b	72. b	73. b	74. a	75. b	76. a	77. a	78. a	79. b	80. b
81. a	82. a	83. a	84. b	85. b	86. b	87. a	88. b	89. a	90. b
91. b	92. a	93. b	94. b	95. b	96. a	97. b	98. a	99. a	100. a
101. b	102. b	103. b	104. a	105. a	106. b	107. a	108. b	109. a	110. b
111. b	112. a	113. b	114. b	115. b	116. a	117. a	118. a	119. a	120. b
121. b	122. b	123. a	124. b	125. a	126. b	127. a	128. a	129. a	

Chapter 6

1. b	2. b	3. a	4. b	5. b	6. a	7. a	8. b	9. b	10. a
11. a	12. a	13. b	14. b	15. a	16. a	17. a	18. a	19. a	20. a
21. b	22. b	23. a	24. a	25. a	26. b	27. a	28. b	29. b	30. b
31. a	32. b	33. a	34. b	35. b	36. b	37. b	38. a	39. a	40. b
41. a	42. a	43. b	44. b	45. a	46. a	47. b	48. a	49. a	50. a
51. a	52. a	53. a	54. a	55. a	56. b	57. b	58. b	59. a	60. a
61. b	62. a	63. b	64. b	65. a	66. a	67. a	68. a	69. a	70. a
71. a	72. a	73. a	74. b	75. a	76. a	77. b	78. b	79. a	80. a
81. a	82. a	83. a	84. a	85. a	86. b	87. a	88. b	89. a	90. b
91. a	92. a	93. b	94. b	95. a	96. a	97. a	98. a	99. b	100. b
101. b	102. b	103. a	104. a	105. b	106. a	107. a	108. b	109. b	110. a
111. b	112. a	113. b	114. a	115. b	116. a	117. a	118. b	119. b	120. b
121. b	122. a	123. b	124. a						

Chapter 7

1. b	2. b	3. a	4. a	5. a	6. b	7. b	8. b	9. a	10. b
11. a	12. b	13. b	14. b	15. a	16. a	17. a	18. b	19. b	20. b
21. a	22. b	23. b	24. a	25. b	26. b	27. a	28. a	29. a	30. a
31. b	32. b	33. b	34. a	35. b	36. b	37. b	38. b	39. b	40. b
41. b	42. b	43. b	44. a	45. b	46. b	47. b	48. a	49. a	50. a
51. b	52. b	53. b	54. a	55. b	56. b	57. a	58. b	59. b	60. a
61. b	62. b	63. b	64. b	65. b	66. b	67. a	68. a	69. b	70. b
71. a	72. b	73. b	74. b	75. a	76. b	77. a	78. b	79. b	80. a
81. b	82. b	83. b	84. b	85. b	86. a	87. b	88. a	89. a	90. b
91. b	92. b	93. a	94. a	95. b	96. a	97. b	98. b	99. a	

Chapter 8

1. a	2. b	3. b	4. b	5. b	6. a	7. b	8. a	9. b	10. a
11. a	12. a	13. a	14. b	15. a	16. b	17. a	18. a	19. a	20. a
21. b	22. a	23. a	24. b	25. a	26. a	27. b	28. b	29. b	30. a
31. b	32. a	33. b	34. b	35. b	36. b	37. b	38. b	39. b	40. a
41. a	42. a	43. b	44. b	45. a	46. b	47. b	48. b	49. a	50. a
51. b	52. a	53. a	54. b	55. b	56. a	57. a	58. b	59. b	60. a
61. b	62. b	63. b	64. a	65. b	66. a	67. a	68. b	69. a	70. a
71. b	72. a	73. a	74. b	75. a	76. b	77. a	78. a	79. b	80. a
81. a	82. a	83. a	84. a	85. a	86. a	87. b	88. b	89. a	90. b
91. a	92. b	93. a	94. b	95. a	96. a	97. a	98. a	99. a	100. b
101. a	102. a	103. b	104. b	105. b	106. a	107. a	108. a	109. b	110. b
111. a	112. a	113. a	114. b	115. b	116. a	117. a	118. a	119. a	120. a
121. b	122. b	123. a	124. b	125. b	126. a	127. a	128. a	129. a	130. b
131. b	132. a	133. b	134. a	135. b	136. a	137. b	138. a	139. a	140. a
141. a	142. a	143. b	144. b	145. a	146. b	147. b	148. a	149. b	150. b
151. b	152. b	153. a	154. b	155. a	156. a	157. a	158. b	159. b	160. a
161. a	162. b	163. a	164. b	165. a	166. a	167. b	168. b	169. b	170. a
171. b	172. a	173. b	174. b	175. a	176. b	177. a	178. a	179. a	180. a
181. a	182. b	183. a	184. b	185. b	186. a				

Chapter 9

1. b	2. a	3. a	4. b	5. a	6. b	7. a	8. b	9. b	10. b
11. b	12. b	13. b	14. b	15. b	16. a	17. b	18. a	19. b	20. b
21. b	22. b	23. a	24. b	25. b	26. b	27. b	28. a	29. b	30. a
31. b	32. a	33. b	34. a	35. a	36. a	37. b	38. b	39. b	40. a
41. a	42. b	43. b	44. a	45. a	46. b	47. a	48. a	49. b	50. b
51. a	52. b	53. b	54. a	55. a	56. b	57. a	58. b	59. b	60. a
61. b	62. a	63. a	64. b	65. b	66. a	67. b	68. a	69. b	70. a
71. b	72. a	73. a	74. a	75. a	76. a	77. b	78. b	79. a	80. a
81. b	82. b	83. a	84. a	85. a	86. b	87. b	88. a	89. a	90. b
91. b	92. b	93. b	94. a	95. a	96. b	97. a	98. a	99. a	100. a
101. a	102. a	103. b	104. a	105. b	106. b	107. b	108. b	109. b	110. a
111. b	112. a	113. a	114. b	115. a	116. b	117. b	118. a	119. b	120. a
121. b	122. a	123. a	124. a	125. b	126. a	127. a	128. b	129. b	130. a
131. a	132. a	133. a	134. b	135. a	136. a	137. a	138. b	139. b	140. a
141. a	142. a	143. b	144. a	145. a	146. b	147. b	148. b	149. b	150. b
151. b	152. b	153. b	154. a	155. b	156. a	157. a	158. a	159. b	160. b
161. b	162. a	163. a	164. b	165. a	166. a	167. b	168. b	169. b	170. b
171. b	172. a	173. b	174. b	175. a	176. b	177. b	178. b	179. a	180. a
181. b	182. b	183. b	184. a	185. b	186. b	187. b	188. b	189. b	190. b
191. a									

ANSWER KEY

Chapter 10
1. b   2. a   3. a   4. a   5. a   6. b   7. a   8. b   9. a   10. b
11. a   12. a   13. b   14. b   15. b   16. a   17. a   18. b   19. a   20. b
21. a   22. b   23. b   24. b   25. b   26. a   27. b   28. a   29. b   30. b
31. b   32. b   33. b   34. b   35. b   36. b   37. a   38. a   39. b   40. b
41. b   42. a   43. a   44. b   45. b   46. b   47. b   48. b   49. a   50. b
51. a   52. a   53. a   54. a   55. b   56. b   57. a   58. b   59. a   60. a
61. a   62. a   63. b   64. a   65. b   66. a   67. a   68. b   69. b   70. b
71. a   72. a   73. a   74. a   75. a   76. b   77. b   78. b   79. b   80. b
81. b   82. b   83. a   84. a   85. b   86. a   87. a   88. a   89. a   90. b
91. b   92. a   93. a   94. a   95. b   96. b   97. a   98. b   99. a   100. b
101. a   102. a   103. a   104. b   105. b   106. b   107. b   108. a   109. b

Chapter 11
1. a   2. b   3. b   4. a   5. a   6. b   7. a   8. b   9. b   10. a
11. b   12. a   13. b   14. a   15. b   16. a   17. a   18. b   19. a   20. b
21. b   22. a   23. b   24. a   25. a   26. a   27. b   28. b   29. b   30. b
31. a   32. b   33. b   34. b   35. b   36. b   37. b   38. b   39. a   40. a
41. a   42. b   43. a   44. b   45. a   46. a   47. b   48. a   49. b   50. b
51. a   52. a   53. b   54. b   55. b   56. a   57. b   58. a   59. a   60. b
61. a   62. a   63. a   64. b   65. a   66. a   67. a   68. b   69. b   70. b
71. a   72. a   73. b   74. b   75. a   76. b   77. a   78. a   79. a   80. a
81. a   82. a   83. a   84. a   85. b   86. a   87. a   88. b   89. a   90. a
91. a   92. a   93. a   94. b   95. b   96. a   97. b   98. b   99. b   100. a
101. a   102. a   103. a   104. a

Chapter 12
1. a   2. a   3. b   4. a   5. a   6. b   7. a   8. a   9. b   10. b
11. b   12. a   13. b   14. a   15. b   16. b   17. a   18. b   19. a   20. a
21. b   22. a   23. a   24. b   25. a   26. b   27. a   28. a   29. a   30. b
31. a   32. b   33. a   34. b   35. a   36. a   37. a   38. a   39. a   40. b
41. b   42. a   43. b   44. a   45. a   46. b   47. a   48. a   49. a   50. a
51. b   52. a   53. a   54. a   55. a   56. b   57. b   58. a   59. b   60. a
61. b   62. b   63. b   64. b   65. b

Chapter 13
1. b   2. b   3. a   4. b   5. b   6. a   7. b   8. b   9. b   10. b
11. a   12. a   13. a   14. b   15. b   16. b   17. a   18. a   19. b   20. a
21. b   22. a   23. a   24. a   25. a   26. b   27. a   28. a   29. b   30. a
31. b   32. b   33. a   34. b   35. a   36. a   37. a   38. b   39. b   40. b
41. a   42. b   43. b   44. a   45. b   46. b   47. a   48. b

Chapter 14

1. a	2. b	3. a	4. b	5. a	6. b	7. b	8. b	9. b	10. b
11. b	12. a	13. a	14. a	15. b	16. b	17. b	18. b	19. a	20. a
21. b	22. b	23. a	24. b	25. b	26. b	27. a	28. a	29. b	30. a
31. a	32. b	33. b	34. a	35. b	36. a	37. a	38. b	39. a	40. a
41. a	42. b	43. b	44. b	45. a	46. a	47. a	48. b	49. a	50. a
51. a	52. b	53. b	54. a	55. a	56. b	57. a	58. a	59. b	60. b
61. a	62. a	63. b	64. a	65. a	66. a	67. a	68. b	69. a	70. a
71. b	72. b	73. a	74. b	75. b	76. b	77. b	78. b	79. b	80. b
81. b	82. a	83. b	84. a	85. a	86. a	87. a	88. a	89. b	90. a
91. a	92. a	93. b	94. a	95. b	96. a	97. b	98. a	99. a	100. b
101. b	102. a	103. a	104. a	105. a	106. b	107. b	108. a	109. a	110. a
111. b	112. b	113. b	114. b	115. b	116. a	117. a	118. a	119. b	120. b
121. b	122. a	123. b	124. b	125. a	126. a	127. a	128. b		

Chapter 15

1. a	2. b	3. b	4. a	5. b	6. a	7. b	8. a	9. a	10. b
11. b	12. b	13. a	14. b	15. b	16. a	17. b	18. a	19. a	20. b
21. b	22. b	23. a	24. b	25. b	26. a	27. b	28. b	29. b	30. b
31. a	32. a	33. a	34. a	35. a	36. b	37. a	38. a	39. b	40. a
41. b	42. a	43. a	44. a	45. b	46. a	47. b	48. b	49. b	50. b
51. a	52. b								

Chapter 16

1. b	2. a	3. a	4. a	5. a	6. a	7. a	8. a	9. a	10. a
11. b	12. a	13. b	14. a	15. b	16. b	17. a	18. a	19. a	20. a
21. b	22. a	23. a	24. a	25. b	26. a	27. b	28. a	29. b	30. a
31. a	32. a	33. b	34. b	35. a	36. b	37. b	38. a	39. a	40. b
41. a	42. a	43. b	44. b	45. b	46. b	47. b	48. b	49. a	50. b
51. b	52. a	53. a	54. a	55. a	56. a	57. a	58. b	59. b	60. b
61. b	62. a	63. b	64. b	65. a	66. a	67. a	68. a	69. b	70. b
71. a	72. b	73. b	74. b	75. a	76. b	77. b	78. a	79. b	80. a
81. b	82. a	83. a	84. a	85. a	86. b	87. a	88. a	89. a	90. b
91. a	92. b	93. a	94. a	95. b	96. a	97. b	98. a	99. a	100. b
101. a	102. b	103. b	104. a	105. b	106. a	107. b	108. b	109. a	110. b
111. a	112. a	113. a	114. a	115. b	116. a	117. b	118. b	119. a	120. a
121. a	122. b	123. b	124. b	125. b	126. b	127. b	128. a	129. b	130. a
131. a	132. b	133. b	134. a	135. b	136. a	137. b	138. b	139. a	140. b
141. a	142. a	143. b	144. a	145. a	146. a	147. b			

ANSWER KEY

Chapter 17

1. a	2. b	3. a	4. a	5. b	6. b	7. a	8. a	9. b	10. b
11. b	12. b	13. b	14. b	15. a	16. b	17. b	18. b	19. a	20. a
21. b	22. a	23. b	24. a	25. a	26. a	27. b	28. b	29. b	30. a
31. b	32. a	33. a	34. b	35. b	36. b	37. b	38. a	39. b	40. a
41. a	42. b	43. b	44. a	45. b	46. b	47. b	48. b	49. a	50. b
51. a	52. a	53. a	54. b	55. a	56. a	57. a	58. a	59. a	60. a
61. b	62. b	63. b	64. b	65. b	66. a	67. b	68. a	69. a	70. a
71. a	72. b	73. a	74. a	75. a	76. b	77. a	78. b	79. a	80. a
81. a	82. b	83. b	84. b	85. a	86. b	87. b	88. b	89. a	90. a
91. b	92. a	93. b	94. a	95. a	96. b	97. a	98. a	99. b	100. a
101. b	102. b	103. a	104. a	105. a	106. a	107. b	108. b	109. b	110. a
111. a	112. a	113. b	114. b	115. b	116. b	117. a	118. b	119. a	120. a
121. a	122. a	123. b	124. a	125. a	126. a	127. b	128. a	129. b	130. b
131. b	132. a	133. a	134. a	135. a	136. a				

Chapter 18

1. b	2. a	3. a	4. a	5. a	6. b	7. a	8. a	9. a	10. a
11. b	12. a	13. b	14. a	15. b	16. a	17. b	18. b	19. a	20. a
21. b	22. a	23. a	24. a	25. b	26. a	27. a	28. b	29. a	30. b
31. b	32. a	33. a	34. b	35. b	36. b	37. a	38. a	39. a	40. a
41. b	42. a	43. b	44. a	45. a	46. a	47. b	48. b	49. b	50. a
51. a	52. b	53. b	54. a						

Chapter 19

1. b	2. a	3. b	4. b	5. b	6. a	7. b	8. a	9. a	10. b
11. b	12. b	13. a	14. b	15. a	16. a	17. a	18. b	19. b	20. b
21. a	22. b	23. a	24. b	25. b	26. b	27. a	28. b	29. a	30. b
31. b	32. a	33. a	34. a	35. b	36. b	37. b	38. a	39. a	40. a
41. a	42. a	43. b	44. b	45. a	46. a	47. b	48. a	49. b	50. b
51. a	52. b								